THE SONIC COLOR LINE

POSTMILLENNIAL POP

General Editors: Karen Tongson and Henry Jenkins

The Sonic Color Line

Race and the Cultural Politics of Listening

Jennifer Lynn Stoever

NEW YORK UNIVERSITY PRESS

New York

NEW YORK UNIVERSITY PRESS
New York
www.nyupress.org

References to Internet websites (URLs) were accurate at the time of writing.
Neither the author nor New York University Press is responsible for URLs that
may have expired or changed since the manuscript was prepared.

ISBN: 978-1-4798-9043-9 (hardback)
ISBN: 978-1-4798-8934-1 (paperback)

For Library of Congress Cataloging-in-Publication data, please contact
the Library of Congress.

New York University Press books are printed on acid-free paper,
and their binding materials are chosen for strength and durability.
We strive to use environmentally responsible suppliers and materials
to the greatest extent possible in publishing our books.

Manufactured in the United States of America

10 9 8 7 6 5 4 3 2 1

Also available as an ebook

THE
AMERICAN
LITERATURES
INITIATIVE
A book in the American Literatures Initiative (ALI), a collaborative publish-
ing project of NYU Press, Fordham University Press, Rutgers University
Press, Temple University Press, and the University of Virginia Press. The
Initiative is supported by the Andrew W. Mellon Foundation. For more infor-
mation, please visit www.americanliteratures.org.

CONTENTS

For my grandma Maryanne (1923–2001), whose lovingly gruff, crumpled-paper-bag voice still carries me.

For my dad, Jeff (1948–2011), who first taught me how to listen, and whose brown Koss KO/747 headphones rest right next to my stereo.

For my son, Martin, who arrived amidst the writing of this book. You teach me to listen anew while letting me think I am teaching you. Your voice will always be my favorite sound. I love you more! Infinity!

ACKNOWLEDGMENTS

"Can you sing out in the pouring rain? / Can you sing out,
can you sing out?"
—Fishbone, "Pouring Rain"

In summer 2015, I was honored to thank Norwood Fisher and Angelo
Moore of Fishbone in person for being my first, funkiest, and fiercest
critical race theorists. Only because music is so very powerful do people
create mechanisms like the sonic color line to contain it.

To my RUSD English teachers Kathy Rossi, Keith Lloyd, Katie Mackey,
and Richard McNeil, who taught us public school kids how to think and
write with a love and rigor that turned many of us toward futures we
thought far beyond our reach. Thank you to art teachers Louis Fox and
Italo DiMarco, for showing me to myself.

I have boundless love for my Riverside home folks: George Campos,
Kim Earhart, Cara Cardinale Fidler, Kelly Herrera, Nova Punongbayan,
Rodrigo Ramos, Joe Spagna, and especially my dearest familia—Julia
Martinez, Sarah Parry, Karin Ribaudo, Jeff Ribaudo, Alison Sumner, Maria
Unzueta-Hernandez, and last but certainly not least, Karen Tongson.
Womb to tomb, birth to earth. Thank you to Juan and Alice and the
Contreras-Martinez families, who helped raise me to be the woman I am
today. The generosity and personal example of the Honorable Joe Her-
nandez II and Gloria Lopez sustained me through graduate school.
Melissa Contreras-McGavin and Bradley McGavin, you are the wind
beneath my wings.

I was fortunate to have a top-notch, affordable undergraduate education at UC Riverside. I first "heard" literature in Katherine Kinney's class;
I still dream of delivering readings as on point as hers. I also benefitted
from the brilliance and generosity of Emory Eliot—gone too soon—
Carlos Cortés, Jennifer Doyle, John Ganim, George Haggerty, Tiffany

Ana López, Peter Mileur (now my Binghamton colleague), Venetria K. Patton, and Margie Waller. Kevin Imamura remains a lifelong friend.

The six years I spent teaching public high school were not a detour from my education but an expressway to its heart. My former students still inspire me, especially Toussaint Bailey, Stephen Brockington, Sara Caro, Kristy Dougherty, J. R. Hale, Sarah Hill, Lakeisha Horne, Don Sargent, Tonya Sherfey, Sett Quinata, and the badass Odie Anaya.

These ideas were nurtured and shaped by my PhD study in American Studies and Ethnicity at the University of Southern California. I am grateful Viet Nguyen, George Sanchez, and Cynthia Young saw potential in my earliest work. Thank you also to USC faculty members who encouraged my research and showed me wonderful examples of professordom: Sarah Banet-Weiser, Alice Gambrell, Ruthie Gilmore, Bill Handley, Lanita Jacobs, Josh Kun, Teresa McKenna, Karen Pinkus, Laura Pulido, David Román, Leland Saito, and Bruce Smith. Sharon Sekhon, now director of the Studio for Southern California History, gave heartfelt support. A timely visit by George Lipsitz convinced me I could feed myself writing about music. Kitty Lai, Sonia Rodriguez, and Sandra Hopwood kept my act together!

I remain especially indebted to Carla Kaplan, Joanna Demers, Judith Jackson Fossett, and Fred Moten. Carla's impeccable research acumen, tough-as-nails love, and insistence on my absolute best motivated me when I needed it most. Joanna's work on electronic music and our walk-and-talks about the nature of "noise" charged me to listen differently. Judith had unwavering faith in me when my way was cloudy and will forever be my finest interlocutor; I am grateful for those nights at her table, drinking tea, listening to Stevie Wonder, and talking over her meticulous green-inked comments. Fittingly, words only inadequately describe my gratitude for Fred's kind and prodigious example; his virtuoso riffs on blackness, sound, music, art, the academy, and politics rock my world then, now, and always.

I have sincere gratitude, love, and respect for the first three USC ASE graduate cohorts (2001–2003), with special shouts to Wendy Cheng, Michan Connor, Carolyn Dunn, Laura Sachiko Fujikawa, Jesús J. Hernández, Emily Hobson, Imani Kai Johnson, Viet Le, Sionne Neely, Daniel Wei Hosang, Nisha Kunte, Lata Murti, Phuong Nguyen, Luis Carlos Rodriguez, Ully Ryder, Anton Smith, Micaela Smith, Karen

Yonemoto, and of course PhDivas Laura Barraclough, Ava Chin, Fiorella Cotrina, Michelle Commander, Araceli Esparza, Perla Guerrero, Nicole Hodges-Persley, Marci McMahon, and Cam Vu. Special amorcito to Hillary Jenks and reina alejandra prado—I love how our friendship continues to deepen. Much gratitude also to comrades across campus: Ruth Blandon, Zoë Corwin, Bridget Hoida, Shakira Holt, Gustavo Licón, Lalo Licón, Patricia Literte, Brooke Carlson, Memo Arce, and Andy Hakim. I remain so thankful for the attentive eye of my dear friend and writing partner Priscilla Peña Ovalle. None of this would have been possible without you, homegirl!

Chapters 1 and 5 began as public talks at the University of Rochester while I was a Predoctoral Fellow at the Frederick Douglass Institute of African and African American Studies (2005–2006). I am especially indebted to my mentor Jeff Tucker, Aubrey Anable, Dinah Holtzman, Cilas Kemendijo, Gloria Kim, Stephanie Li, the late Jesse Moore, Ghislaine Radegonde-Eison, A. Joan Saab, and to Anthea Butler for being absolutely EVERYTHING, still! A heartfelt thank you to Shaila Mehra and to stellar fellows Niambi Carter and Millery Polyné, who not only listened to, read, and shaped countless drafts but also became dear friends.

Thank you to Binghamton University, especially Provost Don Nieman, the Harpur Dean's office, and the Institute for Advanced Studies in the Humanities. My departmental colleagues' enthusiasm and faith in my scholarship, teaching, and blogging heartened me through challenging times. Thanks to David Bartine, Jaimee Colbert, Maria Mazziotti Gillan, Thomas Glave, Aja Martinez, Bill Spanos, Susan Strehle, Libby Tucker, Al Tricomi, and Lisa Yun. My work especially benefitted from the rigorous attention of Donette Francis, Praseeda Gopinath, Joe Keith, and Monika Mehta. I also appreciate the cross-campus support of Nancy Applebaum, Ana Maria Candela, John Cheng, Ariana Gerstein, Robert Ji-Song Ku, Sean Massey, Monteith McCollum, Gladys Jimenez-Munoz, Andreas Pape, Emily Pape, Josh Price, Kelvin Santiago-Valles, Paul Schleuse, Pamela Smart, Wendy Stewart, Nancy Um, Brian Wall, and Michael West.

And of course my graduate students are THE REAL MVPS. 'Nuff respect to Tara Betts and Osvaldo Oyola for always asking the hard questions and being down to geek out on music. To Airek Beauchamp for lovely-yet-rigorous "Theory on Rollerskates" sessions. To Maria Chaves for meticulous research assistance, especially regarding decolonization as verb. Christie Zwahlen attuned my ear toward civic engagement. Wanda Alarcon's work reminds us that DJs save our beautifully complex lives. Natalia Triana-Angel's ability to hear history in music is next level. Thank you also to Barry Jackson for faith and enthusiasm! Several talented undergraduates journeyed with me on this and other projects I'm sure they had initially thought were crazy. Thanks especially to Marva Forsyth, Julian Harrison, Caleb Knapp, Jah-Sonnah MacAlister, Daniel Moore, Felicia Parrish, Michele Quiles, Seneca Sanders, Danny Santos, Dhruv Sehgal, Ashley Verbert, Charles Weiselberg, and Kymel Yard.

Former students, now colleagues/siblings, Liana Silva, Aaron Trammell, and I form like Voltron to make the *Sounding Out!* hive mind—the best team I have ever worked with. Thank you both for unswervingly being there with the quickness—always pushing me to my best and pulling for this project every step of the way, intellectually, emotionally, logistically, and with humor.

I wrote much of this manuscript as a Society for the Humanities Fellow at the A. D. White House at Cornell University. Much respect to director Tim Murray, administrative assistant Mary Ahl, and events coordinator Emily Parsons. For generative conversations, fine critiques, and basement jam sessions, I thank 2011–2012 fellows Eliot Bates, Miloje Despic, Nina Eidsheim, Sarah Ensor, Michael Jonik, Nicolas Knouf, Roger Moseley, Jamie Nisbet, and Jonathan Skinner, with special love to Marcus Boon, Duane Corpis, Ziad Fahmy, Brían Hanrahan, Damien Keane, Eric Lott, Tom McEnaney, Trevor Pinch, and Jeanette Jouili (and the Jouili-Kpai family). You guys rock.

Both sound studies and my own research are intellectually sustained and spiritually nourished by a community of talented scholars including Dolores Inés Casillas, Regina Bradley, Neil Verma, Enongo Lumumba-Kasongo, Alexandra Vasquez, Tavia Nyong'o, Deb Vargas, Deb Paredes, Roshi Kheshti, Shana Redmond, Norma Coates, Marisol LeBron, Alejandro Madrid, Martin Daughtry, Leo Cardoso, Alex Russo, Steph Ceraso, Tara Rodgers, Ashon Crawley, Bill Bahng Boyer, Ben Tausig, Amanda Keeler, Rui Costa, Maile Colbert, Debra Rae Cohen, David Suisman, Mara Mills, Gina Arnold, and Shawn VanCour, who gave chapter 5 a great read. Special appreciation to Frances Aparicio, Fred Moten, Daphne Brooks, Emily Thompson, Gus Stadler, Josh Kun, and Jonathan Sterne for mentorship and those bold early noises in the field! And of course gratitude to the readers, writers, subscribers, and social media supporters of *Sounding Out!*, who motivate on the daily.

To the archivists who gave me keys to kingdoms: Matthew Colbert and David Coppen (Sibley Music Library in Rochester, New York), Jim Farrington (Rush Rhees Library at the University of Rochester), Lea Kemp and Kathryn Murano (Rochester Museum and Science Center), Beth Howse, Aisha Johnson, and Vanessa Smith (Special Collections, John Hope and Aurelia E. Franklin Library at Fisk University), Christopher Harter (Amistad Research Center at Tulane University), Eisha Prather, Katherine Reagan, and Ben Ortiz (Kroch Special Collections at Cornell), Laura Russo (Howard Gotlieb Archival Research Center at Boston University), Alvin Singh (Lead Belly Foundation), and Andy Lanset, archivist for WNYC.

Special thanks goes to those who guided me through manuscript development and production. I am grateful for the motivation and guidance of Anne Bramley, Shakti Castro's meticulous permissions research, and Cecelia Cancellaro's intuitive and surgical editing. At NYU Press, Eric Zinner gifted me with sharp-eyed enthusiasm, patience, and unwavering belief in my project; my series editors and anonymous readers provided necessary nudges to new vistas, and Alicia Nadkarni and Erin Davis tirelessly moved the book along.

I finished this book as I was warmly welcomed to Ithaca, New York. The friendship of SAMMUS, Kebbeh Gold, Nandi Cohen, Ben Ortiz, Travis Gosa, Jessica Gosa, Belisa Gonzales, Phuong Nguyen, Betty Nguyen, Tavo Licón, Sandra Bruno, and Claudia Verhoeven, and Hawk and Ahimsa Tuesdays/Fridays sustained me during the last push.

This book would not exist without the wonderful people who have cared for my son, especially the excellent teachers at the Vestal Jewish Community Center who helped raise him right. Thank you especially to Debbie Mohr (and daughter Hallie) for loving us as family. Denise and Mike Stabile are wonderful grandparents/supporters of this working, writing, researching, traveling single parent, along with Uncle Will Stabile.

Immeasurable love and gratitude to my mom, Pinkie, who always took me to the library, listened to my stories, and encouraged me to go to graduate school (even though it was a crazy idea, Mom!); her vegetable soup fueled many of these pages. To my grandma Mema, who read to me and assembled my very first single-authored publications out of the scraps my grandpa brought home from the paper-cup factory. I also thank my aunt Mary Anne, uncle Greg, aunt Mary, sister Jackie, and brother-in-law Steve; I am grateful for the joy my nieces Molly and Megan and nephew Mason have brought. To those who have passed, forever in my heart and in these pages: my dad, Jeff, Grandpa Smokey, Great-Grandma Irene, Grandpa Walt, and Grandma Maryanne. To my son, Martin—for you, the sun, the moon, the stars, and the book! Finally, I thank my dog, He Who Cannot Be Named (2002–2016), for the countless hours he spent stretched out on my office rug, encouraging me to stay put and write. All the treats are his and any mistakes definitely mine.

Portions of chapter 5 appeared as "Fine-tuning the Sonic Color-line: Radio and the Acousmatic DuBois," in a special issue on radio, in *Modernist Cultures* 10, no. 1 (2015): 99–118, and in Italian as "W. E. B. Du Bois and the Sonic Color-line," in a special issue on W. E. B. Du Bois, in *Studi Culturali* (April 2013): 71–88.

An earlier version of chapter 1 appeared as "The Word and the Sound: Listening to the Sonic Color-line in Frederick Douglass's 1845 *Narrative*," in *SoundEffects: An Interdisciplinary Journal of Sound and Sound Experience* (Fall 2011): 20–36.

Theorizations of the sonic color line and the listening ear appeared in nascent form in "Reproducing U.S. Citizenship in a *Blackboard Jungle*: Race, Cold War Liberalism, and the Tape Recorder," *American Quarterly* 63, no. 3 (September 2011): 781–806, and "Splicing the Sonic Color-Line: Tony Schwartz Remixes Postwar *Nueva York*," *Social Text 102* (Spring 2010): 59–85.

And finally, this book also bears the deep affective traces and influence of Tyisha Miller (1979–1999), a student in the first high school English class I ever taught, and James Martinez (1976–1997), my high school boyfriend's smart and hilarious cousin, both killed by police in Riverside County. I have mourned them both for almost twenty years now; these photographs remind me they were once so very beautifully, heartbreakingly, brilliantly alive.

While both images still wound, the photograph of Tyisha, in particular, bears symbolic resonance: here she performs as Mama Younger from *A Raisin in the Sun* alongside her classmates, who eagerly hand her *"the first present in her life without it being Christmas,"* as Lorraine

Christmas, 1993, Grandma Vera's House, Riverside, California. James second from left.
Photo by author.

May 1996, Rubidoux High School, Riverside, California. Tyisha at center. Photo by author.

Hansberry's stage directions say. In the play, this moment comes as the Younger family ready themselves to leave their squalid tenement apartment to desegregate Chicago's all-white suburbs. I regret that in that moment, I, then a twenty-one-year-old white woman with a lot to learn, focused far too much on the new possibilities for the Younger family; I did not stress enough the blood, bravery, resistance, and death that paid for such possibilities and the violence of the white perpetrators who certainly awaited the family's moving van (as they did Hansberry's own family's). The joy that Tyisha radiates as she accepts the gift of a new future—shining despite murder and time and my misteachings—haunts and inspires.

I have listened to this snapshot of James and this Polaroid of Tyisha for almost twenty years now, hearing their voices and the unyielding whiteness that silenced them. I will always have a lot to learn, but, at long last, this book amplifies what I have heard these many years. May the photograph infuse the phonograph (and vice versa) with the resistant resonance of the past and the present so that we can listen out toward a future world where children of color thrive and freely share their gifts. A world, at long last, worthy of Tyisha's smile, with streets safe for James Martinez Junior, now almost as old as his father ever would be, and his spitting image.

Introduction

The Sonic Color Line and the Listening Ear

Michael Dunn "denied calling the rap 'thug music' but admitted he thought it was 'rap-crap' and that it was 'ridiculously loud.'"
—*The Guardian* coverage of Dunn's murder of Jordan Davis at a gas station in Jacksonville, Florida, November 23, 2012

"Sandra Bland was very combative. It was not a model traffic stop. It was not a model person that was stopped."
—Waller County's district attorney, Elton Mathis, defending the actions of Brian Encinia, who pulled Sandra Bland over for failing to signal during a lane change. Bland was found hanged to death in the Waller County Jail on July 13, 2015, three days after her arrest for "assaulting an officer."

"The student sits quietly at her desk, and remains unresponsive as the officer Ben Fields asks her to come with him. He takes her silence as refusal, at which point he grabs her by the neck, pulls her backward in the desk, forcibly pulls her out of the desk and then slings her body across the classroom. He then yells at her, as she lies prone on the floor, to put her hands behind her back."
—Brittany Cooper in *Salon*, on Fields's violent police attack on a black girl at Spring Valley High School, captured on video on October 26, 2015

We need to talk about listening, power, and race. Willful white mishearings and auditory imaginings of blackness—often state-sanctioned—have long been a matter of life and death in the United States. However, recent events—and large-scale protests testifying to their occurrence and amplifying their impact—have temporarily halted the usual silence surrounding the violent consequences of the racialization of both sound and listening. Toward this end, *The Sonic Color Line* details the long historical entanglement between white supremacy and listening in the United States, contextualizing recent events such as the deaths of Jordan Davis and Sandra Bland within the ongoing struggle of black people to decolonize their listening practices, exert their freedom to sound in safety, diversity, and solidarity, and shift how they are heard in everyday life and in spaces allegedly public.

Without ever consciously expressing the sentiment, white Americans often feel entitled to respect for their sensibilities, sensitivities, and tastes, and to their implicit, sometimes violent, control over the soundscape of an ostensibly "free," "open," and "public" space. When middle-aged white man Michael Dunn murdered seventeen-year-old Davis at a Florida gas station in 2012, for example, he marked his aural territory. Dunn didn't want to hear hip-hop at the pumps, so he walked to the jeep where Davis and his friends were listening to music and demanded they turn it down. When the teenagers refused, Dunn shot into their car and fled.

In July 2015, white officer Brian Encinia pulled over a twenty-eight-year-old Bland en route to her new job at Prairie View A&M University. When she expressed annoyance, Encinia became angry; he called her noncompliant and commanded her to step out of her car. Bland told him she knew her rights and did not need to exit the vehicle or put her cigarette out. Encinia then told her he would "light [her] up" with his Taser, dragged her from the car, and pulled her along the ground until out of his dashboard camera's range. After tackling and handcuffing her, Encinia arrested Bland for "assaulting an officer." Three days later, Bland was found hanged in her cell. As of this writing, Bland's death remains unresolved; Waller County maintains she committed suicide, while her family has filed a wrongful death suit. Even though the Texas Department of Safety director maintains that "citizens have the right to be objectionable—they can be rude," Encinia's actions reveal how white authority figures continue to expect black people to perform more visible, overt, and extreme forms of compliance—through speech, vocal tone, eye contact, and physical behavior—than they ask of white subjects. Unarmed white people who display "noncompliant" behavior do not face violence, punishment, or death at the same rates as black people. An ongoing study by the *Guardian* finds that police kill black people at twice the rate of white people; black people whom police killed were twice as likely to be unarmed.[1] The ability to be audibly annoyed at getting a traffic ticket and live is a contemporary marker of a very old strain of white privilege expressed and embodied through sound.

Silence, on the other hand, offers black people no guaranteed refuge from state and police violence. In October 2015, a young black girl at Spring Valley High School was accused by her teacher of refusing to leave class after using her cell phone; she quietly stared forward at her desk until her school's "resource officer" grabbed and violently pulled her to the ground, desk and all. After he handcuffed and dragged her across the room, he arrested her for "disturbing the school," along with Niya Kenny, who had verbally defended her classmate. "I was crying, like literally crying and screaming like a baby," Kenny described. "I was screaming what the F, what the F, is this really happening. I was praying out loud for the girl. . . . I was just crying and he was like, 'Since you have so much to say, you coming, too. . . . You want some of this?' And just put my hands behind my back."[2] Rather than hear these black girls as children in need of protection, the teacher and school's police force transformed the girls' screams of pain, fearful prayers, and silences into "blackness": dangerous noise, outsized aggression, and a threatening strength.

These sounds, heard and unheard, have histories. If we listen, we can hear resonances with other times and places: segregation's hostile soundscapes, the obedient listening that whites expected of slaves, the screams and prayers of Frederick Douglass's Aunt Hester. Though dispersed by geography, circumstance, and mainstream news coverage insistent that each event is "not about race," the sonic color line inextricably connects them. This book exists to amplify such echoes until we all hear, acknowledge, and end such additions to America's resonant racial history. Double-voiced, this book unfolds in solidarity with everyone already hearing and resisting the sonic color line, offering new language and historical insight for the struggle against the deafening silence of so much death. This book listens as it speaks.

* * *

Race in America is a visual phenomenon. Americans have long understood race as expressed through attitudes about skin color and visible phenotypical differences—such as hair texture and lip contour—and the power differentials resulting from an ideological, racialized visual gaze. As Richard Dyer bluntly states in *White*, "looking and being looked at reproduce racial power relations."[3] When scholars invoke nonvisual idioms of race, they are treated as ancillary to visual indicators rather than as constitutive forces in their own right.

The Sonic Color Line connects sound with race in American culture, showing how listening operates as an organ of racial discernment, categorization, and resistance in the shadow of vision's alleged cultural dominance. While vision remains a powerfully defining element of race, scholars have yet to account for how other senses experience racialization and enact race feeling, both alone and in concert with sight.[4] Neither reifying nor negating vision, this book trumpets the importance of sound, in particular, as a critical modality through which subjects (re) produce, apprehend, and resist imposed racial identities and structures of racist violence. Because racism seems to be a "discourse of power that thinks with the eyes" in a culture driven by an "overdetermined politics of looking," sound has served as a repository of apprehension, oppression, and confrontation, rendered secondary—invisible—by visually driven epistemologies.[5] Far from being vision's opposite, sound frequently appears to be visuality's doppelgänger in U.S. racial history, unacknowledged but ever present in the construction of race and the performance of racial oppression.

To understand the entanglements of sound, race, and technology and the far-reaching material consequences of their collusion, *The Sonic Color Line* presents a cultural and political history detailing when, why, and how listening became a racialized body discipline and how it both informed and was informed by emergent sound technologies. I excavate a century of aural genealogies and a politics of racialized sound to reveal the dynamic relationships between racial ideologies, the development of sound media, and the modern listening practices that shape (and are shaped by) them. Following Kara Keeling, who theorizes "the cinematic" as "a complicated aggregate of capitalist social relations, sensory motor arrangements, and cognitive processes"—at once political, material, sensory, affective, and bodily—I plot a historical narrative that re-enmeshes technology's function as a material "mechanism and modality" of modernity with archival traces of its less apparent—but, as I will show, no less material—reality as a sensory politics flowing from and in tension with the (black) body.[6] I build from studies such as Jonathan Sterne's that "commingle physics and culture" to challenge instrumental, technologically determinant, and self-evidently triumphant narratives of sound reproduction's role in American history, with the insistence that its development and trajectory were indelibly shaped by and through the sonic color line's sonification of race and the racialization of listening.[7] The twentieth-century sound reproduction technologies I explore in the second half of the book—sound cinema and radio, respectively—emerged from and developed in tandem with several key corporeal sonic technologies of the nineteenth century—listening, vocal timbre, music writing, phonography, lynching, and the development of the "black voice"—body disciplines enlisted to mediate, embody, and resist the sonic color line, as the book's opening chapters detail.

The *Sonic Color Line* begins just before the Civil War, when white Southern elites scrambled to shore up slavery as a natural, inviolable system as it came under fire from white Northern abolitionists, black and white presses, and black activists such as Frederick Douglass and Harriet Jacobs. Essentialist ideas about "black" sounds and listening offered white elites a new method of grounding racial abjection in the body while cultivating white listening practices as critical, discerning, and delicate and, above all, as the standard of citizenship and personhood. The book pauses on the cusp of the Civil Rights Movement, at the birth of the racial formation of color blindness in the mid-1940s. American society remains bound by the intertwined political and sensory legacies of color blindness, particularly its narratives—optic and ideological—of racial progress, diversity, multiculturalism, and so-called post-race identity. However, Americans continue to hear, feel, think, and experience race, some leading lives invisibly (and audibly) structured by privilege, while so many othered peoples continue to struggle with exclusions, disadvantages, violence, and the added challenge of perpetually proving the impact of something that no longer officially exists. May this book amplify black performers', writers', and thinkers' historical testimony on the sonic color line; provide useful language for critiquing how race impacts perception; and demonstrate how sound and listening enable racism's evolving persistence.

Like the sounds and resistant practices comprising its focus, this book is diverse and deliberately disruptive. I examine performers who confirmed and strained against the sonic color line. By juxtaposing the racialized reception of their black and white audiences to African American writings from each period, I explore the sonics of black subjectivity and expose modernity's differential listening practices. I read slave narratives by Douglass and Jacobs as engaged with the operatic performances of Jenny Lind and Elizabeth Taylor Greenfield; I listen to echoes of the Fisk Jubilee Singers in Charles Chesnutt's *The Conjure Woman*; I consider collaborations between Louisiana-born songster turned New York City folk singer Huddie "Lead Belly" Ledbetter and Mississippi-born sharecropper's son turned novelist Richard Wright; and I restage a conversation about U.S. radio and race between singer Lena Horne, sociologist and theorist W. E. B. Du Bois, and novelist Ann Petry.

By design, *The Sonic Color Line* presents neither a seamless history of listening nor an encyclopedic taxonomy; it rather takes a cultural materialist approach to a series of resonant events between slavery and the end of segregation that reveals race to be fundamental to any historical consideration of U.S. listening practices (and vice versa). *The Sonic Color Line*'s selective case studies amplify an ongoing historical conversation between black writers and musical performers about listening's role in black selfhood, agency, citizenship, and racial discrimination. I examine musical calls and writerly responses (and writerly calls and musical responses)—across space, time, genre, and medium—as aural performances that together sound out the sonic color line and its impact on American lives. I do not intend my readings to further the neoliberal project of "giving voice to the voiceless" or recovering "lost" sounds. Instead, I make clear how U.S. white supremacy has attempted to suppress, tune out, and willfully misunderstand some sounds and their makers and histories. At the same time, I compel readers to listen deeply to the long history of black agency, resistance, and activism in the face of such silencing.

At once a literary study, performance analysis, cultural history, media study, and critical race theory, this project reveals race's audible contour—*the sonic color line*—and gives an account of key instances in its first one hundred years. I employ multiple methods to ask: What is the historical relationship between sonic and visual racial regimes? How have racialized American listening practices—and attendant sonic racial representations—emerged, spread, and changed over time? How has the sonic color line shaped and been shaped by the rise of audio reproduction technologies and representational discourses such as literature, journalism, and music? To address these questions, *The Sonic Color Line* places African American writers' and singers' ongoing conversations about sound and listening alongside the historical trajectory of theories of U.S. racial formation, the progression of sound reproduction technologies, the shifting sonics of white supremacy, American nationalism, and the everyday racial "structure of feeling" in four eras: the antebellum era, Reconstruction, the Great Depression, and the immediate post–World War II moment.

Through sonically attuned analyses that amplify the aurality of race and the unspoken power of racialized listening, I argue that sound functions as a set of social relations and a compelling medium for racial discourse. Sound has been entangled with vision since the conception of modern ideas of race and it has often operated at the leading edge of the visual to produce racialized identity formations. Overall, *The Sonic Color Line* interweaves original archival analysis with African American literary study to present a holistic approach to the sonics of race and the historical racialization of listening: I investigate materials from the South and the North across the nineteenth and twentieth centuries; I consider the shifting historical relationship between dominant and resistant practices; and I articulate "actual" sounds with textual representations of listening and the auditory imaginary.

To facilitate public conversation about the relationship between sound, race, and American life, I introduce two new concepts: the *sonic color line* and the *listening ear*. The sonic color line describes the process of racializing sound—how and why certain bodies are expected to produce, desire, and live amongst particular sounds—and its product, the hierarchical division sounded between "whiteness" and "blackness." The listening ear drives the sonic color line; it is a figure for how dominant listening practices accrue—and change—over time, as well as a descriptor for how the dominant culture exerts pressure on individual listening practices to conform to the sonic color line's norms. Through the listening ear's surveillance, discipline, and interpretation, certain associations between race and sound come to seem normal, natural, and "right." In the following section, I theorize each term, providing the framework for this book's interventions into African American literary history, sound studies, popular music study, and critical race theory.

The Sonic Color Line and the Listening Ear

I wrote much of this book in coffee shops; inevitably, people asked me what I was working on. White people, in particular, expressed surprise when I told them that I was writing a book on race and sound. I often received off-the-cuff critiques: What could I, a white American woman born in the post–Civil Rights era, know about race? You can't *see* sound, so how could it have a "race"? But when I added that I'm really writing about listening—about how we can hear race—something very telling often happened. "Oh wait a minute," my white (generally) male interlocutor would say, just before conspiratorially dropping his voice. "I get it! You mean like this!"[8] And then, right there in the Starbucks, I'd witness a minstrel show—performances I kept hoping never to hear but that their performers always seemed so eager to give.

Over time, I perfected my part in this American melodrama. "You're only partly right," I'd say, shaking my head and delivering some version of the following monologue: "But not for the reason you think. My book is about where and how you learned that voice—how you came to believe it was 'black,' why you think it sounds funny and weird and sexual, and how you feel like you own it, so much so that you whip it out to a stranger in a coffee shop. That right there, the fact that you and so many white people have this same 'black voice' in their heads, is the sonic color line. And the listening ear explains your erroneous assumption that I would find this voice as funny and weird and sexual as you do because my skin color determines how you think I should listen, what I might want to hear. The listening ear told you to look around and drop your voice to make sure no black person would hear you and lets me know, white person to white person, that we are about to have one of those *really* white moments together, where we will listen to and feel our whiteness through your impression of this vocal stereotype. I am actually writing my book to call attention to these moments, right here, to show the damage they have done and continue to do, and put a stop to them."

Sometimes these exchanges led to arguments, sometimes to deep conversations; most often they resulted in silence. Some days I dreaded these moments. Other days, I wished a dude would. "My book *is* about race," I'd tell them. "It's about whiteness. And we know *a lot* about whiteness—we have been listening to it our whole lives." Despite the many protests of various coffee shop minstrels, their voices told me they heard it too.

* * *

I am indebted to W. E. B. Du Bois for my concept of the sonic color line, particularly his schema of the visual color line in *The Souls of Black Folk* (1903) and his reimagining of that color line as a suffocating plate glass enclosure in *Dusk of Dawn* (1940).[9] Du Bois's profound intellectual shift in the 1940s—from the veil to the vacuum as his preeminent metaphor for race—accounts for the multisensory experience and auditory affect of race that I now theorize as the sonic color line and the listening ear. Far from the first to consider the sonics of Du Bois's work, I build from the scholarship of Alexander Weheliye and others to rethink Du Bois's concept of the veil as an audiovisual entity, one that helps us understand the relationship between sight and sound in the production of racial identity.[10] Using the visual metonym of the veil—an image that redounds in African American literature and thought after *Souls*—Du Bois's key intervention called out the color line and segregation as *causes* of social difference, rather than its "inevitable" result, challenging mainstream turn-of-the-twentieth-century discourse on the "Negro problem."[11]

Du Bois's image of the veil stands in for the ideological barrier whites constructed between themselves and black people in U.S. society and the perceptual distortions resulting on either side. It makes palpable the visual representational processes that render black people either invisible or hypervisible, but never truly seen and known. However, the veil's fundamental visuality invites rather than excludes an engagement with sound, particularly in regard to its evocation of acousmatic phenomena, the emanation of sound from an unseen source.[12] Du Bois's multiply-signifying veil, therefore, comments on race's ocular politics rather than merely describing them. Critiquing the propensity of European modernity to value evidence produced by the eye over evidence generated by the ear—which, according to Charles Hirschkind, Enlightenment thinkers such as Immanuel Kant associated with passivity, self-subordination, and emotional misjudgment[13]—Du Bois asserts that whites' obsession with looking *caused* an extreme distortion of vision. Whites cannot see through their veil of race—a product of hundreds of years of their ignorance, misrepresentation, and self-serving violence—and their loss of vision actually enables them to continue dehumanizing black people, characterizing them as abstract, shadowy "problems" rather than individual, rights-bearing subjects, modernity's sine qua non.

Du Bois noticed the growing connections between race and sound in his second autobiography, *Dusk of Dawn*, written in the grim years leading up to World War II. *Dusk of Dawn* opened not with the bold pronouncements of *Souls*—"the problem of the twentieth century is the problem of the color-line"—but with an "Apology" that such declarations are now impossible.[14] *Dusk of Dawn* sifts through the failure of reason in the face of intractable racism and violence, made palpable by what seemed in the late 1930s to be the apex of white supremacy in both theory and praxis. With admirable yet wrenching self-critique, Du Bois seriously questions *Souls'* assertion that the color line could be breached by a "series of brilliant assaults" on racism's fundamentally flawed logic. Any literary, artistic, or political project challenging race, *Dusk of Dawn* warns, will be gravely complicated by the fact that whites not only have been conditioned to see *and* hear the world differently but also have labeled and propagated this sensory configuration as universal, objective truth. To explain the persistence of race, Du Bois uses the figure of the plate glass vacuum chamber, where the color line, invisible to the eye, manifests itself as a transparent wall. While white and black people remain visible to each other, no sound penetrates the walls. The white people on the outside laugh and point at the trials and tribulations of the black people inside, who are "screaming in the vacuum, unheard."[15]

Du Bois's notion of the visible color line has long had an aural echo, the resonances of which I theorize as *the sonic color line*. The sonic color line is both a hermeneutics of race and a marker of its im/material presence. It enables listeners to construct and discern racial identities based on voices, sounds, and particular soundscapes—the clang and rumble of urban life versus suburban "peace and quiet," for instance—and, in turn, to mobilize racially coded batteries of sounds as discrimination by assigning them differential cultural, social, and political value. The sonic color line produces, codes, and polices racial difference through the ear, enabling us to hear race as well as see it. It is a socially constructed boundary that racially codes sonic phenomena such as vocal timbre, accents, and musical tones. On one level, the sonic color line posits racialized subject positions like "white," "black," and "brown" as historical accretions of sonic phenomena and aural stereotypes that can function without their correlating visual signifiers and often stand in for them, as in the case of the coffee shop minstrel. Through multiple simultaneous processes of dominant representation—as this book's journalistic, literary, and phonographic evidence will show—particular sounds are identified, exaggerated, and "matched" to racialized bodies. For example, Nina Eidsheim argues that white listeners' visual constructions of race in the nineteenth century shifted the sound of black voices, creating a distorted aural effect she calls "sonic blackness." Lisa Gitelman describes how early recording technologies ushered in a new era of blackface minstrelsy in which "sounding black" became more important for white performers than applying burnt cork, positing music as "another possible substance of intrinsic racial difference."[16] White-constructed ideas about "sounding Other"—accents, dialects, "slang," and extraverbal utterances, as well as ambient sounds—have flattened the complex range of sounds actually produced by people of color, marking the sonic color line's main contour.

This book examines how American culture polices the sonic color line at the level of representation, where political powers affix meaning. Representations have a profound role in shaping thoughts, bodies, even notions of reality itself. Racial ideologies are (re)produced through the representational structures of discourse, aural imagery, and performance. While "sounding black" remains linked to looking black, a process I discuss in this book, aural ideas of "blackness" can also trump notions of authenticity proffered via visible phenotype. White radio actors Freeman Fisher Gosden and Charles Correll played the neominstrel characters Amos and Andy, but black actor Frank Wilson was not hired to narrate the 1941 radio program *Freedom's People* because he sounded "too much like a white man" to both white and black producers.[17] These examples point to the instability of sound as a racial determinant and the possibility of crossing the sonic color line; they also highlight that there are very definite ideas "matching" racialized bodies to sounds in U.S. culture. Aural and visual signifiers of race are thoroughly enmeshed; sounds never really lose their referent to different types of bodies despite being able to operate independently of them.

Whiteness, on the other hand, is notorious for representing itself as "invisible"—or in this case, inaudible (at least to white people).[18] The inaudibility of whiteness stems from its considerably wider palette of representation and the belief that white representations stand in for "people" in general, rather than "white people" in particular. The inaudibility of whiteness does not mean it has no sonic markers, but rather that Americans are socialized to perceive them as the keynote of American identity.[19] As dominant listening practices discipline us to process white male ways of sounding as default, natural, normal, and desirable—more on this in a moment—they deem alternate ways of listening and sounding aberrant and—depending upon the historical context—as excessively sensitive, strikingly deficient, or impossibly both.

While never seeming to speak its own name, white sonic identity imagines itself against circumscribed representations of how people of color sound. The binary hierarchy of proper/improper marks one border of the sonic color line; the socially constructed divisions between sound/noise and quiet/loud mark two others. For example, the sonic color line enables particular brands of white speech to become "standard English," as I examine via Charles Chesnutt's short stories in chapter 3 and radio historiography in chapter 5. The sonic color line amplifies the "propriety" of standard white speech, as opposed to—and perpetually threatened by—dialects, accents, and "improper" slang attributed to immigrants and/or people of color. Whiteness's entanglement with "correct speech" has direct material effects, particularly in housing and employment opportunities, as sociologist John Baugh's linguistic profiling research has determined.[20]

The sonic color line also codifies sounds linked to racialized bodies—such as music and the ambient sounds of everyday living—as "noise," sound's loud and unruly "Other."[21] Noise is not merely loudness measured in decibels. Like recordist and theorist Tony Schwartz, I maintain that noise depends on the ear of the beholder. "Noise is an editorial word," Schwartz argues. "When you talk about noise, you are talking about sound that is bothering you. There's no party so noisy as the one you're not invited to."[22] I consider noise a shifting analytic that renders certain sounds—and the bodies that produce and consume them—as Other, what Cornel West describes as "incomprehensible and unintelligible" under white supremacist epistemologies.[23] While cultural uses of "noise" are not exclusive to race—the noise of industry, for example, or of sporting events—I refer specifically to how the sonic color line invokes noise in direct connection to (or as a metonymic stand-in for) people of color, and particularly blackness. The sound of hip-hop pumped at top volume through car speakers, for example, has become a stand-in for the bodies of young black men in American culture; noise ordinances seeking to "tame the boom car monster"—words used in Rochester, New York—allow for racial profiling without ever explicitly mentioning race.[24] Sometimes tolerated, but more often fetishized as exotic or demonized as unassimilable, noise and loudness frequently function as aural substitutes for and markers of race and form key contours of the sonic color line that I map out in this book: *music*/noise (throughout), *word*/sound, *sense*/nonsense (chapter 1), *cultivated*/raw, *controlled*/excessive (chapter 2), *proper*/improper, *assimilable*/foreign, *listener*/performer (chapter 3), *quiet*/loud, *smooth*/rough (chapter 4), and *cold*/emotional (chapter 5).

To expose the historical genealogy of dominant listening practices and to provide new critical tools to deconstruct and dismantle "race" via its sonic register, I offer *the listening ear* as the ideological filter shaped in relation to the sonic color line. The listening ear represents a historical aggregate of normative American listening practices and gives a name to listening's epistemological function as a modality of racial discernment. An aural complement to and interlocutor of the gaze, the listening ear is what Judith Butler calls "a constitutive constraint"[25]: a socially constructed ideological system producing but also regulating cultural ideas about sound. The listening ear enables the key dichotomies of the sonic color line traced in this book; it normalizes the aural tastes and standards of white elite masculinity as the singular way to interpret sonic information. From the antebellum era through the mid-twentieth century, the American listening ear developed through multiple, intersecting representational discourses to process dominant ways of sounding as default—natural, normal, and desirable—while deeming alternate ways of listening and sounding aberrant.

I also build the listening ear from Michel Foucault's theory of discipline and "the way in which the body itself is invested in power relations."[26] Disciplinary processes greatly inform my approach to listening and its tense, mutually constitutive relationship with shifting racial ideologies. Foucault mainly speaks of sensory discipline through visual surveillance and the concept of the gaze, most famously through Jeremy Bentham's Panopticon, the Enlightenment prison whose architecture enabled jailers to watch prisoners without being seen. As Les Bull and Michael Back point out, Foucault's theorizations neglect that Bentham also built auditory surveillance into his prison: a series of hidden, connected tubes allowed the wardens to listen in at will.[27] *The Sonic Color Line* takes up Bull and Back's provocation, using Foucault's insights on discipline and training, to flesh out a "history of listening" that is theoretical, embodied, and sensitive to power, particularly the processes of subjection, racialization, and nationalism.[28] Since the establishment of slavery and the codification of Jim Crow laws in its wake, listening has greatly impacted how bodies are categorized according to racial hierarchies and how raced subjects imagined themselves and negotiated a thoroughly racialized society.

This book identifies the processes enabling some listeners to hear themselves as "normal" citizens—or, to use legal discourse, "reasonable"—while compelling Others to understand their sonic production and consumption—and therefore themselves—as aberrant. Essentially, one's ideas about race shape what and how one hears and vice versa. Although often deemed an unmediated physical act, listening is an interpretive, socially constructed practice conditioned by historically contingent and culturally specific value systems riven with power relations. While speculative philosophic work such as Jean-Luc Nancy's *Listening*—which decouples listening from automatic connection with understanding and reminds us that "to listen is to be straining toward a possible meaning"[29]—has been helpful, I theorize listening as a historical and material practice, one both lived and artistically imagined. I show the dangers and the stakes of grand narratives through archival documentation of a specific racialized filter developed in the United States in the 1840s and the resistance mounted to it by black artists and thinkers. The listening ear is far from the only form of listening; however, it is a stance wielding much power, intersecting with and impacting the many other widely variable practices we experience collectively as "listening."

Occurring at the intersection of class, sexuality, gender, and race, listening offers an epistemological venue for our particular embodiments; our embodiments, in turn, filter incoming sound along various indices of classification and value. A footstep outside a window at night, for example, can have divergent meanings for men and women, and a different resonance for a white mistress than for a black female slave, an example taken up in chapter 2. I use "embodied ear" to represent how individuals' listening practices are shaped by the totality of their experiences, historical context, and physicality, as well as intersecting subject positions and particular interactions with power (the listening ear).[30] I hope that coupling "embodied" and "ear" will remind us of the relationship between ideology and materiality as well as the important interventions of deaf-studies scholars to expand notions of listening beyond an inaccurate focus on the ear as its sole source. Steph Ceraso, for example, urges us to think of listening as "multimodal," vibrations experienced by the entire body and interpreted in conjunction with other senses, while Cara Lynne Cardinale challenges sound studies to consider a radical deafness in which sign language and "look-listening" point to the limits of sound and language (rather than reveal lacks).[31]

Although one filter among many, the listening ear exerts pressure on the embodied ear's numerous listening practices, naturalizing the sonic color line as the singular—and often the most pressing—way to process aural information. In outlining how listening operates as a form of racial subjection, I wish neither to fetishize the listening ear nor to make its own unevenness and complexity into a monolith. Instead, I theorize the listening ear as a singular term because my archive tells me it works by attempting to suppress and reduce an individual's myriad, fine-grained embodied listening experiences by shunting them into narrow, conditioned, and "correct" responses that are politically, culturally, economically, legally, and socially advantageous to whites. At times, the listening ear appears monolithic precisely because that is what it strives to be. From antebellum slavery to mid-twentieth-century color blindness, the listening ear has evolved to become the *only* way to listen, interpret, and understand; in legal discourse, the listening ear claims to be how any "reasonable person" should listen.

"Un-airing" the Past: Methodologies of the Sonic Color Line

I locate my work on the sonic color line as part of a collective project within African American literary and cultural studies to, as Carter Mathes contends, "emphasize the sonic as a conceptual field that might facilitate the radical projection of African American experience."[32] Earlier generations of critics theorized black diasporic writing in terms of sound, particularly Houston Baker, Henry Louis Gates, Paul Gilroy, Hazel Carby, and Stuart Hall, who argued that sound is a large part of what is "black" about black popular culture.

> In its expressivity, its musicality, its orality, in its rich, deep, and varied attention to speech, in its inflections toward the vernacular and the local, in its rich production of counternarratives, and, above all, in its metaphorical use of the musical vocabulary, black popular culture has enabled the surfacing, inside the mixed and contradictory modes even of some mainstream popular culture, of elements of a discourse that is different—other forms of life, other traditions of representation.[33]

Within academia's historically logocentric white supremacist structures, these thinkers launched new ways of conceiving of aesthetics, value, history, theory, and memory. But while they centralized music to reconceive black literary aesthetics, their analysis remained largely structural and metaphoric.[34] Building from these broad strokes, scholars—guided by Daphne Brooks, Farah Jasmine Griffin, Fred Moten, Gayle Wald, and Weheliye—have recently retheorized the relationship between black performance practice and writing as mutually informative. This critical move enables contemporary scholars to engage with the sonics of black cultural production on a more granular level—a "search for resonances" in Emily Lordi's terms and a "listening in detail" in Alexandra Vazquez's methodology—within a wider social and historical context.[35] Scholars can now listen to the unique ways in which African American artists mobilize sound beyond structuring principle and as so much

[handwritten margin note: lots of references]

more than an object: as event, experience, affect, archive, and, as Shana Redmond argues, method.[36]

By tracing a historical conversation between black writers and musicians about the racial politics of listening, this book makes three interventions in the study of African American literature. First, I amplify black performers and writers as theorists of listening, using aural imagery and musical strategies to explore listening as a form of agency, a technique of survival, an ethics of community building, a practice of self-care, a guide through racialized space, a site of racialization, and a mode of decolonizing. Second, current approaches to the sonics of African American literature have focused more intensely on literature and music considered explicitly "experimental," beginning with the black arts movement. By locating my study in the hundred-year period just before the Civil Rights Movement, I break down the experimental/traditional binary, articulating what Mathes calls the "imaginative landscape of experimental sonority" in contemporary black writing with more "realist" forms, such as the slave narrative, framed vernacular tale, and social protest novel.[37] By *listening* to works by writers such as *[margin: 3 Ref]* Jacobs, Chesnutt, and Wright—and foregrounding how these authors conceived and represented listening itself—I argue that we can hear the radical aurality and sonic aesthetics of their work submerged by time, shifts in aesthetics, and limited readings of their artistry as sociological description and/or mere vehicles for racial liberalism. Earlier black writers and musicians experimented with aural imagery to *[margin: music]* radically challenge the mobilization of sound by white power structures, and they did it with *style*. I take seriously Ann Petry's 1950 rejoinder to *[margin: Ref]* critics that the "craftsmanship that goes into [social protest novels] is of *[margin: "It has to be"]* a high order. *It has to be*."[38] Finally, I identify a new signifyin(g) chain within the black literary tradition, the "trope of the listener": scenes focused on characters' listening experience as their primary sense. According to Gates, black literature's "ur-trope" is the "talking book," a recurrent metaphor in the earliest slave narratives such as *The Interesting Narrative* *[margin: Ref]* *of the Life of Olaudah Equiano* (1789). Shifting the discussion from the "talking book" to "the listener" enables us to conceive a more complex interrelationship between orality—what is spoken—and aurality—what *[margin: Spoken → heard]* is heard—as epistemes of knowledge production and forms of resistance to (and within) written expression. By amplifying the trope of the listener, I invite scholars to hear a new "web of filiation"[39] between texts, one that uses sound to signify between genres and across wide swaths of time—revealing dissonances in listening practices *and* uncomfortable historical affinities—and the literary soundscape itself as a form of double-voicedness. Despite the ubiquity and richness of sound in most novels, the visual image still dominates literary analysis; I direct scholars toward literary soundscapes as a subject of critical attention.[40]

Learning to listen differently to race, gender, power, place, and history brought me to "sound studies," not the other way around; however, the field's methodological freedom greatly enabled my scholarship in African American literature, music, and history. As you will see in this book, I meet sound where, when, and in what form I find it, not as an object of study, but as a method enabling an understanding of race as an aural experience with far-reaching historical and material resonance. Recent critiques of the field for its broad perspective on sound mistake methodological innovation for playing fast and loose, claiming "the generalizability of sound, in its most imprecise uses, can sidestep the effects of institutional histories and the structuring influence of entrenched debates."[41] To this description, ironically, I say, "*Exactly!*" One way to read this book is as an extended, historically and theoretically grounded argument for such "sidesteps" in and *as* sound studies, methodological moves made not to avoid contending with established music history, but rather as a strategy of critical sonar to navigate the epistemological terrain that "music"—as a culturally specific, politically charged, and "entrenched" category of value—can obscure. The history of the sonic color line and the listening ear should compel scholars to question music's cultural and institutional privilege rather than assuming it because allegedly "music studies predates sound studies by two millennia."[42] Rearticulating music as a culturally and historically conditioned form of sound in political relation to (and flowing from, and toward) other sounds—none of which exist, as Gustavus Stadler reminds us, "outside of [their] perception by specifically marked subjects and bodies within history"—offers a deeper understanding of *how* and *why* music means, and to whom. *The Sonic Color Line*'s deliberate archival "sidesteps" also function as much-needed historiographical echolocation through and beyond "the overwhelming whiteness of scholars in the field,"[43] tracing a much longer, broader, and blacker history of thinking and writing sound, enabling us to hear theorists, artists, writers, and thinkers silenced by institutional histories built on their very exclusion.

Since I began this research, the field of sound studies has grown exponentially, to the point where we can no longer say the field is "emerging." Work on sound and race has appeared much more slowly—in part because of the processes this book explores—but recent special issues of *Social Text, American Quarterly*, and *Radical History Review* centralized interdisciplinary conversations about sound, race, citizenship, subjectivity, and the body.[44] Liana Silva and Aaron Trammell and I also cofounded *Sounding Out!: The Sound Studies Blog* in 2009 explicitly to address the whiteness and maleness of institutionalized "sound studies" and the field's inattention to power in its research agenda. As editor-in-chief, I publish scholarship directing the field's energy toward sound's social, cultural, and political contexts, in particular how listening constructs and impacts variously positioned bodies.

This book stages four key interventions in sound studies' critical conversation on race and sound. First, I revise the increasingly canonized and overwhelmingly white and male historiography of sound studies, which neglects the work by black writers, thinkers, and scholars on sound and listening dating back at least a hundred and fifty years. I challenge sound studies to consider black artists as theorists and agents of sound, rather than solely as performers or producers. Second, I push existent discourse on sound and race to consider whiteness as an auditory construction. In particular, I identify how black cultural producers have used aural imagery to amplify and challenge how white power structures have mobilized sound to define black racial identities, drawing attention to how whiteness constitutes itself through sonic markers and sounded exclusions. Third, I add significantly to sound studies' overarching project to trace a "history of listening," through meticulous archival documentation of various listening practices and by insisting that histories of listening are always multiple, not only enmeshed in the matrices of social difference and power but also helping to constitute them. Finally, identifying the sonic color line as an externally imposed difference opens up possibilities for new forms of agency through listening. Building from Hall's notion of "decolonized sensibilities,"[45] I show how the proliferation of multiple and diverse black listening practices is itself a form of resistance to the colonizing idea that—in order to have the rights and privileges of national citizenship and at times, shockingly, to be considered human—one has to listen similarly to power: valuing the same sounds in the same ways and reproducing only certain sounds the listening ear deems appropriate, pleasurable, and respectable.

Examining one's listening practices and challenging their predisposed affects, reactions, and interpretations are fundamental for the development of new ways of being in the world and for forging cross-racial solidarities capable of dismantling the sonic color line and the racialized listening practices enabling and enabled by it. Marta Savigliano argues, building on Frantz Fanon, that decolonization "entails learning/ unlearning the preeminence of abstract totalizing Enlightenment logics over bodies and their often absurd techniques of survival."[46] While my use of "decolonization" may seem anachronistic—my book ends shortly before a large wave of uprisings led by black and brown peoples against colonial powers in Africa, South America, and the Caribbean—it highlights that decolonizing does not begin after revolutions but rather that decolonized people *lead* revolutions. Decolonizing begins at colonization, and listening, in particular, is an important method to access freedom, agency, power, and selfhood.

Although intimately intertwined with constructions of "blackness" and "whiteness," the sonic color line and the listening ear have resonance beyond the racialized subject positions of black and white. Other racial and ethnic groups in the United States are subject to aural stereotyping, "linguistic profiling," and discriminatory listening practices.[47] I have written about the racialization of sound in other historical and social contexts—particularly in the cases of Puerto Rican migration to New York City in the 1950s and current anti-immigration legislation directed against Latina/os in the American Southwest—however, this project focuses specifically on the mutually constitutive relationship between sound/listening and the U.S. black and white racial hierarchy between 1845 and 1945.[48] As Sharon Holland argues, "in calls to abandon the black/white dichotomy for more expansive readings of racism's spectacular effects, critics often ignore the psychic life of racism," precisely the site where *The Sonic Color Line* lingers.[49] I do not study the black/white paradigm as the only important difference in the United States, but rather I question how and why the myth of "blackness" and "whiteness" as polarities—one hopelessly abject, the other powerfully "normal"—persists and adjusts to changing demographics and historical circumstances. Despite copious amounts of scholarship documenting the complexities of the U.S. racial spectrum, the black/white binary still retains an enormous amount of symbolic weight and material consequence.[50] The black/white binary has never been about descriptive accuracy, but rather it is a deliberately reductionist racial project constructing white power and privilege against the alterity and abjection of the imagined polarity of "blackness" and the transfer of this power across generations and (white) ethnicities, what Cheryl Harris calls "whiteness as property" and George Lipsitz dubbed "the possessive investment in whiteness."[51] This project does not assume that what is true for some black people is true for all marginalized peoples, as the logic of the black/white binary would have it; rather, my exploration produces a more complicated understanding of how white and black people have mobilized sonic signifiers at particular historical junctures to produce, enable, circumscribe, and challenge dominant notions of "blackness," one of the sharpest edges of the sonic color line, and "whiteness," its bluntest instrument of power.

While my main theoretical emphasis in *The Sonic Color Line* is race, my research remains deeply attuned to gender's impact on listening and vice versa. I regard race and gender as intersectional political identities experienced simultaneously and in a complex, highly contextual relationship; both race and gender—along with sexuality and class—impact how one sounds and listens. *The Sonic Color Line* is mindful of how, as Christine Ehrick argues, "gender is also represented, contested, and reinforced through the aural,"[52] in particular through its detailed examinations of sound and listening in a geographical and historical context. Our experiences of race are necessarily linked to our gendered identities; our gender identities cannot be conceived separately from our racialized experience, an idea infusing this book, beginning with Jacobs's struggle to show the raced edge of the notion that white American women in the nineteenth century had "delicate ears," and concluding with Lutie Johnson, the protagonist of Petry's *The Street*, being stalked aggressively by the particular form of silence black women face in a white supremacist America, what Kimberly Foster calls "the terror of being uncared for."[53]

Petry and several other writers in this book reveal how very deeply the contexts of race and gender continue to matter—and remain controversial—in the reception of so-called universal sounds, such as screams. Although a June 2015 study by psychologists and neural scientists at New York University and the University of Geneva concluded that "screams are the one uncontroversially universal vocalization," I maintain that the sonic color line's disciplining of the senses disrupts notions of "universal" listening. In certain contexts, for example, and depending on the listener, a black woman's scream is heard differently from a white woman's, even if both screams displayed similar properties of pitch, tone, timbre, and volume; the sonic color line maps divergent impacts and meanings for these two sounds, as dependent on the race and gender of the listener as they are on the perceived race and gender of the screamer. Douglass, for instance, notices the sound of his Aunt Hester screaming caused the slave master to whip her harder and longer, while in Wright's fiction, even the *thought* of a white woman screaming sets murders, lynchings, and mass migrations in motion. Both these examples also show how masculinity is experienced through and bound up with listening. While the slave master hears his sexual potency and power in Hester's screams, Douglass hears his inability, as both child and slave, to help his beloved aunt, which drives him toward an understanding of listening as ethical involvement. Wright shows how the white female scream hovers in the nation's sonic imaginary as confirmation of a rapacious black masculinity, and how this sound warps white men toward violence and just plain warps black men, who grow up knowing this scream heralds death.

In examining the relation between raced and gendered perception, I am also careful to interweave rather than collapse the historical processes I see at work in the formation of the sonic color line with the equally complicated, concurrent formation of a sonic glass ceiling. Although far from destiny, biology has a different valence in terms of gender and voice, binding voices in some degree to what Ehrick describes as "physiological parameters of comfortable pitch range" and "voice quality settings." However, Ehrick also notes how "humans can and do place their voices in ways that are consistent with the performative aspects of gender."[54] As with race, the sound of a voice does not *cause* sexism, but rather sexism disciplines the cultural meanings attached to perceived gendered differences in the voice, impacting expressions of race and sexuality as well as assumptions of class. For instance, Liana Silva argues that loudness remains a male privilege in American culture, so women who wield loud voices are dubbed lower class and "noisy, rude, unapologetic, unbridled." Silva calls attention to loudness's special valence for women of color, whose raced identities raise the stakes of respectability politics. Women of color risk being marginalized by men of all races as well as white women, attuned to women of color's expressions of loudness as hostile, immature, angry, less intelligent, and/or divisive. In a society bound by sonic color lines *and* glass ceilings, "loudness," Silva contends, "is something racialized people cannot afford."[55] By theorizing listening as a medium for race and gender hierarchies, *The Sonic Color Line* contextualizes gendered voices within a wider soundscape of music and ambient sounds also subject to raced and gendered policing.

* * *

Traversing multiple archives and utilizing more than one critical method, my interdisciplinary methodology uses archival, literary, and cultural analyses. Through intensive archival excavation and close reading, I "unair" sound and representations of listening in discursive sites where it is not usually looked for: novels, short stories, essays, newspaper coverage, letters, memoirs, etiquette manuals, and advertisements. Bruce Smith describes "unairing" as "acoustic archaeology," a process of "learning to hear, and not just see" evidence embedded in written materials.[56] I locate "unaired" literary sound and embed it in a historical context, tracing the sonic color line and the listening ear through readings that return a sense of proximity to events, people, and perspectives made distant and disparate by traditional archival practice. Through meticulous microhistory, I show how sounds come to us "already listened to," whether we encounter them in print, on recordings, or in our own ears. This book deliberately disrupts the border between "actual" and imagined sound, joining Moten and Smith, who argue that discursive sound constructs, alters, and contests historical memory.[57] *The Sonic Color Line* builds a case for the importance of aural imagery[58] and sonic imaginaries—the multiple ways in which we think, write, and represent sound and listening experiences—to cultural history, breaking new ground while enabling fresh readings of canonical literary texts and performances.

While I stage my interventions at the intersection of African American studies and sound studies, I borrow methodologically from cultural studies. Hall's idea of representation and Roland Barthes's discussion of adjectives in musical discourse provide crucial connective tissue between language and culture that enables my theoretically informed and historically contextualized close-reading practice to intervene at the critical site where audio intersects the literary and both meet the epistemological: language. Because "music is," according to Barthes, "by a natural inclination, what immediately receives an adjective,"[59] evocative reportage of the voice and sound of African American performers reveals a host of racialized aural representations—the sonic color line— and written traces of racialized listening practices—the listening ear. I use close reading to distill American "sonic protocols": culturally specific and socially constructed conventions that shape how sound is indexed, valued, and interpreted at any given moment. Like Marjorie Garber, I believe close reading is less about teasing out *what* something means and much more key to understanding "the *way* something means."[60] Literary texts not only produce and represent their own sounds[61] but also represent and record the process of sound's social production. The hurried, utilitarian diction of journalism and advertising copy—never intended to be pored over—often provides some of the most profound renderings of the sonic color line, while the densely layered poetic language of literature—conflicting, contradictory, and evocative— frequently attempts to replot that same line, constructing representations that urge readers to hear their world differently.

My genealogy of listening in the United States moves through four eras of musical performance and literary production—antebellum slavery, Reconstruction, Jim Crow, and World War II—bridging the nineteenth and twentieth centuries, something few sound studies do. Beginning before the invention of the phonograph enables *The Sonic Color Line* to challenge existing historiographies of sound that give primacy to recording technologies and archives of "actual" sound. Continually privileging recorded texts in the story of sound enacts a kind of technological determinism obscuring how social, cultural, and historical forces mediate sound and audio technologies. While I draw on a number of recorded texts, my study makes a case for written representations as a form of recording, documenting the historical listening practices of the writers themselves. Inspired by Weheliye's understanding of history as "a series of vexed knots that require the active intervention of the critic or DJ,"[62] I "think sound" differently here, digging deeply within the crates of each historical moment under discussion, juxtaposing a wide range of generically diverse sources to create an alternate sense of historical context itself, a transformed "structure of feeling" that takes multiple voices, soundscapes, and socially produced listening practices into account.[63]

The book begins just before the U.S. Civil War, and its first two chapters detail the rise of the sonic color line as a function of slavery and a site of contestation for America's new popular culture industry. Chapter 1 reads slave narratives by Douglass and Jacobs as literary, theoretical, and historical texts, laying bare the starkly racialized sonics of slavery's power differentials to examine how and why whites technologized listening as racial discipline and revealing how slaves used listening as resistance and self-preservation. Douglass's and Jacobs's aural imagery shows how whites constructed sound as irrational and emotional—in Western culture, the province of women and slaves—and mobilized it to fix race and gender in the body. Both develop the trope of the listener to launch pointed critiques of white listening habits and to amplify listening as an avenue of agency for black people in the struggle to hear and free themselves.

However, as chapter 2 makes clear, the antebellum sonic color line wasn't confined to the South. It structured life in the North as well, as I show through analysis of the concert reviews of two female singers who ascended to center stage in the nation's burgeoning popular culture industry: "the Swedish Nightingale" Jenny Lind and Elizabeth Taylor Greenfield, "the Black Swan." The growing conflict over women's rights made these women's voices hyperaudible sites of raced and gendered conflict in the public sphere, and the racialized tropes of audible "whiteness" and "blackness" emerging from the dueling divas' media flurry disciplined the dominant U.S. listening ear with raced and gendered logics inflecting scientific breakthroughs regarding timbre and sound vibrations.

Chapter 3 locates the sonic color line's next big shift during Radical Reconstruction, examining how developing sound recording technology in the 1870s was preceded and anticipated by the intensive repetition of

the Jubilee Singers' corporeal performance and the techniques of phonography explored by writer Chesnutt. Building on Moten's notion of
the intertwined nature of resistance and subjection, this chapter examines "the black voice" itself as a sonic technology of Reconstruction
that interrogated and soothed America's bloody racial history and the
rifts of the recent Civil War. Both the Jubilee Singers and Chesnutt used
the trope of the listener to gain representational control of the historical memory of slavery, challenging dominant racial narratives locating
race in the blood and defining black people as cultureless, uneducable,
and unassimilable. The Jubilees and Chesnutt succeeded in shifting
definitions of "authentic" blackness away from blackface performance;
however, mainstream American media outlets appropriated their representations to shore up a new sonic image of blackness focused on
sounds of suffering.

The sonic color line's third major shift occurred at the intersection
of music, sound cinema, and lynching during the Great Depression
and the Great Migration. Here the sonic color line skewed toward circumscribing public performances of black masculinity, which I trace
by interweaving the late-1930s musical career of Huddie "Lead Belly"
Ledbetter with the early fiction of his friend and contemporary, author
Richard Wright. Folklorist John Lomax strategically sold Lead Belly's
music to white audiences as the thrilling, authentic sound of the "to-be-
lynched" body, enabled by and enabling the sonic color line to "match"
black male bodies with particular voices and musics. But as synchronous
sound cinema displaced "silent" films during this era, the notion of the
"sound track" introduced new possibilities for listening that unsettled
established relationships between sound and the visual image. Using
new cinematic techniques, Wright's fiction from this period challenges
Lomax's representation of Ledbetter by "soundtracking" lynching and
segregation, creating a decolonizing practice intervening in "the ideology of the visible"[64] while simultaneously exposing sound's invisible
ideological freight, carrying lynching far beyond the South and racial
segregation across spatial color lines.

The book closes amidst World War II's immediate aftermath, showing how the sonic color line not only enabled the racial formation we
now know as "color blindness" but also surreptitiously became race's
lingua franca. Radio, in particular, was a technology of the sonic color

line, developing and circulating new acousmatic sonic protocols of racialized sounding and listening no longer dependent on immediate bodily presence. Building upon Ledbetter and Wright's depictions of the sonic color line within segregated Northern cities, I show how radio broadcasts and production practices reproduced raced and gendered urban spaces and enabled the emerging discourse of color blindness. I begin by investigating the subtle racing of singer Lena Horne's voice over the 1940s airwaves, focusing on how and why her vocal crossing— and resistant performances—threatened the nation's underlying racial order. Like Horne, a vocal critic of radio's increasingly subtle racializations and hidden exclusions, Du Bois critiqued radio via his social theory in *Dusk of Dawn*, emphasizing America's movement away from the linear and visual metaphor of the color line to a figuration of race as a plate-glass vacuum chamber, an aural metaphor influenced, I argue, by his work as a behind-the-scenes consultant for CBS Radio's *Americans All, Immigrants All*. Du Bois shows the importance of listening—or the lack thereof—to the "wartime racial realignment" of the 1940s,[65] where mainstream U.S. culture represented the path to equal citizenship and the achievement of the American Dream as straight and true, even as gross inequities and invisible barriers knocked people of color widely off course. Finally, I amplify Petry's contributions to a black radio critique. Whereas Horne's vocal phrasing offered an example of black artistic agency contra the sonic color line and Du Bois's letters and theories the agency of the writer/producer, Petry's fiction evokes the trope of the listener to interrogate the agency of black audiences and their efforts to decolonize their listening and disrupt the sonic color line's (and radio's) deleterious silences. Thinking these artists together illustrates that if color lines are heard—not just seen—the listening ear continues to operate in covert and extralegal ways, even when a society enacts laws turning a "blind eye" to perceived racial difference.

Reconsidering racialization as a sonic practice allows for a deeper understanding of why both race and racism persist, even as "colorblind" formations of race infuse federal law and political pundits insist America is a "post-racial" nation in the wake of Barack Obama's presidency. Although scholars of race have roundly challenged color blindness,[66] it remains the United States' dominant ideology. *The Sonic Color Line* argues that American proponents of color blindness have been able to declare race invisible in the twenty-first century precisely because dominant listening practices grounded in antebellum slavery and shaped by segregation continue to render it audible. In what follows, I jam the sonic color line's aural signals, enabling more equitable listening practices to emerge.

1.

The Word, the Sound, and the Listening Ear

Listening to the Sonic Color Line in Frederick Douglass's 1845
Narrative *and Harriet Jacobs's 1861* Incidents

On July 15, 1836, the *Greensborough Patriot* published an advertisement seeking information on two runaway slaves. The ad's writer, a John W. McGehee, asks readers to join him in searching for

> two negro men, *Solomon* and *Abram,* Solomon is a man twenty years old—black complexion; full face; large mouth; thick lips; coarse voice, large feet; with a burn on his back, received when small—six feet high—well made,—smiles when spoken to—took with him a cloak and frock cloth coat, velvet collar. Abram is about five feet six inches high; black complexion; pert when spoken to; strait[sic], well made man; 26 or 7 years of age; small feet,—fine voice.

Far from unusual, the ad exemplifies the grotesque catalogs commonly printed in Southern newspapers that performatively transformed black subjects into what Hortense Spillers calls "the zero degree of *flesh.*"[1] And one finds several racialized sonic descriptors, tucked away matter-of-factly amongst the litany of white-authored visual stereotypes of "blackness." Cast by the author as simply another "negro" trait to itemize, sonic qualities such as a "fine voice" were, for mid-nineteenth-century whites, becoming as material and identifiable an element of blackness as the already culturally embedded "black complexion," "large mouth," and "thick lips." A keyword search of the University of North Carolina's digital archive of runaway slave ads reveals the ubiquity and iterative quality of such descriptions, with "hoarse voice" first appearing in 1777, and "fine voice" in 1783, with a sharp increase in 1811 that rises throughout the 1830s and 1840s. Other key recurrent descriptors include "loud," "manly," "strong," and/or "whiny," sonic affects amplifying the gendered binary of race for black men as hypermasculine/feminized.

The frequency of such ads suggests white people began perceiving a clear (and rather blunt) difference between the timbral qualities of black and white voices in the nineteenth century. The culturally constructed sonic difference not only marked certain tones, grains, and cadences as "black" but also, by the comparison that ghosts these ads, suggests whites sensed their voices as normative and not easily categorizable. White vocal grains, it seems, could span a range of sounds that were neither "coarse" nor as "loud" or "strong" as "fine" black voices, terms that characterize black timbres as excessive, overly corporeal, and readily describable.

In addition to racializing vocal timbre, the *Greensborough Patriot* outlines distinct, observable differences that whites perceived between black and white listening practices. Whereas whites, by implication, may have any number of reactions to being "spoken to," McGehee limited Solomon and Abram's listening stances to visible signals of obeisance: "smiles" and a "pert" snapping to attention. Notably, McGehee's ad never imagines either Solomon or Abram as speaking first, identifying the breaking of silence as a sonic privilege of whiteness and revealing how slaveholding whites imagined power flowing directly through acts of disciplined listening. White-authored descriptions of their slaves' racialized and power-laden listening countenances appear frequently and consistently in UNC's digital archive; recurrent modifiers that appear either before or after the phrase "when spoken to" in runaway slave ads printed between 1792 and 1840 include having "down eyes" or a "downcast look," being either "slow of speech" or "speaking quick"—the former suggesting modesty in the face of commanding whiteness and the latter displaying rapid deference—or showing a "smiling" or a "pleasant countenance." Only rarely do slave masters describe slaves as laughing when spoken to, or looking whites "directly in the eye," signifying a less-than-submissive listening stance and highlighting how whites read pert smiles and downcast eyes as appropriate visual performances of "black" listening.

Mid-nineteenth-century American whites increasingly used auditory information to inform racial ideologies and to construct racialized identities. Visual fragmentations that dissected black people into metonymic corporeal parts such as "wooly hair, nose flat, lips thick," catalogued in 1854's widely read *The Races of Man*, had long signified the allegedly fixed racial differences justifying slavery's existence.[2] However, as Michael Chaney points out, the trajectory of the "dissolution of the eminence of vision" intersected with "an alternate dynamics of race and vision" fostered by new modes of self-representation by free blacks and former slaves.[3] Furthermore, as Jonathan Crary argues, the rise of commodity culture and ocular-illusion-as-entertainment (i.e., the panorama and the camera obscura) further destabilized visual epistemologies.[4]

Sound both defined and performed the tightening barrier whites drew between themselves and black people, expressing the racialized power dynamics and hierarchical relationships of chattel slavery through vocal tones, musical rhythms, and expressed listening practices marked by whites as "black" and therefore of lesser value and potentially dangerous to whiteness and the power structures upholding it. Functioning as a medium, sound enabled race to be felt, experienced, and affected by white Americans as a collection of fixed sonic desires and repulsions that are taken into the body and radiate out from it. White American elites' use of racialized sonic descriptors drew on a long but spotty history of linking sound to "Otherness" in pre-nineteenth-century America—the "disjointed aural communities" detailed by Richard Cullen Rath in *How Early America Sounded* that unevenly represented indigenous peoples, Quakers, and African slaves as "howling" outsiders.[5] However, the advent of mass print media and popular musical culture enabled white elites to standardize sonic ideas of Otherness on a heretofore-unimagined scale, disciplining readers' listening practices through detailed accounts of listening experiences written by an increasingly professionalized cadre of reporters and critics. Furthermore, white elite discourse increasingly amplified and Othered "black" sounds at a moment of great anxiety over defining Americanness amid sectional tensions over slavery.

At this key historical threshold, white elites' published descriptions of the differences between white and black speech, sounds, environments, and musics spread far beyond intimate speech communities, constructing whites' centrality and dominance as *the* American citizen-subjects at the very level of perception. Even as the nation appeared to be dissolving in the 1850s, white elites represented a powerful sensory experience of racialized sonic citizenship on both sides of the Mason-Dixon Line, a phenomenon that certainly contributed to a relatively speedy reconciliation between Northern and Southern whites after the Civil War. Regardless of their regional location or their feelings concerning slavery, many white elites heard themselves as superior citizens, and they listened to themselves and Others through that privileged, circumscribed, and increasingly standardized filter. I call this dominant racialized filter the listening ear. The listening ear was far from the only listening practice enacted by elite whites during this period and certainly not the only form of listening important in identity construction. As I discussed in the introduction, listening is rich in its multiplicity, and a listening subject develops many filters that operate simultaneously; in fact, a listening subject is *comprised* of auditory information processed through interactive and intersectional psychological filters that include the habits, assumptions, desires, and repulsions shaped by gender, class, national, regional, and linguistic identities. However uneven and diffused, the listening ear's emergence during this period, and its transmission to listeners across the American racial spectrum, more firmly interwove whiteness with Americanness, both normalizing the dyad at the heart of citizenship privilege and making it a visceral, tangible, lived experience at the level of auditory perception. In this way, a subject can touch and be touched by the abstraction of race in the form of sound waves—vibrations were increasingly of interest to nineteenth-century physicists, particularly Hermann von Helmholtz—and a subject can cast one's racial identity out into the world through vocal tones, timbres, music making, soundscape design, noise legislation, music consumption—what Daniel Cavicchi calls "audiencing"[6]—and through publicly enacting shared forms of exclusionary listening. Listening became a key part of understanding one's place in the American racial system, viscerally connecting slavery's macropolitics to lived racial etiquette. The uneven process of building racially disciplined listening through the "'micropenalties' of disciplinary individuation,"[7] as understood by Saidiya Hartman, enabled whites to hear whiteness and blackness as palpably distinct experiences of differing texture, value, quality, and importance, forming what I term the sonic color line.

The racializing of listening, its accordant techniques of body discipline, and the sonic color line enabled by and enabling it, form this chapter's subject. Racialized sonic politics, I argue, profoundly impacted the ability of black people, indigenous peoples, immigrants, and colonized peoples to claim, enact, and sound their rights in American life, with whites representing black people as the least sonically categorizable as human, let alone as potential citizens. Slave owners, in particular, mobilized the sonic color line as an auditory grammar, which they used to discipline slaves to the white-authored subject position of "blackness," even as the border coalescing between "black" and "white" sounds, musics, and listening practices cast sonic differences as natural, essential, and immutable. Black listening subjects challenged white-constructed racialized listening practices in ways both subtle and overt: by mobilizing divergent forms of listening, by recoding certain sounds and listening practices as "white" in defiance of American cultural norms deeming whiteness unmarked and unrepresentable, and by using their own standards to construct an alternate value system and aesthetics for sounds *they* deemed "black." Furthermore, black subjects survived slavery and resisted America's racial hierarchies by becoming proficient in multiple forms of racialized listening, slipping in and out of various standpoints to evaluate the micropolitics of any given situation. Since critics such as Robert Stepto, Henry Louis Gates Jr., Houston Baker Jr., Barbara Johnson, Mae Henderson, and Michael Awkward recalibrated Mikhail Bakhtin to think through African American literary representation, double-voicedness has been a predominant critical understanding of how black-authored literary texts perform cultural work in a white supremacist society, using discursive strategies such as signifying and irony to simultaneously address black *and* white readers on different registers and giving any one text multiple meanings.[8] While, as Dorothy Hale has explored, African American literary critics aligned double-voicedness with W. E. B. Du Bois's concept of "doubleconsciousness" in order to theorize black subject formation through linguistic acts, literary critics have yet to fully explore doubled—and perhaps even tripled—listening practices, the sensory framework that enables the encoding and decoding of doubled address. My exploration of how African American writers represented and deconstructed the sonic color line and the listening ear helps us understand not only the mechanics of double-voicedness—how and why racialized American readers differently experience the same passages, speeches, musics, voices, and ambient sounds—but also how black subjects constituted themselves through and between various conflicted listening practices that they navigated, brokered, and challenged.

The sonic color line emerged as a ubiquitous and palpable force of racialization in nineteenth-century America, particularly in two of the most well-known contemporary critiques of slavery and its mutually constitutive social relations, Frederick Douglass's *Narrative of the Life of Frederick Douglass* (1845) and Harriet Jacobs's *Incidents in the Life of a Slave Girl* (1861). While discursive traces of whites' use of the sonic color line pepper the popular media of the moment, it was first exposed and rebuked in print by Douglass and Jacobs. Particularly when taken together, their work reveals how white masters and mistresses raced and gendered both sound and listening on the plantation, disciplining themselves and their slaves to the listening ear's perceptual frame. Most importantly, both writers detail their resistance to the listening ear's depiction of blackness, highlighting listening as a particularly important site of agency for slaves. African Americans worked to decolonize their listening practices from the inception of the sonic color line, and—co-constitutive with Western imperialization, colonization, and enslavement—they countered the listening ear's pernicious discipline with individual acts of refusal and communal practices strengthening kinship ties across time and space.

Douglass's emphasis on the divergent listening practices of black and white subjects in his *Narrative* shows how they shape (and are shaped by) racial ideologies and everyday disciplinary practices, providing hope that whites could reform their listening ear and that black people can decolonize their listening practices. He exposes and resists the sonic color line while arguing for the importance of slaves' sounds—in particular, women's screaming and mixed-gender collective singing—as fundamental to understanding the sensory experience of racism, particularly the construction, gendering, and limitations of the white listening ear and the uneven physical and psychological restraints of white-conditioned listening practices. My reading of Douglass presents a new perspective on a thinker long considered a champion of written literacy and interracial communication, one that considers black listeners alongside his well-documented appeal to "ethnosympathetic" whites.[9] I show how Douglass also understood that visual and written modes of knowledge, however unstable, enabled whites to increasingly marginalize sound as emotional and unpredictable—qualities associated with blackness (and femaleness)—even as it continued to perform significant racial labor; however, Douglass also took advantage of publication as a venue to challenge whites' limited perception and affirm black listeners' knowledge.

Whereas Douglass's *Narrative* takes on the aural edge of racism, Jacobs's *Incidents* focuses much more on documenting the aural experience of race, particularly for black women rendered doubly subject to white supremacist patriarchy. Douglass explores the divergent interpretations of black and white men as they listen to white men's physical abuse of black women, but he does not represent black women as listeners. In Douglass's *Narrative*, black women sound; in Jacobs's *Incidents* they listen too, developing protective strategies that detect potential sexual abuse and violence in sounds far more subtle than screams. Jacobs's representation of the intertwined relationship between Linda's external experience of place and her internal auditory voicings of family provides new understandings of how black people crafted selves and re-storied antebellum environments through embodied listening practices.

In concert, Douglass and Jacobs expose the partiality of white listening practices and the enabling privilege of whites' purportedly universal interpretations as foundational to white supremacy while simultaneously exploring the sonic color line as a site of possibility, revealing a perceptual gap between black and white audition that harbored life-affirming practices at the microlevel of the senses. Douglass questions the white listening ear's ability to hear across the color line, while Jacobs seeks refuge in alternative sonic modes of knowing, being, and creating community that challenge the sonic color line at its gendered core. This chapter furthers new critical discussions of the slave narrative and performativity that augment long-standing visual analysis with an exploration of the "slave narrative's literary capacities for play and complex signification."[10] I argue that, through their respective literary representations of "listening," Douglass and Jacobs introduced a key trope of African American literature: "the listener." By close-reading scenes where Douglass and Jacobs represent listening as the dominant sense, I identify a new trope that symbolically disentangles audio and visual experience, demonstrating how sound communicated truths about slavery and resistance that the eye always already distorted.

The Rise of the Sonic Color Line

The sonic color line had two key functions in the mid-nineteenth century. First, it helped white elites impose a racialized order on a sense long thought to be unruly and overly connected to the emotions in Western culture, providing white men, in particular, with a socially acceptable range of sounds associated with dispassionate rationality and efficient necessity to aurally communicate their race and class status. Western culture as expressed in the United States characterized the auditory sense as a wellspring of emotional truth rather than an engine of knowledge production, deeming listening ephemeral and uncontrollable next to vision's steady gaze. For instance, Mark M. Smith details how abolitionists permeated antislavery articles with aural images of cracking whips and wailing slaves to recreate slavery's soundscape as an emotional tactic to reach the irrational ears of slave masters.[11] Moreover, the sonic color line enabled the dominant white culture to classify particular sounds as identifiably and essentially "black," fixing race in a sensory domain already branded as emotionally potent and unpredictable. Of course the very process of fixing the racial identity of particular sounds protests too much; whites' imposition of their racial hierarchies in the sonic realm reveals anxiety about the agency possible for black subjects. Listening remains largely invisible under the gaze, located in a complex entanglement of one's internal (and internalized) thoughts, feelings, and emotions. Developing a sonic color line—however uneven, ad hoc, and indeterminate—to verify race's increasingly unreliable visual cues allowed whites to extend both race and racism into the auditory unseen. The sonic color line turned the notion of race inside out; blackness and whiteness could now be *lived and experienced* from within rather than just externally classified. Tethering both an evolving battery of sounds and a limited range of listening practices to black bodies expanded white racism to include new forms of acoustic disciplining that punished racial transgressions and served as violently coercive psychological conformity.

However, listening's enabling invisibility also marked the sonic color line's potential undoing. The singularity of the term "listening" assigns a false simplicity and unity to an act that is not singular but rather represents a potentially vast set of simultaneous and interconnected practices, actions, poses, thoughts, interpretations, and filters; such complexity is precisely why whites sought to narrow its power for black listeners. One's outward display could easily bely listening's workings within, as one of Ralph Ellison's characters, the slave-born grandfather of the protagonist in *Invisible Man* (1952), would advise: "Overcome 'em [whites] with yeses, undermine 'em with grins, agree 'em to death and destruction, let 'em swoller you till they vomit or bust wide open."[12] The seeming amenability that whites identified as "black" listening in fact masked a wide range of alternate, resistant, and decolonizing listening practices.

White fears of black agency were greatly exacerbated by the emerging scientific discourse that emphasized sound as a form of vibrational "touch." For white supremacists, these revelations further necessitated some kind of aural barrier between the races. Notoriously promiscuous, sounds mingle with other sounds in one's encompassing soundscape—sometimes blending, sometimes overpowering, sometimes masking, sometimes rising above—to vibrate inside one's body. While the vibrational quality of sound and its ability to enact "touching at a distance"[13] had been considered by Europeans since at least the seventeenth century, the development of microscopy enabled a closer look into the inner ear; research in the mid-nineteenth century focused on understanding the role of vibration and resonance and their mutual penetration of the ear canal. Marchese Alfonso Corti, an Italian specialist in the new field of anatomy, first drew the hair cells of the inner and outer ear in 1851, cells that resonate with and amplify incoming sound vibrations (outer) and transform vibrations into electric signals in the cochlea (inner). In short, listening became increasingly, thrillingly, and uncomfortably material and erotic, as the notion of being touched by sound vibrations seemed suddenly more concrete and less metaphoric. Arising at the same time, the sonic color line attempted to control the dangerous potential of cross-racial aural traffic—particularly of hybridity, characterized as contamination, and pleasure, deemed aberrant—by providing whites a schematic of disciplined interpretations, predetermined affects, hierarchical logics, and clear racial distinctions for incoming vibrations. However, far from sealing off white desire for transracial crossings and their taboos, the sonic color line affectively delineated the "black" and "white" borders of such encounters.

Simultaneously, Helmholtz began developing his theories of resonance, leading to understandings of pitch, frequency, and timbre that drew explicitly on racialized ideas of musical sound. According to historian of science David Pantalony, "Musical culture was central to German science in the nineteenth century; it inspired inquiry, formed social cohesion and stimulated collaboration between scientists, musicians, and instrument makers," and Helmholtz was an "exemplar" of musical influence.[14] As I discuss in chapter 2, distinctions between forms of European music took on racial overtones in addition to national ones, with Italian music's so-called overly emotional and gestural sonics taking on qualities the sonic color line associated with blackness, particularly irrationality; white Americans increasingly racialized classical music as "white" during the 1850s in the quest to distinguish a distinctly American popular culture, particularly through the visit of white Swedish opera singer Jenny Lind and the Northern tour of black American opera singer Elizabeth Taylor Greenfield. New avenues of acoustic experimentation did not just *explain* musical phenomena but rather flowed from musical training and its influence on nineteenth-century thought. Veit Erlmann notes that Helmholtz "frequently and early on in his career used hearing and music to elaborate key aspects of his theory of knowledge."[15] Unfortunately, there is little existent research on the relationship between nineteenth-century racial science and the growing field of acoustics. However, the rise of the sonic color line alongside the Western scientific "reform of acoustics" suggests that racial science did not need to say anything directly about racial categorization of vocal tone if the very impetus to name and explore the notion of timbre arose from the influence of racially classified music as well as the hyperclassification of difference. The piano, for example, was Helmholtz's conceptual model for the inner ear, where every one of Corti's newly discovered hairs individually corresponded to specific frequencies and would vibrate when struck, just like a piano wire. Helmholtz's theory allowed for the separation of sounds in the ear, even if they are perceived simultaneously. Timbre, the notion that sounds have a peculiar, difficult-to-identify quality that distinguishes the musical tone between instruments producing the same note at the same pitch, then also enables a key tenet of the sonic color line—that men and women of different races have essentially different and discernable vocal tones. Helmholtz's idea regarding separated receptors for various timbres further extends the sonic color line into the realm of the biological, suggesting that listening operates through a hardwired physical form of sonic segregation.

Thus strengthened, however indirectly, through racial science, the sonic color line enabled white elites to tighten slavery's strictures as rising protest destabilized the institution. Mark M. Smith contends that many whites began to question the dominance of sight in racial discourse in the 1850s, after generations of sexual predation by slave masters gave rise to increasing numbers of "visually white slaves." Fears of being unable to reliably see "blackness" in the "one drop rule" society they had set up led white Southerners to construct essential racial difference beyond the visual.[16] Furthermore, as Spillers argues, "it is, perhaps, not by chance that the laws regarding slavery appear to crystallize in the precise moment when agitation against the arrangement becomes articulate in certain European and New World communities."[17] Most obviously, the fight over slavery in America's newly conquered Western territory polarized the country and heightened what Smith dubs "aural sectionalism" between abolitionists and slaveholders. However, even though "Northerners and Southerners heard one another in profoundly and emotionally divisive ways,"[18] they increasingly developed similar listening practices when it came to race. For example, implementing the Fugitive Slave Act in 1850, which demanded all escaped slaves be returned to their masters wherever captured, accelerated the sonic color line's development and extended its reach to the Northern states. On penalty of fines up to 1,000 dollars and six months' imprisonment, every white Northern citizen was legally mandated to report fugitives to the authorities, "after notice or knowledge of the fact that such person was a fugitive."[19] Because "there was not much that could be done to identify such slaves by sight alone," other socially constructed sensory indicators of racial identity became salient, especially culturally identified aural markers of slavery such as "slow speech, accent, dialect, stuttering."[20] These aural markers located slavery within the fugitive body rather than in the institution that produced and conditioned such differences.

Alongside scientific pronouncements and legal compulsions, the ideological foundations of nineteenth-century oratory culture helped define and spread the sonic color line, further stressing the relationship between aurality and rationality. Douglass felt the tension between the two all too well; his narrative is rife with references to Caleb Bingham's 1797 primer *The Columbian Orator*, a popular text that helped define American social standards for sound in the arena of public speaking and beyond. Douglass first purchased the *Orator* at age twelve, after illicitly learning to read. While largely a collection of famous speeches, the *Orator* opens with "General Instructions on Speaking," an essay providing theoretical and practical pointers to aspiring orators. Confirming the rationale behind abolitionists' use of sound as emotional appeal while discouraging its unseemly deployment, Bingham's rules claim that "the influence of sounds, either to raise or allay our passions is evident from music. And certainly the harmony of a fine discourse, well and gracefully pronounced, is as capable of moving us, if not in a way so violent and ecstatic, yet not less powerful, and more agreeable to our rational faculties."[21] By declaring the "influence of sounds" separable from their meaning as "fine discourse," the *Orator* firmly knits aurality to "passion" rather than the "rational faculties." Bingham also expresses an idea key to the formation of the sonic color line and the listening ear, that music and speech are fluid parts of an increasingly organized theory of sounding in which various aural technologies work together to produce the controlled "harmony" of rationality. In attuning the evolving listening ear to recognize and seek out "harmony" in both music and speech, Bingham classified any "violent, "ecstatic," and excessively emotional sounds as threats to the social order.

Championing the sound of restraint, a cultural construct the post-Enlightenment mind-body split associated with whiteness and intellect, *the Orator* harmonizes a modulated "clear" sound with verbal clarity. Because sound can rather unpredictably "raise or allay" emotion, it necessitated a grammar that quelled its potential for excess, aligning it with white bourgeois ideals of "harmony," itself a culturally specific sonic symbol of order, a musical "conciliator of sounds."[22] Bingham's use of "ecstatic" is especially telling; its etymology stems from a Greek root meaning "to put out of place," connoting sound's ability to unseat rationality.[23] It also alludes to the sonic color line, as antebellum whites often used "ecstatic" to describe what they considered the irrationality and excess of black speech, music, and worship.[24] Bingham pronounced "a calm and sedate voice is generally best; as a moderate sound is more pleasing to the ear, especially when clear and distinct."[25]

White elites identified blackness, on the other hand, almost entirely with emotion and corporeality. In an increasingly print-oriented culture, sounds unable to be pinned down to a written, standardized vocabulary created discomfort, which whites resolved by representing nonverbal sound as the instinctual, emotive province of racialized Others. Stereotypical descriptions of black sounds permeated white antebellum writing. Similar to whites' dismissal of slave songs because they did not conform to European notation, they considered sounds such as screams, grunts, groans, and wails signs of "possession, otherness, and wildness" existing "prior to rationality."[26]

Choosing to engage whites' written words and their cultural weight, Douglass struggled to reconcile the constraining conventions of the sonic color line with a revaluation of nonverbal sound that challenged the sonic boundaries of "blackness." The *Narrative* combines oratorical structures such as chiasmus with the masculinist demands of the European genre of autobiography and the currents of radical abolitionist writing, which Alex Black describes as "demand[ing] a reader with an eye for sound."[27] Although representing slavery through nonverbal aural imagery threatened the dominant relationship between "clear" sound and sound logic, abolitionists expected Douglass to perform aural blackness for his white Northern readership, employing emotional forms of address and conventional descriptions of slavery's nonverbal sounds, particularly because he had "heard clearly (and authentically) the ring of the slave whip and the 'clank' of slaves' chains."[28] In fact, Douglass's vexation over performing existent aural stereotypes of blackness may account for the modulation of voice some critics hear in the *Narrative*, especially when compared to the fiery prose of Douglass's speeches.[29]

Perhaps as a result of the sonic color line's pressures, Douglass's *Narrative* represents sound sparingly and iconically. Douglass highlights discussions of prominent sounds identified by the sonic color line and represents (mis)perceptions of the listening ear at key points in his life from his literal and figurative births into slavery—effected by the sound of the master's abuse and the strains of slave songs in the woods—through his young adulthood on various Maryland plantations, where Douglass witnesses emotive outbursts by allegedly reasonable slave masters as well as slaves' resistance to white supremacist structures equating their sound to nonsense and their listening with unthinking obedience. The *Narrative*'s second half tracks his experiences working in Baltimore's shipyards—where he attains written literacy by trading bread to poor white boys in exchange for lessons and becomes "a ready listener" for word of abolition[30]—and his fight with the slave breaker Covey, a conflict sparked by Douglass's refusal to perform "black" listening.

"No Words, No Tears, No Prayers": Douglass and Nonverbal Epistemology

Douglass-as-author challenges the sonic color line and redirects the listening ear by rhetorically inverting dominant associations of nonverbal sound with blackness. At the *Narrative*'s end, for example, his critique of Southern religion parodies the hymn "Our Heavenly Union," altering the lyrics to expose hypocritical white Southern preachers via nonverbal imagery; self-proclaimed upstanding Christians become "roaring, ranting, sleek man-thie[ves]" who "roar and scold, and whip, and sting." Far from utilizing the "sound words" idealized by Douglass's white contemporaries, Southern preachers devilishly "bleat and baa, dona like goats," intimidating the weak with a "roar like a Bashan bull" and sounding off like "braying ass[es], of mischief full." Though they use sound to mask their hypocrisy—no one prays "earlier, later, louder, and longer" than slave-driving reverends, the cruelest masters in Douglass's *Narrative*—nonverbal tones betray their true identities.[31]

Such parody resonates with Douglass's technique of allowing slaveholders and overseers few transcribed words let alone "sound" ones, another method of defying the sonic color line's classification of white elites as eloquent orators à la Bingham. Douglass instead reduces their words to an indistinguishable stream of obscenity.[32] Despite their genteel titles, Captain Anthony, Mr. Plummer, and Mr. Severe are all "profane swearers," an aural image belying the refinement associated with elite Southerners (and their accents). Douglass represents Severe as so obscenely true to his name that he literally curses himself to death. His last words, a rhetorical form freighted with significance in Victorian culture, were but "groans, bitter curses, and horrid oaths."[33] The slaves consider his replacement, Mr. Hopkins, a "good overseer" because he was "less cruel, less profane and made less noise than Mr. Severe," although Douglass's syntax nonetheless marks him as all three.[34] Douglass characterizes Mr. Gore's cruelty nonverbally, the way he does with his representations of Severe and Hopkins; he "spoke but to command" with a "sharp shrill voice" that "produced horror and trembling in [the] ranks" of slaves. Gore primarily communicates through the whip's crack and its lash's sting. Contrary to antebellum idealizations of the word's visual and logical power, Douglass portrays emotive, nonverbal sound as central to white identity.[35]

Douglass also resists the sonic color line by challenging existent stereotypes about black listening. Believed not to possess any of the agency associated with "listening" in the dominant culture—the term having descended from the same Germanic root as "lust" (to desire) and "list" (to choose)—slaves were to respond immediately and uniformly to sounds they heard on the plantation. Under constant violent threat, slaves had to visibly perform the subordinate listening practices that constructed and confirmed slavery's allegedly natural power relationships: "When he [Colonel Lloyd] spoke, a slave must stand, listen, and tremble; and such was literally the case." Importantly, Douglass's first act of resistance against Covey is to "make him no answer and stand with [his] clothes on" after Covey orders them removed. The stakes of refusing to listen as a slave were deadly; the *Narrative* bears witness for Demby, a man shot by Gore for ignoring his orders to come out of a pond. Gore justifies Demby's murder by telling the master his insubordinate listening "se[t] a dangerous example to the other slaves."[36] Some whites considered black listening practices fundamental enough to slavery's "rule and order" to kill over, even as Gore's murderous act protests their allegedly biological nature.

However, the biggest challenge Douglass mounts to the sonic color line comes through recurrent, metonymic scenes of his own listening that reveal the extensive disciplinary practices of the listening ear and their impact on the listening habits of both slaves and their masters. Douglass's textual representation of himself listening to Aunt Hester's shrieks amplifies the centrality of race and gender to the marginalization of sonic epistemologies in the nineteenth century. It shows how listening augmented and deepened the processes of subjection usually ascribed to visuality. I further existent critical conversation surrounding Hester's scream by interrogating if and how Douglass's aural imagery was heard (and by whom), arguing that Douglass's *Narrative* asks, to riff on Elizabeth Alexander riffing on Pat Ward Williams, "Can you be WHITE and (really) LISTEN to this?" or, alternately, "Are you white because of HOW you listen to this?"[37]

Through another rhetorical reversal, Douglass challenges the sonic color line in the Hester passage by revaluing her scream—an extraverbal sound whites associated with blackness—as a vital site of knowledge production. Locating this sound prominently at the beginning and end of the scene, Douglass positions Hester's screams as sounds to be listened to for meaning, rather than dismissed as irrational, collateral noise. Building from Alexander's interpretation of Hester's screams as an important site of knowledge that (re)births Douglass into acknowledgement of himself as "vulnerable and black," Fred Moten theorizes the sound as both ontological and epistemological, a "radically exterior aurality" resistant to and disruptive of the Enlightenment's "overdetermined politics of looking," whose im/possible commingling of terror and pleasure "open[ed] the way into the knowledge of slavery and the knowledge of freedom."[38] Listening to Hester's screams enables Douglass's initial understanding of the conditions of his enslavement while simultaneously fostering resistance. More than involuntary cries of pain, "screams when one was whipped or sold, for example, reminded masters of slaves' humanity . . . inanimate objects, they told whip-happy masters, were dumb and silent."[39] Douglass-as-author emphasizes this resistant role by representing Hester's screams as sonically and syntactically interrupting the scene's visual imagery: "He [Captain Anthony] commenced to lay on the heavy cowskin, and soon the warm red blood (amid heart rending shrieks from her, and horrible oaths from him) came dripping to the floor."[40] By placing Hester's screams in a parenthetical interjection, Douglass amplifies their resistant knowledge by emphasizing Hester's authorship, over and above the role played by Anthony's whip.

Given the existent associations of nonverbal sound with blackness, femaleness, and animalism in nineteenth-century Western culture, the fact that Douglass hears Hester's scream carrying the remotest hint of meaning and agency resists the sonic color line by listening differently. However, both Hester's agency and Douglass's resistance to sonic racial norms have often gone unheard in critical conversations about Douglass's limited representation of Hester as "inarticulate." Critics inadvertently silence her anew by disallowing the possibility that her screams carry meaning. David Messmer, otherwise attuned to the *Narrative*'s aurality, represents Hester's screams as "inarticulate sound" produced by Captain Anthony that "perpetuates the racist concept that slaves were discursively inferior."[41] However, reading Hester's scream only as absence limits meaning to the spoken word, foreclosing the possibility of tonal and/or extraverbal communication. In explicitly challenging the gender hierarchies Douglass enacts—male as powerful (whether as abuser or as narrator) and woman as victim—critics implicitly concede to the dominant social codes separating the logical (white, masculine) word from the emotional (black, feminine) sound and sound from knowledge production. After all, no sound is intrinsically "inarticulate"; the sonic color line's socially and historically contingent aural value systems enable whites to label black sound in this way.

Through the tropic figure of Douglass-as-listener, Douglass-as-author amplifies Hester's screams as his aural and ontological gateway to slavery, a form of knowledge obscured by reigning visual epistemologies but enhanced by the sonic color line. Subtly reminding readers that the dawn of the "age of reason" was concurrent with (and dependent upon) slavery, Hester's screams "awake[n] [him] at the dawn of day," imagery that satirizes (and racializes) the visual iconography of the European Enlightenment. In Douglass's schema, sight and light do not produce the knowledge necessary for enslaved subjects' survival but rather sound and darkness. He finally becomes "so terrified and horror-stricken at the sight [of Anthony whipping Hester], that [he] hid himself in a closet and dared not venture out till long after the bloody transaction was over."[42] Only in the closet's darkness, with the bloody tableau removed from his immediate sight, can Douglass hear alternatives in the layered, indeterminate sound of Hester's scream, which allows him to construct "armor which can take him out of the closet."[43]

Paradoxically, Douglass's armor comes not from hardening his ears but from retaining a radical openness to Hester's cries despite their psychological and emotional toll. Mobilizing limited agency within the confines of enforced listening, Douglass fights the logic of slavery that transforms spectacular violence into routine occurrence. He does not become habituated to Hester's abuse; the screams remain acutely "heart-rending" (a term Douglass uses twice) every time he hears them.[44] Synonymous with involvement for Douglass, the act of listening helps construct the *Narrative*'s ethical framework. Despite being young, terrified, and subordinated, Douglass charges his six-year-old self with an ethics of listening as both "witness and participant" in Hester's torture, precisely the moral enmeshment that the white-produced sonic color line disavowed and sought to discipline out of black *and* white listening.[45] The sonic color line relies on the terror produced by the sonics of white supremacy to produce "black listening" as detached, immediate obedience. Unable (and unwilling) to buffer his ears from Hester's pain—an aural metaphor for rape and a metonym for slavery itself—Douglass represents his younger incarnation as both subject to sonic terror and a defiant subject produced by it.

Douglass-as-author's representation of himself as an ethical listener functions in sharp contrast to the master's muted emotional reaction to Hester's scream, identifying palpable racial differences in listening, not as immutable biological truths but as accrued habits conditioned by the sonic color line and its performative violences. Captain Anthony's listening, for example, oscillates between a titillating sensitivity to "noise" and a willful unhearing. At first, he hungrily attunes his ear to Hester's shriek, imagining himself producing it for his sexual and psychological consumption. An aural fetish for power and sexual violence, Hester's screams stand in for the moans of sexual activity she has refused him while he manifests his control over her at the level of the unseen. To amplify his power, Anthony blocks out anything else Hester says: "No words, no tears, no prayers from his gory victim, seemed to move his heart from its iron purpose."[46] Douglass's repetitive syntax mimics Anthony's "iron" ear, which hears only "no . . . no . . . no" in place of Hester's flood of "words . . . tears . . . [and] prayers," echoing her refusals. While some read this line as evidence of Hester's lack of impact,[47] the fact that Anthony remains unmoved says nothing about the eloquence of Hester's pleas, instead speaking volumes about the narratives white men constructed to absorb and silence such sounds and, in turn, about the ways in which white men as subjects are produced *through* the sonic color line's aural justifications. By evoking Hester's words rather than quoting them, Douglass represents the process through which the master's ear translates human sound into black noise, satirizing the Victorian belief that sound is a direct, universal emotional pathway and challenging his white Northern readers to hear more than absence between those lines.[48]

However, as much as Douglass's image is about control, it also concerns Hester's aural resistance and the methods Anthony uses to suppress it. As Jon Cruz finds, "Far too many of the accounts of owners and overseers that describe black noise also contain a deeper unraveling of noise—an unraveling toward the irrepressible acknowledgement of meaningful emotions."[49] Although "he would whip her to make her scream," once Hester's screams escaped his desire—becoming too loud, too pained, too emotive—Captain Anthony would "whip her to make her hush," smothering her voice and the "irrepressible acknowledgement" of her humanity that it briefly evoked.[50]

By opening his *Narrative* with the multiple meanings made from a sound both desired and suppressed by whites as racialized noise, Douglass resists the raced and gendered performances listening whites expected from black subjects, while simultaneously exposing how elite white men, in particular, come to know their power and experience their privilege through listening. Detailing Hester's scream through his listening experience proves Douglass's "most effective discursive resistance to slavery while a slave depends upon his aural abilities rather than his skills as a literate subject,"[51] while broadening the limited understanding of "aural abilities" as only concerned with the making of (musical) sound and not with the aural literacy that shapes its production and interpretation. I define aural literacy as the ability to accrue knowledge by listening and engaging with the world through making and perceiving sound.[52]

Douglass's representations of listening within a written text contests the artificial and imbalanced dichotomy between orality and literacy and the inherent ocularcentrism embedded within it that privileges the allegedly silent written word. The hybrid forms of aural literacy within the texts I read in this chapter show us that oral and aural ways of knowing the world do not simply disappear or dissolve into written discourse; according to Joseph Roach, orality and literacy are co-constitutive, interactive categories rather than mutually exclusive moments in an evolutionary model of culture.[53] Literary representations of aural literacy amplify the fact that listening continues to be an important epistemology in a society that an overwhelming number of scholars argue has given itself over almost completely to the eye. By placing

Douglass-as-child inside the darkened closet, Douglass-as-writer enacts listening as a literary trope of decolonization, one that explicitly challenges the dominance of slavery's spectacular visuality. Douglass does not define listening as an unconscious, universal, biological given but rather as a socially constructed and embodied act of aural literacy: an intellectual, physical, and emotional openness to sound that shapes and is shaped by one's subject position. Listening operates simultaneously in the *Narrative* as a site of meaning and as ethical involvement. When listening, Douglass intimates, one always has some skin in the game.

Subsequent iterations of Douglass-as-listener reinforce the act of listening as a racially dichotomous and mutually exclusive experience both structured by and structuring everyday life on the plantation. Unlike visual spectacles, which can dissipate when removed from view, the aural imagery of Hester's scream leaves echoes and traces that reverberate in Douglass's memory and bleed throughout the *Narrative*. His iconic description of the multiple racialized experiences of listening to slaves sing, in particular, explores the impact of the sonic color line on both slavery and the fight against it.

"In the Sound": Listening to Slaves Sing

Although a qualitatively different aural image from Hester's cries of pain, the Great House Farm sequence immediately following evokes the trope of the listener to reveal how the tones of slave song also sound out the "soul-killing effects of slavery."[54] Douglass-as-protagonist joins his fellow slaves in permeating the woods with musical projections of presence, and Douglass-as-author plays with the racialized assumptions of the elite white listening ear that slave songs were a meaningless collection of "wild notes" signifying contentment.[55] Given his white reader's likely assumption that these tones, however "wild," expressed less pain and violence than Hester's shrieks, Douglass's meditation on the memory of singing and listening to these songs recasts his vulnerability to sound as a willful openness to both the everyday pain of slavery as well as the knowledge produced "if not in the word, in the sound."[56]

However, while Douglass's representation of listening to Aunt Hester utilizes spatial proximity to create a sense of uncomfortable intimacy among differently raced listeners and readers interrogating the supposed universality of sounded pain, the trope of listening in the slave song sequence relies on time to effect distance, this time questioning the sonic color line's representation of musical sound. For Douglass-as-protagonist, the experience of listening to his voice join fellow slaves in song complements and echoes Hester's expressions of pain and re-sistance. Unlike his childhood memory of the scream, the slave songs Douglass exhumes refuse to remain in the past, creating a dissonant aural effect. Remembering the songs years later—yet crying fresh tears—Douglass-as-author represents his experience of listening as doubled, enabling him to examine himself "within the circle" of slavery while simultaneously questioning how his interpellation into an American identity—however uneven, partial, and limited—impacts his sensory perception of the past and present.[57] Does becoming free and "American" mean becoming attuned to the increasingly rigid contours of the white supremacist sonic color line that tunes out the cultural production of slaves as senseless noise? Douglass admonishes his readers that the "mere hearing" of the slave songs should automatically "impress some minds with the horrible character of slavery," especially according to dominant norms about sound's emotional impact; however, his doubled listening experience enables an understanding of how the sonic color line has already primed white Northern ears to hear "the singing, among slaves, as evidence of their contentment and happiness."[58] The proximity of the slave song passage to the Hester scene connects the erotic sensitivity and obdurate tuning out of the Southern master's ear with white North-erners' inability to hear slave songs as anything but plantation fantasy and/or amusical gibberish. Interrogating the universality of musical value forwarded by Western culture, Douglass notes how slave songs were dismissed as "apparently incoherent," "unmeaning jargon" by cul-tural outsiders trained to consider sound as superfluous or secondary to meaning.[59] While Douglass highlights his own ability to cross the encircling confines of the sonic color line and maintain a dual listen-ing practice, he also seriously questions whether traffic across the sonic color line can flow in the other direction.

Douglass not only models the complex, self-reflective fluidity of his own listening practices but also calls upon the trope of the listener to expose the mutability of the sonic color line, challenging his white readership to listen beyond their racialized expectations and desires.

His double-voiced text hails his white Northern readers as listeners, using aural imagery to evoke their spatial, ideological, and perceptual distance from slaves and amplify their potentially surprising and discomfiting connections with the sensibilities of white Southern elites. Douglass urges his white Northern readers to place themselves "deep in the pine woods . . . in silence," quieting their racially conditioned reactions so that the slaves' songs may breach the listening ear's distorting filter.[60] Douglass charges white readers with an ethical responsibility to hear African American cultural production with alternate assumptions about value, agency, and meaning, particularly regarding the relationship between the written word and nonverbal sound laid out by texts such as *The Columbian Orator*. Only then may they hear black voices in sonic resistance to the system denying them personhood, "every tone a testimony against slavery."[61] Exceedingly aware that sound is always already enmeshed in the sonic color line and skeptical of sentimental appeals to sound as truth, Douglass's aural imagery issues a challenge to dominant notions of truth produced and disseminated through the listening ear. The *Narrative* both manipulates and resists the sonic color line, denaturalizing the racialized listening practices of both blacks and whites, exposing them as one of slavery's habituating violences.

The musical imagery of Douglass's *Narrative* has been read predominately as hearkening to the potential connections to be made through cross-racial listening, what Jon Cruz calls "ethnosympathy."[62] However, as Carla Kaplan finds, African American literature "often seeks to dramatize its *lack* of listeners" and the impossibility of reaching competent, let alone ideal, readers.[63] In fact, Douglass closes the slave song passage with the "singing of a man cast away upon a desolate island," an aural image likening enslavement to the isolation of being perpetually without a listener or interpretive community.[64] Even as Douglass's work appeals to the power of sound for legal, political, literary, and ontological representation of slaves' experiences, his doubled ears hear the dehumanizing physical violence of Hester's beatings in both the slave songs and in the deleterious interpretive violence performed by white listeners who ignore, misunderstand, dismiss, and/or (mis)interpret black cultural production for their own ends.

However, Douglass's challenge to the sonic color line stops short of fully examining gendered oppression. In fact, by privileging and universalizing male sonic experience, Douglass affixes a gendered meaning to the sounds that is uncomfortably aligned with dominant nineteenth-century modes of understanding sexual difference. Douglass casts the collective singing of the slaves as, at heart, an expression of the individual masculine proclivity to create expressive culture out of the experience of social death, while Hester's individual screams represent a collective expression of pain, suffering, and resistance. Although these sonic labors are intimately intertwined, their sources remain distinct; Douglass represents the female scream as raw material to be transduced into masculine song. Such a gendered division of sonic labor comes about not only because Douglass works within dominant American ideas connecting women to emotional expression and men to artistic production but also because he depicts the acts of listening to these sounds—however diverse—as a form of congress between men: between Douglass and his master in the Aunt Hester scene and between Douglass and an imagined white male abolitionist reader in the case of slave singing. The biggest silence in the *Narrative* is not the lack of Hester's words, but rather Douglass's failure to represent Hester as a listener, her embodied ear understanding and representing her own screams and intervening in the masculine power relationships formed over her bloody body and through her voice's strained grain. His *Narrative* also remains silent on how the slave singers use listening to connect through—and in spite of—their profound isolation.

Refining the "Listening Ear": *Incidents in the Life of a Slave Girl*

Whereas Douglass evokes the trope of listening only a few times in his *Narrative*, Harriet Jacobs represents the pervasiveness of listening in *Incidents in the Life of a Slave Girl*, exploring it as both an intimate vehicle for oppression and a covert method of resisting slavery's unrelenting isolation. A first-person narrative told through the perspective of Jacobs's pseudonymous persona Linda Brent, *Incidents* intertwines the stories of Brent's harrowing fight against physical and sexual abuse and her protracted struggle for freedom for herself and her children.[65] While Jacobs mobilizes many of the generic conventions of the slave narrative, she concerns herself less with revealing the salacious and violent events of slavery for her white Northern readership and much more with communicating how Linda Brent perceives slavery's traumas, particularly how she listens to them. In detailing Brent and her family's sonic understanding of their experiences as slaves, Jacobs emphasizes aurality as an indispensable mode of literacy, imagination, and memory, both personal and historical. Open to pleasure in spite of continuous exposure to pain, Brent's embodied listening recognizes sound's fundamental importance to slavery's power relationships. Laying important groundwork toward what later emerges as decolonizing listening in the work of Richard Wright, W. E. B. Du Bois, and Ann Petry, Jacobs also reveals listening as a fundamental epistemology crucial not only for ensuring slaves' survival but also for enabling an evolving understanding of one's self. I close-read Jacobs's *Incidents* somewhat against the grain as both a literary and a theoretical text, exploring how she mobilizes the trope of the listener to posit the importance of aural literacy in everyday life. I also articulate how Brent's listening practice—a form of queered listening Yvon Bonenfant calls "listening out," an "unusual reaching" toward others[66]—evolves through four key periods in her life: girlhood, young womanhood, entrapment in the garret, and her eventual freedom.

Jacobs's story emphasizes the diversity, contingency, and mutability of listening while also charting her own difficulty in reshaping her embodied praxis. Like Douglass, Brent spends her early childhood away from slavery's immediate horrors; her grandmother, a free woman, raises her after her enslaved parents' deaths. Also like Douglass's, her initiation into slavery's gendered economy occurs through listening, although it is not the experience of listening to a slave's scream that marks her as a gendered subject, but rather the moment she has to endure "foul words" whispered into her fifteen-year-old ear by her sexually abusive master, the aptly named Dr. Flint. As Jacobs bluntly states, "Slavery is terrible for men, but it is far more terrible for women."[67] Refusing to accede to the master's relentless advances even as she recognizes his aural abuses as a constituent part of a female slave's life—"I shuddered, but I was constrained to listen," Linda describes[68]—she eventually takes a white lover, Mr. Sands, to spite Flint and exact some control over her body and her desire. She has two children with Sands while remaining subject to her master's rage and her mistress's jealousy. When Flint refuses to let Sands buy their children and threatens their sale, Linda goes into hiding in her grandmother's garret. Nine feet long, seven feet wide, and only three feet tall, this tight space hides Linda for seven years. Battling atrophy and illness, Linda listens hungrily for her children's voices, overhears valuable information from the street, and uses her listening practices to retain familial connections. Linda eventually ends up a fugitive in New York, where she works as a nurse to a wealthy white family, saving money to free her children and build a family home. *Incidents* ends with Linda and her children struggling against new oppressions, ostensibly free but wrestling with Northern racism; slavery, white supremacy, and the vagaries of the dominant white listening ear exert a discomfiting influence on her perceptions long after her escape.

"It Was Not Long before We Heard the Tramp of Feet and the Sound of Voices": Aural Literacy and the Auditory Imagination

Without dismissing the eventual necessity of written literacy, Jacobs's *Incidents* identifies aural literacy and auditory imagination as crucial skill sets slaves attain as a consequence of enslavement. Both can be honed as potential sites of freedom and resistance that evade the sonic color line and the listening ear, even as they ultimately trade upon and operate within these disciplinary forces. While Jacobs avoids pitting aurality against written literacy, she expresses much more skepticism than Douglass regarding America's dominant cultural narrative equating written literacy with freedom. Jacobs has a "troubled relationship with language," Holly Blackford writes, which is "associated with patriarchy, rape, violation, and abolitionist appropriation."[69] Initially, Linda's ability to read further enslaves her, as Dr. Flint sends her sexually abusive notes and demands written responses. For these reasons, Jacobs instead concentrates on articulating the literacies that slaves already possess, especially their ability to glean important, lifesaving knowledge from the minutest of auditory details. Through the cultivation of a sophisticated aural literacy that detected discrepancies in listening practices—that those on top of the power structure labeled particular sounds as "black" and interpreted them as markedly different from sounds deemed "white" (read: normal, human)—slaves accrued knowledge, prevented punishment, fostered resistance, preserved memories, and constructed cultural identity.[70] Linda's son, for example, hears a wayward cough stray from Linda's attic hiding place, and even though years have passed and he has no idea of her location, he immediately recognizes the sound. For years afterward and without mentioning his suspicions to anyone, he protects his mother by steering whites and neighborhood children away from that side of the house. As Jacobs highlights, whites may have kept slaves from the written word under threat of extreme corporeal punishment and defined their sonic profiles by enforcing the sonic color line, but some slaves sought agency through alternative sensory modes of communication, information gathering, and self-expression. In defiance of the white elite listening ear that defined black listening as biologically determined obedience and nonverbal communication as repugnant, Jacobs mobilizes the trope of the listener to reveal the complexity of black listening practices and revalue the written word as only one form of literacy among others.

In addition to providing crucial information for everyday survival, Linda's skilled aural literacy equips her with an important site of imagination in defiance of the sonic color line's historical erasure of the sounds of black family presence and its classification of black listeners as reacting solely—and simply—to immediate external stimuli. Jacobs depicts Brent's vibrant auditory imagination as peopled with the voices of family members past and present, remembered sounds that strengthen her forcibly ruptured familial bonds while spurring her to take the necessary actions to free herself and her children. In *Listening and Voice*, phenomenologist Don Idhe describes the auditory imagination as a "mode of experience [wherein] lies the full range from sedimented memories to wildest fancy" that interweaves imagined sound with perceived sound and forms "an *almost continuous* aspect of self-presence" through the expressions of one's inner voice. Idhe argues that Western scholarship has severely neglected the auditory imagination because Enlightenment ideologies assume thought to be a disembodied activity rather than one experienced through and activated by the body.[71] In contrast, Jacobs's literary representation of Linda's auditory imagination relates the power of embodied knowledge as personal and social resistance, as Linda experiences the remembered voices of her family members as interwoven with the sights and sounds of slaves' collective historical memory of their enslavement. She experiences copresence not only in the context of her own voice but also through the voices of family members—dead and living—that challenge the social death of slavery's official narratives declaring black slaves as without history, culture, and family.

Triggered by visits to sites important to the history of her family's enslavement, Linda's vivid auditory imagination enables her to re-story a landscape with events all but erased by acts of white supremacy. I borrow the term "re-story" from Neil Campbell, who extended Gary Nabhan's concept to the contested landscapes of contemporary Western American literature. Without eliding its specificity, I find the term useful to understanding how Jacobs depicts Linda's ability to layer African American histories, memories, and counternarratives onto the Southern plantation, a space physically and narratively dominated by whites.[72] Using her auditory imagination, Linda re-stories this seemingly serene landscape with memories of her family's presence that whites have deliberately suppressed and erased. For example, when Linda visits her mother's grave on the eve of her decision to run away, she ruminates on the cloying sense of "death-like stillness" that marks its sacredness to her and the profound loss represented by unmarked graves: people silenced in both life *and* death, forced to the outskirts of their communities and removed from official narratives of American history, culture, and identity. But Linda's mother does not remain silent; Jacobs writes, "I received my mother's blessing when she died, and in many an hour of tribulation I had seemed to hear her voice, sometimes chiding me, sometimes whispering loving words into my wounded heart."[73] As discussed earlier, nineteenth-century American culture considered a person's last words important (and quite revealing of character). Here Jacobs evokes the Victorian sentimental practice of listening for a loved one's last words but emphasizes the materiality of her mother's voice and its ability to console Linda far into the unseen future. While Blackford interprets Linda's memory as a projection of her conflicted feelings regarding the remaining female figures in her life, namely Mrs. Flint and her grandmother Marthy's "*double power to abuse and nourish*," I counter that Linda's specific evocation of her mother's sound must be heard and respected, particularly because voices possess unique links to memories of individual people.[74] Slavery's power dynamics sought to lump slaves together as an indistinguishable mass, a practice Hartman calls "fungibility."[75] Forbidden to keep written or material items of remembrance such as letters, family Bibles, locks of hair, jewelry, or other treasured heirlooms, slaves held on to and rehearsed their loved ones' heard memories, challenging dominant depictions of sound—and slave families—as amorphous and ephemeral, here and then gone. Through her auditory imagination, Linda resists slavery's fungibility and erasure. Linda internalizes not only the sound of her mother's voice but also the sonic experience of being parented by her, in discipline and in comfort, and she evokes this memory when she seeks motivation or a model for her own parenting. Jacobs shares the knowledge and actions produced through Linda's (re)enactment of her mother's sonic legacy without exposing its specific content, an act of agency in the face of her undoubtedly and uncomfortably curious white readership.

A second evocation of the trope of the listener, this time in reference to her father's vocal timbre, amplifies the specificity of Linda's auditory imagination and its ability to hear histories deliberately squelched by the white listening ear. Her father's faded grave, marked only by a small wooden board with writing "nearly obliterated," contrasts with her sharp memory of his voice: "I passed the wreck of the old meeting house, where, before Nat Turner's time, the slaves had been allowed to meet for worship, I seemed to hear my father's voice come from it, bidding me not to tarry till I reached freedom or the grave. I rushed on with renovated hopes."[76] Linda projects the sound of her father's voice onto the plantation's built environment as a reminder of its bloody history and of slaves' claims to it. She also connects his voice to slaves' resistance. Although Linda's recollection genders resistance—her mother associated with comfort and her father with overt rebellion—that both of them speak to her in rapid succession foreshadows how Linda eventually combines these strategies. Her auditory imagination provides her with the knowledge that her dream was once theirs too.

In carefully attending to the sound of her dead parents' voices, Linda's auditory imagination both re-stories the plantation landscape with her ancestors' presence and constructs subversive narratives that defy the sonic color line's constricting definitions of black sonic subjectivity. Cavicchi argues for the importance of the auditory imagination in the antebellum period as a narrative force. In particular, "soundless 'interior' hearing," of the type experienced by Linda Brent, "became an important factor in conversion stories, often acting as the catalyst for the dramatic 'turning' that precipitated being 'born again.' Sounds of thunder, bells, and birds were all carefully examined for evidence of either God's grace or Satan's temptation."[77] Jacobs, in fact, does not describe Brent as remembering voices; rather she "seemed to hear" the interior sounds rise from external objects such as the wreckage of the worship house.[78] Linda also hears the sounds of her living-but-absent children's voices as tones that bind her to life and spur her to risk everything to secure their freedom. Jacobs's use of the trope of the listener powerfully connects Linda's decision to escape slavery with popular cultural narratives of religious conversion.

Linda also cultivates her auditory imagination as a method of narrating the events of her life when no other means are available. An unacknowledged precursor to Charlotte Perkins Gilman's 1892 short story "The Yellow Wallpaper," in which the thwarted female protagonist unlooses her visual imagination upon the wallpaper's whorls when forbidden from writing, *Incidents* depicts Linda using environmental sounds as emotional touchstones. Jacobs, for instance, invests the sound of Linda's grandmother's gate with her feelings. After her master threatens her with rape, Linda visits her grandmother for solace. Finding her angry and disapproving due to the Mistresses' lies, a devastated Linda describes, "With what feelings did I now close that little gate, which I used to open with such an eager hand in my childhood! It closed upon me with a sound I never heard before."[79] Here the trope of the listener again marks the gendered passage through the "bloodstained gate of slavery," for Linda the indescribable sound of a literal gate closing upon her physical safety, sexual agency, and dreams of a loving domestic life. Furthermore, as a slave mother-to-be, Linda realizes her limited control—if any—over her children's future. Jacobs embeds Linda's horrific realization in the sentence's very syntax; as a child, Linda eagerly opened the gate, but now the gate "closed upon [her]." The gate remains visually familiar but sounds with a new pitch, re-storying the built environment with the utter transformation of Linda's world. Jacobs revisits the gate later on, mobilizing its sound to mark another sorrowful threshold: Linda's loss of her daughter to servitude. From her attic cell, Linda listens to the sounds of her daughter leaving her grandmother's house to become her father's family servant: "I heard the gate close after her with such feelings as only a slave mother can experience."[80] In Linda's auditory imagination, the gate's click sounds out the distance between herself and her white Northern abolitionist readership, women who claimed sisterhood with black women without attempting to understand the pervasive impact the lack of freedom over one's body has for slave women, down to the very level of sensory perception.

Jacobs further explores the differences between white listening practices and those developed by slaves, using rich description to detail the white supremacist assumptions enabled by and encoded in the sonic color line, revealing them as specific sonic symbols of American patriarchy and white supremacy rather than universal affective experiences. The most powerful example occurs when Linda, crouched in her darkened attic cell, overhears a performance of the conventionally sentimental popular song "Home Sweet Home" and uses her auditory imagination to challenge the nostalgic idealization of the white woman as wife and mother to the nation. The breakaway hit from the 1829 opera *Clari, Maid of Milan* and arguably the nineteenth century's most popular song, "Home Sweet Home" was most famous for its refrain "'Mid pleasures and palaces though I may roam, / Be it ever so humble, there's no place like home."[81] Given the song's brisk sales—and the copious "Home Sweet Home!" needlepoints adorning American homes—Jacobs's readers would have been familiar with its lyrics, melody, and overdetermined cultural meanings that helped shape evolving ideas of middle-class domesticity. While Douglass asks his white readers to imagine the sound of the singing of a "man cast away on a desolate island" as representative of slavery's isolation, Jacobs presents her readership with the imaginative listening practices of a slave mother cast away in an isolation chamber, eavesdropping on white American middle-class culture.

As she listens as a slave mother, Linda's auditory imagination unravels the foundations of the song until they no longer "seem like music," stripping away its European musical trappings and the listening ear's dominant cultural associations. Jacobs positions Brent as an invisible interloper overhearing a song whose strains are clearly not meant to serenade the ears of a slave mother with no legal right to *herself*, let alone her children. Linda remembers sitting and

> thinking of my children, when I heard a low strain of music. A band of
> serenaders were under the window playing "Home Sweet Home." I listened

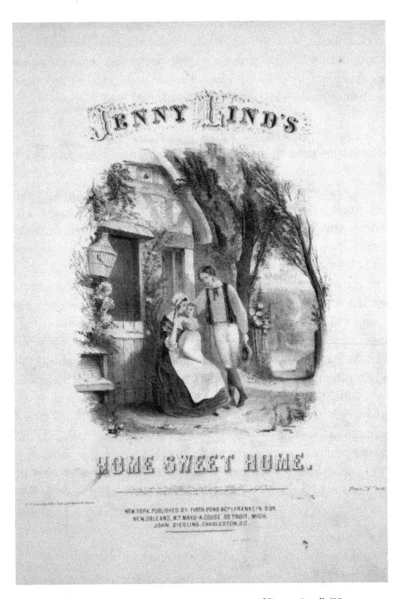

1854 sheet music from Samuel Owen's arrangement of "Jenny Lind's 'Home Sweet Home,'" one of countless versions sold in the mid-nineteenth century reinforcing normative white domesticity.

until the sounds did not seem like music, but like the moaning of children. It seemed as if my heart would burst. I rose from my sitting posture, and knelt. A streak of moonlight was on the floor before me, and in
the midst of it appeared the forms of my two children. . . . I felt certain
something had happened to my little ones.[82]

For Brent, there is no place that *is* home; the song's conventional
sentimentality remains inaccessible, and its sound brings pain and fore-
boding. Reversing white descriptions of black music as "noise"—and
nodding to Douglass's "if not in the word, in the sound" epistemology—
Brent listens to "Home Sweet Home" by breaking it down to the sounds
she hears constituting it: "the moaning of children." Moaning, a sound
Moten argues "renders mourning wordless . . . releasing more than
what is bound up in the presence of the word,"[83] strips away the lyrics of the song and unlocks its suppressed suffering. The moaning
Brent hears reclaims "Home Sweet Home" as specifically for her. Heard
through a slave mother's auditory imagination, "Home Sweet Home"
brings not aural assurances of domestic bliss, but rather sonic reminders of the painful toll slavery exacted upon children forced to follow
the "condition of the mother." The challenge that Linda Brent's auditory imagination presents to the dominant cultural narratives about
sound structured by the sonic color line and racialized by the listening
ear amplifies listening's potential as a resistant practice for slaves, offering a method of strengthening family bonds and histories in the face of
an institution bent on destroying both at once and a perceptual framework enabling a limited experience of agency over themselves and their
environment.

"Joy and Sadness in the Sound": Listening as Epistemology

Jacobs's self-reflexive representation of Linda Brent's evolving listening
experiences evinces the sonic color line's presence and makes palpable
the terrible resonance of the listening ear on slaves' self-perceptions and
apprehensions. By tracking Linda's listening practices through changes
in age, geography, and social status, Jacobs constructs listening not as a
fixed biological trait but as a flexible process capable of change (albeit
with great effort); Jacobs imparts this lesson to white *and* black readers.

Listening practices may seem natural and immutable, but as Pauline Oliveros would later argue, listening is actually "a process developing from instantaneous survival reactions to ideas that drive consciousness. The listening process continues throughout one's lifetime."[84] Jacobs represents listening as a responsive and evolving mode of learning for slaves in particular, crucial to self-understanding, accruing knowledge over time and remaining vigilantly attentive to imminent danger. For slaves, Jacobs indicates, matters of survival intertwine intimately with "ideas that drive consciousness," and the episteme of listening equips Linda with some sustenance and protection, as well as her capacity to imagine a life and identity outside of "slave." *Incidents* represents Linda's practiced ability to perceive echoes of the past in the present—knowledge key to her survival—but also tracks how her ear adapts to new ideas, locations, and iterations of the sonic color line. Four distinct moments and geographies shape Linda's auditory experience and demand new modes of listening: her childhood with her family at her first mistress's home, her girlhood on the Flints' plantation, her young motherhood in the "loophole of retreat" in her grandmother's attic, and her time as a fugitive in the urban North.

In Linda's childhood, listening emerges as a key way to obtain truths, however painful, despite the sonic color line's narrowed definition of black listening abilities. Raised in "fortunate circumstances," Linda doesn't learn she is a slave until age six, upon her mother's death, when she listens to her friends and family unfold her family's genealogy. Although she describes her mistress as "kind"—she teaches Linda to read, does not beat her, and allows her to remain with her grandmother—Linda finds herself no less in slavery's clutches. Through listening, she learns whom to listen to and whom to regard with distrust. Upon death, Linda's mistress does not free her as promised but arbitrarily bequeaths her to a five-year-old niece. Thus disciplined to listen to the promises (and interpret the kindnesses) of white people with skepticism, Linda quickly understands that words can be twisted, promises broken, and sworn oaths denied, even as some words whites speak become ironclad truths with great consequences for her and her family. Finally, as I have mentioned, the comforting exchanges she has with her mother, father, and grandmother during this time help shape her aural literacy and auditory imagination while enabling lasting aural bonds.

When twelve-year-old Linda arrives at the Flints', her listening practices shift dramatically upon encountering the listening ear of her new
master and mistress, both of whom unsparingly discipline her via aural
terrorism. They forcibly attune her to the aural markers of slavery's
raced and gendered power relations: the equation of slave listening with
obedience, the master's deliberately "cold words and cold treatment,"
the spectacular sounds of violence, the master's sexually abusive whispers, and the controlling power of silence.[85] Almost immediately, Linda
learns the obedient listening expected of slaves by observing her brother
Willie's conundrum when his father and his new mistress simultaneously demand his attention. She describes how he

> hesitated between the two; being perplexed to know which had the
> strongest claim upon his obedience. He finally concluded to go to his
> mistress. When my father reproved him for it, he said, "You both called
> me, and I didn't know which I ought to go to first."
>
> "You are my child," replied our father. "and when I call you, you should
> come immediately, if you have to pass through fire and water."
>
> Poor Willie! He was now to learn his first lesson of obedience to a
> master.[86]

Witnessing Willie choose between the listening ear's demand that he
court his father's reproach—devastating their familial relationship and
acknowledging its tenuousness—or risk physical punishment by ignoring his mistress teaches Linda the relationship between listening and
power. Not only does she observe Willie concede to whites' primary
authority, but she also sees how the listening ear and its power to enforce
listening as obedience uncomfortably link the roles of master and father.
Willie's experience influences Linda to reject listening as obedience; as
Stephanie Li notes, Linda "avoids creating the double-bind that entraps
her brother," never calling her children to her nor demanding public
displays of love.[87] In contrast, Linda spends time listening to her children,
coming to know and love them through this practice.

The second listening experience marking the abrupt end to Linda's
girlhood occurs the night she earwitnesses Mr. Flint beating a slave, an
act of violence and aural terrorism that reveals the limits of language
and further conditions her gendered relationship to the master's power

and the sonic color line. Signifying on the imagery of the Hester scene in Douglass's *Narrative*, Jacobs's *Incidents* de-emphasizes violence's spectacular qualities, embedding it into a larger economy of gendered violence. "I shall never forget that night," Linda recalls. "Never before, in my life, had I heard hundreds of blows fall, in succession, on a human being. His piteous groans, and his 'O pray don't, Massa' rang in my ear for months afterward."[88] Unlike Douglass's graphic audiovisual description, Jacobs's representation of the unnamed man's beating is almost completely aural, an editorial choice that depicts heard violence as itself terrorism rather than merely its by-product. Her use of "never before" signifies how such aural terrorism creates a new understanding of her subject position and hints that this will not be the last time she hears such sounds; the usual rhetorical companion, "never again," never comes. Jacobs asserts the slave's humanity *before* she describes his "piteous groans," and she reduces the master to the metonymic rise and fall of the whip, using this machinelike sound to reveal him—rather than the slave he beats—as inhuman. Whereas the interchange between Douglass's Aunt Hester and his master possesses a disturbingly personal and erotic intensity, Jacobs's scene casts violence as rote and institutional. Not that the master's abuse remains free of desire, as the relentless rising and falling of the whip alludes; Flint beats the man because the man has (rightly) accused him of fathering his wife's child. While Douglass represents Hester only through her screams, Jacobs relates the slave's linguistic *and* extralinguistic pleas; however, rather than humanizing him further, as so many of Douglass's critics argued a transcription of Hester's words would have accomplished, the man's cry "O pray don't, Massa" works to the contrary. Andrew Levy explains how the word "Massa" functions as a strategic rhetorical appeal to the "power of deference" to stop the attack, as well as a calculated literary technique to enhance the "expressive appeal" of Jacobs's text to her white Northern readers.[89] Without foreclosing these possibilities, I suggest the scene affirms Douglass's conclusion that words alone will not stop the master's whip, while also considering how words themselves, in certain contexts, can lead to further enslavement by verbally performing the sonic color line.

In another key shift from Douglass's iconic imagery, Jacobs avoids linking the male slave's screams to black musical culture, instead representing song as an excruciatingly brief exercise of agency—how the slaves might hear it—rather than reaching across the sonic color line to challenge the listening ear's misrepresentations. In Jacobs's depictions of slaves singing at Johnkannaus and a Methodist town meeting, she highlights their experience of choosing when and how to use their voices in a manner pleasing to themselves.[90] Both the singing and its attendant listening experiences provided slaves with fleeting feelings akin to freedom, producing powerful affects that operated neither as false balm nor empty diversion but rather as a crucial exercise of will and imagination. Jacobs invites the possibility of enjoyment through song, one that Douglass's representation forecloses: "If you were to hear them at such times, you might think they were happy. But can that hour of singing and shouting sustain them through the dreary week, toiling without wages, under constant dread of the lash?"[91] By representing a very limited, momentary pleasure in "singing and shouting," Jacobs resists dominant abolitionist articulations of common humanity between black and white people through images of pain and suffering while suggesting that sounds produced within the sonic color line's bounds have power, meaning, and value. In the word *and* the sound then, singing provided slaves a communal experience of vibrational, emotional, and psychological possibility—however temporary and transient—outside of bondage and the listening ear's binaristic logic. Jacobs's imagery intimates that if slaves, whenever possible, attuned themselves to the truth and value expressed through their own voices, they would increasingly be able to hear it as well. By listening differently to their singing—what I identify as decolonizing listening—they would strengthen their auditory imaginations and redirect their listening practices away from the listening ear's obliteration.

To deconstruct the listening ear and to underscore the boundary she redraws between slaves' cries of pain and shouts of song, Jacobs embeds the sounds of screams within slavery's larger sonic economy of sexual violence, an institutional soundscape naturalized by the sonic color line as business as usual. Challenging her white Northern readership to hear slaves' suppressed screams-within-screams—and perhaps rattling black readers into the radical openness of Douglass's listening practices— Jacobs counters the screams' physical dissipation by using aural imagery to reveal the interconnection between slavery's violences and their lingering systemic, terror-inducing, and often silent resonances, particularly for the sold-away and the dying. In Jacobs's sonic economy, the screams of the man Flint beats perform as an audible herald and spectacular mask for its quieter but no less brutal expressions. Following the incident, Linda describes how whispered speculations arise amongst the slave community as they look to his wife's fair newborn child; the couple's quarrelling reverberates across the quarters. However, all these sounds abruptly cease when Flint sells both man and woman away. Not only does Flint profit from his cruelty, but he also "had the satisfaction of knowing they were out of sight and hearing."[92] Flint engineers the sights and soundscape of the plantation to satisfy his own sensory desires and to uphold his self-image, remixing screams with silence in order to retain his power and standing. As the slave trader leads the mother of Flint's child away, she yells, "You *promised* to treat me well," breaking the master's silence and publicly revealing the open secret of his abuse and paternity. Flint counters by blaming her because she refused to collude with his sonic and sexual designs: "You have let your tongue run too far, damn you!" Together, the screams of the whipped would-be father and the protests of the sold-away mother reverberate and bleed together in the narrative's soundscape as Jacobs ends the chapter with a vignette relating the aural torture of another young slave mother by her mistress, who shouts obscenities into her ear as she lies dying from a difficult birth of "a child nearly white."[93] Jacobs's aural imagery connects sounds that the listening ear deems isolated institutional by-products, exposing them as constitutive of the gendered violence at the heart of the slave economy. Neither necessary aural collateral damage nor raw material for redemption, the sounds of men and women screaming reveal both public pain and secreted social and familial relations. Related just pages before Flint's first attempt at rape, Linda's memory of these screams and their suppression foreshadows—presounds?—the aural abuse Linda will experience when the master and mistress initiate her into the plantation's sexual economy. Here, too, Jacobs resists the listening ear's perception of slavery by deliberately mingling two sounds the sonic color line would separate, slaves' screams and the master's and mistress's abusive whispers.

Paradoxically an aural contrast and an analogue to slaves' screams, the master's whispers terrorize and discipline Linda to slave womanhood— the third major listening event marking the end of her childhood—

and the obedient listening demanded by her prurient master and the sonic color line writ large. Without denying the importance of screams, Jacobs insists slavery's most devastating sounds were its least audible: the hushed—and pervasive—whispers of rape and sexual abuse that envelop young women in rage, shame, depression, and fear, sounds rarely amplified in nineteenth-century society. Her editor, abolitionist Lydia Marie Child, worried that "many will accuse [Jacobs] of indecorum for presenting these pages to the public," and Jacobs herself declared it "would have been more pleasant to me to have been silent about my own history."[94] However, in recreating the master's whispers, she breaks the protective silence surrounding sex slavery and its impact on black women, revealing the "character of men living among them." From Flint's first visceral assault with "stinging, scorching words, words that scathed ear and brain like fire," everything in Brent's life changes, from her feeling of security, to her relationship with her grandmother, to her sense of herself as a woman.[95] I disagree with Li that Brent defers to "describing her master's abuse as an attack of language" in an attempt to avoid "representing his body as danger to her sexual virtue."[96] Vocal cord vibrations *are* material representations. Jacobs's descriptions do not replicate the master's language; rather, he attacks her with sounds, physical vibrations emanating from his body and violating hers. The combined /s/ sounds of "stinging," "scorching," and "scathed," for example, mimic Flint's whispers, while the image of fire suggests the heat of her master's breath forcing itself into her ear canal and sound's metaphoric ability to burn the foundations of her life to cinders. Rather than avoiding a scandalizing discussion of rape, this scene uses sound and listening to represent rape itself, including the life-altering trauma Linda experiences afterward.

In Linda's account, slaveholding whites enact an aural terrorism in order to discipline black women's listening practices, altering their minds, bodies, behavior, and well-being. Answering the silence of Douglass's *Narrative* regarding Hester's listening experiences—perhaps Hester screamed so loudly to drown out the master's "horrid oaths" forced into her ear—Linda relates how slave girls are "reared in an atmosphere of licentiousness and fear. The lash and the foul talk of her master and his sons are her teachers."[97] Revealing how sexual violence drives so many of slavery's horrors, Linda's evocative image aligns the

serpentine sonic boom of the master's whip with the vibrational un-
dulations of his tongue in her ear—and both with his phallus (and its
successive generations). Another of Jacobs's deft sonic connections, the
linkage of whip and whisper provides a stark contrast with the discourse
of Victorian innocence and "true womanhood." In such a dangerous atmosphere, Jacobs shows the importance of slaves' precise listening practices
for survival.

Just as Jacobs makes explicit how Linda's slave masters' enforcement
of the sonic color line disciplined her, she also conveys how engagement
with the listening ear's racialized perspective filters Mistress Flint's listening across the sonic color line, a process leading to further abuse of
black women. Jacobs explains:

> White daughters early hear their parents quarrelling about some female
> slave. Their curiosity is excited, and they soon learn the cause. They are
> attended by the young slave girls whom their father has corrupted, and
> they hear such talk as should never meet youthful ears, or any other ears.
> They know that the women slaves are subject to their father's authority
> in all things; and in some cases they exercise the same authority over the
> male slaves.[98]

The quarrelling tone, in particular, shunts the white girls' initial "youth-
ful" "curiosity" toward an admiration (and for some a replication) of
white patriarchal power, a sonic experience that prompts them to hear
their racialized difference from the black girls who "attend" them,
silencing fledgling possibilities for gendered solidarity. The moment
when white girls' ears become attuned to their fathers' power—and, by
extension, their own—functions as the flip side to the "bloodstained
gate" of slavery described by both Douglass and Jacobs.

Jacobs's representation of the tortuous relationship between Linda
and Mrs. Flint exemplifies how the listening ear operates at the intersection of gender and race. When Mr. Flint begins abusing Linda, she
comes to Mrs. Flint expecting refuge and sympathy. However, Mrs.
Flint continues to turn a cold ear to Linda's woes even as she extracts
lurid information about her husband, exerting racial and sexual authority over Linda and blaming her for inciting Mr. Flint's lust. Mrs. Flint
wields listening as a medium of domination, extracting Linda's story in

what amounts to a public inquisition rather than an intimate confession; after asking Linda to swear on a Bible, she "order[s]" her to speak. Meeting Mrs. Flint's listening ear with her own skillful aural literacy, Linda quickly realizes that Mrs. Flint only approximates sympathy for her ordeal; her extraverbal sounds express primarily self-concern. Rather than hearing a plea for help, Mrs. Flint interprets Linda's words as evidence of a rivalry for Mr. Flint's affections. Mrs. Flint chooses to torment rather than help Linda, creeping to her at night to "test" her by whispering into her ear while she sleeps, allegedly to ferret out Linda's "true" response to Flint. By forcing her tongue, lips, and breath into Linda's ear, Mrs. Flint terrorizes Linda à la Mr. Flint to seize racialized power over her, performing her own desire for Linda's sexual submission by ventriloquizing the voice of the white patriarchy. By exposing Mrs. Flint's dominating listening practices and their kinship to patriarchy, Jacobs exposes the seams of "true womanhood." While Child's introduction frames *Incidents* as Jacobs's attempt to regender herself as a "lady" by confessing to the "delicate" ears of white Northern readers, Jacobs's narrative instead challenges the listening ear as a paradigm, revealing gendered assumptions about listening as they are crosscut by the sonic color line. Through the character of Mrs. Flint, Jacobs "ungenders" Southern white women by exposing the notion of "delicate ears" as a deliberate artifice that shields white women from black women's suffering and enacts racialized subjugation.[99]

Jacobs represents Mrs. Flint's manifestation of the dominant white listening ear as a "petty [and] tyrannical" instrument of what Hartman delineates as "everyday subjection," one that manifests a particularly insidious flexibility in its constant vigilance for new aural markers of black Otherness to extend the sonic color line's reach.[100] In close quarters occupied by black and white bodies, visual distinctions alone could not guard against intimate exchange. Here whites used the sonic color line to maintain distance through aural performances of racialized power relations, segregating blackness from whiteness without physical separation. Mrs. Flint's listening ear fluctuates rapidly between radical hardness and a heightened sensitivity to racial difference in the smallest everyday detail. She persistently marks sounds produced by black bodies as noise: sound that does not belong, sound that is out of place, sound that must be continually policed. Mrs. Flint, for example, beats

Linda because the sound of her new winter shoes "grated harshly on her refined nerves."[101] Jealous of the sexual attention forced on Linda by her husband and threatened by Linda's love for her free grandmother—provider of the shoes—Mrs. Flint amplifies the small squeak to an epically "horrid noise." She perceives the creaking shoes as signaling the threat of the hypersexual black female body in her primary arena of power as the (re)producer of legitimate offspring and heirs. To reassert her authority, Mrs. Flint forces Linda to remove the shoes and, quite literally, toe her sonic color line through miles of biting cold snow. The listening ear enabled whites to experience a different world within the same spaces they occupied with black people, one protected by its deliberate imperceptibility even as white listeners meted out punishments large and small for trespasses of the sonic color line.

By representing the world-within-a-world of the racialized listening ear alongside depictions of resistant listening by slaves, Jacobs shows readers how black subjects began to decolonize their listening practices even under white surveillance. By manipulating her masters' expectations of how she will listen, for example, Linda sometimes turns her proscribed listening position into a mode of resistance without overtly transgressing the sonic color-line—sometimes "listen[ing] with silent contempt" and at other times concealing the knowledge of her pregnancy by remaining silent—allowing her some psychological disassociation from Flint's abuse and a modicum of control over her body. Kevin Quashie argues for "the sovereignty of quiet" in black culture and history in his book of the same name, noting how "the expressiveness of silence is often aware of an audience, a watcher or a listener whose presence is the reason for the withholding—it is an expressiveness which is intent and even defiant."[102] By strategically concealing anger and fear, Linda's silences refuse the Flints' pleasure at her "shuddering." Beyond resistance, Linda uses her silence as an opportunity to listen to others' listening, a metacognitive practice enabling new forms of listening and selfhood to emerge.

Linda's listening deliberately creates space for (and affirms) black lives, sounds, and familial relationships, a form of decolonizing listening. In a scene revealing listening's potential for empathy amid terror, for example, Linda inhabits her brother's aural experience as Flint forces him to listen while he punishes Linda: "I felt humiliated that my brother should listen to such language as would be addressed only to a slave. Poor boy! He was powerless to defend me; but I saw the tears, which he strove vainly to keep back."[103] In listening to her brother listen, Linda understands how masculinity intersects with race for her brother, who—similar to the young Douglass—experiences his own enslavement in his inability to help his sister. Like her brother and Douglass, Linda refuses to harden her ear against slavery's violence. In another instance, the Flints place Linda in the position of listening to her own daughter, left alone outside, "crying that weary cry which makes a mother's heart bleed." Initially, she feels "obliged to steel [her]self to bear it" to protect them both from worse punishment.[104] However, the trauma of hardening her ear and its near-disastrous result—her daughter cries herself to sleep in the mansion's crawl space and barely escapes a poisonous snake—spur Linda to action. She very deliberately rejects both black listening-as-obedience and the callousness of the slave masters' listening ear, risking her own life by sending her daughter to her grandmother's without asking Flint's permission. By listening to her daughter in the ethically involved manner Douglass fights to maintain, Linda begins to decolonize her listening practice from slavery's violent and dehumanizing discipline, opening herself to the dangerous vulnerability of love and connection.

The third major geographic shift in Linda's life—the seven years she spends hidden in her grandmother's garret, nearly all her young motherhood—mobilizes the trope of the listener to make material the sonic color line's claustrophobic effects on black subjects and amplify listening as a strategy to survive and resist isolation. Literary critics have analyzed this space—only nine feet long and seven feet wide—as a representation of a grave (social death), a cell (slavery as incarceration), a womb (rebirth), an image of the Middle Passage, a symbol of the restriction on women's lives (the "confinement" of pregnancy and child-rearing), and a signifier of the African American literary trope of the "tight space" that black people occupy, metaphorically and materially, in U.S. society. Building on *Incidents*' critical history, I argue that sensory deprivation factors into all of these prior readings, particularly in the case of sight. An inversion of Douglass's Aunt Hester scene, here a slave mother, trapped in a darkened crawl space, listens to the sounds of her children laughing and playing to "comfort [her] in [her] despondency."[105] Linda's cramped space of imprisonment, therefore, also functions as an isolation chamber in which listening remains her primary link to the world.[106] While not completely removed, her senses of smell, taste, and touch are severely restricted. For the first few months, Linda cannot see; she knows the passage of time "only by the noises [she] heard; for in [her] small den day and night were all the same."[107] Both before and after she carves out a small peephole in her garret, listening binds Linda to life and provides comfort, even as her heightened aural literacy demands she bear the psychological weight of listening to herself as "noise" and continually strain for the sound of her master's approach.

The isolation chamber of the garret heightens Linda's attention to the myriad ways the white listening ear demands that black people listen to themselves as "noise." Every sound the fugitive Linda makes threatens to reveal her body as out of bonds/bounds; therefore, she turns the listening ear against herself, policing her every movement and suppressing even the subtlest bodily functions. Although there is a certain amount of power and satisfaction gained in being an unseen listener—culling important intelligence, as Linda points out, without need of the eye—being constantly on the ready during "countless" nights filled with intermittent blasts of information devastates her nerves. After years of being "warned to keep extremely quiet," "even [her] face and tongue stiffened, and [she] lost the power of speech." When her ability to communicate atrophies, Linda experiences a concomitant loss of self. Although Linda never fully loses her ability to listen, she yearns for its sociality to be unfettered, revelling in moments where her oppressive quietude is broken: "It was also pleasant to me to hear a human voice speaking to me above a whisper."[108] Linda embraces not only the meaning of conversational exchange but also the delightful experience of sound itself, which signifies a material difference between slavery and freedom. The sudden increase in volume provides Linda with a brief blast of freedom, including the agency to make "noise," the liberty to move one's body without hypervigilant attention to its every sound, and the ability to have a conversation with a loved one at a desirable volume without constant fear. Linda's brutal experience in the garret's isolation chamber calls attention to the sonic restrictions slaves faced within the sonic color line's circumscription, using the trope of the listener to amplify how slaves must listen through and beyond the listening ear's deleterious representations of their bodies, voices, and culture as "noise."

However, rather than understanding Linda's listening only as reactive practice dealing only with "noise," Jacobs highlights listening as an active practice of desire, a casting out toward sounds that provide Linda with a certain quality of touch, even love, in her isolation. Rather than withdraw, for example, Linda carefully attends to her children's sounds, continuously stoking her maternal relationship, however painful: "Season after season, year after year, I peeped at my children's faces, and heard their sweet voices, with a heart yearning all the while to say, 'your mother is here.'" Linda's grandmother also frequently brings the children to play within Linda's earshot, knowing the sounds "comfort [Linda] in her despondency." [109] As Bonenfant's work on queer listening argues, listening provides comfort and self-recognition because vocal sound, in particular, functions as "a kind of intimate, human-generated touch" that vibrates bodies and caresses the surface of the skin. Bonenfant argues people listen differently to sounds they desire—as opposed to unbidden sounds, such as Flint's whispers—using the body to "listen 'out' for (reaching toward) voices that . . . will gratify." [110] In Bonenfant's terms, listening out for her children's voices allows Linda to feel their presence. Linda listens out for her grandmother, too, who, over the course of Linda's confinement, develops a wordless code to communicate with her. "She had four places to knock for me to come to the trapdoor," Jacobs writes, "and each place had a different meaning," an act of vibration creating pleasurable expectation for Linda and maintaining a material link with her family. [111] Gradually, the furtive whispers of her grandmother and other family members come to replace Flint's. Even as it warps her body and silences her voice, the isolation chamber queers Linda's listening, enabling her to hear beyond the sonic color line's confines and imagine an alternate relationship to her body's experiences of love, pain, desire, survival, and motherhood.

The final phase of Linda's evolving listening practice, the process of liberating herself from a lifetime of the listening ear's discipline, proves arduous and uneven, even as Linda finds herself on the clamorous streets of Philadelphia, New York City, and Boston. Here Jacobs shows listening's mutability, however stubbornly filtered through the past and ghosted by echoes of former geographies. Once in the North, Linda struggles with feeling psychologically mired in the South; listening functions here as a conduit for wrestling with the emotional consequences of slavery, sexual abuse, and her long period of entrapment. After meeting her first free black acquaintance, the Reverend Jeremiah Durham, Linda realizes how slavery still stigmatizes her in the "free" North. Durham suggests Linda shouldn't recount her sexual abuse lest it "give some heartless people a pretext for treating [her] with contempt." The shock of the idea that Northerners might shun her for her master's licentiousness impacts Linda viscerally. She notes, "The word *contempt* burned me like coals of fire," hearkening back to the "scorching" words of Mr. Flint and connecting them to the political economy of gender that would silence her. The realization of a larger system of racialized gender connecting North and South fills Linda with dread, causing her to seek the solitude she had so recently left behind: "I went to my room, glad to shut out the world for awhile."[112] Linda arrives in the North listening out for signs of freedom, connection, and family life but learns that her raced and gendered identity still demands she continue to listen for danger.

A theme echoed by Douglass and throughout the texts I explore, the notion that the North falls short of its promises of freedom for black people—that it is, in fact, part of a national system of white supremacy—finds deep expression through Jacobs's representations of sound and the trope of the listener. While the urban North and the rural South present strikingly different visual tableaus, black writers use aural imagery to amplify how the sonic color line facilitates profound ideological similarities between the regions that defy the eye and, by design, elude the listening ear. Upon finally making contact with her daughter, Ellen, for instance, Linda hears familiar echoes of her own sexual abuse as a slave. When Linda asks Ellen if her white family treats her well—Ellen works for them as a slave in fact if not in name—Linda hears "no heartiness in the tone" of her "yes." Listening through the words to her daughter's tone—the aural literacy key to her daily life as a slave—Linda realizes her daughter's danger; she eventually finds out the brother-in-law of Ellen's mistress "poured vile language into her ears" just as Mr. Flint had done to her.[113] Similarly, Linda finds her son, Benny, facing a different kind of aural racial abuse. After the Americans and "Irish-born Americans" at his apprenticeship discover that he is "colored"—a fact that "transformed him into a different being" in their estimation—they now hear him through the sonic color line's filter: "They began by treating him with silent scorn, and finding that he returned the same, they resorted to insults and abuse."[114] While Benny does not feel immediately constrained to listen—and he resists through returning some of the scorn—the sounds of cold tones and communicative silences nonetheless shape his self-image, life chances, and material circumstances as they did Linda's. Such examples of slavery-honed aural literacy foretelling Northern violence for Linda and her family not only map the sonic color line's profound reach but also characterize how it enacts "slavery" and "freedom" as mobile racialized sensory orientations resistant to physical borders.

In "Listening," Roland Barthes claims the "freedom to listen is as necessary as freedom of speech." [115] However, as Douglass and Jacobs show, such freedoms were imagined through and enabled by New World slavery and explicitly denied to slaves. Upon her arrival North, Linda experiences a thrill at consciously reorienting her senses from slavery to freedom; she wonders at even mundane Northern street sounds, particularly loud female voices hawking groceries. But like Douglass's remembering of the sound of slave songs from his writing desk, Brent's listening continues to inhabit a dissonant space of doubleness and fugitivity, where freedom of speech intertwines with the freedom to listen, and echoes of an aural literacy honed by slavery both affirm and haunt sounds signaling freedom. Linda can, for perhaps the first time since her youngest days, listen to others without being first attuned to the sound of her own body as betrayal—modulating her tones, worrying who would hear, and dreading the consequences if overheard—but the filter of slavery's "silent days" culls such moments as strange, fragile, and devastatingly conditional, especially with the Fugitive Slave Act in effect.[116]

However, precisely because Jacobs focuses so intently upon how slavery shaped Linda's listening practices, her new auditory experiences of freedom present an intimate portrait of her struggle to decolonize listening. However much Linda still wrestled with the dissonant traces of abuse, she eventually begins to hear the world differently. Although, as a fugitive slave, she remains marginalized and in constant danger, Linda exercises agency through listening via the capacity to listen out for pleasurable sounds while simultaneously shifting the dominant cultural narratives of sound she must endure. Fittingly, the sound of Linda's children "laugh[ing] and chat[ting] merrily" punctuates the climax of Jacobs's narrative: the moment when Linda finally has both of her children under the same roof, "one of the happiest of [her] life" because she feels free to listen, to speak, to mother, to comfort, and to be comforted in turn.[117] The painful fleetingness of her experience makes it no less transformational, reaffirming Linda's practice of "listening out" across chronological and geographical distance while challenging the internal devastation the sonic color line has wrought on her ability to hear freely and hear herself as free. While *Incidents* closes with Linda far from freedom, Jacobs's attentiveness to listening as a resistant and self-making practice and her rendering of the evolving trope of the listener are important literary interventions in the cultural politics of listening in antebellum America.

Resisting Ethnosympathy: Jacobs's Critique of Douglass

Even as Jacobs reveals the sonic color line's permeability and the possibilities of an eventual decolonization of listening for black subjects, Linda's auditory sojourn in the North openly questions her white readers' ability to reform the listening ear and its material effects. Jacobs's focus on listening as a racialized practice suggests a deep sensory dimension to Hartman's claim that "empathy is double-edged; for in making the other's suffering one's own, this suffering is occluded by the other's obliteration."[118] Even if her white readers could consciously imagine themselves in Linda's position, Jacobs implies their own senses—honed by years of race privilege—would always imagine this experience differently. The danger of empathy means not only that Jacobs's readers would begin to feel *for* themselves, as Hartman implies, but also that they are limited to feeling *as* themselves; because their privilege enables them to imagine their bodies and feelings as universally human, they do not even recognize how their sensory limitations erase and misunderstand the Other's experiences. Jacobs's constant reminders of how racialized listening practices produce (and are produced by) the sonic color line attempt to disrupt its propensity for misrecognition, mishearing, and silencing.

In order to disrupt the "delicate ears" of her privileged, white Northern female audience, Jacobs offers listening instructions in the style of Frederick Douglass but in signifying contrast. Rather than suggesting a trip to the pine woods to hear slaves sing, Jacobs suggests to her readers: "If you want to be fully convinced of the abominations of slavery, go on a southern plantation, and call yourself a negro trader. Then there will be no concealment; and you will see and hear things that will seem to you impossible among human beings with immortal souls."[119] In representing her readers as active "negro traders" rather than unseen eavesdroppers, she comments on the culpability of the North in accepting Southern slavery and the recent passage of the Fugitive Slave Act, which essentially made all Northerners slave catchers. For Jacobs, the truth about slavery does not lie solely in slaves' cultural exchange but also in whites' acts of aggression, abuse, and terror. Whereas Douglass's instructions invite the shedding and reforming of white identity, Jacobs's distinctly demand the assumption of a classed, raced, and gendered subject position. By asking her privileged female readers to imagine themselves across the lines of gender and class as morally repugnant figures, Jacobs calls attention to the literary conceit of such pleas for better listening. While Douglass's request launched a wave of "ethnosympathetic" listening—in which white abolitionists sought deeper meanings in the cultural productions of slaves—Jacobs's instructions thwart white empathy through listening, seeking a disidentification through dissonant shock and horror at the brutal acts of allegedly cultured, civilized, and religious whites.[120] For Jacobs's wealthy Northern white female readership, beginning to understand their culpability and, most importantly, agency in the institution of slavery meant stripping away various layers of "concealment" that class, gender, and geography provided. Rather than using sound to bring her white readers closer—as Douglass often does—Jacobs's aural imagery emphasizes vast cultural, social, and political distances between herself and her readers, particularly in scenes involving motherhood or sexual abuse. Understanding the distance created by the sonic color line, Jacobs insinuates, may be the best path to eventual solidarity for black and white women.

While Douglass and Jacobs both represent America's sonic color line and the antebellum listening ear of the white elite as fundamental problems, their respective narratives present markedly divergent interventions. Douglass holds out for universal perception, representing "black listening" in order to reveal it as simply "listening" and depicting the listening ear as a correctible distortion caused by white supremacist ideology. Jacobs, on the other hand, understands the listening ear as a constituting element of whiteness itself; she identifies black forms of listening as mobile oppositional forces capable of reshaping the very notion of black selfhood. The white-authored sonic color line causes much emotional, psychological, and material damage in *Incidents*, but Jacobs's representations suggest that, rather than countering its stereotypes to reform white listening habits and gain their acknowledgement on its "other" side, black subjects may ultimately find liberation and agency through asserting their cultural difference from the listening ear and more deeply exploring their own listening practices and the new worlds listening can create. However, while Douglass's listening instructions sparked entire modes of cultural criticism and inquiry across the sonic color line—Cruz argues Douglass's introduction to black music enabled its "central role in the rise of modern modes of cultural interpretation"[121]—Jacobs's caveats and detailed exploration of black listening practices remained an underground current of critique, but one no less central to the development of black politics, aesthetics, and self-making practices. Far from mutually exclusive, both perspectives—the desire for universal equality and the quest to alter the very terms of "universality"—resound and reecho in the voices and literary texts examined throughout this book.

As we will see in following chapters, the sonic color line only increases in importance beyond the South, far outliving formal chattel slavery and allowing developing forms of racism such as segregation and color blindness to thrive in its wake, particularly through successive shapings of the listening ear. Expected to emanate from black bodies, the sonic color line's perpetually "Othered" sounds shift alongside the rise of the American entertainment industry, dramatic changes in audio technology, and so-called discoveries in racial science, performing the unspoken vibrational work of racial production.

2.

Performing the Sonic Color Line in the Antebellum North

The Swedish Nightingale and the Black Swan

Swedish opera singer Jenny Lind was one of nineteenth-century America's first bona fide "stars." This chapter complicates Lind's vast critical history by considering the impact of her 1851 U.S. tour—one of the first of its kind—on shifting notions of racial identity during the antebellum period, particularly the consolidation of "whiteness" and its growing association with "racial purity" as crafted by racial scientists. More than just a protofeminist phenomenon or an example of P. T. Barnum's preternatural marketing talents, Lind and her soprano gave American crowds a palpable whiteness they could hear *and* feel, contributing to a sonics linking U.S. citizenship and white supremacy. White American critics heard and championed Lind's voice as a standard-bearer for race-feeling and bodily discipline; Lind's sound enabled whiteness to script its vibrational presence at the heart of the rising American popular culture industry. The sonic color line not only regulated "black" sound but also deemed certain sounds publicly expressive of whiteness.

In contrast with Lind—and despite excellent historical recovery work by Black scholars in the late 1960s—Elizabeth Taylor Greenfield, the Natchez-born, Philadelphia-raised former slave who dared sing Lind's repertoire in white concert halls, remains largely a footnote. Unlike the overwhelming raves about the unifying melodies emanating from Lind's white body, white elite critics' reviews of Greenfield perceived her singing as noise, primed to intensify white America's festering divisions of race, class, gender, and region. However, scholars have underscored the importance of Greenfield's performances, particularly as sonic challenges to America's racial regime and as evidence of what Nina Eidsheim calls "sonic blackness," the attribution of "black" qualities to classical voices based on visual impression.[1] In particular, Julia Chybowski's recent biographical history of Greenfield's first American tour makes an impeccable argument for her legacy as well as the necessity to interpret (rather then recite) Greenfield's nineteenth-century newspaper reception. This chapter uses similar archival methods but places "The Black Swan" in a broader American context concerning the racialization of sound. I reveal a more complex perceptual process at work in Greenfield's print reception, particularly how the collusive relationship between sight and sound deliberately interweaves the racial gaze and its aural counterpart, the listening ear.

Greenfield's reviews perform race rather than merely reflect already-circulating racial ideologies, and I trace how white *and* black audiences attempted to resolve her performances' perceptual challenges. I agree with Chybowski that Greenfield's white audiences were much more conflicted over Greenfield's performances than Eidsheim suggests, but I maintain that such diversity drove attempts to locate Greenfield's voice—in and of itself—as either "black" or "white." Nervous that Greenfield sounded "white," white reviewers feared her ability to vocally "pass" and potentially best Lind. Others remained terrified Greenfield produced "black" sounds in white performance spaces, thereby "contaminating" the operatic tradition and valorizing "low" culture. Certain that either their eyes were deceived *or* their ears were playing tricks, many white reviewers either "whitened" Greenfield's voice—disembodying it and locating it firmly in Lind's style and tradition—or "blackened" its sound to match the cultural meanings her visible body represented. By criticizing Greenfield's voice for betraying "blackness" *or* "whiteness," nineteenth-century critics shored up the sonic color line by training readers' ears to detect both. Black Northern critics, rarely discussed in Lind and Greenfield criticism, challenged the emerging sonic color line by re-presenting the women's voices against broader social contexts, particularly slavery, and by discussing the role of listening in identity construction and community formation. For many free black antebellum subjects, hearing Greenfield's voice—whether in person or in print—worked to decolonize listening and create alternate experiences of blackness away from and in resistance to the listening ear.

In amplifying the differing expectations and receptions of the New York debuts of Lind and Greenfield—two singers whose performances were inextricably tied to each other even as their lives remained worlds apart—this chapter traces the rise of the sonic color line in the antebellum North and its codification through the listening ear: normative listening practices tied to (and linking) whiteness, masculinity, and citizenship. Whereas the sonic color line operated in the South as an everyday mode of racial discipline, its Northern analogue trafficked in stage spectacles, heightened—and increasingly popular—performances of race, gender, and sexuality that prodded, provoked, and shaped everyday understandings of race. Although sonic stereotypes of race circulated prior to Lind's and Greenfield's tours, their similarity, popularity, and proximity—which Chybowski notes overlapped for seven months and placed them in Boston, the hotbed of abolitionist activism, only days apart—coupled with the singers' visibly different racial subject positions, provided the American press with the opportunity to sound out and circulate sonic racial difference, reaching audiences far beyond the North's concert halls.[2] Reporters' and critics' copious descriptions of Lind's and Greenfield's respective voices revealed and performed the racialization of listening practices in the antebellum North.

The white antebellum press pitted the racially divergent dueling divas against each other, locked in symbolic battle over the keys to America's burgeoning (and increasingly stratified) "kingdom of culture" while calling attention to race's sonic dimensions. If Greenfield, a former slave with little-to-no access to continental European training, could sing Bellini's "Do Not Mingle" as well as (if not better than) the acclaimed "Swedish Nightingale," what did that say about the antebellum racial hierarchies?[3] Did hearing expertly performed "white" music emanating from a black woman's body unsettle dominant ideas about race for white American audiences increasingly divided over the abolition of slavery? Or did Greenfield's transgressive potential amplify the "whiteness" Lind produced, hastening the construction of a dominant listening ear attuned to an emerging sonic color line?

My argument unfolds in three sections. First, I historicize the sonic color line and the respective tours of Lind and Greenfield in the contexts of the Fugitive Slave Law, popular performances of minstrelsy, and the women's rights movement in order to show how the public appearance of two differently raced female bodies greatly enabled Northern versions of the sonic color line and the listening ear. By defying the strictures of "true womanhood," Lind's and Greenfield's performances confronted predominately male audiences and critics with raced and gendered expectations regarding comportment, desire, and presumed links between womanhood, emotion, and the body. The second section compares archival traces of the white and black press receptions of Jenny Lind's 1850–1852 tour. In order for white Americans to claim the virtuosity of Lind, they raced her voice as supremely and purely "white," linking it to her visual phenotype even as they disavowed the imprint of her gendered body on its "angelic" sound. I focus specifically on descriptions of Lind's "timbre," the latest vocal technology theorized by German scientist (and musician) Hermann von Helmholtz that identified unique vibrational qualities of sounding bodies even when playing (or voicing) the same note. The third section performs parallel archival analysis on Greenfield's press receptions, both to excavate the sonic color line and the listening ear as they coalesced in the North and to argue for her 1851 tour as a "sonic slave narrative," a form Daphne Brooks provocatively pursues in her recuperative research on Blind Tom—an African American pianist who performed a generation after Greenfield's debut—in which she reads archival traces of Tom's stage performances as "a kind of alternative narration of the bondsman" and an "archive of sound commentary about the world in which he lived and performed."[4] I embed Greenfield's story within this growing body of literature, meticulously weighing out the constraints the white elite listening ear placed on her voice with what its vibrations bespoke of Greenfield's life in the North and her struggle for agency and self-definition. Like Frado, the protagonist of Harriet Wilson's 1859 novel *Our Nig: Sketches from a Free Black*, Greenfield experiences—and sounds out—the subtler brutalities of white supremacy, and her sonic slave narrative makes audible the connections between the power dynamics of Southern slavery and the discrimination, economic insecurity, and extreme vulnerability of "free" black life in the North. White audiences and critics struggled to separate her voice from her black female body, banishing explicit "blackness" from its sound—which nonetheless lingered in many white listeners' expectation of her failure and their emphasis on her voice's "flaws"—while simultaneously refusing to locate her voice as "feminine." While the black press praised Greenfield's voice—a strong corrective to the sonic color line's racialized parsing of timbre—critics remained deeply divided over what the experience of listening to Greenfield should signify to black listeners, particularly when her voice so often vibrated within the walls of segregated concert halls.

At stake across Lind's and Greenfield's audience reception is the construction and normalizing of the white American citizen subject and the consolidation of "whiteness" through sonic experience and perceptual discipline. The voice presented a powerful medium through which new expressions of race traveled in mid-nineteenth-century America, part of what Kyla Wazana Tompkins calls the nineteenth century's "early expression of biopower."[5] But voice alone cannot cement the relationship between the sonic color line, citizenship, and racial identity; white American listeners had to be attuned to the sounds of race embedded in musical styles and vocal timbres, and the unprecedented circulation of print media during this era provided a medium for just that.[6] In the era before the invention and mass marketing of sound reproduction, detailed written accounts served as listening experiences in their own right, a form of recording and a technology of discipline shaping a national listening ear attuned to race and its intersections with gender, class, sexuality, and citizenship. Greenfield's 1853 memoir, a promotional document composed largely of clippings, calls the press "the living voice and oracle of our times."[7] Across multiple branches of contemporary print media, an important conversation about race, voice, and listening took place in the antebellum North that standardized the racial rhetoric of the sonic color line and circulated it across a nation increasingly enthralled by the rapidly growing popular culture industry and its spectacular representations of celebrity. Adjective by adjective, a handful of elite listeners published reviews that performatively affixed vocal tones and styles to essential notions of racial identity, constructing the grammar of the sonic color line and casting it far beyond any immediately visible onstage presence.

Because white reviewers and other power brokers cast value judgments made via the sonic color line as universal standards, free black people in the North faced immense external and internal pressure to conform to the white elite listening ear. As the archive reveals, black writers well understood the paradox that, while whites *became* white (and experienced and exercised whiteness) through the selectivity of their listening, mobilizing the strictures of the listening ear would not guarantee black people the same access to power and privilege; in fact, aural conformity could inflict great damage upon black subjects. Black sonic resistance to the listening ear involved a complicated negotiation between several strategies. Some black listeners challenged white assumptions; others exposed the link between fluency in whites' sonic expectations and full citizenship privilege, while still others recognized the listening ear as partial and challenged its limitations. The added layer of the sonic color line pitched racial identity in America as a shell game: a perpetual oscillation between aural and visual markers of race, each one signaling the other yet both capable of operating alone, with citizenship privilege as its constantly shifting stake.

Black subjects' internalization of the sonic color line and the listening ear's raced value system represented what Christina Sharpe calls "monstrous intimacy," a marker of the trauma of slavery and its diachronic echoes.[8] At the very moment of the sonic color line's inception, black writers such as Frederick Douglass, Harriet Jacobs, and Martin Delany fought its influence, using a variety of press platforms and textual strategies to intervene in the discursive recording of American popular music, politicizing white press reviews in the contexts of slavery, exposing their partiality, and asking their readers to question the overwhelming popularity of Lind's voice and the marginalization of Greenfield's. This chapter brings these little known writings into critical conversations in African American literature, particularly concerning what Brooks calls "the politics of black listenership." Furthermore, I place the genre of the slave narrative and the trope of the listener in the context of "the larger matrices of print culture studies—a field that has rarely attended to Black texts."[9] Crafting liberatory listening practices was, I argue, an important part of antiracist struggle, and the voices of Lind and Greenfield—in both their textual and vibrational forms—presented opportunity and challenge in the praxis surviving this period, the decolonization of listening.

Historicizing the Sonic Color Line: The Fugitive Slave Law, Minstrelsy, the Women's Rights Movement, and Immigration

The rise of a recognizable sonic color line in the 1840s and 1850s operated at the confluence of massive historical and ideological shifts in politics, popular culture, and racial science. To riff on Hortense Spillers, if Elizabeth Taylor Greenfield had not existed, it was very likely she "would have [had] to be invented" by a tenuous United States fiercely riven with sectional conflict over slavery in the wake of the Compromise of 1850.[10] And she almost was. Even before Greenfield entered Buffalo, New York's concert scene in fall 1851, reporters clamored for a black songstress rivalling Jenny Lind. The day before Lind's American debut, the *Detroit Advertiser* printed a provocation concerning a "black *Prima Donna* arrived in London who promises to be a formidable rival of Jenny Lind's," closing with the popular platitude, "*Where's Barnum.*"[11] Evoking Barnum was, by the mid-nineteenth century, a common joke signalling a commodification-ready novelty.[12] That Barnum managed Lind meant the joke cut both ways; in America, buying and selling blackness was already a familiar practice—indeed a constitutive quality of the nation—and Lind herself was now one of Barnum's colossal humbugs, her white Nordic womanhood transformed into an audiovisual spectacle.

As controversy over the Fugitive Slave Law intensified, the popular white working class practice of minstrelsy moved to the center of American culture, trafficking in its own influential aural representations of "blackness" (and "whiteness" through negation). Scholars such as Eric Lott, Michael Rogin, William J. Mahar, and Jayna Brown have shown that the complexity of minstrelsy extended beyond a crude exercise of white domination, a truth nonetheless compatible with one of its most enduring effects: an array of sonic stereotypes. Minstrelsy's aural practice involved distorted dialect, exaggerated intonation, rhythmic speech cadences, and particular musical instruments such as the banjo and bone castanets allegedly lifted from "the plantation" (but more likely heard in Northern spaces of interracial interaction: waterfronts, taverns, and neighborhoods such as New York's Five Points).[13] Minstrelsy shaped the antebellum content of "black" sounds and normalized the listening ear across class boundaries.

At its apex when Lind and Greenfield emerged, minstrelsy impacted the singers' receptions in ways that emphasized their divergent relationship to sounds the increasingly cross-class white listening ear deemed "black." For example, although minstrel troupe Buckley's Serenaders burlesqued Lind on the New York City blackface stage three years before her arrival—and *both* she and Greenfield included sentimental Stephen Foster favorites such as "Old Folks at Home" in their repertoires—Lind's reviewers raised minstrelsy in order to mark her distance from it, in terms of both race and class.[14] In contrast, Greenfield would never be able to attain such distance from minstrelsy no matter what her repertoire. Even given her many deliberate similarities to Lind, Greenfield often met with audiences "straining their ears to catch pure negro minstrelsy," as charged by *The Albion* in 1853.[15] Only partly due to Greenfield's phenotypical blackness, minstrelsy comparisons provided the listening ear with a resolution to the cognitive dissonance many whites experienced when confronted with her vocal talents. One confused, angry white Clevelander allegedly demanded a refund because he had "been told that this woman you call the Black Swan ain't nobody but Jenny Lind blacked up."[16] The layered image of "Jenny Lind blacked up" characterizes Greenfield's blackness as both deceptive *and* authentic, a minstrel act explaining her "white" sound to an increasingly cross-class listening ear and a genuine exception proving the sonic color line's rule.

Taken alongside the masculine domain of minstrelsy, mid-nineteenth-century American conflicts over women's suffrage and the increasing emergence of white women into the public sphere revealed a distinctly gendered filter enabling the sonic color line and the listening ear, particularly in the case of the discourse evoking Lind's and Greenfield's sounding bodies. The discourse of minstrelsy fragmenting Greenfield's body into *"genuine negro features, including the feet, hair and hands"* remained quite distinct from the classical music-driven rhetoric surrounding Lind, whose reviewers made brief, modest remarks about her body in marked contrast to voluminous notes about her voice.[17] Calling Lind a "performed effigy," Rebeccah Bechtold traces nineteenth-century complaints that the dozen or more engravings of Lind could not capture her physicality. It was not only that audiences thought the images inaccurate but also that Lind's body could not be visually represented.[18] Unlike minstrelsy, which operated through a dramatic, even grotesque corporeal emphasis, classical concert performances disavowed singers' physicality. As feminist musicologist Susan McClary argues, one of the claims for European high musical culture's supremacy focused on its perceived ability to "transcend the body" and concern itself "with the nobler domains of imagination and even metaphysics."[19] Of course, the goal of transcendence through music—particularly the overt sublimation of any erotic encounter—remained fraught for female performers, because Victorian emphasis on essential gender difference within the female reproductive body caused a "pervasive cultural anxiety over women as obstacles to transcendence."[20] As a result, the antebellum concert stage hosted intensified gender policing; plots emerged involving "monstrous vampish women preying on poor helpless males," and aural motifs marking "femaleness" found expression through both music and voice.[21] The same gender codes restricted bourgeois white female bodies from becoming grist for paper sales; therefore, male audiences' unspoken (but palpable) sexual desire for Lind produced a massive slippage between her body, largely left undescribed, and the sound of her voice, rendered in fine detail, an erotics that played out in the fetishizing of the many Jenny Lind products available for purchase: gloves, bottles, statuettes, handkerchiefs, and the trademark furniture that still bears her name.[22]

Because Jenny Lind's bel canto voice embodied the "feminine range," Greenfield's vocal explorations of the lower registers had especially high stakes. Revealingly, one critic declared that Greenfield's "excesses in deep bass developed a power quite monstrous, compared with any other female voice we have heard."[23] Being visibly black and female, Greenfield bore the additional weight of dominant associations of "blackness" with masculinity and hypersexuality. A priori denied the subject position of "woman" by the same white supremacy that deemed Lind its supreme yet elusive embodiment, Greenfield relentlessly faced what Spillers calls slavery's "ungendering."[24] "She takes easily the lowest chalumeau note of the clarionet," remarked the *Tribune*, "and when it is taken it is worth nothing. The idea of a woman's voice is a feminine tone; anything below that is disgusting; it is as bad as a bride with a beard on her chin and an oath in her mouth."[25] At once crossing gender boundaries and the sonic color line, critics called Greenfield's voice a "disgusting" noise. "Bearded bride" also summons the bearded lady of the freak show—another popular form of antebellum entertainment that scholars such as Rachel Adams and Linda Frost argue had an important function in constructing race and gender norms—queering the image of the in/authentic "Jenny Lind blackened up" while eroticizing the black female body as sexually available. Particularly when heard through cultural anxieties over the women's rights movement— "manly" women and feminized men cropped up in political cartoons depicting potential outcomes of women's suffrage—Greenfield's voice, at once eroticized and masculinized, exemplified a "defensive slippage among the 'feminine,' the racial Other, and popular culture."[26] In his travel memoir *Old England and New England* (1853), British expatriate Alfred Bunn describes seeing Greenfield one evening and then returning to the same hall the next night for a treatise on women's rights from the bloomered "Miss Lucy Neale (Stone, we beg the lady's pardon)." Lott argues that the joke here, the deliberate mix-up between "Lucy Neale," the commonly known minstrel character and song, and Lucy Stone, the prominent women's rights speaker, represents a deliberate bleed between Greenfield's performances, minstrelsy, and the women's rights movement.[27] This chain of burlesque marks female bodies as key sites over which white male culture brokers drew the sonic color line, containing the transgressive power of Lind's and Greenfield's voices in their gendered and eroticized bodies and effacing the increasingly entwined—and vocal—women's rights and abolitionist movements,

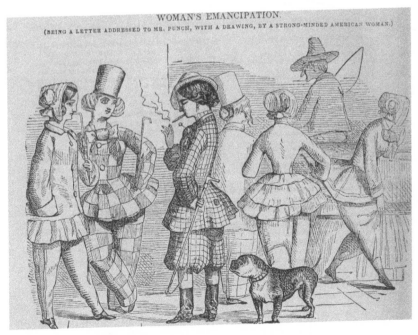

Political cartoon picturing women smoking, wearing hats and "bloomers," carrying canes, and engaging in other "masculine" activities, "Women's Emancipation," *Punch*, 1851, reprinted in *Harper's*, August 1851.

"where upper-class white women took leadership roles and associated with African Americans."[28]

However, the sonic color line divided white women from black women, and the listening ear amplified perceived differences in the face of abolition and women's rights activism, devaluing Greenfield's voice and appearance while representing Lind's soprano as the embodiment of the tenets of upper-class Victorian femininity, even as her performances immanently subverted them. Writer Washington Irving, for example, idealized Lind as "enough to counterbalance, of herself, all the evil that the world was threatened with by the great convention of women" at the same time as the Seneca Falls architects cited Lind as an example of the power of a (white) woman's voice in a public forum, a move that simultaneously refuted the reigning logic of gender supremacy and affirmed the racial order of things.[29] Susan B. Anthony and the Reverend Antoinette Brown mentioned only Lind's performances in their respective speeches at the Women's Temperance Meeting at New York's Metropolitan Hall, although Greenfield had also performed there by 1853.[30] Brown, in particular, evoked Lind as the embodiment of the universal woman deserving of a public hearing—"if they thought her anything besides a woman," Brown said, "they thought she was angelic"—muting Greenfield's struggle with white supremacist patriarchy and ironically aligning women's rights with white feminine ideals.[31]

Whereas Lind could be "angelic" to white feminists and antifeminists alike, Greenfield could only dubiously borrow an angel's voice, as a critic in the *Springfield Review* made clear: "It was amusing to behold the utter surprise and intense pleasure which were depicted on the faces of her listeners; they seemed to express—'Why, we see the face of a black woman, but hear the voice of an angel, what does it mean?'"[32] The syntax here depicts "black woman" and (white) "angel" as dichotomous, mutually exclusive identities bisected by the sonic color line, conditioning the sounds expected from racially categorized bodies by highlighting the perceived dissonance between Greenfield's voice and body. Some white critics thus barred Greenfield from the category of "angel"; for them, her visible blackness only emphasized the sound of white femaleness emanating from her mouth. Even when attempting to divide sound from race's visual bias, white listeners still deemed Greenfield's black body a visual flaw to overlook, turn away from, and/or remove from view to reveal the potential for white sound within.[33] In the face of such silencing and redirection toward whiteness, the association between Lind's voice and the women's rights movement affirmed and strengthened the color line, enhancing white female exceptionalism and contributing to the profound silencing of black women in the movement.

Making Greenfield's body hypervisible amplified Lind's voice, while disavowing Lind's bodily presence assuaged some of the cultural anxiety over white women's emergence into public space. White reviewers' general practice of ignoring Lind's body in print depicted Lind's voice as a perfect vessel for the vibrational power of whiteness, erasing female difference under the standards of race and female equality. The *Water-Cure Journal*, for example—a New York newspaper devoted to physiology and hydropathy—reported that American listeners could expect Lind's voice to "harmoniz[e] so well with her appearance," which, ironically, it never describes.[34] The perceived ethereality of her bodily transcendence performs the aspirational femininity of "true womanhood," a gendered performance seeking to abjure desire, transform raw sentiment into mannered sentimentality, and mystify bodily functions, including reproduction. Her voice, ultimately (and ironically), "evoked this transformation in her physical attractiveness and that conjured forth the audience's emotional response."[35] Aligning Lind's voice with her body—hearing one as echoing the other—allowed whiteness to be material yet ethereal, a powerful yet, as George Lipsitz has noted, "invisible" experience of transformation.[36]

Yet another contextual layer intersecting with the cultural filters of slavery, minstrelsy, and the women's rights movement in the development of the sonic color line, rising European immigration to the United States also impacted the receptions of Lind and Greenfield, making questions of citizenship, nationalism, and social class much more audible. Beginning around 1825, Irish and German immigrants arrived in large numbers, transforming American urban spaces and the composition of the country's working class. Lott notes the rise of "a virulently male white supremacy" during this period, as the middle classes set themselves apart from the working classes and native-born workers challenged new arrivals. "The rhetoric of race that was a specific product of antebellum America's capitalist crisis," Lott writes, "thus equated working-classness with blackness as often as it differentiated between them, an antinomy with properly equivocal results." Nell Irvin Painter connects American fascination with Northern European racial identity during this period to a rising tide of "Teutonic/Saxon race chauvinism" in response to anti-immigrant sentiment, which shaped the idea that "to be *American* was to be Saxon." Lind, in particular, provided an opportunity for Americans, in the face of what Europeans considered their crass capitalist bent, to prove their ability to appreciate and reproduce the "finer values" of Northern Europe.[37] Though only in the United States a short time, Lind's voice and diverse repertoire offered wealthy white audiences an audiovisual representation of the "right" kind of assimilated immigrant, one skilled in the increasingly high-status European concert tradition and able to entertain with discretely packaged culture of the "old country" such as her "Swedish Echo Song," yet still prove herself fully assimilated into American popular culture by closing with ditties such as "Home Sweet Home." Gustavus Stadler's exploration of Lind through the prism of nineteenth-century conceptions of "genius" reveals how her exceptionalism was racialized as white and, eventually, adopted as distinctly American. He notes the American press heightened Lind's display of skill and talent through very prominent reminders of her Scandinavian heritage.[38] Ironically, anti-immigrant sentiment also placed many white reviewers in the uncomfortable position of "embrac[ing] Greenfield as 'American' in the 1850s, when a sense of a distinct national culture was growing in the U.S."[39] Rather than broadening the racial umbrella of citizenship, however, claiming Greenfield as "American" stoked fears regarding the agency of free blacks in the North and the outcome of abolition for white Americans. It also postulated that black people must prove themselves exceptional to be considered "American."

Occurring alongside the work of racial and gendered differentiation performed by minstrelsy—"class turbulence with a racial accent," as Lott argues—Lind's and Greenfield's performances also shored up the class dimensions of the sonic color line by offering an opportunity for the elite listening ear to separate U.S.-born, middle-class white men from the immigrant, working-class "b'hoys" and "g'hals."[40] Lind has been called America's first modern pop star, not only because of her ability to draw a fanatical crowd but also because Barnum's marketing strategies sold her image to a broad audience, heterogeneous, as Steve Waksman notes, "in most regards other than race." Waksman argues that the diversity of Lind's audiences separated her cultural impact from minstrelsy's, which engaged a much narrower audience of working-class white males in "more overt mechanisms of racial performance and representation."[41] However, the fact that Lind's singing drew a big tent—especially taking into account the phenomenal sales of her sheet music—does not make her performances any less racially performative than those of the minstrel stage, it only meant the white press did not explicitly mark and reference Lind's as such. Lind's racial identity as a white European woman may have seemed unremarkable to white American audiences, however class and gender diverse, but it remained fundamentally pervasive and highly performative.

"A Sincere and Hearty Welcome": Jenny Lind and White American Audiences

The sound of Jenny Lind's U.S. debut was as much clamor as melody. Barnum's relentless marketing campaign whetted public appetite, so much so that the proprietors of New York City's Castle Garden—at the time the city's largest venue—demanded assurances that Lind's September 11 performance would be orderly and civil. While this may have been true inside the hall—an innovative color-coded system helped concertgoers find their seats—even Barnum was not entirely prepared for the pandemonium outside. The city police, still fledgling in 1850, were summoned to the Battery to control the ticketless throng hoping to glimpse the Swedish Nightingale's arrival. Although public ticket auctions drove the price up to a dramatic average of 6.38 dollars (around 76 in 2013 dollars), Barnum created far more demand than Castle Garden could accommodate.

Lind's debut exacerbated New York's growing class divisions and anti-immigrant tensions, particularly when enterprising Lind fans arrived via boats on the Hudson River, dexterously maneuvering their crafts under Castle Garden's open windows. The New York Tribune—the nation's largest and most influential paper with a weekly circulation of 200,000—described the flotilla of "two hundred boats and a thousand persons" as "a noisy crowd of boys in boats," with "boy" of course a reference to the Bowery "b'hoys." The Tribune also suggested the river interlopers intentionally disturbed the bourgeois audience with "a hideous clamor of shouts and yells, accompanied by a discordant din of drums and fifes," an aural image of instrumentation integral to Irish, Welsh, and African American folk traditions, hinting at the potential soundscape for a revolt by racialized im/migrants.[42] However, neither boundaries of flesh nor finance could ultimately prevent the "powerful voice of the nightingale" from wafting freely over the Hudson; the *Herald* intimated that Lind's soprano calmed even the "hardest kind of looking customers," performative aural imagery depicting music's ability to soothe the proverbial "savage beast."[43] The *Herald*'s alleged quelling perhaps accounts for the *Evening Post*'s dramatically disparate depiction; however, the paper's decidedly liberal abolitionist bent under editor William Cullen Bryant underscored the combined power of race and class ideologies to shape auditory perception. Revealing how the sonic color line could be mobilized to racialize immigrants and enhance intraracial class distinctions within whiteness, the ensuing press uproar over the noise of "Lindmania" in New York also, ironically, depicted the desire of Americans of all stripes to hear Lind's "powerful voice." Never itself the cause of unrest, Lind's soprano appeared to the white American print media as the antithesis of noise and disorder, a sound uniquely able to unite a divided citizenry in a moment of severe social, civil, and political conflict.

Lind's white audiences became a spectacle in their own right, sharpening the nationalist edge of the sonic color line and amplifying the identity-making qualities of nineteenth-century white "audiencing." In his discussion of America's shift toward a culture of professional music making and listening, Daniel Cavicchi argues that "Barnum was inviting Americans to examine—and enjoy—their own participation in Lind's tour."[44] Doing so marked audience members as culturally savvy and allowed them "the opportunity to be 'in' on something," a satisfying affective experience created via capitalism. Intimately related to the marketplace, whiteness also presented a profound "something" for Lind's audiences to be "'in' on," and the moment when they began paying to appreciate themselves as Lind's audience enabled audible connections between whiteness, capitalism, and Americanness to become lived sensory experience. The fact that Lind's concerts so often became a proving ground for race and its performative protocols attests to the powerful alchemy of the sonic color line's racial formation; journalists and critics freely speculated as to whether or not the American masses would erupt into violence or col-

JENNY LIND AND THE AMERICANS.
From our own Reporters.

CORONATION OF JENNY THE FIRST—QUEEN OF THE AMERICANS

"Jenny Lind and the Americans," *Punch*, October 1850.

lectively abide by the established codes of white bourgeois respectability Lind performed and traded so profitably in. For example, the satirical London newspaper *Punch* represented Lind's reception as inappropriately fanatical in "Coronation of Jenny the First—Queen of the Americans," insinuating that the American public's reaction to Lind revealed a crisis of whiteness as much as it crowned its glory.

The cartoon chides Americans for their worshipful adoration of a European public figure—"Long Live our QUEEN Jenny," a placard reads—and a woman at that, while also representing Americans' fervent emotional excitement as unbecoming to British understandings of "whiteness." Visually, the artist juxtaposes Lind's unblemished alabaster skin with the smudged faces of her prostrate audience and her composed, upright posture with fans' frenzied motions and faces twisted with passion and desire. Sonically, the Americans' open-mouthed contortions suggest an unruly wall of noise bearing down on the stoic, tight-lipped Lind. The many visual elements of class ridicule at play here—unkempt hair, uncouth plumes of tobacco smoke, raggedy clothing—only intensify the racialized threat of noisy, emotive nonwhiteness of the type I discussed in chapter 1, a connection made most acutely by the painted-face Native American caricature at the crowd's center. Other men in the crowd possess exaggerated "Indian" features—hooked noses, down-turned eyes, long, loose hair—implicating a particularly American threat of racial amalgamation at play in the sight and sound of Lind's excessively expressive audiences. A simultaneous dig at American deco-rum and the disorderliness of its democracy, *Punch*'s image of the silent, composed Lind facing an onslaught of racialized noise heralds a mas-sive breach of whiteness's borders while offering Lind's voice as its aural reparative.

The fact that the U.S. press routinely dubbed excessive Lind fandom as a pathological sickness—referring to it as "Lindmania" or "Jenny Lind Fever"—reveals many white American elites also feared the racial devolution intimated by *Punch*, as do the many articles detailing re-spectful audience deportment, a border of the sonic color line where the audible markers of race met racialized body discipline. A symptomatic piece from the *Saturday Evening Post* explicitly denounces the fervor over Lind and demonstrates how antebellum thought bound up musical sound with racial science:

> But what a commentary is such an enormous compensation to Jenny Lind, upon the moral and intellectual position of some of our people. How grossly is music overvalued by them in comparison with nobler things. For music is the lowest of the arts. It does not seem to require so much elevation of character as either painting, sculpture, or poetry. An ability for it is often found, in fact, in company with inferior endow-ments. Degraded races, such as the negro, may excel in it. The English and the Americans—the noblest specimens of the Circassian race—are far surpassed by other nations of the same great branch, in music. . . . Na-tions with their hearts filled with the music of great deeds, have but little time for the music of brass and catgut.[45]

Deeming "Lind Fever" the sign of a debased humanity, the *Post* piece both constructs the antebellum sonic color line and attunes its readers to the sensory orientation of the "Circassian" listening ear, which should seek the silent, immaterially lofty "music of great deeds" rather than the base blaring of "brass and catgut" associated with essentialized blackness and its naturalized abilities to "excel" in "the lowest of the arts." Refusing any hints of New World racial amalgamation and conflating racial with national identity, the anonymous author reasserts the shared racial ancestry between England and America questioned by *Punch*.

A larger majority of the representations of Lind's audiences served an inoculating effect, as Waksman notes, shoring up the sonic color line by deflecting accusations of noisiness and challenging implications that any large American crowd leads to social disorder.[46] "For its size," qualified the liberal *Tribune*, "the audience was one of the most quiet, refined and appreciative we ever saw assembled in this city," an early instance of "quiet" as an aural signifier for whiteness.[47] *The Albion*, a weekly addressing a British American readership, counterintuitively embraced New York City's raucousness, reframing crowd noise as an acceptable, even distinctively American, hospitality:

> At the close of the applause, there came up from the vast area a noise as of distant thunder. The hum of anticipation and excitement of congregated thousands—*Jenny Lind was coming!* She came; and her reception baffles all attempt at description. . . . Seven thousand people, a moment before reasonable and quiet, became suddenly frantic, they clapped their hands, they stamped, they shouted, they roared, they waved their hats, their handkerchiefs, walking sticks and umbrellas, and showered bouquets upon the stage.[48]

Like the *Tribune*'s description, *The Albion*'s representation emphasizes its initially "reasonable and quiet" decorum, affirming "quiet" as a sonic standard for whiteness and connecting it with rationality and body discipline. Although seeing Lind causes the audience to break its quiet, *The Albion* affirms their noisiness as agency, a "sincere and hearty welcome." Using copious verbs—"roared," "stamped," "shouted"—*The Albion* skillfully avoids the term "noise," with its negative connotations of blackness and working-class b'hoy culture, and carefully directs all raucousness toward the welcome of a worthy figure. As constructed through reviewers' descriptions of Lind's audiences, the sonic color line does not limit whiteness to its signature refined quiet, rather it empowers elite whites with the agency to make sound unabated when the listening ear deems it necessary, meaningful, and appropriate.

"It Harmonizes So Well with Her Appearance": Lind and the Sound of White Womanhood

The startling conventionality of Lind's reviews—especially considering the newness of U.S. popular music criticism in general and the lack of news wires and publicity infrastructure—suggests that if the sight of Lind caused sonic behavior that threw the boundaries of white identity into question, critics could nonetheless call upon the sound of her voice to reaffirm and strengthen the sonic color line. The bulk follow this pattern: first, a description of the audience's respectability, the venue's elegance, and the first sight of Lind ascending the stage, then an extensive description of Lind's voice, usually tracking its moves song by song, hitting her high notes, and detailing any low moments. Nineteenth-century music writers' meticulous attention to sound reveals how they understood themselves as documentarians as much as critics, charged with transforming an ephemeral event into a recorded performance. Cavicchi's intensive study of music lovers' diaries finds written accounts were used "not simply as tools, but as stand-ins, indices, for music performances themselves."[49] An 1857 reader letter to *Dwight's Journal of Music* testifies to music writing as a technology of recording and reproduction. Signed "An Up Country Doctor," to emphasize both the author's status and inability to attend urban concerts, the letter details how the author "read the programmes of these delightful concerts . . . with an avidity and relish almost equal to listening to them. Listening, did I say? I *have* listened, with the aid of your own interpretation."[50] Written accounts also scored and circulated the experiential sonic elements of a concert defying musical notation: stylistic flourishes, unique timbres, the vibrational warmth of the venue, unfortunate mistakes, and unusual triumphs.

Writing as a technology of sonic recording and reproduction disciplined disparate geographic groups of white elites to hear themselves and Others through the filter of an increasingly specific battery of aural imagery, sonifying race and racializing listening far beyond any one concert hall. To amplify the rough footprint of the emergent listening ear in the

Northern states, I have culled adjectival commonalities found in Lind's 1851 press reception—"controlled," "pure," "clear," and "brilliant"—terms symptomatic of music writers' shared assumptions and similar lexicon across time and space. Music writers' mediation of vocal performances such as Lind's and Greenfield's served to shape, however unevenly, the listening ear, and their commonalities help us understand the American popular music industry's mutually constitutive relationship with the sonic color line and the print media's role in enabling its widespread iteration.

One of the most prevalent terms elite white listeners used to describe Jenny Lind's voice, "control" described not so much a specific sound of the sonic color line but the way it worked to transform timbre's potential passions into a performance of authority, perfection, and emotional self-discipline. New York audiences racialized Lind's restraint—her mastery of the physical and musical boundaries she pushed but did not cross—as well as her perceived discipline over her body and emotions. Seemingly without fail, Lind limited her sound to the composed note, holding the power of her voice in perpetual check and bending any excesses to a select affective palate. *The Albion* initially described her as a "Vocal Sphinx," emotionally inscrutable to the point of seeming aloof: "She sings earnestly, but there seems to be *something held back*, and to this we attribute in a great measure to the appearance of coldness."[51] However, in a review published two months later, the music critic "J.P." recanted his earlier disappointment, finding an aesthetically pleasing erotic tension in her emotional control: "There is at times in her a combination of feeling, of happiness *pressed down yet running over*, and something of *heart*, which made me long to shake hands with her."[52] For this listener, Lind's power lay in her ability to show audible signs of *"heart"* at the very moment that control and decorum *"pressed down"* upon it, enabling the patriarchal fantasy of white female sexuality as at once carnally desirous and excessive yet corporeally transcendent. J.P. exhibits what Bechtold calls a "heightened demand for the sensational experience of physical intimacy—even if that intimacy was merely constructed from Lind's residue."[53] Rejecting coldness as a descriptor, J.P. thrilled at what he interpreted as the sound of Lind's struggle with (and ultimate triumph over) feeling, an image leading him to fantasize about violating her by "shak[ing] hands," a gesture both congratulatory and erotic in its fetishistic depiction of touch and (barely) restrained desire.

The racialized edge of white male critics' fetishization of Lind's vocal restraint becomes more apparent when contextualized within American critiques of Italian opera. Utilizing language similar to descriptions of black excess I tracked in chapter 1—*too* emotional, *too* bodily, *too* unrestrained (and therefore inarticulate)—American critics tellingly claimed Italian opera "privileged sound over rhetoric."[54] The white press frequently mobilized Lind as a force to purge operatic singing of the corporeal and vocal excess they heard in Italian performers. Most reviews compared Lind's Parisian-trained stylings favorably to Italian virtuosos, using her voice as an affective aural boundary between Northern and Southern Europe and white and nonwhite. While Italians were technically categorized as "white" Europeans in the mid-nineteenth century, racial scientists nonetheless placed them on the lower end of the American racial spectrum, with the Nordic whiteness of someone like Lind at the apex.[55]

Particularly when imagined favorably against an allegedly overemotive Italian style, Lind's New York performances illustrated how white men felt bodily restraint could—and should—be an audible marker of white femininity. As Richard Dyer argues in *White*, while whites thought the "non-white soul was prey to the promptings and fallibilities of the body," they felt the "white spirit could both master and transcend the white body." While "that spirit itself can't be seen," whites materially manifested their spirits through disciplined body training, posture, and restrained movement.[56] When *The Water-Cure* reviewer remarked that Lind's voice "harmonizes so well with her appearance," he alluded to her ability to "master and transcend" her physicality and harmonize it completely with her spirit, an image that both empowers Lind and genders her vocal prowess as a passive bodily emanation.

Importantly, whiteness as spirit-body could be received as well as transmitted. Kyla Schuller argues that "body was understood as a 'biocultural' formation . . . [and] affective experiences mold the plastic body of the civilized races."[57] Given this plastic sense of the body, Lind's bourgeois white audiences could increase their own corporeal mastery by listening intently to her vocal authority and restraint—not just an audible experience of whiteness but an auditory transmission of it. Furthermore, for Lind's elite white male listeners, perceiving Lind's voice constructed the white female as an object filtered through the listening ear—a siren whose song enticed yet performed as an "everlasting barrier against which the tides of man's sensual nature surge."[58] Connecting Lind's public voice to her private female body paradoxically allowed reviewers to embrace yet mute the power of both.

White critics also celebrated "purity" in Lind's voice, a concept already freighted with raced and gendered meanings now mobilized toward the aural production and perception of whiteness. *The Albion* heralded the "purity and brilliancy of [Lind's] intonation," for example.[59] American critics made easy associations between purity, white European operatic traditions, and the "correctness" of the sounded voice—breaths, emphasis, pronunciation, pitch, and mouth all in their expected places—that both foreshadowed and enabled the public debates over the standardizing of American English that I discuss in the next chapter. "Purity" as a rubric also racializes gender; although Lind was near thirty when she arrived in New York, reviewers usually described her as a "girl," associating Lind's aural purity with her unmarried, white female body and a chaste but tantalizing virginity. Sherry Lee Linkon connects the repetitive, almost obsessive nature of critics' use of "purity" with anxiety over the culturally pervasive ideal of true womanhood and the question of whether or not "good" (white) women had a place in the public sphere.[60] A pervasive Victorian code of white middle-class female behavior dominant from about 1820 to 1860, "true womanhood" espoused tenets of sexual purity, religious piety, submissiveness, and domesticity.[61] Linkon does not discuss, however, the racial edge to true womanhood, which by its very definition was an aspiration available only to white middle-class women.

In the application of "purity" to Lind's powerful, palpable sound—embodied yet ethereal—listening surfaces as a structured site of white heterosexual erotic exchange at a safer distance; accounts of Lind's voice function both to discipline white women's singing and speaking voices and to train the elite white masculine listening ear *how* to listen to them. The *Tribune*'s European correspondent declared that "Jenny's voice is essentially poetical. The emotions it excites are basically those raised at sixteen, reading some delectable passage or falling into some fine frenzy with the classic face of the opposite sex. It is entirely pure."[62] The

Tribune's listener infantilizes Lind's voice as perpetually on the verge of sexuality, remaining neither cognizant of nor consumed by desire. His description simultaneously expresses his own charged erotic attraction and deliberately deflects it from the physical realm, channelling it into the mental consumption of a "delectable passage" or a nondescript, removed "classic face." The sonic color line and the gendered politics of the listening ear allow Lind's voice to remain "entirely pure" in the Victorian sexual economy, even as it bears the impression—and the blame—for a "fine frenzy" of erotic sonic exchange.

Previous accounts of this period examine "white purity" almost exclusively in the context of visuality and/or representational absence. However, aural representations of purity such as those heard in Lind's voice engendered a feeling of racial presence that vivifies the absence of visual representation without despoiling it. The July 1850 fashion plate of Lind from *Godey's Lady's Book* emphasized the visual edge to Lind's hyperwhitened "pure" aesthetic while amplifying its copresence in her voice.[63] *Godey's* depicts Lind with a luminous glow, her skin's paleness indistinguishable from her signature white dress and both set off by contrast with the inky background. Lind's brightness both illuminates the surroundings and keeps their indiscriminate, sludgy blackness at bay. Notably, the still—taken from Vincenzo Bellini's *La sonnambula*, in which Lind played the title role—represents Lind in performance mode, but silent and closemouthed, avoiding the racialized "caught in the act" vulgarity that a gaping mouth would imply; as Wazana Tompkins notes, the white mouth was "far from a mere physiological site for the ingestion of nutrients . . . [it] is public space whereupon the racialized erotics of the modern encounter are played out."[64] Lind's closed mouth performs white female "purity" even in midsong, positing sonic "purity" not solely as silence or quiet but as an idealized sound made without singing, palpable but not visceral. *Godey's* represents Lind's singing as the very last act of music making, an emanation from the spirit of the controlled white body, seen in Lind's sharply upright posture and her firmly mannered hands. Because this drawing—and many similar images—circulated for months before Lind's arrival, its representation of audiovisual white female purity undoubtedly shaped the sonic color line as well as the way the listening ear imagined the sonic "purity" of Lind's voice.

Jenny Lind.

Jenny Lind performs *La sonnambula*, *Godey's Lady's Book*, 1850.

The aural image of "purity" as "singing without singing" enabled the vibrational transmission of whiteness's alleged connection to spirit and intellect. Many Americans turned away from Italian opera as a result. "Anti-virtuostic" singing—a xenophobic movement music scholar Gillen D'Arcy Wood calls "virtuosophobia"—had been ascendant in England and the United States since the eighteenth century, a practice that self-consciously eschewed the "bravura mode of music, language or display" of Italian performers.[65] Out of an array of words used to describe "anti-virtuostic" performers—"crisp," "precise," "clear," "true," "natural"— musicians and critics settled on the term "pure" as the sine qua non of the new antistyle. Purity, in particular, became associated with Lind's brand of coloratura soprano singing, especially the premium she placed on crisp intonation and adherence to timing. Taken in broad strokes, Lind's white press reception represented the purest voice as the least bodily, celebrating yet disavowing the training that enabled Lind to skillfully and willfully use her body as sonic evidence of white feminine purity.

Even though Lind's repertoire drew heavily from Italian opera, and Bechtold has argued that Lind's controlled sentimentality "revised antebellum perceptions of virtuosity," her personal writings reveal her musical philosophy as antivirtuostic and contributed to the sonic color line's racialized discourse regarding mental and physical discipline to produce "pure" sound.[66] In an 1868 personal letter addressed to a Swedish music professor, Lind describes her talent as "simple and natural," based on an intellectual understanding of song lyrics rather than bodily production of sound. In line with contemporary racial science—which, according to Schuller, defined race "as a relative account of the body's affective capacity"—Lind stated bluntly, "No stupid person can sing with expression."[67] In fact, Lind only knew that "everything was prepared when [she] deeply and quietly studied the meaning of the words and when [she] drew a thread, so to speak, through the whole poem." Then, Lind concentrated on pronunciation, as for her, "singing was really musical speaking. When words are properly pronounced the production of tone is remarkably facilitated." Lind's emphasis on speech articulation and tone production harmonizes with Caleb Bingham's widespread notions of "clear" sound and logic detailed in chapter 1, particularly Frederick Douglass's negotiations with and challenges to the dominant Western idea, submerged in Lind's letter but no less present, that whites identify nonwhite "Others" by a perceived inability to "properly" harness emotion and crisply articulate language. Throughout the letter, Lind emphasizes the challenge of her craft and her triumph in shaping her instrument, a move countering dominant patriarchal assumptions that essentialized women as effortless singers—nightingales, after all, do not have to practice—yet strengthening the sonic color line's emphasis on whiteness as "a correct declamation and careful phrasing" that must be combined with the "right development of the *inner being*." Lind made clear, however, that for her "inner being" to surface and "react upon the body," she had to keep her body and voice in check; in particular, she noted, "my timbre must obey my feelings."[68] Lind's usage of Helmholtz's new term "timbre" both subscribed to his contemporary theories about sound—that musical tones were complex combinations of fundamental vibrations and overtones that sounded uniquely across resonating bodies hitting the same note—and revised him in concert with white body discipline. Lind characterized her timbre as a given yet malleable entity, one whose unique purity could only be realized through restraint. Expressed in the parlance of scientific theories of music, Lind's theory of crisp note-bound articulation of tone sonified and naturalized what antebellum American culture considered a fundamental constitutive quality of whiteness: the ability to forge raw emotions into tempered sentiment. The massive success of Lind's performances—informed by scientific theory, launched as "pure," and received as such by America's emergent white elite listening ear—enabled (and was enabled by) the antebellum sonic color line between audible sounds of white sentiment and black sentimentality, articulateness and inarticulateness, "pure" notes and "dirty" ones.

Lind's white reviewers described her voice with adjectives typically reserved for light, such as "brilliant," "clear," and "silver." This created a synesthetic crossover between visual referents to race and the sonic color line. For example, *The Water-Cure Journal* lauded the "crisp silvery quality of her upper notes," while *Godey's Lady's Book* recognized Lind's "wonderful voice, its clearness, its brilliancy," and *The United States Democratic Review* complimented Lind's "silver tones."[69] According to Dyer, silver had long held a privileged representational relationship with whiteness; he quotes Renaissance painter Lomazzo's theorizations that "among the elements [white] represents water, among metals, silver, and among theological virtues, hope which must be *pure* and *impeccable*," all qualities heard in Lind's voice by white reviewers.[70] At once fantasy, distortion, and performative manifestation of the sonic color line, Lind's "silvery" voice mediated and made audible the glowing visual representations that preceded her American performances.

Critical to the history of racial formation, Lind's synesthetic critical reception made it difficult to parse whether sight dictated sound in the construction of "whiteness" or whether sound confirmed and shaped sight. Visual experiences certainly triggered racialized perceptions of sound, but imagining only a one-way transmission from sight to hearing oversimplifies the complex and multidirectional audiovisual nature of race. When confronted with Lind's singing white female body, white music critics and audiences transferred visual idealizations of whiteness onto her voice; however, reviewers and audiences also arrived at the concert hall schooled in the listening ear's racialized sonic grammar. When Lind fulfilled the listening ear's expectations, the experience intensified visual perceptions of her harmonized racial and gender identities and enabled a powerful affective experience of whiteness—a "singing without singing" at once vibrational, visual, *and* sonic—capable of deep impressions upon the racial imaginary and the performances and perceptions flowing from and constructing it.

Furthermore, Lind's critical reception transmitted racialized impressions of the sound of her voice far beyond her immediate physical presence to a much more diverse audience than the moneyed white elite, diffusing distinct auditory markers of whiteness into far-flung and disparate local contexts. As Ziad Fahmy's critique of the visual bias of Benedict Anderson's concept of imagined communities helps us understand, "print is important, yet we must not ignore that it is often digested in a living (embodied) communal context and hence is very much enmeshed within a framework of orality,"[71] as well as, I would add, in a sonic context where printed aural imagery functions to discipline everyday perception. For many of Lind's white listeners, the sonic color line worked as an audiovisual feedback loop enabling them to imagine *and* experience their own whiteness as material—both alone and in concert with real and imagined peers—while sensing that the identified sounds of whiteness confirmed its visual qualities and its sight could accurately anticipate its sound. The filter of the listening ear—unevenly assembled from stage, print, sheet music, education, and everyday performance—contributed to a growing sense of whiteness as *the* national American identity just prior to the Civil War.

"The Thrilling Voice": Black Americans Listen to Jenny Lind

Black presses in antebellum America crafted "a broad intellectual persona within the black community," as Elizabeth McHenry argues, while remaining attuned to the fight against slavery and racism.[72] Even before Lind's arrival, editors' selective coverage heard her voice against the backdrop of her marked silence on abolition (and, eventually, Greenfield's struggles to be heard). About a year and a half before the Castle Garden concerts, Frederick Douglass's *North Star* reprinted a review of Jenny Lind's English performances by British critic Douglas Jerrold that anticipated (and surely influenced) the tone of her American press. Practically, curating reprints allowed black presses to cover a wider geographical area, but they also operated as a resistant citational strategy, exposing racism in the white press. In the case of Jerrold, Douglass starts the excerpt with racialized audiovisual imagery of "lightness" common to Lind's press; Jerrold described Lind's voice as "bright and evanescent as the summer rose," a sound sure to be remembered by British fans "as one of the glorious lights which gave 'the purple lustre' to their youth." Jerrold pushes racial rhetoric further than most white American press reviewers, using Lind's voice as a metonym for the growing consolidation of whiteness as a global racial identity, identifying in its sound "an affinity with the Scandinavian ways of thinking and feeling" that crossed national boundaries and bridged "superficial and unimportant" regional inflections. Douglass surely thought his black readers would find Jerrold's commentary revealing from the opening, exclusionary "We":

> We have an affinity with the Scandinavian ways of thinking and feeling upon all important and essential subjects, and therefore it is that a dissimilarity between our ways and their ways, in superficial and unimportant manners, is full of charms for us; we call it fresh and novel and agreeable. If the dissimilarity were radical, we should call it unpleasant, shocking, and intolerable, even in its most trifling manifestations. In short, it is because the gods of the Northern nations "are our gods," that we do not quarrel with them when we find "their ways are not our ways."[73]

While Jerrold, an openly radical liberal, theorized how the audibly Swedish Lind could earn such high praise above and beyond homegrown

British singers, his statement also inadvertently exposed the sonic color line, particularly how it operated to amplify whiteness and minimize "superficial and unimportant" ethnic variance across borders, while disciplining the white elite listening ear to remain attentive to the "radical" dissimilarity of racial difference within national lines. More than simply predicting the heights of fame that Lind eventually reached, Douglass's citation gestured toward decolonizing listening, offering his readers a critique of how and why Lind held such fascination for the white elite listening ear and anticipating why Greenfield, though a Mississippian, would never receive similar enthusiasm in American concert halls. In addition, Douglass's coverage of Lind's American tour revealed—and stayed with—the fact that Lind never publicly questioned slavery and, even though she regularly donated half of her earnings to charity, gave no money to abolitionist groups. William Lloyd Garrison's *The Liberator* reprinted an open letter from Barnum explaining Lind's silence as a sign that "she prizes too dear the glorious institutions of our country to lend the slightest sanction to any attack on the union of these United States." Garrison responded by calling Lind's abstention and Barnum's justification "Ludicrious and Pitiable!"[74]

Media critiques and representations of alternative and decolonizing listening practices from the black and abolitionist presses negotiated the entry of black listeners into America's concert halls as agents with their own sonic value systems, whose pleasures sometimes intersected with white American audiences' but oftentimes diverged. While Lind's purported "control" registered with black reviewers, for example, they often cast it as a form of silence, listening instead for moments where she pushed her voice beyond strict adherence to concert music's norms. According to the *National Era*'s Cincinnati correspondent, Lind's songs offered "nothing apparently more than a fine exhibition of correct and highly finished musical expression and in most of them nothing to arouse the sympathies or ignite the passions, [yet] there is yet *a something* which charms alike the undisciplined and disciplined ear."[75] The anonymous critic challenges "highly finished" as the apex of musical value, celebrating moments when an undefined but yearned-for "*something*" breaks through the stranglehold of the "disciplined ear" and beckons to the allegedly "undisciplined" as well. White presses also noted Lind's appeal to the "undisciplined" ears of working-class whites and immigrants—never mentioning black audiences—but as a by-product and/or a strategy to quell unrest. The *National Era*, on the other hand, listens out for the connection offered through Lind's *"something"*—a vague signifier gesturing toward a queered sound—representing the brief moments conveying a resistant passion as the strongest notes of her performance.

Black reviewers took Lind's silences into account, as well as the sonic color line's ability to silence dissent by evoking her voice and performances. A particularly egregious example of such silencing involved Douglass himself at a meeting of abolitionists held in Boston's Faneuil Hall in November 1850, just two months after Lind performed there. Douglass found himself literally silenced by anti-abolitionist protestors chanting Lind's name and imitating her distinctive yodel. Determined to "prevent the abolitionists from being heard, and to show them that there must be an end to their folly," the increasingly surly audience greeted one of Douglass's cospeakers, William H. Channing, with "Three cheers for Jenny Lind!" When "Mr. Channing foolishly persisted in his desire to be heard, Jenny Lind was again cheered, as were also Webster, Cass, Winthrop, Bunker Hill, and the ladies in the gallery, etc."[76] Whether earnest, ironic, or both at once, the crowd's hearty cheers for Lind placed her alongside some of the most powerful white male anti-abolitionist figures in Massachusetts, evoking her availability as a symbol of a particular kind of white supremacy, patriotism, and antifeminist patriarchy. When Channing and eventually Douglass tried to speak above the crowd's jeers, "about fifty whistlers struck up a medley of 'Yankee Doodle,' 'Dandy Jim,' and one fellow, more shrill than his companions, gave an excellent imitation of Jenny Lind's 'echo.'" The shrill, cross-gender performance of Lind's signature sound as anti-abolitionist battle cry—interwoven with minstrel tunes and popular ditties—simultaneously sent up and channelled Lind's cultural power as an icon of whiteness at both symbolic and material levels.

In a different venue, Harriet Jacobs also called attention to Lind's voice as a metonym for white Americans' ability to silence black American resistance and suppress slaves' suffering, representing Lind's performances as an opportune distraction for white Northerners from the violence wrought by the Fugitive Slave Act. "But while fashionables were listening to the thrilling voice of Jenny Lind in Metropolitan Hall,"

Jacobs wrote, "the thrilling voices of poor hunted people went up, in an agony of supplication, to the Lord, from Zion's church. Many families who had lived in the city for twenty years, fled from it now." Jacobs uses sound here as both a metaphor for race and a representation of its relationship to power, describing how the listening ear's discipline enabled the ornate voice of one white woman in a concert hall to drown out thousands of cries for help on the streets outside it, providing white ears with a narcissistic and anesthetic "thrill" that dulled them to the Fugitive Slave Act's "beginning of a reign of terror for the colored population."[77] Jacobs's selection of "thrill" to describe the voices of both Lind and the black supplicants neatly anticipates Reconstruction's twist on the sonic color line by ten years—when fashionable white people suddenly begin to find black suffering "thrilling" in its commodified, concertized form via the Jubilee Singers—but here Jacobs's repetition indicts whites for sensationalizing what they heard as emotive entertainments while real people they knew (and often depended upon) needed advocacy and protection. Taken together, these examples expose a similar circulation of white power and agency enacted through and enhanced by listening. The sonic color line not only demarcated the "whiteness" and "blackness" of sounds in the case of Lind but also functioned as a rubric by which the dominant white listening ear determined which sounds to amplify in the contentious antebellum political landscape and which sounds to ignore, suppress, and drown out.

"Surely a Wonder of the Nineteenth Century": Elizabeth Taylor Greenfield

In 1852, two and a half years after Lind's Castle Garden run, the New York Police again arrived at an opera venue to handle a potential riot, this time at Metropolitan Hall, at the edge of the new Broadway arts district. Unlike at Lind's chaotic opening night, the Met's proprietors did not task the police with securing the building's perimeter *after* an unruly crowd gathered, but rather stationed them *inside* the building's lobby, allegedly as a preventative measure; the promoters worried more about the social temperature of the paying customers inside than about ticketless interlopers. Thankfully, the rumored riot—spread via whisper campaigns—never actually happened, although other forms of violence permeated Greenfield's Northern tour.[78]

Before discussing the representational violence the white American press served Greenfield, I linger a moment in the gossip-fueled gasps of potential riot, investigating how the sonic color line operated as an advance guard for the nation's social hierarchies, producing imagined sounds for the elite listening ear that carried devastating material results. In the case of Greenfield, the listening ear's auditory imaginary produced a different brand of "singing without singing" to the one Lind exemplified, rendering the sound of a black woman's operatic song as dangerous and anxiety-producing before Greenfield even sang a note. The sound of opera itself posed little obvious danger; Metropolitan Hall routinely hosted Lind and other famous white European divas of the period. Although very few preceded her, Greenfield was not the first African American performer on New York City's stages. Lott points out in *Love and Theft* that black performers were fairly commonplace in the antebellum era, even in the North, and various white-produced distortions of black musical culture had circulated widely in American culture since the 1830s.[79] So why then, given New York's familiarity with female divas and black performers, did threats of violence precede Greenfield's performance to the point that the *New York Herald* reported that "a very large posse of police was in attendance in the hall"?[80] Even as the term "posse" connoted criminality—and cast the lone Greenfield as offending outlaw rather than potential victim—the white press coverage largely sidestepped obvious structural elements of race, gender, and class conflict at play.

Perhaps, in the wake of the Fugitive Slave Law and the recent publication of Harriet Beecher Stowe's *Uncle Tom's Cabin*, the tensions of American social hierarchies boiled too close to the surface to need naming. The 1849 Astor Place riots, after all, had occurred just a half mile from Metropolitan Hall at the edge of Five Points, a neighborhood comprised mainly of Irish immigrants, free blacks, and fugitive slaves; by 1850 more than half of New York's population was foreign born, and anti-immigrant nativism inflamed class tensions. On May 10, 1849, 5,000 people gathered to heckle and protest Charles Macready's appearance at the Astor Place Opera House, a British Shakespearean actor whose "kid glove" dress code and pricey performances made him a symbol of exclusivity and class-based oppression.[81] The police arrested eighty-six people; the aftermath left twenty-two dead and over one hundred and fifty wounded, largely by the actions of the soldiers supposed to quell the unrest. Even though published reviews from Greenfield's Buffalo and Rochester performances characterized her audiences as the most "respectable, cultivated, and fashionable people of the city," the proprietors of the Met clearly worried this would not be the case in an increasingly class- and race-stratified New York City.[82] Would working-class minstrel audiences from Five Points show, expecting raucous comedy instead of arias? Would black audiences, whom the Met's promoters had deliberately barred, attempt entrance, even though Greenfield promised to perform to a mixed-race crowd at the Broadway Tabernacle a few days later? Or if New York's most fashionable class would in fact attend—at one dollar, Greenfield's ticket price was expensive, although nowhere near as high as Lind's—would their presence at a black woman's concert ignite class resentments still smoldering from Astor Place? As Garrison's *The Liberator* wryly remarked in Greenfield's defense, "What a commentary on the civilization of New York City, that the Chief of Police, with all his forces, should be required on such an occasion!"[83]

Anti-abolitionist violence also loomed large in New York City, particularly in the wake of the riots of 1834. Over four heated July days, whites burned the homes and churches of prominent abolitionists and free blacks; one of the flash points occurred in the Bowery Theatre, where an angry mob descended to avenge allegedly anti-American remarks made by English-born stage manager George Farren.[84] Greenfield's promotional *Memoir* told of her "great apprehensions" about performing in New York—even after three concerts in slaveholding Baltimore—because of its reputation as "the great theatre of the Abolition Controversy."[85] Greenfield, who lived in Philadelphia when several thousand anti-abolitionist rioters burned down Pennsylvania Hall in 1834, knew she faced immense danger even in the North, particularly for her associations with white people—something Chybowski notes that modern scholars reading nineteenth-century sources do not fully appreciate[86]—and was undoubtedly all the more careful because she knew a black woman's safety did not rate white police concern.

To many white listeners, Greenfield's voice threatened to set off untold conflict, unlike Lind's, which could pacify social unrest. Greenfield onstage represented opera in the hands of the *wrong* people—or in the hands of those whom American whites did not consider to be legally, socially, and politically people at all. While opera had not yet cemented its status as "sacred" high culture in the United States, it arose in Europe as a sonic complement to colonialism and remained historically identified with whiteness and power. For Europeans, Timothy Taylor argues, the "development of opera provided a way of dealing with the powerful 'discovery' of other peoples, from home and abroad; opera—especially once combined with a powerful new musical language, tonality—offered new and effective ways to (re)present and control difference."[87] Given this history, in which European thinkers, culture producers, and scientists placed people of color, particularly black people, in an evolutionary prehistory to European modernity, the sound of opera signified the Other's fixed position at the bottom of the "Great Chain of Being" and on one side of the sonic color line; the West did not imagine opera as a sonic blueprint revealing how to break such boundaries.

Therefore, the question of whether or not Greenfield's "voice of great sweetness and power"[88] would master the masters—both the operatic composers of her repertoire and the sovereign white citizens assembled before her—hung menacingly in the antebellum air. Her sound, particularly as imagined by white audiences, carried much more symbolic heft in regard to the reigning racial order than that of Lind, whose performances thrilled through exemplifying and expanding existent aural understandings of race. Greenfield's performances of Lind standards "Do Not Mingle," "I Know My Redeemer Liveth," and "Home Sweet Home" challenged her audiences and basically forced the white press to discuss her, a black woman and former slave, in the same sentences as the pure, cool, light, silvery Lind.[89] Furthermore, by unabashedly flaunting a vocal compass that, beginning with E in the bass clef and running up to C in the treble clef, sounded both higher and lower than the Swedish Nightingale's, Greenfield operated as both a threat to the sonic color line and an exceptional case enabling white elites to consolidate and strengthen it.

White American listeners seemed to fear and crave the challenge Greenfield's voice presented to the sonic color line, even as they attempted to neutralize it. The sobriquet the white press thrust upon Greenfield after her Buffalo debut, the "Black Swan," amplified American audiences' contradictory reaction. A gendered practice typical of the concert stage, bird nicknames celebrated female performers' (alleged) purity, sweetness, and delicacy, even as such names circumscribed their talent as "natural" and God-given; after all, birds sing without instruction or scientific performance theories. Greenfield's name stands out amongst her white peers', however, as explicitly racial rather than ethnic or national such as "the Swedish Nightingale" or the "Irish Swan." Many white papers, particularly proslavery publications such as the *Herald*, refer to her simply by her sobriquet—rarely by Miss Greenfield or even Elizabeth—a silent-but-loud reminder of her (former) slave status; African Americans were not accorded the titles of "Mr." or "Miss/Mrs." that signified adult personhood and the rights and respect implied therein. To further circumscribe Greenfield's transgressive potential, the *Cincinnati Enquirer* denied her even the second-class dignity of the "Black Swan," calling her the "African Crow." "Black Swan" signified as a triple entendre, referring not only to Greenfield's race but also to her alleged lack of cultivation—swans are not known for their singing abilities; they honk rather than harmonize—and her cultural status as a freakish novelty. Swans were believed to be ephemeral singers, flashes-in-the-pan who sing their "swan songs" shortly before death. The term "black swan" had long been a colloquialism for things considered rare or nonexistent; the *Oxford English Dictionary* traces its written usage back to the fourteenth century and its origin to Roman poet Juvenal.[90] Until Dutch explorers saw black swans in Western Australia, Europeans simply assumed the creatures did not exist. By affixing "Black Swan" to Greenfield, white elite critics announced the aural presence of the Other in a previously white space, publicly drawing the sonic color line and disciplining the white listening ear through expectations simultaneously too low and too high.

Greenfield's reception in the mainstream white press shaped the notion that talented, visibly black performers who reached outside the boundaries of "black" sound were always already exceptions to the sonic color line. While certainly, as Alex Black claims, "there was no uniform way in which Americans in this period perceived African American performers"[91]—especially, of course, if we understand "American" as a multiracial category—close rhetorical analysis reveals similarities across Greenfield's white press that affirmed aural stereotypes shaped in slavery and constructed additional boundaries of the sonic color line. Just as they did for Lind, white press reviews across the Eastern states tended to follow similar rhetorical conventions, opening with positive reports from other cities, describing the fine audience and excellent venue, discussing Greenfield's singing as beautiful yet flawed, and closing with the suggestion that she needs "cultivation" to truly succeed. The rapid emergence of rote conventions across time and distance suggests a deep-seated cultural anxiety over Greenfield's sound, as if deviation from the press materials or previous responses might put reviewers in dangerous territory. However, whereas Eidsheim claims antebellum white listening practices resulted from passive ignorance—the sum total of "limited exposure to the sounds of black classical singers" and "white audiences' limited perceptual frameworks," particularly in regard to minstrelsy[92]—I lay bare the sonic color line and the listening ear as discernable practices and active, biopolitical microprocesses, however uneven, enabling white American elites to collectively mediate the growing threat of racial realignment.

The emerging presence of the sonic color line resolves the seeming epistemological conflict between voice and vision by revealing that, in actuality, neither the voice *nor* the body actually get first "dibs" on audiences' senses. Black and Eidsheim present contradictory arguments regarding race and sound. Black argues Greenfield exhibits a "*resonant body.* This term emphasizes the influence a performer's voice had over the way the reviewer saw her body." By contrast, Eidsheim uses Greenfield to posit the existence of "sonic blackness," a phenomenon suggesting Greenfield's audiences' auditory perception was distorted by their visual perspective.[93] The sonic color line, however, articulates the socially constructed, historically contingent relationships *between* sight and sound, voice and the body—how each collapses into the other at various moments in time—directing a complex traffic between the senses, much more feedback loop than unidirectional causal relationship. The coalescing sonic color line offered white audiences a way to regulate intense emotions stirred up by Greenfield's performances, channelling them along culturally available racial fault lines explaining the seeming disconnect between her body and voice.

The sound of Greenfield's voice emanating from her black female body created a pleasurable (and discomfiting) aesthetic confusion for white audiences. One of the most common reactions evinced by white reviewers involved a profound sense of racially inflected (but not automatically unpleasant) surprise at the seeming disparity between her visual blackness and her sonic whiteness. As the *Boston Evening Transcript* bluntly remarked, "Although colored as dark as Ethiopia, [Greenfield] utters notes as pure as if uttered in the words of the Adriatic."[94]

Unlike Lind's performances, where racialized ideas about sound remained ostensibly invisible, Greenfield's onstage appearances were always preceded by public dialogue about race. Without an overt conversation in print media, Lind's voice sounded a confirmation of her talent and ideologies of white supremacy, whereas Greenfield's voice turned the sonic color line into a trip wire, enacting a particularly white form of explosive astonishment that set the terms for the listening ear's perceptual bracketing of her skill as unusual, freakish, exotic, novel, rare, and exceptional. "If all, or half, of her musical powers be true," heralded the *Boston Evening Gazette*, "she is surely a wonder of the nineteenth century."[95] Reading across her clippings shows that rarely, if ever, did critics engage in the painstaking song-by-song vocal critique of Greenfield's performances as they did for Lind, both an obvious snub and a sign that critics could not (or refused to) move past Greenfield's sheer existence. By reproducing their shock in print, her reviewers encouraged a wide swath of white Americans to linger in their racial surprise at Greenfield's vocal abilities and the socially constructed mismatch between her white-sounding voice and her black-looking body, a "wonder" long outlasting the nineteenth century.

While sound scholars usually speak of disembodiment in terms of recorded voices—a legacy of R. Murray Schafer's neologism "schizophonia," the splitting of an "original" sound from its aural reproduction[96]—the case of Greenfield's white audiences reveals how the sonic color line technologized listening to produce such a split before the advent of recording capabilities. Steven Connor argues that "sound, especially sourceless, autonomous, or excessive sound will be experienced as a lack or an excess; both as a mystery to be explained and an intensity to be contained."[97] Many of Greenfield's white reviewers advocated a kind of "blind" listening to complement the initial surprise at hearing

Greenfield's voice—particularly as impressive or beautiful—claiming she was best heard while looking away or closing one's eyes. Popularized by German operagoers, "blind listening" allegedly increased aesthetic pleasure and mitigated the perceived crudeness of the act of singing. In Greenfield's reception, "blind listening" became a race ritual, as articles launched into meticulous racialized physical descriptions of Greenfield, implying that her visible blackness would skew even the most musical ear's assessment and that closing one's eyes would enable white listeners to judge Greenfield's voice more objectively, for better or worse. Carla Peterson argues that because white reviewers "had difficulty reconciling the blackness of the diva with the beauty of her voice," Greenfield's audience "sought to obliterate the body altogether."[98]

Even as some white critics advocated "blind listening" in regard to Greenfield, most employed overwhelmingly detailed (and crudely racist) descriptions of her body that triggered her voice's inaudibility. Critics interwove the rhetorics of the sideshow, the slave auction, and the minstrel stage to physically describe Greenfield, all three contexts evoking grotesque, hyperbolic soundscapes performing racial difference and dehumanizing black women with representational and corporeal violence. With a hawker's air, the *Morning Courier and New-York Enquirer*, a Whig paper with a proslavery bent, proclaimed Greenfield a "fine looking negress of about thirty years of age." Another review recommended a "blindfolded" audience *and* fragmented Greenfield into racialized body parts as if at auction, calling attention to her "crispy hair" and describing her as "a dark mulatto, quite stout, with a broad, full face, genuine negro features."[99] The *New York Herald* dubbed Greenfield a "biped hippopotamus," conjuring up the animalistic language used to report earlier public exhibitions of Saartjie Baartman ("the Hottentot Venus") and Joice Heth, an enslaved woman whom Barnum purchased in 1835 and commodified as "George Washington's 161-year old nurse."[100] The visceral minstrel grotesquerie printed about Greenfield could not be more different from Lind's ethereal representation; critics disembodied both women's voices, but for very different purposes. Lind's reviewers largely made brief, modest remarks about her body and voluminous notes about her voice, fetishizing the purity of her sound to disavow their desire and to emphasize Lind's scientific approach, preserving her true white womanhood through a deliberate desexualizing. The institutional structures of slavery, however, constituted Greenfield's body as always already available for white consumption and desire, enabling white reviewers to obsessively fragment and catalogue its audiovisual difference, experienced as both thrilling and abject. Reframing "racial surprise" as a form of utter disbelief allowed white listeners to deflect potential erotic exchanges via musical vibration and defer the upending of social hierarchies.

Greenfield's reception also contains several sonic terms such as "uncultivated," repeated across time and geography, whose accretion helped construct the sonic color line and condition the listening ear as a racialized auditory filter. Already a narrow and racialized term specifically referencing European concert training, "cultivation" operated as an aural racial shorthand that identified sonic traces of Greenfield's "blackness" and labeled them as natural, uncontrolled/uncontrollable, and inarticulate. The *Morning Courier and New-York Enquirer* described Greenfield as "far less cultivated than we hoped to find her; she having yet to learn how to deliver her voice, and her scale passages being given without the slightest articulation of successive notes, but with a continuous sound, such as produced by running a finger up a violin string."[101] Defining cultivation in more detail than most, the *Courier and Enquirer* charged the voice with representing the last audible evidence of a singing process deeply rooted within the body's ability to "deliver" a properly controlled voice. The sound of blackness, then, to elite white listeners, aurally signalled a deeper inability to master biology and emotions, detected in such qualities as running notes together in one "continuous sound," a reference to the melismatic technique of African and Middle Eastern traditions.

Chybowski's biographical research into Greenfield further solidifies that white reviewers' almost obsessive focus on Greenfield's lack of cultivation—in both her life and voice—stemmed from the narrowed filter of the listening ear in formation rather than from transparent perception. She describes how Greenfield's mistress moved her to urban Philadelphia from her Natchez, Mississippi, plantation at an early age, where Greenfield had both formal schooling and private tutoring, including voice and piano training; she was already a music teacher when she decided to support herself by touring after her former mistress's death left her homeless and penniless. Precisely because Greenfield had so much in common with her Northern audiences—"Aspects of her performance seemed familiar to them," Chybowski writes[102]—and her biography had the rags-to-riches quality attractive to industrializing America, many elite white reviewers strained to hear a lack of cultivation that not only marked her as straight off the plantation but also conceptualized the limits of the black body to produce art music. Maintaining European training as the only way in which a voice may be properly "cultivated" both disavowed Greenfield's documented training and denied black performance practices cultural legitimacy as musical disciplines that honed voices and ears, an exclusion that continued when the Jubilee Singers toured the Northern states in the 1870s. In either case, by recording racially conditioned listening experiences in unselfconsciously universalized rhetoric and then circulating them in newsprint, critics identified and performed the sonic color line for their readers and attuned their perceptions to the values and aesthetics of the elite listening ear.

Connected to and applied to Greenfield's voice almost as often as "cultivation," the adjective "natural" also possessed racialized aural implications that reflected and shaped the sonic color line, especially its usage in the nineteenth century as culture's binary opposite. Greenfield had "good natural powers of voice," according to the *New York Morning Express*, "but without the slightest scientific cultivation; a black diamond, in the rough, and without the least polish."[103] The black diamond metaphor suggested that no matter how much "polish" Greenfield received, her essential blackness would remain unaltered. Furthermore, "scientific cultivation" here refers to emergent methodologies of vocal training articulated by Lind and their connection to efforts by American scientists to systematize and standardize English pronunciation. Alexander Melville Bell wrote *A New Elucidation of the Principles of Speech and Elocution* in 1849 as a disciplinary practice manual to correct "defective articulation" by helping deficient speakers "*angliciz[e]*" their "dialectic vowel habits" or to "naturaliz[e]" tendencies toward "extravagant delivery," amongst other vocal qualities deemed socially undesirable. Bell's theories focused in particular on the proper positioning of the tongue, lips, and throat to produce sound "correctly," what he would come to call a "universal alphabet."[104] The emergent scientific discourse of elocution not only provides an important context for the use of "uncultivated" and "natural" as sonic terms but also challenges the notion that white reviewers' racist descriptions of Greenfield's voice stemmed only from a visually skewed mishearing. White audiences also understood Greenfield's body as a sonic vessel, worrying over her ability to properly sound her repertoire from the inside out.

Descriptions of Greenfield in the same outlets vaunting Lind's ability to control her singing deny Greenfield access to her forms of self-possession and body discipline, emphasizing the effortlessness of Greenfield's singing as a sign of the inevitable material traces her raced body will leave in her voice. Such contrasts show how the sonic color line crosscut nineteenth-century patriarchy. The elite white male purchase on the listening ear and the ability white men possessed to identify and circulate the sonic color line via print media interpellated and implicated white women in racialized listening practices even as white women continued to occupy a slippery sonic and political space regarding gender; Lind sings effortlessly like a bird when compared to white male singers, for example, but suddenly possesses far more agency and scientific control when the white press pits her against Greenfield. She also simultaneously gains in sweetness, a specifically white feminine sonic marker; Chybowski notes that whenever the term "sweet" is applied to Greenfield, the menacing and masculinizing term "power" is never far behind.[105]

Rather than confirming Greenfield's gender—as the sonic color line does for white men—or investing her voice with the liminality of white women's—alternately sweet and strong, natural and cultured—the sonic color line racializes black women to all but erase their sonic presence. Some white listeners dealt with their racial surprise at Greenfield's virtuostic performances by consciously splitting her very wide vocal range into two distinctly raced and gendered domains as they listened: one voice white and feminine, the other black and masculine. For example, the *Toronto Globe* claimed she could "go as low as Lablanche [a male opera singer known for his especially deep voice] and as high as Jenny Lind, a power of voice perfectly astonishing."[106] Bifurcating Greenfield's voice, a practice formed at the listening ear's intersection with patriarchal ideology, preserved white audiences' astonishment—a refusal to acknowledge Greenfield's fluid vocal spectrum as skill and not sideshow novelty—thereby deflecting her performative challenges to American cultural norms of race and gender and denying Greenfield's agency in publicly performing her full range. In Spillers's terms, Greenfield's vocal performance deliberately refuses the "traditional symbolics of female gender," creating a new sound signifying her "*claiming the monstrosity*" thrust upon black womanhood—"that locus of confounded identities"—in hopes of enacting "a radically different text for a female empowerment, one not bound by codes of white masculinity."[107] Her lower notes, in particular, and her bold decision to cast them out from her body, form an archive of resistant sonic commentary, what Brooks calls a sonic slave narrative, vibrating through the air and surfacing in fits, starts, and breaches in her reviews, enabling later readers to perceive the sonic color line and her struggle to free herself from the listening ear's normalizing vigilance.

The listening ear, as represented and shaped by Greenfield's reviews, attempted to contain her defiantly "monstrous" threat to the sonic color line and its gendered protocols. Greenfield's "*double* voice of extraordinary sweetness" signified excess, an unusual sound that reified sonic gender norms rather than rendering them deficient.[108] Whereas "blind listening" allowed white listeners to distinguish strains of a "white" voice from Greenfield's "black" body, her racially resonant lower notes seemed to drive white listeners to scrutinize her body with redoubled intensity, recognizing, suddenly, sound's potential to fool them—or make fools out of them. In a description of a Greenfield performance, Harriet Beecher Stowe first discusses the power of Greenfield's voice in terms of new scientific understandings of timbre and the language of sentiment but then proceeds to check this power by describing its ability to mislead: "Her voice, with its keen, searching fire, its penetrating vibrant quality, its timbre as the French have it, cut its way like a Damascus blade to the heart. She sang the ballad 'Old Folks at Home,' giving one verse in the soprano, another in the tenor voice. As she stood partly concealed by the piano, Chevalier Bunsen thought that the latter part was performed by one of the gentlemen."[109] By the time she designated herself Greenfield's advocate, Stowe had already exhibited questionable ethical practices in her professional relationships with black women; when Jacobs wrote her seeking literary guidance as she started *Incidents in the Life of a Slave Girl*, for example, Stowe rebuffed her, offering instead to incorporate Jacobs's story into *her* next book, which Jacobs furiously refused. While Stowe raved about Greenfield's

talent, she represented Greenfield's voice only in respect to its sentimental influence on white audiences and limited her repertoire to the
Stephen Foster–penned minstrel tune. Furthermore, by raising the notion of timbre in reference to a black woman's voice, Stowe belied an
anxiety about its potential physical impacts on listeners—if audiences
could resonate sympathetically with Lind's vibrational whiteness, what
might the impact be of the "penetrating vibrant quality" of Greenfield's
voice? Greenfield's voice confounded Stowe in regard to gender, and
she responded by splitting it in two, disembodying Greenfield, "partly
concealed by the piano," and masculinizing her voice through Bunsen's anecdote. Stowe found Greenfield's voice powerful but ultimately
unreliable, at once a weapon of heartrending emotional truths and a
technique of concealment and duplicity, an estimation that reproduced
racial stereotypes of "blackness" alongside dominant mid-nineteenth-
century attitudes about sound.

Many critics confined Greenfield's range to the upper feminine *or* lower
masculine registers. High voices registered as feminine in nineteenth-
century culture—a judgment that lingers still—and Annie McKay notes
that, in the era before amplification, American social norms generally
considered white women's voices weak, quiet, and unable to articulate
at a high enough volume for crowds to hear; only postpubescent males,
"and only exceptional ones among them," had the right depth of voice for
successful public performance.[110] Some reviewers tied the existent sonic
protocols of gender to racial categorization, further separating Greenfield
from the category of (white) womanhood by fixing her natural talents to
the deeper ranges and connecting low tones to the aural stereotypes of
"blackness" coalescing in the sonic color line. One press clipping naturalized her voice's movement down the scales, for instance, noting that "the
ease with which she passed from the highest to the lowest notes seemed
without an effort."[111]

Although the listening ear enabled some whites to hear Greenfield's
"masculine" tones as reassuring sonic confirmations of her blackness, others mitigated her breach of gendered vocal conventions by
circumscribing her sound as female. Using pointedly domestic metaphors, the *Evening Post* declared that Greenfield "seems much more at
home in her upper than in her lower voice." "The introduction of the
deeper voice in the treble songs was a singularity," professed the *To-*

ronto Globe, "but it was also an unpleasing offence against the ear."[112] Notably, fewer papers took this tack and pointedly stopped short of declaring Greenfield's female voice feminine; it remained merely a female analogue to her "unpleasing" masculine voice rather than an essential characteristic of womanhood. No matter what the ultimate result, through the very process of willfully interpreting Greenfield's voice as either female or male, the listening ear came to perceive black women's voices as ineffable and unstable, located in a shifting space between the low vocal pitches of black masculinity and the hyper-feminized voices of white women, a perpetual site of fantasy and racial surprise.

In particular—and in contrast to the many white male expressions of longing littering Lind's press—Greenfield's vibrational embodiment of racialized sexuality stoked the erotic desire of liberal white women, exhibiting how gender identity differently impacts the listening ear's racialized affect and revealing how white feminists used black female voices as an enabling site of fantasy regarding power, gender, sexuality, and the reimagining of womanhood. As Cavicchi argues, music was already "especially suited for the purpose of self-making, since it represented an intensely emotional and sensual experience that could create a heightened, vaguely erotic, intimacy with another."[113] For some white female listeners, the sound of music created by a female Other amplified the erotics of encounter. Greenfield's *Biography*, published in 1855, includes this letter from a female well-wisher in Buffalo, specifically citing her low notes as a cause of "trembling":

> If I was enchanted with your "Entreat Me Not," and enraptured with the aria from "Garcia," how perfectly amazed was I at the basso of the Rover's song! I trembled for you, thinking every moment you should fail; while at the same time I knew that one of the chief charms of your voice, is the perfect ease and freedom from effort, which you appeared to possess. There is one thing which Miss Greenfield must allow a stranger to suggest—and it is on the subject of her dress. The dress itself was handsome, but why wear that *white lace berth*? Some bright rich colour would suit so much better—or something darkly delicate; indeed, before a European audience, I think Miss Greenfield might adopt the *Oriental Style* of dress with the best effects.[114]

The Buffalo listener fantasizes about Greenfield's difference by stripping her of her *"white lace berth"*—the sartorial signature of Jenny Lind—and dressing her in "some bright rich colour" or "something darkly delicate," emphasizing Greenfield's raced and un/gendered Otherness, transformed by the listener's imagination into *"Oriental Style"* rather than African phenotype. Amazed at the ability of Greenfield's "basso" to push beyond the typically feminine range, the Buffalo listener hears Greenfield's voice as singular and thrills at the feeling of *her listening ear* split in two. While she listens out for—hopes for?—Greenfield's failure, she also relishes Greenfield's "ease and freedom" in the masculine domain.

While it is important to understand white critics' fascinated responses to Greenfield's unique vocal range, it should not be at the expense of Greenfield's agency in choosing to develop and highlight the full compass of her voice, in spite of the harsh, sustained criticism she received for doing so. Given her considerable talents, she could have selected a different repertoire that showcased her voice's upper registers, representing it as firmly located in the white feminine domain of the "head" region of the body. It would seem that the best way to outdo Lind would have been for Greenfield to emphasize her ability to transcend Lind's upper limits rather than the depth of her lower tones, perceived as housed in the chest. To quote Elizabeth Wood paraphrasing Wayne Koestenbaum: "The break between the registers (called Il Ponticello, the little bridge) is the place *within* one voice where the split between male and female occurs, and that failure to disguise this gendered break is, like falsetto, fatal to the art of 'natural' voice production." Greenfield not only failed to disguise her voice's "little bridge"; she chose to flaunt her fluid movement between the voice's gendered spheres, even performing entire songs in the baritone register. Moments of disruption appear in her white press, showing how, for some listeners, Greenfield's performance actually unsettled the listening ear. "Her voice here was masculine and rich—and at the same time soft—" waxed the *Cleveland Plain Dealer*, "devoid of that burr with which most *bona fide* male voices are encumbered."[115] The Cleveland critic raises the possibility that the "*bona fide*" may not always be best and that Greenfield's singular "voice" managed to merge the best qualities of male and female sonic identity to create something strikingly different and unencumbered.

However, as Brooks reminds us in *Bodies in Dissent*, focusing only on white audience reactions "occlude[s] any consideration of black audiences and, perhaps most importantly, the artists themselves."[116] Greenfield performed her identity-confounding sonic agency first and foremost so *she* could hear it vibrating through the rarefied air of architectural sites designed in the most literal way to amplify the sounds of white supremacy, aligning pleasure and politics in a powerful public act of self-making. Greenfield's performance of what Sharpe calls "monstrous intimacy" in America's concert halls created a space where "desires and positions are produced, reproduced, circulated, and transmitted . . . breathed in like air."[117] By casting her defiantly un/made and re/fashioned selves into that hostile air and enveloping herself in their monstrously beautiful sounds, Greenfield offered herself and others an intimate, vibrational performance of her body *and* voice in dissent.

White Ravens and Curbstone Sofas: The Black Press on "the Black Swan"

White papers downplayed Greenfield's extensive ties to free black people, choosing instead to focus on her relationships with white patrons in order to identify any "polish" heard in her voice with whiteness. However, in the 1830s, the largest population of free black people in the United States called Philadelphia home. Although the majority worked in the margins of the economy, Greenfield forged a different path, inspired to use her musical talent by the small but prominent free black elite community of entrepreneurs, religious leaders, reformists, and musical professionals.[118] Her wide-ranging black press reviews, then, represent and critique Greenfield as a peer rather than an outsider, interested in her sound as both an embodiment of the limitlessness of black capability and a sonic expression helping to forge black identity and solidarity via listening. Her sonic slave narrative—and the black press's public reading of it—wrestled with the issue at the heart of Douglass's narrative, the drive toward individual achievement and its tense relationship with responsibility to one's community, a group forged both by the external pressures of white supremacy and by internal drives toward cultural expression and political solidarity.

Existent black press reviews of Greenfield are few, but a close reading of four key conversations about her performance offers distinct portraits of how free black people in the North constructed and understood listening as a political and potentially self-defining act. Against the backdrop of Douglass's conception of listening as radical openness and Jacobs's articulations of community listening, I examine how the trope of the listener appears in Mary Shadd Carey's *Provincial Freeman*—a bold antislavery paper published out of Windsor (and later Toronto), Canada, by the first black woman publisher in North America—Henry Bibb's *Voice of the Fugitive*, also of Ontario, and Douglass's *North Star* and *Frederick Douglass's Paper*, both out of the abolitionist hotbed of Rochester, New York. All four papers took pride in Greenfield's performances and commended her bravery and vocal superiority—the *Provincial Freeman* and the *Voice of the Fugitive* a bit more tenaciously and consistently, perhaps because of their location outside the United States—but diverged in their interpretations of Greenfield's decision to perform a classical repertoire in largely segregated venues. Greenfield unsettled the notion of "race" in a different way for members of the black press, sparking a public dialogue about the nature of freedom—individual and communal—and its relationship to black subjectivity.

The debates in the black press about Greenfield's decisions—especially whether she actually had choices—allowed for crucial public debate about whether and how to self-identify as "black" during the antebellum period, and whether or not sound and listening operated as vehicles for the construction and expression of a black subjectivity not bound by white supremacy. The unspoken questions framing the *Provincial Freeman*'s reports of Greenfield's travels and *Frederick Douglass's Paper*'s discussions about her audiences included: What should black agency sound like and to whom, particularly considering America's rapidly coalescing listening ear? Must artists such as Greenfield use their voice primarily to challenge the white-authored sonic color line "without the circle"? Or should they devote their talents to amplifying music self-identified with black life and the antislavery struggle, with the primary objective of enacting a palpable cohesion for black audiences "within the circle"? In other words, should the sound of a black person's voice on the American stage operate as a weapon against white supremacy or as balm and inoculation for black audiences struggling against it? Can it function as all of these things simultaneously without dissipating into none of them?

The flip side of the debate about Greenfield's choice of repertoire and venue concerned the cultural politics of listening: how agency and freedom can and should be understood, experienced, and expressed through auditory perception. Can one participate in American musical culture—as an American—without adopting the listening ear's racialized perceptual frame regarding music? If music sounds racial difference and vocal tones vibrate communities into being—as the case of Jenny Lind reveals—can one self-identify as black and listen with aplomb to Lind's and Greenfield's operatic singing? Is listening to European art music a radical act of claiming American cultural citizenship, or does it validate America's white supremacist hierarchies? Does the freedom to listen, so eagerly sought by Linda Brent, entail limitless individual choice? Or do black listeners understand freedom as also entailing an obligation to develop collective listening practices mediating and articulating the individual's responsibility to the social? Douglass, Martin Delany, and the anonymous reviewers of the *Provincial Freeman* do not resolve these questions, but their discussion of Greenfield's performances sets the terms for ongoing debate so much earlier in U.S. cultural history than scholars have previously thought, at the very burgeoning of American popular culture.

All four papers championed Greenfield's talent, but only the *Provincial Freeman* reported consistently on her career—publishing short news items about her travels and lengthier reviews that enabled readers' sustained interest—and the paper remained steadfast in its support of her chosen repertoire. The paper honored Greenfield's talent in word and in deed, defending her against charges levelled by the white-run *Providence Daily Journal* that she was "being derelict in her duty and the cause of humanity by not singing substantial songs, such as would interest the masses; not associating with colored people, etc." by placing Greenfield in the larger contexts of class privilege and American cultural citizenship. Having black skin and having been a slave did not automatically make a person a reformer, the *Freeman* argued, and human self-interest—heightened by the interrelationship of freedom and capitalism in America—distributed itself across the color line. Greenfield should not be held to a different—and higher—standard than all American performers operating in the capitalist marketplace, especially not by a white paper. While the *Freeman* paper drew the line at the "doubly servile" practice of "court[ing] the favor of white people . . . simply because they are white," the paper's editorial staff affirmed that the exercise of freedom for black subjects such as Greenfield entailed pursuing a music of one's choosing and finding the largest number of audience members to appreciate one's efforts and talents.[119] That Greenfield's audiences happened to be white only proved that race and class operated in connection to the listening ear to determine musical value.

Delany, one of the earliest proponents of black nationalism in the United States, also celebrated Greenfield, claiming her as an important example of how black subjects challenged the damaging internalized effects of white racism and how the sound of black talent unfettered can be healing for black audiences. Representing Greenfield as both inherently talented and fiercely determined in his controversial 1852 book *The Condition, Elevation, Emigration, and Destiny of the Colored People of the United States*—published a month after *Uncle Tom's Cabin*—Delany declared her to be "among the most extraordinary persons of the present century" in the antebellum North; for him, the use of the universalizing "persons" both suggests the uniqueness of Greenfield's talent and makes a more Douglass-like move toward full inclusion. He continues to revel in Greenfield's voice—both its highest highs *and* its lowest lows—as a symbol of agency and a vehicle of liberation for suppressed black humanity and talent befitting what Robert S. Levine describes as his "transnational or proto-Pan-African vision of the distinctive qualities of and connections among blacks throughout the world."[120] Importantly, he discussed the training Greenfield received as a perpetually vulnerable black woman and hailed Greenfield's resolve "to let out her voice" in spite of Lind's performances, not only undaunted but performing the radical action of "steal[ing] an opportunity when no one listened."[121] Combining the concept of theft—so often applied to fugitive slaves—with the rhetoric of the American Dream, Delany depicts the spaces of neglect inadvertently created through the listening ear's suppression as covert sites to foster decolonization, nurture talent, and launch cultural campaigns for black equality.

However, in other venues, such as *Frederick Douglass's Paper*, Delany expressed concern about the limits of Greenfield's agency in the white public sphere. Although Lind faced scrutiny for working with Barnum, his agreement to handle her public business kept her status as a white woman of leisure intact. In the case of Greenfield, Delany wrote a public letter to Douglass, exposing Greenfield's manager, the white, Barnumesque Col. Wood, as an "*unprincipled* hater of the black race" and "a most uncompromising supporter of the fugitive slave law" who wielded undue influence. With imagery both raced and gendered, he claimed Col. Wood turned Greenfield into "the merest creature of a slave": handling her money, reading her mail, isolating her by barring black visitors, and encouraging her to exclude black audience members.[122] The *Freeman* doubled down on Greenfield's agency in the face of such claims, however painful, hailing her freedom to perform whatever music she chose in the highest-status venue possible, whereas Delany reconciled his pride in Greenfield by calling out slavery's power dynamics thinly disguised as Northern capitalism.

Frederick Douglass's Paper had tracked Greenfield's segregated performances for a year prior to publishing Delany's letter, and the paper's coverage included much more polemic reviews of Greenfield than the *Freeman*, initially raving about Greenfield's talent and then insisting black audiences weigh the beauty of her singing voice with her seeming lack of a public voice in the antislavery fight. The only published statement that can possibly be attributed to Douglass reads: "The Conduct of the Black Swan (if not exaggerated) should be reprobated by the colored people. She should no longer be called the Black Swan, but the White Raven.—F.D."[123] In a sonic, visual, *and* gendered slight, *Douglass's Paper* calls Greenfield out for silencing the political blackness of her voice in white mimicry—ravens are known for their uncanny ability to copy any sound—and his reproach attempts to discipline his readers' reactions to Greenfield's performance from an uncritical pride to a knowing mistrust. Douglass's assessment of Greenfield's performances did not stop *Douglass's Paper* from printing positive reviews of her Rochester performances, however, which heralded "the magnificent quality of her voice, its great power, flexibility, and compass; her self-taught genius, energy and perseverance."[124] While such coverage seems inconsistent, the juxtaposition performs Douglass's belief that no essential meanings should be attached to blackness, that the sound of Greenfield's voice was social, contextual, and subject to the racialized differences of listening he detailed in his *Narrative*.

The black press made abundantly clear that whites were not the only audience for Greenfield. Similar to the way that Lind's press worked to spread the sound of her voice to those geographically, racially, and/or economically unable to attend her concerts, black newspapers reprinted descriptions of Greenfield's "wonderful powers" to their readerships, circumventing formal segregation and amplifying her impact beyond her immediate and often hostile white audience. A brief passage from abolitionist Henry Bibb's paper, the *Voice of the Fugitive*, depicts antebellum black audiences stealing their opportunity to listen—and listen differently—using a perceptual praxis I place alongside Douglass's and Brent's resistant efforts as the foundations for a decolonizing listening practice, one capable of consciously stripping away destructive internalizations of the listening ear's filter, revaluing sounds damaged by its interpretations, and amplifying them toward liberatory ends.

Black men and women gathered outside Greenfield's performances, listening to the Black Swan's voice in ways that materially, symbolically, and interpretively freed its vibrations from the sonic color line. Using rhetoric and imagery that anticipated W. E. B. Du Bois's 1903 *The Souls of Black Folk* by fifty years, the *Fugitive*'s reviewer described how "my friends and I had a curbstone sofa, notwithstanding there were hundreds of seats unoccupied. And as Miss Greenfield sang, and the echo on her voice fell on our ears we were ready to say—'*Your praise the birds shall chant in every grove,/and winds shall waft it to the powers above.*'"[125] While never forgetting how and why they were barred from the half-filled venue, these anonymous listeners' decolonizing practice concentrated on how the escape of Greenfield's voice makes them feel, an affect transforming the cold comfort of their third-class "curbstone sofa" into the only site where the powerful inspiration of her voice—revalued as a renegade "echo" slipping the boundaries of the sonic color line—can truly be heard. The writer expresses the group's elation via a giddy couplet from Alexander Pope's 1709 Edenic pastoral "Summer." The allusion's cultural cache amplifies the racially mingled nature of Greenfield's sonic address, vesting Greenfield's voice with the acclaim denied it by the listening ear. Importantly, the couplet hints at how her voice will make a radical move beyond the immediate circumstances of the segregated concert house as a sonic slave narrative that will inspire and connect black listeners from "every grove," rising as offering and appeal to the higher "powers above" for the end of Southern slavery and its related Northern injustices.

The image of the curbside listeners revelling in Greenfield's voice returns us to the key shifts in musical listening that occurred in the 1850s, particularly regarding self-making through intense affective experiences. Even though whites physically barred them from many concert halls, many of Greenfield's black audience members refused the position of cultural eavesdropper the sonic color line outlined for them; rather, they listened out for her remote echoes from curbstones, church pews, and column inches, transducing them into an intimate sonic embrace of agency. On the other hand, many white listeners, privileged with the best seats in the house, used resistant microperceptual tactics to distance themselves from the potential for intimate erotic exchange with Greenfield's voice, a physical and emotional vulnerability they welcomed so eagerly at Lind's performances. Greenfield's performances thrilled, impressed, and ultimately terrified her white audiences because her audiovisual presentation threatened to undo all of the cultural work Lind's angelic body and clear voice had performed the year before. Instead, Greenfield's performances flaunted the instability of sight and the indeterminacy of sound, especially as markers of allegedly essential racial and gender identities, driving whites to employ multiple, even conflicting tactics—Look away! Look more closely! Keep her to the lower registers! Push her to the higher!—to resolve the threat she posed. Black reviewers alternately suggested that whites needed to see several Greenfield performances, without looking away, until they were able to finally resolve the dissonant conflict that racial ideologies had created between their ears and their eyes and hear the voice of an angel as compatible with the body of a black woman.

However confused and conflicted, the complex snarl of white negotiation with and resistance to Greenfield's voice gave rise to the feeling that the listening ear simply needed to get better at detecting and enforcing the sonic color line and its related classed and gendered boundaries, a belief that would dramatically increase following the Civil

War. Arising from slavery's power dynamics and gaining traction across the United States through popular performances and their newspaper "recordings," the antebellum sonic color line functioned as a portable and preventative aural membrane for whites, enabling them to transform the full human complexity of the sounds produced by black people into conventional and easily classifiable sounds of "blackness." The sonic color line's simplification not only strengthened racial hierarchies but also psychologically buffered whites from the self-altering connection and the titillating vibrational and emotional intimacy they felt music so affectively capable of.

Whether white audiences ultimately loved, hated, or felt indifferent toward Greenfield did not ultimately matter as much as their development of an ideological boundary beyond which her sound became spectacle, a form of consumption that systematized and channelled the intense emotions her performances stirred up along culturally available fault lines. Whites could listen to black difference at a distance, without ever deeply engaging it. The antebellum sonic color line naturalized the socially constructed, historically contingent relationship between the voice and the body, suturing the two together as essentially raced entities via the listening ear. Although broadly configured and communicated through uneven practices as diverse as the violently enforced structures of the plantation soundscape, widely circulated written "recordings" of musical performances, and auditory etiquette at Lind's and Greenfield's respective concerts, the idea that white American identity could be experienced and expressed through specific timbres and shared listening practices became widespread racial common sense.

While relentless in its pursuit, the listening ear's resistant pushback never entirely silenced Greenfield, nor could it mute black agency and its resonant sonic traces in American culture. Greenfield toured Europe, donated performances to raise funds during and after the Civil War, and opened a voice studio in Philadelphia offering black students the opportunities whites denied her. While I have devoted much critical labor to identifying how white supremacy operated at the level of aural perception in the mid-nineteenth century, I have done so to uncover the seams of its power and expose its holes, large and small. Without fetishizing the struggle, pain, and abjection black men and women endured simply to know, announce, and assert themselves in antebellum America—let alone shift worldviews and paradigms—we absolutely must take stock of the fact that, even in the face of the severe distortions of the sonic color line and the listening ear, Elizabeth Taylor Greenfield continued to tour, powering through Lind's repertoire and vibrating concert halls with the full range of her voice. Ostensibly free but entangled in the punishing limits of the sonic color line and the economic indenture faced by black performers in America's popular music industry, Greenfield's voice performed the entangled agency and subjection Douglass heard in his Aunt Hester's screams while sounding her powerful beauty.

Greenfield insisted on vibrating herself into vocal presence *as she heard herself*, on the lower frequencies. Twenty years later, from within the hard-fought but vulnerable walls of Reconstruction-era Fisk University, a historically black institution founded in 1866, the Jubilee Singers crafted a signature sound as indebted to Greenfield as to the vernacular music of their recently freed parents, turning the sonic color line into a tightrope of agency for black performers and writers exploring how "blackness" would sound during America's first attempt at multiracial democracy.

3. 11|12

Preserving "Quare Sounds," Conserving the "Dark Past"

The Jubilee Singers and Charles Chesnutt Reconstruct the Sonic Color Line

When the Jubilee Singers first toured the Northern United States in 1871, Henry Ward Beecher—cousin of *Uncle Tom's Cabin* author Harriet Beecher Stowe—asked them to begin their concert behind a curtain, enacting the "blind listening" that white critics so often recommended for Elizabeth Taylor Greenfield. As reverend of the wealthy white Plymouth Church in Brooklyn, Beecher was known for theatrics, but his decision to unveil the Jubilee Singers represented more than a dramatic reveal; W. E. B. Du Bois later asserted that Beecher wanted to hide the group "lest pious Congregationalists see their black faces before they heard their heavenly voices."[1] Beecher claimed it was a preventive measure; he worried his flock would take the troupe for white minstrels and automatically deem their sound unsavory.

However, Beecher's ruse had a much more complicated resonance, both metaphorically and viscerally. He also thought the Jubilees' best opportunity for winning his congregation's pocketbooks lay in delaying their conditioned sensory impressions of the group, whom their own white agent, Gustavus Pike, described as "poorly clad untutored colored students" in these early years.[2] However, the preacher's actions also turned the church curtain into a screen upon which he projected a version of black identity dependent upon sound as a mediating force. Before the first strains of "Steal Away," Beecher introduced the group by constructing, authenticating, and anchoring their "blackness" firmly in the sounds of slavery rather than in the sight of their ostensibly free bodies. "They will charm any audience sure," Beecher reportedly told his friends. "They make their mark by giving the 'spirituals' and plantation hymns as only they can sing them who know how to keep time to a master's whip."[3] While initially seeming to circumvent the sonic color line's linkages between phenotype and sound, Beecher's plot actually reduced the group's complicated hybrid of African American and European musical forms into two separable voices: one bearing the sonics of white supremacy and the other a "charming" blackness still circumscribed by white desire and temporality. Beecher's theatrical re-embodiment validated Reconstruction-era cultural politics that severed "black" from categories of beauty and value, a practice enabling America's growing white middle class to consume black cultural products without canonizing them or enacting equitable policies for their makers. By allowing the invisible yet palpable timbre of the Jubilee Singers' voices to precede the visible materiality of their bodies, Beecher echoed antebellum "racial surprise," conditioning his audience to receive the group as sonic mediums for grief, nostalgia, and racial release. During Reconstruction, liberal whites like Beecher helped construct and naturalize the notion of "the black voice" as more affective, truthful, and expressive than other voices, a musical sound whose tones, timbre, rhythms, and cadences remained mired in the past and colored with the whipcrack of subjection.

Rising to prominence in the late nineteenth century—one of America's most intensive periods of racial reorganization—the Fisk Jubilee Singers challenged America's sonic color line and altered the dominant listening ear. The years of Radical Reconstruction—beginning with the Reconstruction Act's passage in 1867 and ending when the federal government removed peacekeeping troops in 1877—represented a "profound social revolution" and a sweeping effort to transform the United States into a truly interracial democracy.[4] The group fashioned a new musical form from slave songs and European concert technique that functioned as an aural image of slavery that challenged the harmonious strains of plantation nostalgia. In publicly pairing their visibly black bodies with audibly "black sounds" forged in slavery, the Jubilee Singers performed the sonic color line as a tightrope for black performers, a site of agency and potential empowerment where negative constructions of blackness could be "inverted," but only through dangerous performances that risked affirming the listening ear by constructing new sonic representations of "blackness."

Fastidiously dressed in Victorian finery and singing "spirituals" in a muted pianissimo, the Jubilee Singers audiovisually performed what Alexander Weheliye dubs "sonic afro-modernity," where sound offers "more flexible and future-directed provenances" through which black subjects understand themselves and (re)negotiate their participation in Western modernity.[5] I build from Weheliye's theorizations about the critical relationship of black culture with both modernity and twentieth-century sound technologies but insist that the story of late-nineteenth-century sound reproduction technologies must include the Jubilee Singers, who technologized their voices and bodies through daily training sessions and grueling performance schedules. The Jubilee Singers developed their performances as a "technique of the self" enabling them to reproduce and conserve the echoes of slavery within modernity's call and craft a sonic citizenship that neither erased black cultural traditions nor depended on white male citizenship standards.[6] The Jubilee Singers' concerts also functioned as a technology of conservation and reproduction predating the phonograph—along with Blind Tom, as Stephen Best argues—amplifying the sound of black agency during the Radical Reconstruction years and enabling its reverberation long after the original group dissolved in 1877, the year the infamous "compromise" ended many hopes that America would become a multiracial democracy.[7]

The Jubilee Singers' unique sonification of citizenship, I argue, inspired prominent literary chronicler of the eras of slavery and Reconstruction Charles Chesnutt to represent the stakes of the group's sonic interventions into race, sound, and American identity. In his 1899 short story collection *The Conjure Woman*, set twenty years earlier in Reconstruction, Chesnutt constructs a series of encounters between former slave Julius McAdoo and white Northern entrepreneurs John and Annie, who employ Julius for odd jobs as they transform the "old plantation" they have purchased into a "modern" vineyard.[8] Although Chesnutt centers each tale on Julius's storytelling performance—a remembrance of slavery written in visual dialect—he frames Julius's words with John's and Annie's standard-English musings. Using John and Annie to consider a liberal formation of the listening ear, Chesnutt inverts the trope of listening to examine the logistics necessitating double-voicedness as a strategy of black resistance in literature and everyday life. In Chesnutt's writing, double-voicedness—the crafting of a story, song, or artistic performance to speak different messages simultaneously to different audiences—mutually constitutes the sonic color line.[9] Double-voicedness exploits the divergences in listening and interpretation created by the sonic color line and lived racial experience. While the sonic color line enabled segregation's portability into potential interracial contact zones after the Civil War—such as the concert hall, the "new plantation," and so-called local color literature—and made segregation a sounded process and heard experience, double-voicedness enabled the survival of black selfhood and sensibility within and beyond white attempts to totalize segregation. The double-voicedness of Chesnutt's fiction worked toward decolonizing black listening; it called attention to the listening ear's white supremacist orientations, affirmed alternative meanings and sounding practices, and dismantled essentialist theories about listening. During Reconstruction, the antebellum white elite mode of disgust and fascinated racial surprise began to give way to desire and racial release via consumption. If sound enabled whiteness to be experienced as visceral vibration, could blackness be consumed the same way? If so, could the sonic color line bind, frame, and contain such experiences to enable white enjoyment without a concurrent transformation?

In *The Conjure Woman*, Chesnutt's double-voicedness is both literal and figurative. While John's and Annie's musings begin and end each story, Julius narrates the central tale. Within Julius's embedded monologues, Chesnutt uses his vernacular sound and his aural imagery of slavery to sound out and resist John's and Annie's deliberate historical amnesia. Julius re-stories the site of the "old plantation" at the moment John and Annie attempt to transform it as part of the industrializing "New South." But over and above any immediate impact on John and Annie (or, by extension, Chesnutt's white readership), his use of Julius's voice also issued a call to black readers familiar with its resonance. Thomas DeFrantz and Anita Gonzales describe the pull of the "known sound" on black listeners: "When we know the sounds being referenced by a literary text—'know' the sound, in the deep way of having lived with it and its progenitors—we experience the text at hand in unexpected arousal." For black listeners, Julius's narratives offered the resistant power of conjure and storytelling as historical archive and relayed what DeFrantz and Gonzales describe as black sonic expression's "unexpected pleasure."[10] The stories' outer frame presented metacommentary about the seeming impossibility of breaking through the Reconstruction-era listening ear's resistance. This allows readers to hear an early form of "microaggression," the affirmation of racial hierarchies through casual, everyday interaction and theoretically unintended offenses, and recognize microaggression's entanglement with the sonic color line and the listening ear.

This chapter juxtaposes the reconstructive sonics of the Fisk Jubilee Singers' performances and Chesnutt's *The Conjure Woman*, arguing that both experimented with techniques of sound reproduction and double-voicedness to challenge the sonic color line and change the tenor of the cultural memory of slavery. Whereas the Jubilees hybridized "white" concert styles with black vernacular forms, Chesnutt integrated "black" speech sounds, storytelling traditions, and sonic imagery with the European frame tale. The Jubilee Singers mobilized the "strange" sounds of slavery to challenge familiar categories of "music" and "citizenship," while Chesnutt used the familiar representation of black dialect to represent the classed and gendered complexity of the listening ear, revealing the sympathetic listening practices of white liberals as potentially dangerous and frequently inhumane.

This chapter articulates a relationship between the artistic projects of the Jubilee Singers and those of Chesnutt through their engagements with sound's vibrational qualities, the challenges they posed to the listening ear's understanding of black bodies as mediums channelling plantation nostalgia, and their resistance to the sonic color line's categorization of black performers as technologies of repetition and preservation. First, I think through "preservation" and "conservation" and contextualize these logics with the reigning racial thought of the moment—ethnology—and examine how black thinkers technologized the voice as a mode of resistance to racial science and social Darwinism. Then, I present original archival research tracing how the Jubilee Singers used their bodies as archival technologies of conservation to enhance their agency and decolonize listening in both the contemporary moment and in the historical record. Finally, I close-read three tales from Charles Chesnutt's *The Conjure Woman*: "The Goophered Grapevine," "Po' Sandy," and "The Conjurer's Revenge." These stories, written in succession and published twenty years after the original Jubilee Singers tour, reflect on Reconstruction's sonic color line and its contribution to the years of intensified racism and segregation following the *Plessy v. Ferguson* "separate but equal" decision (1896). The divergent listening experiences Chesnutt details account for the Jubilee Singers' bifurcated press reception, revealing that although middle-class white Northerners and poor black Southerners increasingly shared the same physical spaces during Reconstruction, white supremacist ideology and vastly divergent experiences of racial identity had acculturated them to different perceptual worlds, greatly impacting their mutual understandings of the past, interpretations of present inequities, and their visions of the future in the rapidly industrializing United States. The conjure stories present a counternarrative of slavery and a profound critique of the reconstructed listening ear, showing how the same white Northern liberal elites whom Chesnutt and his narrator Julius—and, by extension, the Jubilee Singers—thrilled so very deeply also deliberately misheard and tuned them out in order to maintain white privilege.

Vibration, Preservation, Conservation

While the sonic color line arose, in part, to contain the perceived physical impact of vibrational blackness on white ears, such power opened up new forms of agency for black performers, particularly via live performance. Rethinking music as "vibrations," Gayle Wald argues, encourages scholars to engage sound's emotional affects and to recognize its function as "a tool in struggles over space, including spaces that symbolize the nation." Through the example of Marian Anderson's 1939 performance on the steps of the Lincoln Memorial—a moment I return to in chapter 5—Wald theorizes the role of vibrations as a sonic form of black agency, able to cross the visible markings of segregation as well as to radiate out to black embodied ears through time, space, and white misdirection. In what follows, I extend Wald's theorizations, channelling the pianissimo pulses of the Jubilee Singers and their echoes in Chesnutt's writing as Reconstruction-era calls to what she describes as the "social practice of utopia," in/audible appeals to an interracial democracy to come.[11] As culture workers helping forge the national memory of slavery, the Jubilees and Chesnutt used embodied, vibrational strategies to conjure the sounds of the still-resonant "dark past"—in the words of Jubilee Singer and arranger Ella Sheppard—to reconstruct a useable history for themselves and their audiences, one making space for black citizenship.

Ella Sheppard Moore, soprano and arranger for the original Fisk Jubilee Singers. Image courtesy of the John Hope and Aurelia E. Franklin Library Special Collections at Fisk University.

Wald argues that while vibrations might seem "a slippery and impracticable concept" for twenty-first-century scholars, they were fundamental to nineteenth-century musical experiences.[12] Drawing from private listening journals, Daniel Cavicchi writes, "Nineteenth-century listeners talked about hearing a musical performance as an astonishingly physical experience. . . . Music lovers were attuned to the power and quality of performed sound at a visceral, almost intuitive level," an effect heightened by Victorian-era bodily restraint.[13] Indeed, Jubilee Singer Sheppard mentions vibrational acoustics in the handwritten journal she kept during the 1870s; while the band's director may have based a show's success on the audience's enthusiasm and monetary donation, singer Sheppard considered her corporeal experience of primary importance. While recognizing that an 1874 performance in Providence, Rhode Island, provided a "good house" for the group, for example, she noted she "seldom enjoy[ed] a concert in this hall. Sound falls flat and dead." A concert at Oberlin that same year, she wrote, was "not one of our best. Poor house for sound."[14] Projecting their voices without electric amplification into white churches, concert houses, and vast public halls, the Jubilee Singers used the properties of contemporary acoustics to announce their presence, amplify their virtuosity, and channel their vibrations to create a spectacular visceral imagining of a reconstructed America for themselves as much as their audience. In a later reminiscence, Sheppard described how at the group's public debut at Boston's World Peace Jubilee concert—a post–Jenny Lind musical spectacle featuring approximately 1,000 orchestra members and 10,000 chorus singers performing to 30,000-plus people—the Jubilee Singers left their mark by singing part of "The Battle Hymn of the Republic" in "a key three half steps higher than usual." Their voices cut through the maelstrom of music and other voices, all working in E flat, the key allowing the most instruments to harmonize. The group practiced this vibrational intervention for weeks; the result, Sheppard noted, ensured they could "enunciate with perfect accuracy of pitch and purity of tone every word and every part of a word." There had been some derision as the group mounted the stage—the reaction Beecher had imagined from white audiences—but it ended when they sang "with apparently one voice, pure, clear, and distinct." Sheppard recalled, "The audience of forty thousand people was electrified." For the Jubilees, the vibrational experience of what Fred Moten and Daphne Brooks theorize as "the ensemble" was paramount.[15]

Just as Wald argues that Anderson's singing sent out a vibrational call to future black culture workers, the wake of a Jubilee Singers performance touched the young Chesnutt via the *Christian Union*, a New York newspaper edited by the very same Beecher who staged the "blind listening" stunt. Beecher's paper's favorable recounting of the concert resonated in the twenty-one-year-old Chesnutt—a peer in age, sentiment, and region with the Fisk students—as a "hopeful sign" allowing him "to cherish a fond hope that, in this age of improvements, this country of rapid changes, the time of that recognition [of black equality] is not very far off."[16] Vibing on the Jubilees' utopian imaginings, Chesnutt eventually embarked on a literary career to reframe the past, to incite change, and eventually, he hoped, to enjoy his own artistic agency. "I shall write," he wrote colleague George Washington Cable following a rejection, "as every man must do, to please editors, to please the public, and who knows but that perhaps at some future day, I may best be able to please others by pleasing myself."[17] The Jubilee Singers' example and the "great revival" their tours set off across the United States also sparked a reconsideration of black vernacular forms in a man raised in a standard English–speaking, black, middle-class home in Fayetteville, North Carolina, impacted by the listening ear's standardization yet simultaneously compelled by the Southern storytelling traditions he overheard at his father's grocery store. Much like the Jubilee Singers, Chesnutt was, as John Edgar Wideman describes, "a man who straddled two worlds."[18] A teacher, Chesnutt lamented his rural black students' pronunciation and sought to "unteach" their home language, yet in a journal entry dated March 11, 1880, he wrote of a seemingly conflicting desire to curate "a collection of the ballads or hymns which the colored people sing with such fervor."[19] He admired their vibrational power in the face of contemporary communication technologies, just as Sheppard did: "Their originality lay in their simplicity and in that force which accompanies simplicity. The thunderbolt inspires us with awe; while the same force, confined in a battery, and transmitted along the wires of a telegraph, only excites our admiration."[20] Using electrical power as a metaphor—the consummate invention of modernity—Sheppard and Chesnutt present black sonic culture as both timeless and timely, conducted within, through, around, and via white technological developments, but not dependent upon them. Although the song collection never surfaced, Chesnutt published his own reworking of black vernacular in the *Atlantic Monthly*, 1887's "The Goophered Grapevine."

Chesnutt's dialect stories honor the power and agency vibrating within black sonic culture even as they reveal the sonic color line's shifts during Reconstruction, from whites' blanket rejection of any black sound as inferior noise to increasingly subtle forms of marginalization. Glenda Carpio describes how white American audiences "dismissively consumed" Chesnutt's work, a phrase that also rings true for the Jubilee Singers.[21] In *The Conjure Woman*, Chesnutt uses John and Annie as cyphers for the hungry yet dismissive listening ear of white Northern liberal men and women. Many white Northern liberals evinced a postbellum fascination with black culture as a source of novel entertainment, emotional release, and soul-wrenching edification, even as they tuned out elements heard as threatening to white cultural supremacy. Whereas the sonic color line once divided human from subhuman, the dominant white listening ear now racialized the border between sounds rejected as hopelessly raw and strange and those embraced as "cultivated" and therefore assimilable to the modern American nation.

One of ways whites deliberately misheard black sound during Reconstruction and its aftermath was through the filter of ephemerality. The listening ear characterized slave songs, stories, and folk practices as fading remnants of a dying culture, destined to pass from American cultural memory as black freedmen and women conformed to white sonic norms. The white Northern crowds encoring the Jubilee Singers and the white Northern couple repeatedly eliciting stories from Julius thrill both from black sound's alleged physical sensations and from what they hear as a ghostly sense of pastness. As John Wesley Work, musical arranger, curator, and director of the Fisk Jubilee Singers from 1904–1923, acknowledged on the group's fortieth anniversary, "It was fully expected that when these schools drew in their companies of singers, this music would die."[22] Therefore, rather than straining to hear the new ways in which black cultural workers hybridized American modernity, many white listeners focused on the songs as heard signs of a past rapidly receding. In the parlance of the still-thriving Spiritualist movements of the period, black performers working in vernacular forms functioned as mediums for a nation consumed by guilt and grief after the Civil War. Molly McGarry describes how mediums offered a "collapsing of time," producing sonic openings into "the past preserved in the present for the future."[23] White listeners used black singers and storytellers as sonic experiences of collapsed time, capable of momentarily conjuring a preserved antebellum soundscape to vibrational life.

White experiences of black performers as mediums shifted the sonic color line, as a segment of liberal white listeners began to freight black vernacular with pathos that enabled dramatic collective episodes of mourning, transcendence, and racial release. The Jubilee Singers' press resounds with reports of audiences weeping and wailing; Chesnutt's Julius frequently moves John's wife, Annie, to tears. Black cultural workers brokered cultural power through evoking such catharsis, manipulating white desire and surviving and maneuvering within it. McGarry's work reminds us that the position of the medium in nineteenth-century culture remained liminal and precarious—caught betwixt and between the past and present and treated as a passive vessel "who received no credit for her own intellectual, verbal, or performative skills."[24] The white audiences of the Jubilee Singers, Julius, and Chesnutt consumed their sonic representations of slavery, but the listening ear heard natural talent rather than artistic praxis.

Although it seems ironic that white Northern elites would seek to preserve the ephemerality of slave culture, it makes sense when contextualized within the late-nineteenth-century ethos of preservation. McGarry's discussion of mediumship as preservation dovetails with Jonathan Sterne's argument that the cultural pervasiveness of technologies of preservation such as canning and embalming—developed to solve the problem of mass battlefield corpses—gave rise to the phonograph during the 1870s, a device, Thomas Edison argued, for "gathering up and retaining sounds hitherto fugitive." McGarry argues that white middle-class Americans' desires to communicate with the dead arose within, among, and through nineteenth-century "new media" such as photography and telegraphy, while Sterne asserts that, *"for its early users, death somehow explained and shaped the cultural power of sound recording."*[25] Permeated by death and invested with spirituality, recording technologies, McGarry and Sterne both argue, developed from the desire for preservation as a white bourgeois impulse, which also meant recording was shaped by racialized listening and helped shape the listening ear in turn.

The 1870s were at once the high point of American mediumship, the beginnings of mechanical sound reproduction, and a critical moment of racial reorganization. During this period, white Northern liberals sought to stabilize the sonic color line through recursive contact with "black" sounds, capturing "fugitive" upstart ephemera within a preservationist frame that attempted to fix the past meanings of black sonic expression (and the meanings made of the past). In turn, the listening ear conditioned the entry of black tones, timbres, musical arrangements, and historical soundscapes into the newly (and reluctantly, for most whites) interracial nation and its increasingly profitable popular culture industry.

Nowhere was the twinned phenomenon of preservation and iteration in the newly dominant white middle-class Northern listening ear
more evident than in the Jubilee Singers' complex relationship with
George White, their white director, tour manager, and arranger. Born
in New York and educated in Ohio, White served in the Civil War and
moved to Nashville in 1866 on assignment for the Freedman's Bureau,
eventually landing a position at Fisk. His own music training was intermittent; however, he was known for being so "accurate of taste" he
could "exac[t] from his scholars just the tones and harmonies that
captivated the people."[26] The group's initial audience consisted of local
African Americans and radical whites, and White taught the group a
concert repertoire a là Lind and Greenfield. "A fine concert given by
colored people is entirely a new thing," he told Fisk President Adam
Spence.[27] The group intentionally varied their repertoire during their
first Northern tour, which soprano Maggie Porter Cole remembered
was planned along the former route of the Underground Railway. The
group represented themselves as Reconstruction's success story: young
modern black American subjects benefitting from new educational opportunities and showing sympathetic whites "what we did do, and what
we could do after Freedom."[28] But most white audiences were interested
in the sounds they perceived as giving material heft to the notion of
black difference. After weeks of running in the red and falling ill from
lack of nourishment, warm clothing, and decent housing, the Jubilees
earned two hundred and fifty dollars from their "surprise" performance
of "Steal Away" at Beecher's church (approximately 4,800 in 2015 dollars), and they retooled their lineup to emphasize spirituals.

The decision to share the songs with White ended up dramatically reshaping their sonic qualities while retaining traditional black diasporic
musical elements such as a capella vocals and a call-and-response structure. As Gordon recalled, "He [White] was wonderful in the interpretation of those old Negro melodies. He would keep us singing them all
day until he was satisfied that we had every soft or loud passage to suit
his fastidious taste. We sometimes thought him too exacting, but we
who are left know too well that our success was through the rigid training received at his hand."[29] Gordon's memories of White's "too exacting"
listening practice highlights several important elements of the listening
ear, particularly the tension between the desire to preserve a specific

aural image of black vernacular culture via repetitive "rigid training" and the conflicting need to "interpret" it according to European musical values. Gordon notes White's diligence, skill, and listening abilities in the passage, as do other Jubilee Singers, including Porter Cole, who said White heard the slave songs "as my mother sang them when a daughter was taken from her arms."[30] However, Gordon's and Cole's descriptions also reveal White's uncanny listening as a function of his racial power and privilege. Most immediately, Gordon's reflection that the group members knew "too well" the importance of White's influence suggests tension. Furthermore, Gordon's unsettling image of White keeping the group "singing . . . all day" echoes slavery—the song's context of production—and, while Cole's comment does not say that White heard the songs as a slave might, it suggests that he could preserve the sounds of slavery's gendered violence against her ancestors. Accuracy of sonic repetition does not automatically coincide with an ethics of listening. At the very least, White's insistence—especially combined with the enthusiasm and monetary support from white Northern audiences— may have precluded the Jubilee Singers from singing new songs evoking contemporary styles and experiences and/or obtaining more classical music proficiency as contralto Mabel Lewis desired.

In memoirs published on the group's fortieth anniversary, the remaining Singers drew boundaries around White's influence, affirming the decision to reframe and sing their parents' songs as their own, an act I read as a countermove to the listening ear's desire to preserve performances whites have deemed "authentic": isolated, historical, captured, passing, past, dead. Sheppard actually arranged most of the Jubilee Singers' music; it was her ear that negotiated between the music that was "sacred to our parents" and the sound "[the group] called the white man's music." She remembered the group's initial hesitance to perform spirituals even amongst themselves, feeling they were "associated with slavery and the dark past, and represented the things to be forgotten."[31] As Porter Cole put it, the group felt the songs were "for God and our parents' talks with God . . . they were not for white men's ears."[32] At Fisk, black students gathered in secret to sing songs like "Go Down, Moses," modulating their voices in the muted pianissimo that eventually became the Jubilee Singers' trademark. Criticism and biographies of the Jubilee Singers often attribute the students' practice of closeting the spirituals to fear and/or embarrassment on their part; according to Spence, "the door was shut and locked, the window curtains were drawn, and, as if a thing they were ashamed of, they sang some of the old time religious slave songs."[33]

Fred Moten and Stefano Harney's theorization of conservation, however, enables a long-overdue revaluing of the Fisk students' decision to steal themselves away (like Douglass and Jacobs before them) and allows scholars to recentralize the singers in their artistic performance and listening practices. "Anywhere you can stay," Moten and Harney advise in *The Undercommons*, "conserve yourself, plan. A few minutes, a few days when you cannot hear them say there is something wrong with you."[34] The Fisk students performed crucial identity work in those precious moments away from the listening ear that always already heard black voices, songs, and stories as "something wrong." In those few moments stolen from liberal white surveillance, Fisk students used pianissimo as a tactic to check the sonic color line and the listening ear at their door, creating and conserving a self-crafted—and self-crafting—site of *marronage* away from the brutality of redoubled racism and the more subtle but no less violent acts of postemancipation white disciplining Saidiya Hartman calls the "fashioning of obligation."[35] Meanwhile, biographer and Fisk president Spence assumed the students quieted themselves to keep their songs from escaping, never for a second doubting himself as the most important listener in the room.

The narrative logic of preservation has held sway in what Brooks identifies as "white reformist histotextuality."[36] History shaped by sonic color line credits White and Spence with "discovering" and "saving" the songs (and, ultimately, Fisk University itself) because they recognized the songs' appeal and exchange value. White critics' overwhelming praise—in tandem with the rapid growth of industrial capitalism and the American popular culture industry—further obscured the singers' agency. I argue here that only through their group performance of *marronage*—a kind of musical conservation "within the circle," as Douglass had phrased it, or qua Moten and Harney, "the downlow lowdown community"—did the Singers negotiate their relationship to their parents' sonic legacy, hearing the agency that was expressed in the songs and that they themselves possessed.[37] Note the careful syntax in Sheppard's remembrance: "Had Mr. White or Professor Spence suggested such a thing, we certainly had rebelled. It was only after many months that gradually our hearts were opened to the influence of these friends and we began to appreciate the wonderful beauty and power of our songs but we continued to sing in public the usual choruses, duets, solos, etc. learned at school."[38] According to Sheppard, the experience of performing this music together in a radically different historical setting enabled the group to imagine how, why, and in what form they might share the songs with white listeners. Sheppard does not credit the groups' teachers with recognizing their music's worth; rather, her syntax suggests that the group began to "appreciate the wonderful beauty and power of our songs" as a dynamic performative experience capable of altering subjectivities and rearticulating social relations, just as it happened in microcosm in their rooms.

Thinking through "conservation" as sonic political strategy enables a deeper understanding of what Brooks calls "the complexity of the black performance *experience*" for the performers themselves.[39] Following Moten and Harney, I understand "conservation" as a resistant praxis and use it here as a strategy of black resistance to the rigidity of the liberal listening ear and its use of the sonic color line to unify aural interpretations, fix stereotypes, and preserve contemporary forms of blackness out of existence. Moten and Harney theorize conservation as a challenge to acts of order, preservation, and the violence of capturing fugitive acts, sounds, and ideas. Unlike preservation, which seeks to fix the past and arrest change, "conservation is always new. It comes from the place we stopped when we were on the run. It's made from the people who took us in. It's the space they say is wrong, the practice they say needs fixing."[40] Through arrangement and private and public ensemble performances, the Jubilee Singers adapted their parents' sustaining songs to seek new forms of deliverance, conserving their own power and asserting their citizenship in Reconstruction's violent world.

Born of the vibrational space the sonic color line demarcated as "wrong" and of sounds that the listening ear declared "need[ed] fixing," the Jubilee Singers' new versions of the slave songs conserved their lives physically, psychologically, emotionally, and communally, with and in each other's presence. Their music also offered black audiences opportunities for conservation; Douglass, for example, hosted a private meeting with the group in his Washington, DC office in February 1874, when he was transitioning from editing *The New National Era* to presiding over the Freedman's Bank. Sheppard's journal describes the group's humility in meeting "our noble orator" and her surprise at the honor of spending over an hour with him. "We did not intend to remain so long," Sheppard wrote, "but he (Mr. D), began to sing some slave melodies for us which took some time for Mr. Seward to take down."[41] A profound vibrational exchange occurred in the gaps of Sheppard's matter-of-fact account. As a fugitive slave just twenty years before, Douglass could not remember these songs without involuntary tears. Douglass's impromptu concert speaks to the singers' transformative power and sound's ability to collapse time and link spaces in painful yet profound ways. While Seward preserved the songs via notation, Douglass's performance—"for us" as Sheppard pointedly noted—conserved a continuum amongst him and the group and connected the confining spaces of the ante- and postbellum moments: the closet in which the young Douglass hid while his Aunt Hester screamed in pain and resistance, the cloying woods covering the songs of fellow slaves, the ramshackle rooms of Fisk University where the students sang in secrecy, the relative grandeur of Douglass's DC chambers, and the regal concert halls of America and Europe where the Jubilee Singers performed. Again, Moten and Harney write: "Fugitive publics do not need to be restored. They need to be conserved, which is to say moved, hidden, restarted with the same joke, the same story, always elsewhere than where the long arm of the creditor seeks them, conserved from restoration."[42] In recognition that the listening ear sought preservation for black sound to restore white supremacy via an imagined "old plantation," Douglass's performance encouraged the Jubilee Singers to "change the joke and slip the yoke," as Ralph Ellison later phrased it:[43] restart with the same songs, mobilizing the acoustics of elsewhere (vibrating from yesterday's hidden spaces) to conserve themselves and the resistant story of a new black public.

Like the Jubilee Singers, Charles Chesnutt understood the body as a sonic agent of conservation, particularly through the new technology of phonography. As a young man planning a legal career, Chesnutt ambitiously taught himself Pitman shorthand, a written form of recording he placed in a technological continuum with the newest sound reproduction devices; his handwritten journals (now in Fisk University's special collections) show him diligently practicing his craft. "My journal is a sort of mental Phonograph," wrote Chesnutt in 1880, "into which I speak my thoughts by means of the pen; and at any future time I can recall them by simply opening the book."[44] Chesnutt understood phonography as a powerful technology that "deserves to rank, and does rank, in the mind of those who know its uses, with the great inventions of the nineteenth century; along with the steam engine, the telegraph, the sewing machine, and the telephone."[45] Somewhat uncannily, his conclusions regarding phonography's value came about after listening to Douglass. In October 1880, Chesnutt recorded a speech by Douglass for the *Raleigh Signal*. In a later reflection, Chesnutt described Douglass's "eloquence as a mightier power than the lash, the bloodhound, and all the machinery of unholy laws," theorizing transcription as a technological means to conduct and conserve Douglass's specific vocal power against racism past, present, and future.[46] For Chesnutt, phonography was "more than a labor-saving invention. Its greatest value—its most important use—is as a conservator of thought." Chesnutt's use of "conservator," with all of its legal resonance, bestows upon the phonographer the obligation to conserve history's so-called ephemera from loss, distortion, and embalming via preservation. "When Socrates talked of the unknown god," Chesnutt proclaimed to fellow stenographers at a meeting "—phonography would have laid the world under a debt of gratitude which no homage could have paid."[47]

Although phonographers use writing as a recording device—the trademark curls, curves, and stabs of shorthand—Chesnutt argued that listening remained the phonographer's most important tool of conservation. With "memory and exactness," the phonographer meets his subjects where and how they speak, serving as a medium for an accurate historical record. For Chesnutt, exactness flourished in the listener rather than in the record itself. Sometimes, Chesnutt described, the attuned ear of a legal stenographer may be called upon to "write what the judge meant to say," rather than simply transcribe words said, especially if the judge's phrasing is garbled or the grammar is incorrect.[48] Listening for conservation entailed an intimate listening through, beyond and in spite of words, one that worked to create a useable past rather than a perfectly preserved one. He also saw stenography as conserving truth from future manipulation, as the practice served an important role in "checking the utterances of public speakers."[49] For Chesnutt, stenography underlined the importance of speech and sound as history and empowered listening as a powerful historical (and historicizing) force.

While Chesnutt viewed stenography as productively at odds with his creative work, a strong connection existed between the two practices as technologies of conservation that empowered—and critiqued—listening as an epistemology. *The Conjure Woman*, in particular, offers a doubled listening experience; Chesnutt gives the sense of conserving both the sound and content of Julius's stories—alternate audiovisual histories of slavery—yet he embeds them within John's and Annie's misinterpretations. In order to better understand how and why Reconstruction-era white Northern audiences interpreted black song, story, and sound as they did, the next section examines how ethnology, the dominant social-scientific discourse regarding race, imagined the act of listening.

"None for the Long Ears": Ethnology, Social Darwinism, and the Cultivation of Listening

The increasingly social Darwinist racial discourse of the late-nineteenth century dovetailed with cultural concern over listening as a critical and epistemological practice. Earlier in the century, scientists interested in audition understood listening as an essential, fixed, and emotive practice related to physical reception. However, with the publication of Hermann von Helmholtz's *On the Sensations of Tone* in 1875, listening seemed much more flexible, shifting, and connected to notions of cultural evolution. Veit Erlmann argues that Helmholtz, influenced by German music, reconceived listening as the "interdependence of auditory resonance and rational choice." Musical appreciation became an outward sign of inner evolution and listening an act of discernment reflecting and shaping key (white) American social norms of discipline, culture, and value. Helmholtz's theories align with racial science when he locates listening as an "internal affair" rather than merely an external vibrational response.[50] After Darwin's theory of evolution disproved polygenesis—the idea that different races descended from separate groups—racial scientists continued to locate race in the body, but increasingly in the brain instead of in external characteristics. Therefore, even though white and black bodies may have similar physiological processing capabilities via the ear, racial scientists maintained the crucial element of listening actually happens in the psyche. Through practices such as craniometry—skull measurements allegedly linking brain size with mental capacity—racial scientists claimed thought and reason as the province of a more highly evolved Caucasian race. The combination of evolutionary theory and racial science further politicized the sonic color line between music and the merely musical, plunging white American music critics into a national crisis. Were the nation's composers up to snuff, and, more importantly, could American audiences actually appreciate European art music?

Frederick Nast's 1881 admonishment to poor listeners in *Harper's* illustrates how the relationship between musical ideology and perception became wedded to a classed and raced notion of American national identity. While the bulk of the article critiques all the major performances in New York City that year, including a brief mention of the Jubilee Singers, it concludes with a harsh listening lesson, allegedly from Wolfgang Amadeus Mozart himself (but clearly an allusion to the Greek myth of King Midas).[51] "Mozart's Father once told his son, 'Consider that for every connoisseur there are a hundred wholly ignorant; therefore, do not overlook the popular in your style of composition, and forget to tickle the long ears.' Mozart replied, 'Fear not, Father, respecting the pleasure of the multitude; there will be music for all kinds of people, but none for long ears.'" And then, Nast extrapolates:

> Too many American musicians, knowing the fate that has attended the larger compositions in the past, wrote for the 'long ears' only, and the result is an enormously long list of extravaganzas and music of the most ephemeral character. The only characteristic American music hitherto is the product of the lowest strata of its society. The plaintive slave songs, and their echoes the plantation melodies and minstrel ballads, have won popularity wherever the English language is spoken; but . . . in a few years [they] will exist in memory only. The chief hindrance to the development of a national school of music lies in the diverse character of our population. . . . American music cannot be expected until the present discordant elements are merged into a homogenous people.

Nast uses Mozart's father to represent an absolute division between the sensitive "listening ear" of the rarified musical connoisseur and the dull "long ear" of the "wholly ignorant." Nast goes on to suggest that the nonhuman listening of the "long ears"—which respond only to the bluntest of stimuli, like a mule's ears involuntarily twitching when "tickle[d]"—has caused the apparently dismal crop of American concert composers, who seek recognition through "ephemeral" appeals and "extravaganza[s]" (a musical insult in the nineteenth century). "Long ears" functions as an aural metonym for the "lowest strata of [American] society," the classed and raced social Others whom the writer labels "discordant elements"—noise alterior and perhaps destructive to the nation—and blames for the United States' perceived lack of harmony and homegrown culture, specifically newly freed slaves and the not-yet-white working class. Nast awards the Jubilee Singers a victory of sorts, deeming their songs the original "characteristic American music" that "plantation melodies and minstrel ballads" merely echo; however, to Nast's iteration of the listening ear, the "plaintive slave songs" and their debased parodies sound sour notes against which the category of a real, lasting (read: formal European-style) "national school of music" can be imagined. However, Nash worried that "American music" would remain a fantasy until unruly "long ears" are somehow assimilated to homogenous "listening ears."

The "long ears" parable is symptomatic of a larger project in nineteenth-century American music criticism: disciplining listeners to identify and separate music from the merely musical and delineating the boundary between good ears and bad. Outside of the tuning fork—which trained artists for the European musical hallmark of "pure" tone—and the recently introduced metronome that helped internalize fixed tempos, no other mechanical devices existed to enhance a listener's technical experience. Therefore, music journals like *Dwight's* devoted much column space to training readers to detect "good" musical tone, "proper" room acoustics, and appropriately "cultivated" voices; the disciplining of the listener's ear was arguably more important than a musician's training. A *London Times* review of the Jubilee Singers depicts the reward of a trained "listening ear" as the pleasure of a sonic fit with a trained musician's sound, and anything less produces dissonance and discomfort: "Though the music is the offspring of wholly untutored minds, and therefore may grate upon the disciplined ear, it possesses a 'peculiar charm.'"[52] Although the *Times* labels the Jubilees' performance as "music"—unlike most U.S. papers—it links listening to culturally specific forms of education and deems pleasure obtained by listening to the Jubilee Singers in excess of normative "disciplined" ideas about music. As disciplinary and performative as they were descriptive, passages about listening nudged readers into aligning their listening practices with musical *and* racial ideologies.

Critics often referred to process of honing one's ear as "cultivation," an extremely loaded term in the late nineteenth century because "cultivation" operated as shorthand for both racial and class identities, especially when contextualized with the ferocious debates over Reconstruction, the Civil Rights Bill of 1875, rising immigration, violent labor strikes, intensified military action against indigenous peoples, and the rise of U.S. imperialism. Not surprisingly, the white press usually referred to the Jubilee's white audiences as "the most cultivated classes" of American society, while dubbing the performers "uncultivated singers."[53] As I discussed in the previous chapter, "uncultivated" had a limited musical context that was itself racialized—it referred specifically to European concert training, either of the ear or the voice—yet gatekeeping music reviewers unselfconsciously universalized it. Maintaining that European training was the only way a voice could be properly "cultivated" denied black performance practices cultural legitimacy as musical disciplines. Coming, then, from musical channels deemed illegitimate, the Jubilee Singers' voices sounded "artless" and "childish" to white music critics, their songs deemed the "rude," "wild," "inarticulate" "offspring of wholly untutored minds," even in articles heaping on praise.[54] In addition to foreclosing alternate forms of cultivation, deeming the Jubilee Singers "uncultivated" patently disregarded White's training of the group as well as Sheppard's arrangements of the songs. It also glosses over the question of access to "cultivation," an expense available to only the wealthy, well-connected, and overwhelmingly white.

There is a clear slippage between critics' use of the term "cultivated" as a musical category and the ways they essentialized it in reference to classed, gendered, and raced bodies. For example, no matter how unseemly white audiences reacted to a Jubilee Singers performance— crying, cheering, being "moved and melted" in public—reviewers rarely questioned their privileged designation as "cultivated." On the flip side, no matter how polished the Jubilee Singers' visual and aural presentation, the white press represented them as perpetually on the verge of cultivation, rarely an embodiment of it. The liberal Boston *Independent*, for example, praised the Singers' "modest and decorous behavior and their evident intelligence" yet called them "uncultivated singers from the Southern plantations."[55] In spite of the Jubilee Singers' innovative hybrid arrangements, white critics did not apprehend them as heralds of an interracial and multicultural modernity but rather as "plaintive and touching" sonic throwbacks straight off the plantation. Critics presented the sound of the Jubilee Singers to the American "listening ear" as a form of aural voyeurism, appeasing white desire for real and raw black sound while transforming it into a rallying cry for the white labor yet to be done toward black "cultivation."

Distancing Jubilee Singers' performances from the valued category of music was perhaps the most damaging way white critics willfully tuned them out. Most white press reviews, for example, lack the dense description of the musical repertoire and vivid vocal renderings that were part and parcel of nineteenth-century musical discourse. Reviewers instead devoted inches to the group's history as former slaves, the fundraising mission of Fisk University, and flat, stock description of their "peculiar," "indescribable," "pathetic," and "plaintive" (yet "wild" and "thrilling") voices. With such a recalcitrant, limited, and racialized category of music firmly entrenched within American culture, white critics struggled to find the words that would reward what they heard as a powerful emotive experience yet simultaneously contained the Jubilees' power via the sonic color line, thwarting any potential breach to the category of "music." The group's black audiences, however, questioned the necessity of homogenization and fought racial science's theories about "cultivated" ears on two fronts: by showing black audiences' appreciation of European music and by questioning white audiences' ability to truly hear the Jubilee Singers.

"This Is Not All of Progress": The Jubilee Singers in the *Christian Recorder*

Philadelphia's *Christian Recorder* took a keen interest in the Jubilee Singers because of the paper's role as the mouthpiece of the African Methodist Episcopal Church (AME) and because of its secular mission to "record" African American history in the sense that Chesnutt argued, a narrative conserved as it was *meant* to be, for use in the immediate tumult of the present as well as the future. The oldest black-owned newspaper still in circulation, the *Recorder* had a brief run before the Civil War—even boasting Southern distribution via shipments to black Union regiments—and reemerged in 1861 to great popularity.[56] "The pages of the AME *Christian Recorder* following the Civil War," historian Julius Bailey argues, "reveal a contested site in which major issues of the day remained contentious and secular history was parsed for its revelation and correlation to a broader social history."[57] The Jubilee Singers positioned themselves precisely at this juncture, singing spirituals under the banner of the American Missionary Association yet visually and sonically affecting a modern black American subjectivity, neither reconciled nor amnesiac. The group's aesthetics sounded out the possibilities of a nation free of the sonic color line by its assimilation to/through blackness, rather than blackness vanishing through assimilation.

The *Christian Recorder*'s Jubilee Singers coverage, therefore, is best understood through the paper's present-focused editorial filter, which neither repressed nor lingered in slavery's memory but rather conserved what was useful from the recent past to fuel antiracist efforts and contemporary struggles over black identity formation. Benjamin T. Tanner, former director of several freedman's schools in the South and a consistent advocate for higher education for black Americans, helmed the paper from 1867 to 1885, spanning the original Jubilee Singers' first tours and the rise of unprecedented mass media production in the United States. Tanner made the *Recorder* an "all-inclusive newspaper" known for bold stances against racism and its active role in reuniting family members torn apart by slavery, war, and the tumult of Reconstruction. He also used the *Recorder* to develop a "reading people" by advocating for women's education and literacy; the 1861 article "Ladies Should Read Newspapers" reveals a relatively progressive view of gender politics and a strong stance on the importance of black people's engagement with the contemporary fight for equality. In engaging with contemporary racial ideologies and increasing violence, Tanner felt "American was the foremost identity for blacks in the United States"—arguing against advocates for African emigration—and sought to "uplift" the public perception of black people, particularly in regard to social Darwinism as justification for white supremacy. Tanner adapted uplift theory, a recurrent topic in the *Recorder*, to decouple evolutionary theory from racial essentialism, calling attention to the historic influence of black people on American culture, history, and society and highlighting successful black Americans. The Jubilee Singers' sonic blending of slavery's oral traditions with the aural customs of European concert music appealed to Tanner's vision regarding the *Recorder* and the way black citizenship in America could look *and* sound.

In its extensive coverage of the Jubilee Singers, the *Christian Recorder* carefully contextualized the group's sound and performances in contemporary struggles over black subjectivity. The paper celebrated the Jubilees' efforts on Fisk's behalf while critiquing the hypocrisy of America's white reception and the limits of the sonic color line and the listening ear it revealed. The coverage expressed little wonder at the Jubilee Singers' talents and little-to-no "strangeness" or peculiarity at their sound—both frequent aural images from the white press— suggesting both a familiarity with their music and a taken-for-granted sense of black personhood, capability, and achievement rarely found in contemporary white auditors. Furthermore, the *Recorder* used few, if any, repeated adjectives to describe the Singers' voices, choosing instead various nonsonic descriptors such as "very neatly" or "good" that tend to be song- and singer-specific. Such description focused on the Jubilee Singers' musical performance as subject rather than object, depicting their music as an acting vibrational force rather than a commodity to be beheld, possessed, or captured: "Their excellent singing won all hearts," reported T.S.M. after an 1873 performance. "The first note they struck rang through the room," the Reverend Newman Hall proclaimed after the Singers' first concert in England, and it "silenced every murmur and thrilled all hearts."[58] Another key difference concerned the paper's representation of the group as a mixed-gender ensemble comprised of individual singers with various talents. The white press reception rarely distinguished between the singers or mentioned the group's gender composition, representing the sound en masse and the individual singers as fungible. In reading hundreds of white press articles, I have never encountered a quote from a group member, let alone extensive first-person accounts or detailed updates on the singers' welfare such as those the *Recorder* published. Whereas the white press focused on their repertoire, the *Recorder* revelled in the "successful basso" of Frederick Loudin and the "bewitching" singing of Jennie Jackson and Maggie Porter, a traditionally gendered description, to be sure, but one nonetheless endowing black female voices with the attractiveness once accorded Jenny Lind's.[59] The *Recorder's* representation of the group as an ensemble built from the commitment and sacrifice of talented individuals functioned as an analogue for emerging Reconstruction-era modes of black community building and uplift.

Because the *Recorder* understood the Jubilee Singers as contemporary artists engaging postemancipation racial politics with sound, its writers worried about their representational impact on black Americans, expressing ambivalence about their project and its stakes. While writers evinced overall pride and goodwill—"May God bless them and protect them and give them great success," read the paper's send-off as the group headed to England—they also expressed doubts concerning their ability to get a fair hearing in an increasingly racist America.[60] The Washington, DC correspondent, for example, praised the Singers for "developing from among us the highest and most varied musical talent ever attained by people of the same race," but then challenged (at length) an unnamed white DC paper's remark that "the colored people of this country would only rise to influence and powers, if at all, through their music." The DC correspondent recognized both an opening and a foreclosing in the group's appeal to whites. The sonic color line enabled the white listening ear to mask black voices clamoring for social, economic, and political gains by amplifying the black voice's arresting power as pleasurable entertainment and a historical referent to enslavement. Demanding the listening ear open itself to both at once, the correspondent vehemently responded: "This is not all of progress. We cannot all become renowned as vocalists. . . . We will soon prove to the world, despite the contrary predictors of a Washington paper, that we can rise by means other than by treading the boards of the concert or opera."[61] Evoking recurrent creaking and groaning, the phrase "treading the boards"—referring to onstage pacing—the writer radically diminishes black performers' sonic variety into a sonic by-product, marking American entertainment as a particular (and potentially futile) form of black labor fraught with repetition, exhaustion, and silencing. In articles laced with nascent class conflict and a growing investment in respectability politics, the *Recorder* also critiqued audiences for their perceived overinvestment in entertainment. A letter to the editor from "Carrie" bemoaned the poor attendance of J. E. M. Gilliard's lecture on "The Colored American," placing the blame on the "too exclusive cultivation of our musical powers (or any other single gift)." Whereas "cultivation" of the ear marked race and class status on the other side of the sonic color line, Carrie suggests that, for black people, it threatened to drown out voices arguing for other paths to political and economic equality. She urges black audiences to "summon half the enthusiasm that greeted the *Jubilee Singers*" the next time an important speaker comes to town.[62]

The *Recorder* also analyzed *how* and *why* white people professed such love for the group while demanding an ethics of listening across the sonic color line. One *Recorder* article quoted the *New York Tribune*—a liberal paper that had opposed slavery under Horace Greeley's editorship—to question the motive behind the white listening ear's attraction: "We are glad to hear that this [the group's] great success *has not taken at all from that modesty and simplicity*, which was one of their chief charms." Directly referring to the sonic color line, the *Recorder* admonishes: "Exactly what the writer means by the words we have *italicized* we know not. Our supposition is, however, that he refers to that first lesson which most white men give to colored, 'keep yourselves in your place.'"[63] This critique calls attention to the disciplinary function of the white listening ear, first, by refusing to grant the terms "modesty" and simplicity" any taken-for-granted sonic referent to blackness and, second, by pointing out that white desire for the "charms" of black sound depends upon an accompanying perception that they occupy their proper "place" according to the sonic color line. By breaking this boundary, the Jubilee Singers appealed to an ethical standard of listening beyond the listening ear's "first lesson." The *Recorder* questioned the listening ear's desire for the Jubilee Singers to function as a sonic technology of repetition and preservation. "Without an exception they [the Jubilee Singers] are all superb singers," reported the *Recorder* in 1875. "That their audiences are of the same opinion is evidenced by the almost unreasonable demand for repetitions."[64] Another reported that, at the London Tabernacle, Reverend Charles Spurgeon had to intervene on the group's behalf because there was "so much encoring called for" that the congregation might have to "make night caps of their pocket handkerchiefs."[65] Given that white Northern audiences largely looked down upon the black cultural tradition of participatory call-and-response religious sermons, such excessive vocal and noisy approbations sounded disrespectful to some black listeners, an aural sign that the Jubilee Singers remained distanced from the esteem given to European art music. Amidst the thunderous applause, the *Recorder's* reviewers recognized the ethical breach of the "almost unreasonable" demands for encores, calling attention to its physical and, eventually, psychic toll.

The *Recorder* concerned itself with the impact of repetitive encoring because black freedom demanded different ethical practices *and* enabled new sensory orientations, sounds, and listening practices. White audiences' repetitive encoring threatened the Singers' art—and, by extension, black cultural production—with arrested development. "One thing is noticeable to he who keeps his eyes open," a *Recorder* reviewer noted.

> The students are themselves fast outgrowing these songs of their grief-stricken parents, and in singing not a few of them they themselves seem to enter into the spirit of the audience, and are constrained to smile at the weirdness of their own music. While this detracts somewhat from the entertainment, it is certainly no more of what ought to be expected. Freedom has its fruits as well as slavery.[66]

The reviewer hearkens his readership to keep their own "eyes open," noting that the audience's desire to use the Singers to conjure "their grief-stricken parents" constrains the Jubilee Singers' experiences of freedom in the contemporary moment and the creative "fruits" it could bear. Freedom, as Harriet Jacobs detailed in *Incidents in the Life of a Slave Girl*, involves both listening and sounding according to one's needs, desires, and values—areas where the Jubilee Singers remained constrained. The writer represents the group's sensibilities as forged outside the circle of slavery, and therefore they cross the sonic color line freely, "seem[ing] to enter into the spirit of the audience," as Reconstruction enabled them to do. While, certainly, the gestural image of listening characterizing the group as "constrained to smile at the weirdness of their own music" suggests that traversing the sonic color line leads to double consciousness in the Du Boisian sense—that the Jubilee Singers hear their "own music" through the dominant listening ear and judge it strange—here the *Recorder* suggests strangeness accrues because the Jubilee Singers' relentless repetition of their repertoire betrays their own desires, experiences, and shifting sensibilities. Did the listening ear's positioning of the Jubilees' sound as antebellum communiqué deny them opportunity to sonically explore and express their freedom?

Importantly, the *Recorder* did not just speculate about the difficulties the group faced in sounding the chasm between white and black citizenship privileges; it also featured Frederick Loudin's firsthand insights from the 1875 European tour. Loudin sent the *Recorder* clippings from the Singers' foreign press, availing American readers of the group's warm and dignified welcome from European royalty and dignitaries at events *besides* their musical performances, interracial social settings exceedingly rare in the United States, and increasingly illegal.[67] Loudin's clippings frame the Jubilee Singers' performances not as odes to a preserved past but as the sonic signature of black people's contemporary struggle for freedom, legal subject status, and citizenship. His material also allowed the *Recorder* to represent a different perspective on the Jubilee Singers' sound once away from the American listening ear, aligning it with modernity rather than freezing it in the slave past. While the British eventually proved to have a listening ear of their own—hearing the Jubilee Singers through the filter of their imperialist project in Africa and the missionary work of David Livingstone—the *Recorder* curated clippings and correspondence reports that focus less on British assertions of the Singers' "weirdness"[68] and more on detailing the shifting contemporary context of race framing the Singers abroad. Loudin's clippings embed descriptions of the Jubilee Singers' divergent international soundscape, one filled with cries of "Shame!" after the Jubilees told 500 Good Templars in Yorkshire they were barred from lodges in their own country, quietly imbued with the voices of European royalty with whom the group "conversed freely," and permeated with music from Covent Garden, the Crystal Palace, and all the many venues the Singers could enter "without any thought of *being barred on account of color.* All this in monarchical England, and yet democratic America shrugs her shoulders and cries out 'nigger.'"[69] Loudin's account offered up the Jubilee Singers' experiences to its "members" back at home, urging them to take pleasure in the group's displays of musical virtuosity and share in a different sensory experience of freedom in the relative absence of America's particularly virulent racism. By sharing his disciplined attention to the "rightness" of his sensory experiences of equality, Loudin challenged both the well-worn racial logic deeming black sensory perception as nonnormative and the contemporary racial science that sought to cultivate black sonic praxis out of existence. Loudin identified the white supremacist gaze and its aural analogue, the listening ear, as aberrant, "blinded," and "deaf[ened]" by color prejudice (rather than a critical stance with which freedmen and -women should aspire to assimilate). Through Loudin's missives, the *Recorder* intimated that some of the most crucial work of Reconstruction needed to happen within white Americans' sensory orientations, at the site where ideology meets perception.

Just a decade after the original Jubilee Singers disbanded in Luneberg, Germany, in 1878, writer and phonographer Charles Chesnutt also began to critique white listeners' consumption of black vernacular forms, culminating in his first collection of short fiction, 1898's *The Conjure Woman*. Chesnutt's era already seemed far removed from the Jubilee Singers' success, rife with the increased violence, disenfranchisement, and social alienation whites visited upon black people after the federal government abandoned the Reconstruction project and, in 1883, declared the 1875 Civil Rights Act unconstitutional. Loudin and the original Singers barely survived into this period; quite literally, their relentless touring and practicing physically and emotionally drained many well before they broke up: founding member Benjamin Holmes died of tuberculosis in 1875; Julia Jackson suffered a stroke in Germany in 1876; and Ella Sheppard developed severe throat issues in 1875. Loudin, angered by the irony of the increasing similarities between slavery and the university's treatment of the students as fungible objects, wrote to then-Fisk president Erastus Cravath: "You seem determined to drive ahead as if we were all superhuman and in fact as we are killed, you put in a new one."[70] Symptomatic of larger post-Reconstruction power dynamics, Loudin's damning critique exemplifies the stultifying pressure white supremacist expectations placed upon freedmen and -women. Still reeling from slavery's inhumanity and material impacts, black Americans now faced white expectations of them as "superhuman" performers, workers, and citizens: a technology of repetition for white consumption (and redemption).

The transactional yet erotically charged relationship Chesnutt depicts between his characters Julius—the elder black storyteller—and John and Annie, the new owners of the "old" plantation, embodies Loudin's condemnation of the listening ear's post-Reconstruction political economy. The pattern where John and Annie occasion a story from Julius—at least they *think* they occasion it—and then either reward or disregard Julius remains the same for all of the tales published in the original collection.[71] Through this conventional frame, Chesnutt depicts how John and Annie's racialized listening practice imagines Julius as a technology of repetition for their listening pleasure. Using imagery almost indistinguishable from the Jubilee Singers' white press, Chesnutt represents John's fantasy of Julius's performance in "The Goophered Grapevine," the opening story to *The Conjure Woman*; as Julius begins to speak, John immediately assumes that Julius "seemed to lose sight of his [white] auditors . . . living over again in monologue his life on the old plantation."[72] The phrase "over again" points to the black storyteller as a technology of repetition, one that allows John to eagerly conceive of himself as an unseen eavesdropper across the sonic color line, hearing the real, raw sounds of authentic "blackness" unchecked by the physical presence of whiteness, and fulfilling an intimate desire of the white listening ear to hear the black voice as a medium-like collapse of time that preserves the "old plantation" and provides sonic access to it. Whereas Douglass once asserted that white listeners could hear something truly horrible about slavery if they hid themselves in the Southern pine woods and listened across the sonic color line, he urged Northern white auditors to hear *through* their embodiments, in order that the slave song would enable them to realize at last their agency in and responsibility for slavery and provoke immediate action. Chesnutt depicts John as a willing, even desirous, listener in the woods, seated on "a pine log, lying under a spreading elm" *alongside* Julius, suggestive of the overt changes in the racial order since Douglass's time.[73] However, like many of the Jubilee Singers' white auditors, John listens to Julius's stories through the post-Reconstruction fantasy of the white listener's absence, which allows John to resist the deeper truths Julius embeds in his tales and to point blame for white supremacy elsewhere while still conceiving of himself as reasonable and progressive. Critics have asserted that Chesnutt's use of the term "monologue" in John's description of Julius points careful readers to acknowledge Julius's racial performativity and, therefore, the social construction of race—and I do not disagree—but it also links Julius to the history of racialized stage performance in the United States and suggests John's desire to be entertained by what he imagines as Julius's solipsistic (and ever-available) repetition.

"Monst'us Quare Sounds": Charles Chesnutt's *The Conjure Woman*

Engaging with the trope of the listener unites Chesnutt with the Jubilee Singers' virtuostic rescripting of black vernacular forms and performs an immanent critique of the notion that persistent black sonic performance can fundamentally alter white supremacy. And even if it could do so, at what cost to black artists? Chesnutt gestures at the paradox at the center of his work by naming his main character Uncle Julius McAdoo, signifying on Joel Chandler Harris's Remus—and the white practice of referring to all older black men as "Uncle"—and makes reference to Orpheus McAdoo, the famed singer (and North Carolinian) in Chesnutt's Ohio social circle. McAdoo began as a Fisk Jubilee Singer (and toured with Loudin in 1879) and then founded his own troupe to tour South Africa in the 1890s. The group began the tour performing spirituals but finished performing as a minstrel troupe.[74] Chesnutt's Julius embodies Orpheus's ambivalence, the challenges the Fisk Jubilee Singers faced, and his own struggles with the slippages the dominant white listening ear made between minstrelsy and black vernacular expression, along with the dubious affective and monetary rewards they gave both, with little concomitant gain in civil rights and citizenship privilege.

Chesnutt wrote during the era long called the racial nadir due to the virulence of legally sanctioned white supremacy and the rampant violence of lynching. During this era, spanning thirty years after the end of Radical Reconstruction, white governance dramatically disenfranchised black citizens, enacting poll taxes and restrictive voter laws, reinstitutionalizing a version of slavery in the South, and introducing segregation to the country at large. Chesnutt himself witnessed an 1898 riot in Wilmington, North Carolina—a majority black city just a hundred miles from Fayetteville—in which whites effectively ended the political ascendancy of the black middle class by stuffing the ballot box, spreading propaganda about black men raping white women, burning the black newspaper office, and murdering black men and women in the streets. However, literary scholars Barbara McCaskill and Caroline Gebhard recently recalibrated this period as more than the sum of white political control and mass disenfranchisement of black Americans. Following Chesnutt's lead—he came to call this period "Post-bellum—Pre-Harlem" in an eponymous 1931 essay—McCaskill and Gebhard argue that black writing between Reconstruction and the Harlem Renaissance made bold interventions into the racial politics and discourse of the era while working to strengthen and sustain fledgling black institutions, particularly schools, presses, and political organizations.[75]

Like the Jubilee Singers, and many black artists from the "Post-Bellum—Pre-Harlem" period, Chesnutt began his career working in standard English and European artistic forms only to find that the work that America's still-majority white audiences most sought from black artists had, in some way, to acknowledge the sonic color line, which automatically paired dialect and/or black vernacular structures with bodies visibly or socially marked as "black." Black artists at the time remained tenuously dependent on the white publishing and entertainment industries and therefore had to negotiate their artistic and political visions with the foundational white supremacy of these institutions. A spectrum of coping strategies emerged. The Jubilee Singers merged the formal properties of black spirituals with lyrics sung in standard English, reinterpreting the sonic color line as a porous boundary accessible via "New Negro" uplift but also open to cultural blurring, whether white audiences heard it or not. "The result is still distinctly Negro and the method of blending original," Fisk Alum and Chesnutt contemporary Du Bois wrote in *The Souls of Black Folk*, "but the elements are both Negro and Caucasian."[76] Chesnutt, however, chose a literary form for his conjure tales that neither completely separated nor sonically blended European and African American storytelling traditions but nonetheless traded on white desire for so-called black sounds. Chesnutt embedded the trope of the listener within the structural conventions of the frame narrative to create a tale of two dialects wrought by very different yet intertwined histories and valued quite differently by the listening ear.[77]

"The conception of a pure Aryan, Indo-European race has been abandoned in scientific circles," Chesnutt wrote in "The Future American," published a year after *The Conjure Woman*, "and the secret progress of Europe has been found in racial heterogeneity, rather than in racial purity."[78]

Although not without controversy—both then and now—Chesnutt's decision to use dialect writing emerged from his desire to write *away* from the graphic minstrelsy of white representations of blackness and a complementary desire to write *toward* the hybrid sonics of the Jubilee Singers. As wielded by white writers peddling plantation nostalgia, dialect writing starkly visualized and actualized the sonic color line for white readers at what should have been a profound moment of racial restructuring, heightening perceptions of sonic difference to nullify black knowledge, cultural and artistic traditions, intellectual history, and acts of historical witness precisely as black people entered America's public sphere. Following *The Conjure Woman*'s publication, Booker T. Washington urged Chesnutt to seize the

> golden opportunity to create sympathy throughout the country for our cause through the medium of fiction. Joel Chandler Harris [white author of the Uncle Remus tales] and Thomas Nelson Page [white author of *In Ole Virginia*, a romanticized version of "the Old South"] and others have done indefinite harm through their writings.

Chesnutt responded: "It has been the writings of Harris and Thomas Nelson Page and others of that ilk which have furnished my chief incentive to write something upon the other side of this very vital question."[79] Harris's and Page's nostalgic representations of happy slaves and kind masters on the old plantation gained traction as formal Reconstruction abruptly ended and whites reconciled across the Mason-Dixon Line via the economic exploitation of vulnerable black workers and the indefinite deferral of African Americans' citizenship rights. Both writers used the convention of graphic dialect to represent the perceived gap between black "difference" and the listening ear's sonic ideals of reasonable, intelligent, literate citizenship. "Black speech," notes John Edgar Wideman, "the mirror of black people's mind and character, was codified into a deviant variety of good English. . . . [It] implied lazy, slovenly pronunciation if not the downright physical impossibility of getting thick lips around the King's English."[80] Post-Reconstruction white-authored visual displays of so-called black dialect did not merely reinforce the sonic color line, which deemed black speech incorrect and inferior; rather, its ubiquity expanded the sonic color line's precision and reach.

White publishers' almost default use of dialect to convey black speech enabled the listening ear to become an increasingly cross-class sensation. Graphic dialect affirmed to lower-class whites who did not speak standard English that sharp differences existed between their speech and their black neighbors' (even when sonically undetectable, particularly in Southern communities), and as nativist politics began to mount after new waves of European immigration, white listeners could hierarchize European immigrants' linguistic variety as temporarily "ethnic" rather than essentially racial. Most devastating of all, culturally sanctioned use of what Houston Baker called "the graphics of minstrelsy" also fixed the sonic color line as a boundary of intelligibility, basically giving whites permission to dismiss "black" speech as nonsense (however fascinating, entertaining, or enthralling the listening ear occasionally found it).[81] The stakes, therefore, of Chesnutt's project were impossibly high: Could the fraught form of dialect literature operate to reconstruct and conserve the cultural memories of slavery and Reconstruction without reinforcing the sonic color line and bolstering the dismissive agency of the listening ear, all while one steadily published and earned a living (and respect) as a writer?

That Chesnutt deftly navigated the hegemony/resistance edge of dialect writing has been thoroughly argued. His professional correspondence with Walter Hines Page, his editor from *The Atlantic*, revealed a careful attention to decisions concerning sound and spelling. Chesnutt decided to consistently spell "you" as "you," for example, rather than "yer" because the latter would not be true to how it sounded when spoken, and he felt it would be distracting from the story to keep changing the spelling of "you." "I do not imagine I have got my dialect, even now," he wrote Page, "any more uniform than any other writers of the same sort of matter."[82] The inconsistencies mark his dialect as more sensitive and "real" than other writers', even though in the same letter he remarked: "The fact is, that there is no such thing as negro dialect; that what we call by that name is to express, with a degree of phonetic correctness as to suggest the sound, English pronounced as an ignorant old southern negro would be supposed to speak it, and at the same time preserve a sufficient approximation to the correct spelling to make it easy reading." To Chesnutt, the idea of "negro dialect" is a fictional device in the truest sense of the word: an invented visual representation of sound connected to—and reinforcing—the notion that black Americans are out of time ("old"), out of place ("Southern"), and out of step ("ignorant") with modernity. It is certainly not a vehicle of some essential anthropological or biological truth about black speech. Therefore, I build on arguments by Wideman, Gates, and Gavin Jones regarding Chesnutt's against-the-grain use of dialect writing by embedding the dual dialects represented in the stories—black vernacular *and* standard English—within the racialized politics of listening that frame the collection.[83] I also argue that by signifying on the trope of listening in his first three conjure tales, Chesnutt urges readers to contextualize so-called dialects in a larger sonic politics and a thoroughly racialized soundscape; how one listens to and makes meaning of the screech of a saw in "Po' Sandy," for example, or the silences of a club-footed former slave in "The Conjurer's Revenge" reveals as much as, if not more than, "dis" or "that."

"The Goophered Grapevine," the first tale in *The Conjure Woman*, sets up the racialized conditions of communication throughout the collection.[84] Set in fictional Patesville, North Carolina, "Grapevine," like most of Chesnutt's conjure tales, begins and ends with first-person narration by John. The meat of the story, however, comes from Julius's tale of slavery. Post-emancipation, Julius has continued to live at the old McAdoo plantation, cultivating its grapes for sustenance and profit. Because the U.S. government stopped short of giving former slaves legal rights to the land they worked and the wealth they created, Julius turned to storytelling as a mode of resistance—verbal conjure—to deflect John and Annie's economic encroachments on Patesville's black community. In "Grapevine," Julius attempts to convince the couple not to buy the plantation through a tale explaining how greedy master McAdoo had Aunt Peggy—a free conjure woman appearing in several of the stories— "goopher" his grapevines to prevent slaves from supplementing their meager diets, setting off a tragic chain of events. While they ultimately close the deal to buy the land—John tells the reader the mild climate is

necessary for Annie's tenuous health and his new business enterprise—
Julius convinces them of his indispensible knowledge (among other
things, he mentions that only he knows which grapevines have been
conjured). John offers Julius a position as a coachman as "compensa-
tion" for losing his grape business, a narrative device setting up the
characters' frequent encounters and commenting on liberal whites' expectations of black assimilation into the industrial economy.

Chesnutt characterizes John and Annie as types for liberal Northern
whiteness. John's name conjures up the anonymous legal placeholder
"John Doe" (as well as a sly reversal of the traditional "John and the
Old Master" vernacular story form); "Annie" evokes the black colloquialism "Miss Anne," a derisive term for a white woman connoting ar-
rogance, condescension, and racist behavior.[85] Chesnutt gives them no
surname, adding an additional layer of allegorical anonymity. Certainly
John's "standard" English, Northern mannerisms, and listening habits
served as a touchstone for the readership of the white literary magazines
regularly publishing Chesnutt. However, as Wideman points out, Chesnutt's representation of John's inner thoughts (and Annie's dialogue)
is *also* written in dialect via Chesnutt's phonographic ear; John's often
awkward, reserved speech seems far less "normal" and universal than
literary conventions (then and now) might have portrayed, particularly
when juxtaposed with Julius's fluid storytelling passages. "These variet-
ies of speech," Wideman says, "describe two different worlds; each speech
form (speech community) represents a version of reality," versions that
Chesnutt, like Douglass, Jacobs, Greenfield, and the Jubilee Singers
before him, knew intimately and trafficked between.[86] To challenge
the sonic color line dividing these "different worlds" and, ultimately,
to decolonize the racialized listening practices upholding it, Chesnutt's
use of dialect depends upon—and plays with—automatic associations
of "white" speech with truth telling, reliability, and reason and "black"
speech with ignorance, entertainment, and fantasy. Naturalizing this
arbitrary division allowed white liberal listeners to distort the cultural
memory and political meaning of slavery; in turn, the construction of
warped histories of slavery *enacted* the divergent sensory experiences
enabling new forms of white supremacy to emerge. John's belief that he
and Annie are the perfect listeners for Julius's remembrances enables
John to disavow his own stake, both in terms of the immediate issue at

hand—Julius's life and livelihood in Patesville—and the historical, economic, and social legacies of slavery that enabled him to profit from his move to the South.

"The Goophered Grapevine" sets up the relationship between Julius's aural performance of race and the racialized erotics of the listening ear's demand for and consumption of "blackness." John describes being compelled by his perception of the strangeness of Julius's diction, "not grasping the meaning of this unfamiliar word . . . conjure." John also remarks that Julius's vocal tone piques the couple's interest, an attraction based on the sonic color line and the thrill of listening across it: "He imparted the information with such solemn earnestness, and with such an air of confidential mystery, that I felt somewhat interested, while Annie was evidently much impressed, and drew closer to me."[87] John describes being attracted by the "solemn earnestness" and "confidential mystery" of Julius's voice—a decided break from minstrelsy's image of black people as perpetually comedic, yet one still insinuating that Julius's belief in conjure is foolish—images recalling the purportedly "strange" qualities of the Jubilee Singers' performances as well as white auditors' desire to believe such enchantment is for their ears alone. Chesnutt's phrasing lends ambiguity to the encounter, decoupling Julius's vocal qualities from biological essentialism and suggesting that Julius, a master storyteller who understands the racial etiquette of the sonic color line, stages this "confidential mystery," as Julius adds particular "air[s]" when he sees fit, stoking his white listener's desires. Revealingly, whether or not Julius performs his blackness appears to matter less to John and Annie than the performance itself. The couple's feeling that Julius labors for them heightens the listening ear's receptivity and the erotics of the encounter.

"Po' Sandy," Chesnutt's second conjure tale, uses aural imagery of violent and/or ambient sounds to examine how the sonic color line enabled different sensory perceptions of the legacy of slavery and its continued impact on the Southern landscape, its inhabitants, and Reconstruction's alleged failure. "Po' Sandy" opens with Julius, now officially employed, driving John and Annie to buy lumber for a new plantation-style outdoor kitchen. En route, the group encounters the sounds of a sawmill, and Julius finds John's and Annie's reactions to its buzzing insensitive, prompting him to recount a tale that recodes the sawmill's sound as a

noise signifying encroachment and terror rather than a herald of industrial progress. Julius's tale recounts the murder of a slave named Sandy
by his master. Whites called Sandy "a monst'us good nigger," an ironic
title critiquing how white supremacy warped language: to be "good" in
this context leads to pain, punishment, and an almost complete loss of
agency. The master's children fight over "borrowing" Sandy so much, for
example, that the master begins lending him out on a rotating schedule,
with no concern for Sandy's health or well-being; the master even sells
Sandy's first wife while he is away. Sandy becomes so psychologically
dissociated by his constant movement that he "hardly knowed whar he
wuz gwine ter stay fum one week's een'ter de yuther." The very sound of
his name in the mouth of whites reminds of his lack of self-possession:
"'hit's Sandy dis en Sandy dat, en Sandy yer en Sandy dere, tel it 'pears
ter me I ain' got no home, ner no marster, ner no mistiss, ner no nuffin." His second wife, Tenie—a conjure woman—responds to his pain by
revealing a secret: she can transform Sandy into a tree so that he at last
may have roots on the land where he has lived and worked his entire
life. "You won't hab no mouf ner years," Tenie informs him, "but I kin
turn you back oncet in a w'ile, so you can git sump'n ter eat, en hear
w'at's gwine on."[88] Once a tree, Sandy can neither speak nor listen, an
image of aural terror and social death. Sandy follows Frederick Douglass through the bloodstained gate and Linda Brent into the attic but cannot tap into listening's agency, knowledge, and life-sustaining connection
in order to keep himself and his family together. Most chillingly, Sandy
remains vulnerable to slavery's wounds and the master's desire: a wood-
pecker drills a hole in his arm; a fellow slave scars his leg while chopping
turpentine boxes; and, horrifically, the master decides that Sandy would
provide the perfect raw material for *his* new kitchen, so he chops him
down and planes him, a graphic and murderous pre-echo of John and
Annie's current mission and a clear challenge for Julius: Can his storytelling performance enable theoretically sympathetic whites to hear the
very material terror of white supremacy lingering in their contemporary
moment?

The sawmill's sound functions as an aural metonym for the sonic
color line in "Po' Sandy," amplifying how John's, Julius's, and Annie's
very different subject positions impact how they hear their lived environments. John immediately interprets the mill's din as a sonic marker

of the South's economic recovery through the industrious efforts of men like himself. He sublimates the mill's sound to the background of the group's conversation with no change in his outward demeanor; it remains merely a "whir" that "was not unpleasing."[89] Julius, on the other hand, foregrounds the sound and shares its visceral and emotional impact: "Julius observed, in a lugubrious tone, and with a perceptible shudder:—'Ugh! But dat des do cuddle my blood!'"[90] Julius's visceral reaction invites John and Annie (and, by extension, Chesnutt's readers) to listen more deeply to industrial sounds and the memories they prompt. However "sympathetic," Annie still cannot quite hear the mill sound or Julius's entrée, asking him: "Does the noise affect your nerves?" While well-intentioned and born of concern, Annie's use of the word "noise" channels Julius's discomfort into an easily definable medical malady suggestive of her own experience. Nineteenth-century American medical care treated middle- and upper-class white women as nervous and excitable due to the female reproductive system; doctors considered "noise," in particular, a vitality-draining threat for women's more easily exhaustible nerves, often prescribing rest away from urban clamor as a sedative for "nervous" women.[91] The couple's move to Patesville may have partly been inspired by a perceived necessity to escape "noise."

Julius's interpretation of the buzz saw's sonic output rejects the listening ear's gendered explanations—John's capitalist sound and Annie's medicalized noise—and he uses Sandy's tale to communicate how and why he listens to the Southern soundscape as he does. Filled with emotion, Julius tells Annie, "I ain' nervous"; he counters John's description of the saw as "eat[ing]" through the trees—an image of necessary consumption—with a fine-grained sonic evocation of the saw's violence: "dat saw, a-cuttin' en grindin' thoo dat stick er timber, en moanin', en groanin', en sweekin', kyars my'memb'ance back ter ole times, en 'min's me er po' Sandy."[92] Deftly moving the perspective from the triumphant saw to that of the felled tree, Julius anthropomorphizes its sound as "moanin', en groanin'," endowing the tree with agency, however restricted and aggrieved, to protest its destruction. Julius then links the tree's sound of pained resistance to his memory of Sandy, showing sound's power to retain histories visually erased and culturally suppressed.

Chesnutt's frame dramatizes the possibility of speaking and listening across the sonic color line while revealing how the listening ear produces barriers that guard against potential breaches. Chesnutt shows both the cultural currency of Julius's performative vocal tone—what John describes as a "pathetic intonation"[93]—and the listening ear's resistance to it; in the conjure tales, the sonic color line deflects head-on engagement and reckoning with slavery's legacy. Almost immediately after Julius finishes, John disavows the story's implications and deflects a sympathetic response, defensively enacting a self-consciously analytical perspective. He distances himself by launching into a literary categorization of the tales told "from the lips of older colored people" and dismissing "deep interest" in these stories as a feminine weakness, noting that the most tragic seem to be "poured freely into the sympathetic ear of a Northern-bred woman."[94] John's remark shores up the defenses of the listening ear, at once dismissing black storytelling artistry as a natural torrent of words and conjuring up the incendiary erotics of white America's deep-seated fear of miscegenation. Linking black male speakers to white female listeners also casts the political relationship between white Northern women and black (male) abolitionists—quite strong in the antebellum moment—as a temporary enchantment rather than a powerful intersectional affinity; by the time "Po' Sandy" was written, the coalition had all but evaporated after leading white feminists refused to support black male suffrage and to organize on equal terms with black women. Finally, the image of black words "pouring" into a white ear alludes to the play-within-a-play staged by the titular character in Shakespeare's *Hamlet*, a scenario, of course, staged to evoke a public response of guilt from Hamlet's uncle. In the play—designed by Hamlet to mimic real-life happenings—a man murders his brother, the king, by pouring poison in his ear while he sleeps; he then seduces the queen. John's literary allusion characterizes Julius's story as an erotic poison designed to corrupt white listeners and expose their guilt for the "tragic incident[s] of the darker side of slavery."[95] Through John's insinuations, Chesnutt critiques the white listening ear's disposition toward black voices, an interweaving of fear and fascination that simultaneously sensationalizes and nullifies black expression.

But Julius persists against the listening ear's defenses by telling a story that explicitly confronts the pain caused by racialized listening practices, especially the quotidian terror whites systemically enacted against black people during and after slavery. Perhaps because of the soundscapes circulated in slave narratives and on abolitionist circuits—the creaking chains, cracking whips, and women's wails discussed in chapter 1— whites represented slavery's violence as largely spectacular, which, as Saidiya Hartman notes, paved the way for new forms of brutality and coercion after its official end. Revealing the connections between slavery's violence and the brutality of the convict lease, sharecropping, and industrial labor systems that followed, Hartman argues that "slavery is less the antithesis of free labor than an intemperate consort, a moral foil, a barbarism overcome, and the pedestal on which the virtues of free labor are decried."[96] Hartman's analysis explains how and why Chesnutt's kaleidoscopic layering of history—he writes at the end of the nineteenth century yet sets his stories twenty years earlier, and then Julius's tales twenty or more years before that—allowed him to blur time and upend narratives of progress. Embedded in multiple presents, the stories set in slavery resonate violently into the Reconstruction, and John's and Annie's refusal to hear them as anything other than entertainment only amplifies history's impact on the lynchings and race riots of Chesnutt's contemporary moment. Chesnutt's aural images of terror move fluidly across the multiple overlapping chronologies attempting to contain them. Sandy's resistant "creakin', en shakin' en wobblin'"[97] vocalize the pain of enslavement, forecast lynching's horrific sounds, and make audible the fundamental yet often invisible processes of American capitalism that continued well beyond emancipation, bio-disciplines carried out silently in psyches or on balance sheets: whites transforming black men and women into objects and then conjuring objects into capital and infrastructure. The frame of "Po' Sandy" casts John and Annie (and by extension the reader) as witnesses to white people's transformation and fragmentation of black people, particularly through Julius's characterization of the listening experience of Sandy's wife Tenie, who witnesses his demise.

Tenie's frustrated attempts to publicly account for Sandy's murder offer up another image of racial terror to challenge the sonic color line within and without the story. Unable to stop Sandy's murder nor even to conjure him back so that they may share last words, Tenie opens herself to the full horror of Sandy's death. She is the only person present who hears, understands, and truly marks the violence taking place. At first, Tenie loudly expresses her grief, guilt, and concern for Sandy, "a-hollerin' en cryin' ter her Sandy ter fergib her," a public display her master immediately silences by locking her up in the smokehouse— where meats are "cured" and toughened—"'tel she got ober her spells."[98] Mars Marrabo, in contrast, freely exercises his sonic power, dominating the plantation soundscape with his unchecked and "monst'us mad" outbursts; his is the true craziness in this scene. The master's expressions of madness terrorize his black listeners, especially when coupled with his power to label and define them. To the antebellum listening ear, emotions expressed by female slaves—what Moten calls "the resistance of the object"—became sonic markers of insanity rather than relatable human sentiment.[99] As Mars Marrabo's angry accusations point out, slave masters understood these sounds as interfering with the plantation's productivity. More than once, Julius refers to Tenie as "'stracted" rather than "crazy," suggesting Mars Marrabo worried mainly about the possibility of losing Tenie's labor. Tenie, trapped in the smokehouse and undoubtedly listening to Mars Marrabo's rant, takes a different tack to sound her pain. Tenie waits until no longer emotionally overcome—her silence being the price of being "'lowed to go 'roun' de plantation"— then approaches Marrabo and tells him what happened with the calm directness of "reason" (ironically, a value he himself has not displayed). Marrabo soundly rejects her story, calling her "de wuss 'stracted nigger he eber hearn of." Tenie, grieving Sandy's death and seeking a public reckoning, begins to haunt the plantation with her painful truth, going "'roun' moanin', en groanin' en shakin' her head."[100] Tenie resists the institution that devoured Sandy by echoing and repeating the sounds he made as the saw tore him apart, recasting them as sounds of mourning and remembrance.

Paralleling the divergent listening practices in the story's frame, master and slaves listen to Tenie's moanin' en groanin' quite differently, marking the sonic color line and exposing both the power and the limits of the listening ear. Mars Marrabo continues to tune Tenie out as crazy, diminishing her emotional breakdown as "no harm to nobody ner nuffin." He remains stubbornly determined to extract all possible use from her body as he did from Sandy's, deeming her well enough to nurse the slave children. However, the other slaves refuse to let the master silence Tenie and erase Sandy's murder. Tenie's bold act of radical openness to Sandy's pain enables a resistant auditory imagination and the kind of decolonizing community listening Jacobs depicted in *Incidents in the Life of a Slave Girl*, when Linda Brent experiences her ancestors' sonic memories embedded in the Southern landscape and built environment. One by one, the slaves hear the doubled sounds of Sandy's death and Tenie's grief emanating from the master's new kitchen built from Sandy's dismembered body. Julius recounts how the slaves reported that "dey could hear sump'n moanin' en groanin' 'bout de kitchen in de nighttime, en w'en de win' would blow dey could hear sump'n a-hollerin' en sweekin' lack it was in great pain en sufferin'."[101] The phrase "moanin' en groanin'" expresses complaint as well as sadness, and the slaves use this sound to disrupt the plantation's spatial politics, sounding out the hallowed ground enclosed by the kitchen's wooden walls. The slaves' decision to listen together to Tenie's grief refuses to let her stand alone in her "pain en sufferin" and soundly rejects the master's labelling of her as "crazy." If Tenie's reaction to Sandy's death is "crazy," her community's decision to hear and sound Sandy's "moanin' en groanin'" along with her declares that they all must, in fact, be "crazy." Eventually, Julius remarks, "Dey wa'n't naer nigger on de plantation w'at would n' rudder take forty dan ter go 'bout dat kitchen atter dark." By listening together, the slaves resist Tenie's silencing and sonify the daily violence they experience. Eventually, the master stands alone in his refusal to listen. Even the master's wife, for whom the kitchen was built, "wuz skeered ter go out in the yard atter dark."[102] However, Julius, and by extension Chesnutt, leaves the nature of the mistress's fear open ended: Is it Sandy's ghost that terrifies her? The sound of Tenie's pain? Or the thought of collective action by the slaves? All three?

Upon reexamining the community listening in this scene, I can't help but think of the December 2014 protests in New York City against the lack of indictment for white Staten Island police officer Daniel Pantaleo, who choked an unarmed black man named Eric Garner to death, essentially for speaking out against the officer's harassment of him for selling "looseys" (untaxed single cigarettes). To the grand jury, the idea that the officer murdered Garner seemed as fantastical as a man turned into a tree and felled for lumber. But, like Tenie and friends creaking and groaning over Sandy's body, crowds gathered in New York City to chant Garner's last words—"I can't breathe"—over and over, playing back the recording of Garner's voice over loudspeakers—"I can't breathe"—and using them as a Twitter hashtag to seek justice and sound out community on the Internet—#Icantbreathe. Protestors made connections to slavery; one man told *the Guardian*, "It goes back to the foundations of the country. We've been dehumanised since we've been here, and we are being dehumanised now."[103]

No matter what the nature of the mistress's fear or the master's obdurate tuning out, the slaves' decision to listen to Tenie's grief and amplify Sandy's murder made an impact: Master Marrabo eventually tears down the kitchen and uses the lumber/Sandy's body to build a schoolhouse. However, the slaves continue to haunt the space, making plain that even beneficial changes to the built environment cannot buy their silence nor erase the master's crimes. Officially, Julius notes, the schoolhouse was only used in the daytime because "on dark nights folks gwine 'long de road would hear quare soun's en see quare things." Here Julius shows the remembrance of the sounds of Sandy's death—and Tenie's visitations—as double-voiced, sounding out grief *and* cover for meetings outside of the master's surveillance.[104] In this way, the slaves of the Marrabo plantation turned white Western ideals of rationality and empiricism against their believers and cultivated a space of privacy, communal interchange, and decolonial knowledge ("quare soun's") away from power's prying listening ear. Colloquially, slaves called these sites "hush harbors," and Vorris Nunley argues that the meaning-making practices black subjects developed in these sites formed an epistemological rhetorical tradition, African American Hush Harbor Rhetoric, a sustaining "tradition/genealogy of danger" reaching back to the Middle Passage and forward to our contemporary moment.[105] By telling the tale of "Po' Sandy," Julius also dedicates a new hush harbor on the same hallowed ground: his tale convinces his employers to buy new wood from the mill and allow his church to meet in the old schoolhouse. The rededication of the schoolhouse as the Sandy Run Baptist Church operates as a double-voiced reminder of slavery's still-palpable presence, but also of the fiercely liberatory ends of Reconstruction-era Hush Harbor Rhetoric; Sandy's successors know the South remains, sometimes quite literally, a dead end—a "sandy run"— yet they must continue to seek liberation—"Sandy, run!"—even if it means uprooting themselves to go north, the subject of my next chapter.

Through Julius's story of Po' Sandy's and the kitchen's material transformations, Chesnutt shows how the white listening ear's limitations are both a fundamental problem and an enabling opportunity for black performers. Julius implicates his own story as a "quare sound" that the listening ear would dismiss and/or misinterpret, a provocation for John and Annie to hear beyond their preconceptions, of course, as several critics have suggested.[106] However, he simultaneously offers the story's black readers an alternate epistemology to the sonic color line, a decolonizing of listening that flips the script on white supremacist value systems that dismiss such stories as "quare sound," even to the ears of many Reconstructed white listeners thrilling at music and oratory performed by black Americans as pathetic, beautiful, pleasurable, and/or humorous. Julius's come-up at the frame tale's end suggests that, unbeknownst to white listeners who understood themselves as central to any American cultural production, the sonic color line produced and preserved distortion, allowing black culture workers to channel white listeners away from the primary ontological purpose of their stories, songs, and other forms of Hush Harbor Rhetoric. At the same time that he queers the very notion of "quare," Chesnutt (re)invests black readers with agency to "quare" their sounds to exclude or misdirect white listeners, hostile and well meaning alike, to create a community of listeners and conserve its presence within the white listening ear's misinterpretations.

Within and without the narrative frame of both "The Goophered Grapevine" and "Po' Sandy," the markedly different listening practices of black and white people reveal three key tensions at the heart of black literature from and about the Reconstruction period. How could black writers challenge the official historical narrative of American slavery without completely privileging dominant modes of knowing, speaking, and listening? Tenie falls silent in death, after all, and the master "didn' shed no tears," not to mention that nostalgic Northern newcomers John and Annie want to rebuild the outdoor kitchen not more than a generation later.[107] How can black cultural producers write (and, in the case of the Jubilees, sing) the "quare sounds" of blackness into the American cultural imaginary in a way that conserves the beauty, power, and meaning of their distinction to (many) black listeners yet simultaneously attack the white supremacist value system of the white listening ear that deems blackness "quare" in the first place? And, especially acute for postbellum culture brokers like the Jubilee Singers and Chesnutt who have mastered (and take pleasure in and meaning from) black *and* white forms of expression, how to (Re)construct listeners, black and white, to hear the hybrid sound of American citizenship rather than disjointed dispatches from an evolutionary continuum reaching toward the apex of the white listening ear?

While many critics argue the answer to these questions lies in Julius's ability to coax a sympathetic response from John and Annie—and much has been made of Annie's response to Tenie's plight—I argue that reading these moments with an increased understanding of the complexities of racialized listening enables us to understand how listening across the sonic color line is not inherently progressive. In fact, John's and Annie's perception of themselves as enlightened, liberal whites possessing the generosity and patience to listen to Julius maintains white supremacist racial hierarchies and threatens to produce new forms of inequality. " 'What a system it was,' [Annie] exclaimed, when Julius had finished, 'under which such things were possible!' " Annie understands that the physical and emotional violence Marrabo inflicted upon Tenie and Sandy was part and parcel of slavery, yet she still fails to acknowledge white agency in creating the system "under which such things were" not only "possible" but normalized as necessary, even fundamental. Furthermore, Annie's syntax reflects the dominant post-Reconstruction understanding of slavery as past, in spite of Julius's warning that any structure containing lumber cut from Sandy's body "is gwine ter be ha'nted tel de las' piece er plank is rotted en crumble' inter dus.'" The way Annie phrases her sympathy makes the emotional connection she offers up contingent on accepting her view that slavery is a thing of the past. While John agrees with Annie's perspective on slavery, he distances himself from her sympathy with a gendered dig at her credulity: "Are you seriously considering the possibility of a man's being turned into a tree?" It does not cross John's mind that his expectations of black storytelling are at odds—he demands spectacular difference in black narrative and diction yet simultaneously expects Julius to evoke a strict sense of realism—or that he has taken Julius's story at face value and missed a crucial employment of metaphor, a very common literary technique. John expresses "amazement" not at Julius's story (or his storytelling ability) but at Annie's willingness to believe. She immediately refutes John's accusations, aligning herself with the listening ear's dominant rationality and communicating that while she extended herself across the sonic color line to take in the sound of Julius's voice and entertain the meaning of his story, she did not leave her values and rational epistemology behind.[108] True to the framework of sentimental fiction, and to the politics of empathy examined by Hartman in which sympathetic whites often replaced suffering black bodies with images of their own, Annie expresses empathy toward the grieving wife Tenie rather than toward "Po' Sandy" or Julius, right in front of her, whose voice lingers in the air between them. And much like the Jubilee Singers repeating their performances, city after city, across the Northern United States and Europe, Julius repeats more tales of black slaves' pain and suffering for John and Annie throughout *The Conjure Woman*—to liven up their Sunday afternoon, pass a rainstorm, convince them not to fire his nephew, allow him to eat their leftover ham—yet no lasting discernible movement occurs in John and Annie's racial politics. Being compelled to bear historical witness to an audience who, however polite, cannot or will not listen or act on it—one of the new conditions of the sonic color line at the turn of the twentieth century—evokes a new violence, another critique Chesnutt's conjure tales casts back to the Jubilee Singers' emotionally wrought audiences.

However, just as Brooks urges scholars to remember that the Jubilee Singers performed for themselves as much as they did for their audiences, if not more, the trope of the listener prompts a consideration of Julius's aural experience and the power and transformation possible through listening to his own voice telling these stories. In the third tale, the aptly named "The Conjurer's Revenge," Julius transforms himself by listening to himself voice the memory of his friend Primus. In this tale, the conjurer begins to turn Primus into a mule for stealing his pig but dies in the process, leaving Primus with a clubfoot. After Julius finishes the story, Annie pronounces it a failure: "That story does not appeal to me, Uncle Julius, and it is not up to your usual mark. It isn't pathetic, it has no moral that I can discover, and I can't see why you should tell it. In fact, it seems to me like nonsense."[109] Annie's criticism reveals a number of assumptions of the (female) white listening ear: that African American folk tales should be told mainly to "appeal" to white listeners and that African American stories are successful insofar as they hit the "mark" of evoking white sympathy. Tales that do not meet these criteria, Annie informs Julius, are "nonsense," a close analogue to "noise." During Annie's dismissal, John notes Julius "looking puzzled as well as pained," although he assumes that Julius's discomfort arose because he "did not seem to understand why" he failed to please her. But Julius, empowered by his experience as conservator of the tale, responds with his own critique: "'I'm sorry m'am,' he said reproachfully, 'ef you doan lack' dat tale. I can't make out w'at you means by some er dem wo'ds you uses, but I'm tellin' nuffin but de truf. Co'se I didn' see de cunjuh man tu'n im back, fer I wuzn' dere; but I be'n hearin' de tale fer twenty-five yeahs, en I ain' got no 'casion fer ter 'spute it.'"[110] Julius criticizes Annie for using an external and unfamiliar standard to judge his story, a sensation Du Bois dubbed double consciousness just four years after Chesnutt's collection was published: the "sense of always looking at one's self through the eyes of others, of measuring one's soul by the tape of a world that looks on in amused contempt and pity."[111] Instead of remaining caught between the listening ear's Scylla and Charybdis for black artists—minstrel entertainment (John's desire) and moral instruction (Annie's expectation)—Julius disrupts the dynamic by reasserting what his tale accomplishes for *him*: a very visceral connection of his voice to the ancestors he has listened to over the last twenty-five years. Julius empowers himself through the material connection he hears through his voice, and he states unequivocally that telling the truth he has "be'n hearin'" challenges the listening ear's desire to package blackness as the sonic color line imagined it.

Julius's belief in his voice reasserts the primacy of listening and asserts aurality as a vehicle capable of conveying experiences never visible to the eye in the first place. Unlike Primus, whose clubfoot remained as evidence of his sudden (and vexed) transformation, former slaves and their descendants largely bore the marks and memories of their experiences in sites unseen. The most important truths of slavery, Julius tells Annie, cannot be seen; they can only be voiced and listened to. Isn't it a "monst'us quare" world that places the burden of proof on the aggrieved, when evidence of the oppressor's spoils still echoed in the air?

4.

"A Voice to Match All That"

Lead Belly, Richard Wright, and Lynching's Soundtrack

When Richard Wright met Huddie "Lead Belly" Ledbetter in August 1937, both men faced artistic crossroads. Ledbetter had just returned to New York City after spending several months in Shreveport, Louisiana, trying to support himself and his wife, Martha Promise, even as the newly released *Negro Folk Songs as Sung by Lead Belly* by John A. Lomax and Alan Lomax sold for 3.50 dollars a piece. Ledbetter had received only ten dollars total for contributing his life story, name, and over forty-five songs to the volume. Even though *LIFE* reported in April 1937 that Ledbetter "may well be on the brink of a new and prosperous period," it remained to be seen that summer.[1] Financially destitute, Ledbetter struggled to break his exploitative five-year contract with John Lomax that guaranteed Lomax 50 percent of Lead Belly's profits (along with full control over his bookings). Unhappy playing for the white academic audiences Lomax had preferred for Ledbetter since his release from Angola Prison in 1934—including a gig at the Modern Language Association's annual meeting—Ledbetter had yet to transition to the leftist folk crowd that comprised his fan base into the 1940s.[2] Ledbetter's visible and sonic performance of the historical legacies, economic inequities, and the social indignities of Jim Crow made Northern black urban audiences uneasy—not to mention the middle-class concern over what white America would make of the hustlers, unfaithful lovers, gamblers, and drunks populating Lead Belly's repertoire—resulting in slight black press coverage.

Himself no stranger to poverty, exploitation, and criticism, Wright also faced harsh challenges as a black professional writer. Having arrived in New York City just two months before meeting Ledbetter, Wright began to second-guess leaving his Great Migration home of Chicago, especially after his transfer to the New York Writer's Project fell through, and he begrudgingly became the *Daily Worker's* full-time

Harlem correspondent. Wright liked the paper in theory—the *Daily Worker* regularly employed black workers and addressed black issues— but the job meant taking a pay cut and reintegrating himself into the communist network after seriously questioning the party line. The pace and workload also interfered with his own writing; in the six months Wright occupied the Harlem desk, he filed forty signed articles (and an estimated 100-plus anonymous pieces), and he regularly complained of twelve-hour days.[3] What is more, Wright found himself writing what he considered tedious propaganda. On the rare occasion he covered cultural events instead of the news beat, Wright scholar Michael Fabre noted, the tone of Wright's articles markedly changed; readers caught glimpses of the passionate skill Wright would soon bring to *Uncle Tom's Children, Native Son,* and *12 Million Black Voices.*[4] His most compelling cultural feature, "Huddie Ledbetter, Famous Negro Folk Artist, Sings the Songs of His People," published August 12, 1937, provided Wright with a public site to work through the most prominent theme of his early fiction: the price young black men paid in the United States for the quality he described in Ledbetter as the "inability to take injustice and like it."[5] Wright's foray into music writing also enabled him to make sharp rejoinders to skeptical New York leftists, who heard Lead Belly as too apolitical and licentious—simultaneously "too black" and "not black enough"—to black papers, wrestling with the politics of respectability, that would not feature Lead Belly, and to John Lomax's paternalism. The occasion also sparked a friendship, at once perfect and unlikely, between the fifty-year-old singer-songwriter and the almost thirty-year-old (and still-unknown) writer, during what were likely lonely times for both men.

Wright befriended Ledbetter just before Ledbetter broke with Lomax. The power-laden, and by now mythic, Ledbetter-Lomax relationship— legal, emotional, material, symbolic, and sonic—reveals a worn edge of the sonic color line during the Depression-era United States: the sound of black masculinity as a threat. To critique this closed circuit of desire—fearful and fascinated white listeners consuming the sounds of a dangerous racialized sexuality they themselves have conjured—I unsettle the Lomax/Ledbetter dyad at the heart of Lead Belly's critical history through his sonic and personal connections to Wright and Wright's resistance to what Hazel Carby describes as Lomax's "aesthetics of the folk," "a fictive ethnicity of blackness which, when performed, enabled Leadbelly's incorporation into the national community."[6] New Lead Belly compositions addressing contemporary racial politics such as "Bourgeois Blues" and "Scottsboro Boys"—actively discouraged by Lomax—especially excited Wright, who quoted the latter prominently in the *Worker* and encouraged readers to attend Ledbetter's benefit concert for the Scottsboro legal defense fund: "Go to Alabama and ya better watch out / The landlord'll get ya, gonna jump and shout / Scottsboro Scottsboro Scottsboro boys / Tell ya what its all about."[7] Ledbetter's use of "jump and shout" pits the pleasure of sonic resistance against the pain of white violence; the last line's missing subject enables it to invoke the Scottsboro Boys' voices and definitively vest Lead Belly as one to "tell ya what its all about."

Around this time, Wright made the final edits on "Blueprint for Negro Writing," the manifesto that would assert his writerly authority and challenge his contemporaries to shun individual accomplishment and seek political and aesthetic inspiration from the collective "racial wisdom" of black folklore and music. Published in the black literary magazine *New Challenge* in October 1937, the essay also rebuked John Lomax's curatorial practices and his use of a simplistic realism to depict black lives "devoid of wider social connotations [and] devoid of the revolutionary significance of [their] nationalist tendencies."[8] Realism devoid of a social justice context, Wright argued, fed white voyeurism and commodified a sounded black pain as an intrinsic trait rather than an indictment of white racism. Whereas Lomax's brand of authenticity aestheticized black suffering and depended upon continued cultural isolation, Wright's "Blueprint" suggested that black folk aesthetics "carri[ed] the highest possible pitch of social consciousness" that recognized "the interdependence of people in modern society"; it yearned for connection across the sonic color line instead of remaining perpetually Othered by the listening ear.[9] Sound remained, according to Wright, the most liberatory force of black expression, particularly the "deepest vernacular." "Not yet caught in paint or stone, and as yet but feebly depicted in the poem and the novel," Wright intones, "the Negroes' most powerful images of hope and despair still remain in the fluid state of daily speech. How many John Henrys have lived and died on the lips of these black people?"[10] Particularly when understood alongside his relationship to Ledbetter, "Blueprint" reveals Wright's desire to merge the lived sonics of black life with the power of written words as historical testaments and weapons of protest. Writing sound, or more accurately, writing *listening*, became an important artistic strategy in Wright's social realist literary experimentation. Wright evokes the trope of listening to enmesh realism within black literary traditions while signifying on prior representations of listening in African American literature as a vehicle for knowing, being, and self-making.

This chapter examines historic traces of Ledbetter's first performances in New York alongside the early fiction of his friend and contemporary Wright, a juxtaposition that helps us understand how the sonic color line shifted in regard to black masculinity, Jim Crow violence, and the tense cultural politics of black artistic representation in the 1930s and early 1940s. As the divergent press receptions reveal, white and black audiences heard in Lead Belly different strains of what Eric Lott calls "the sound of Jim Crow." Although Lott's analysis catalogues many of its material traces—the "strident masculinism" of Howlin' Wolf's gravelly voice in "Back Door Man," for example—he concludes that the sound of Jim Crow was not a stable sonic artifact but an affective auditory grammar of "terminal exile."[11] This chapter builds on Lott's analysis by examining how American audiences recognized the sound of exile, contextualizing this period within the tightening cordons of the sonic color line and its impact on segregated listening. In other words, what modes of listening enabled Jim Crow? And what forms of listening did Jim Crow produce? How did Jim Crow listening impact the lives of white and black Americans during the 1930s and beyond?

To answer these questions, I structure my discussion of Ledbetter's and Wright's sonics a bit differently from preceding chapters. While retaining a similar comparative, historical, and methodological framework, I take a different rhetorical tack, interweaving analysis of Lead Belly's press reception with readings of Wright's fiction, with Lead Belly's struggles serving as an inspirational call for various artistic and critical responses from Wright. This structure evokes a greater sense of interchange between the two artists—rhetorically invoking what gaps in the historical record have obscured—and provides a sense of movement akin to that of African American migration from the South in the 1930s and 1940s, the beginning of what would come to be called "The Second Great Migration" following the first (and smaller) exodus during World War I. During the Depression era, black Americans created movements—migratory, activist-oriented, and artistically experimental—and experienced crossings on an unprecedented scale, and in this chapter, I use the particular biographies and artistic choices of Ledbetter and Wright to access a collective "soundtrack" linking racial violence in the South with Northern urban segregation (and white liberal responses to it). I also amplify the agency of the millions of black men and women who apprehended this flow and challenged their ensnarement in it through listening. By oscillating across regional boundaries and between these two men, I specifically examine how the sonic color line enabled segregation and gendered forms of white supremacist violence against the black male body, as well as how sonic representations of the black male body and black listening practices impacted the sonic color line in turn. I anchor the various forms of traffic in this chapter—artistic, corporeal, material, visual, auditory—through a new understanding of lynching and segregation as conjoined practices of sonic terrorism, and the resistant forms of listening that black people enacted during this period as part of growing efforts to decolonize themselves and the nation.

While this chapter will not—and cannot—reconstruct the sound or content of Ledbetter and Wright's private exchanges, it places their creative work, contemporary struggles, and historical legacies in conversation. Through a process akin to what Brandon LaBelle describes as "letting out the nested audibility and emotional force within history,"[12] I amplify the reverberations of their 1937 meeting that shudder through song lyrics, the interweave of vocal grain and guitar chords, and the words published by them and about them: essays, short stories, novels, letters, reviews. I do not seek a sense of "authenticity," a socially constructed, racially heirarchized category of value that dogged both Wright and Ledbetter throughout their (too) short careers. Instead, I re-sound aesthetic claims about "the folk" and the black male voice by Lomax and others against an ever-present backdrop of lynching in the South and other forms of Northern racial violence less spectacular but no less lethal: segregation, economic exploitation, "dead end" jobs, and brutally isolating incarceration. While Lead Belly's biographers have long miscast him as "apolitical," Wright's critics have erroneously considered him anti-blues, even anti–black vernacular culture. I offer my tandem exploration as an important corrective to both reductions.

Lynching, in particular, was an act of terrorism that seemed deliberately stripped of a soundtrack as whites circulated its photographic traces in American mainstream culture. While introducing James Allen's controversial collection *Without Sanctuary: Lynching Photography in America* (2000), musician and cultural critic Hilton Als felt the need for a "soundtrack to these pictures, which, when viewed together, make up America's first disaster movie," a cinematic reference echoing Wright's mission and technique.[13] Gustavus Stadler, however, argues that the silence of lynching was due to technological limitation rather than design. Stadler documents that "descriptive specialty" recordings of "lynchings" circulated in catalogs and at county fairs in the 1890s, often in conjunction with new sound recording technology. While live, on-site recording capabilities existed only in dreams in the 1890s, many people nonetheless believed in the veracity of these recordings. Stadler shows how their appearance at the dawn of the recording industry heralded "the saleability of the voice of racial violence" coupled with the "indelible whiteness of phonographic listening in the 1890s,"[14] factors that link the Jubilee Singers' grueling live repetition of slavery's pain in the 1870s with the stories of sharecropping, imprisonment, and hardscrabble Southern life Ledbetter summoned from his twelve-string acoustic guitar in the 1930s. However, despite white efforts to fix black performances within a matrix of white supremacy, capitalism, rapid technological change, and the listening ear—"the imagined sounds of slaughter," Stadler notes, "were heard as so well suited to the technology"[15]—black artists actuated new forms of agency within "marketability." Engaging white desire for the "black voice," singers and musicians creatively used white-run recording studios to create and conserve a sonified black modernity, voicing the pains and pleasures of black self-making and embedding sonic details of black history within the grooves of records circulating far beyond their geographic and temporal origins. The connection Stadler excavates between racism, violence, and recording also means that, as Paige McGinley argues in *Staging the Blues*, "records do not tell the whole story"; we must be more attentive to the role of live performance as a site where black blues artists such as Ledbetter embodied political struggles, bent the sonic color line's implied rules, and double-coded sounds to inflame and thwart the white listening ear[16] while making new forms of black selfhood audible to one's self and to audiences able to hear it: present, imagined, and remembered.

Lead Belly's performances, for example, anticipated Als's motivation for a "soundtrack to lynching," not just via songs such as "Gallis Pole" and "In the Pines (Where Did You Sleep Last Night)" that sonically and lyrically reference it, but also through sonic negotiations with his hypervisibility as a "to-be-lynched" body, his commitment to a "songster" performance style that integrated dance with (hi)storytelling, and his political commitment to antiracism and antifascism, evidenced by his many rally and benefit performances. Though not a musician, Wright must be considered alongside Lead Belly—and both with Billie Holiday's performances and recording of "Strange Fruit"—as sonic renderers of lynching, creating representations that sound its affect, aftermath, and the way it shapes—and is shaped by—listening. Using aural imagery and point-of-audition description, Wright created written descriptions of sound as ambient soundtracks of American racism, disrupting lynching's ocularcentrism and voyeurism, rechanneling the gaze of lynching through the ears of fictional protagonists Big Boy and Bigger Thomas. Using literary descriptions of sound to intervene in the gap between what (white) America sees and what it knows about racial violence, Wright links the overt Southern brutality Big Boy overhears to the subtle—but still terrorizing—sounds of Northern manifestations of white supremacy and white liberalism surrounding Bigger in icy Chicago. Offering sound as an epistemological point of entry to the psychological impact of racial violence, Wright's work amplifies the audibility of segregation itself, particularly the sonic color line, the racialized practices of audition and their brutal stakes, and the necessity for black people to decolonize how they hear themselves and their surroundings.

In penning a soundtrack for white supremacist violence, Wright turns Lead Belly's music inside out, emphasizing the sounds shaping it, the soundscapes lodged deeply within it, and the sonic color line conditioning its reception. Wright's fiction, inspired and inflected by Ledbetter, reveals sound as a key modality of white supremacy's assault upon black psyches, attempting to fill in the gaps of an incomplete, visually based system of discrimination colonizing black consciousness with palpable violence. In Wright's fiction, whites Other blackness as "noise"—in order to better identify, isolate, and eradicate black people—while black people remain vulnerable to random intrusions of whiteness's ferocious noises, sounds that create an illusion of omnipresence and all-encompassing power. The "soundtrack" of lynching spoke audible truths about the institutional causes and intimate effects of racial violence and showed how dividing black sound from visual blackness enabled whites to hail black people as "to-be-lynched" bodies to surveil, condemn, and consume. Wright's work, like that of Douglass, Jacobs, and Chesnutt before him, voices a skepticism regarding how—and if—black truths will ever be heard by whites, a skepticism actualized by Ledbetter's white press reception. However, Wright also directs black readers' attention to how the sonic color line functions as both a spatialization of whiteness and as an internalized norm artificially propping up white people's sense of mastery and entitlement while dangerously diminishing black people's physical, emotional, and psychological well-being. For Ledbetter and Wright, sound operated as a medium of lynching's terror and as a homeopathic treatment for the listening practices wrought by racial exclusion, a call to decolonize listening or die trying.

On the Road but Off the Record: Ledbetter Meets Wright

The Great Migration of Southern black people to the North and West indelibly shaped the sonic color line's intensification and spatialization. Jim Crow laws shifted the sound protocols of the new "separate but equal" South, while the tenor of urban neighborhoods, workplaces, and public spaces signalled whether or not newly arriving Northerners would be accommodated, conditioned, and/or de facto excluded from urban spaces. While the migration did not gain its full momentum until World War I, black people had already begun to leave the South in the closing decades of the nineteenth century, as Southern whites reseized power following the U.S. government's withdrawal of its troops and its commitment to Radical Reconstruction. Southern white men—many of whom still maintained property and wealth—regained control of local and state governments by enacting "Black Codes" that policed black mobility and labor, while simultaneously barring newly enfranchised black men from voting through restrictive laws, poll taxes, and terrorist violence. Once the Supreme Court voted down 7–1 Homer Plessy's right to ride the "whites only car" of the East Louisiana Railroad in *Plessy v. Ferguson* (1896), the "separate but equal" doctrine facilitated new Jim Crow laws seeking to segregate white and black people from cradle to grave. Furthermore, whites punished black people disproportionately via a biased legal system that kept black people from jury service and enabled heavy sentencing and extended time in contract labor camps for minor infractions such "speaking loudly in public"[17]; whites instituted a convict-lease system that was all but slavery and often a death sentence for black men (and emotional and financial devastation for their families). White courts rarely, if ever, held white people accountable for crimes they committed against black people, including murder. Post-Reconstruction white supremacy created a political system demanding black people's constant vigilance and self-policing. Wright described "answering all of his [boss's] questions with sharp yessirs and nosirs," in his harrowing 1937 essay "The Ethics of Living Jim Crow," being "very careful to pronounce my *sirs* distinctly, in order that he might know that I was polite, that I knew where I was, and that I knew that he was a *white* man."[18] In the segregated South, sonic details such as intonation proved a ready, reassuring metonym for the force of the entire system, and such command performances, scenes of subjection as Saidiya Hartman calls them, proved a constant source of microterrorism and a reminder of the always already conditional nature of black people's freedom.

Over the next six decades, millions of black people resisted Jim Crow's caste system by leaving the South. "The first mass act of independence" by black people fundamentally transformed urban space and altered the "social and political order of every city it touched,"[19] a move also experienced, expressed, and communicated through sound. In "Scottsboro Boys," written shortly after Ledbetter's arrival in New York, he "tell[s] all the colored people / livin' in Harlem *swing* / don't you ever go to Alabama" lest they face the white Southern racial violence and discriminatory practices that made so many leave their friends, family, and ancestral homes behind. In *Who Set You Flowin'?* Farah Jasmine Griffin identified the genre of the migration narrative within the African American literary tradition, thematically connecting a vast archive of visual art, music, and literature that documented, represented, processed, and imagined black migrants' moves north and west; in addition to "offering a catalyst for leaving the South," many migration narratives share scenes of "confrontation with the urban landscape" and use aesthetic methods to explore "the process of changing the sights and sounds of the cities they inhabit."[20] Upon arrival, migrants faced "new fast ways of speaking and carrying oneself," for example, and had to adapt to people "not speaking or being friendly" as in the South.[21] Many black Northerners, often recent migrants themselves, worried about the new arrivals' "country" ways shifting the soundscape and drawing white scrutiny and discrimination. Here the white hegemony of the sonic color line echoed within increasingly densely populated neighborhoods hemmed in by the residential color line; in black communities, sound became a site of class conflict and a key material signifier of the stakes of respectability politics, particularly for middle-class urbanites. *The Chicago Defender*'s preemptive "do's and don'ts" list from 1917, for instance, told new migrants: "Don't Hang Out the Windows" and "Don't Use Vile Language in Public Places"; the Chicago Urban League distributed printed cards bearing rules such as "3. Do Not Carry On Loud Conversations in Street Cars and Public Spaces," which disparaged migrants from exercising newfound freedom to sound, listen to, and audibly inhabit public space.[22] Whites did, in fact, identify and use the "noise" of black neighborhoods to justify segregation and "white flight." In addition, arbitrarily enforced noise ordinances and periodic citywide noise abatement campaigns made black neighborhoods in New York City vulnerable to aggressive and invasive policing.[23] Some white employers began to use "voice tests to weed out those from the South." Although many migrants propelled themselves north via what Jodi Roberts calls "the crucial role of optimism," such conviction proved difficult to channel once enmeshed in the shifting spatial and sonic politics of race in Northern cities.[24]

Thirty years into the Great Migration's possibilities, upheavals, and disenchantments, people continued to arrive in the North, Ledbetter and Wright among them, two artists who would find a hush harbor in the other as they charted bold but somewhat lonely paths through New York's white leftist circles. Although far from strangers to Harlem, both men defied New York's residential segregation by living outside it: Ledbetter in the East Village and Wright in various Brooklyn neighborhoods, renting a room in Fort Greene from a white family, the Newtons, while writing *Native Son*.[25] Certainly, the two men had meaningful biographical details in common that would have supported each finding a vital familiarity in the other, such as their upbringings on plantations turned sharecropping plots in the Deep South—Ledbetter in Caddo Lake, Louisiana, and Wright in Natchez, Mississippi—their eventual migrations to Southern urban centers (Dallas and Memphis, respectively) before deciding to head north, and the mutual challenges of being black artists in the white public eye.

However, in confronting unexpected archival silence regarding Ledbetter and Wright's friendship—prolific letter writers, both—I have come to the conclusion that both men intentionally kept their relationship "off the record" in order to create an aural safe space of camaraderie, artistic exchange, and down-home feeling that could remain their own, especially beyond the prying eyes of the Federal Bureau of Investigation, which had begun surveilling members of the Communist Party. The FBI compiled files on both Ledbetter and Wright during the early 1940s.

Outside of Wright's *Daily Worker* clipping, then, the specifics of his relationship with Ledbetter remain unknown. Only scant references appear in Ledbetter's papers. Ledbetter biographers Kip Lornell and Charles Wolfe quote extensively from Wright's *Worker* article but devote few sentences to their friendship, simply calling Wright "one of Huddie's drinking buddies in New York."[26] True enough, Wright and Lead Belly often crossed paths at communist-sponsored events, leftist rallies, and folk concerts in the late 1930s–early 1940s; Wright emceed at least one of the events in which Lead Belly performed, 1942's "Folk Songs on the Firing Line."[27] Michel Fabre, author of several books on Wright, characterized their relationship in the context of Wright's interest in black folk culture, revealing Lead Belly's "Irene" as Wright's favorite song. Fabre also suggested Wright honed his ear and "supplemented his knowledge of the blues" through conversations with Ledbetter and had great respect for the way Ledbetter "used words as weapons."[28]

In what follows, I will move beyond inference toward artistic influence, listening for resonances of Ledbetter's sound and struggle in Wright's fiction. This is not to say Ledbetter's oeuvre shows no traces of mutual inspiration. Although I have yet to fully trace its provenance, I

```
Bigger who is native son when he was born
He had something in his mind
Was eatin' on him - then he just wouldn't be kind
That made him have evil  mind

There was Bigger who was a native son
There was Bess she thought he was her friend
But you  see what he had done.
Then there was Mary and Jane who was a white
girl and a man who Bigger tried to  frame.

Mary taken Bigger for a ride
And Jane was sittin' by her side
Then Bigger couldn't kill feel good
That mean he began tothink  that they was makin fun.
This is what the native son done.
```

First three stanzas of "Native Son," an unsigned song found in the Sean Killeen Lead Belly Collection at Cornell University's Kroch Special Collections.

found a song entitled "*Native Son*" amongst Ledbetter's papers, accompanied by a handwritten summary of the novel.[29]

While both pages are undated and unsigned, the fact that Ledbetter kept them until his death in 1949, nine years after *Native Son*'s publication, indicates opportunity to have performed the song, even if he himself did not write it. Whether Ledbetter composed, played, or just collected the song, I believe it to be black-authored, based on how the song both assumes and prioritizes Bigger's state of mind, beginning the story of *Native Son* not with the murder of Mary but with a description of how racism "was eatin' on" Bigger's mind. No matter its authorship, the song's presence in Ledbetter's personal archive pays tribute to Wright's literary skill and both men's tenacious ability to wrest artists' lives from the violent white South.

While material evidence may be hard to come by, Wright's oeuvre contains biographic and aesthetic echoes of Ledbetter's influence. The themes of Wright's early fiction suggest Ledbetter's personal history stirred him: Ledbetter had an itinerant and violent youth on the East Texas-Louisiana border and served multiple murder sentences on Southern chain gangs. In his *Daily Worker* review, Wright described Ledbetter as the type of man called a "bad nigger" by Southern landlords, the very words he later contracted to form the name of *Native Son*'s protagonist: Bigger. Ledbetter was a lesser-known but no less important influence on the development of Bigger Thomas—a character Wright described as "not just one Bigger, but many of them, more than

I could count and more than you suspect"—alongside well-documented motivations such as the false imprisonment of the "Scottsboro nine" in 1931 and the 1938 trial of Robert Nixon in Chicago.[30]

Although Wright was himself "No Stranger to the Blues," to sample a Lead Belly standard, his literary contemporaries disparaged his interest in the music's personalities, aesthetic forms, and encompassing soundscapes. In her 1938 review of *Uncle Tom's Children*, writer and folklore scholar Zora Neale Hurston, famously called Wright "tone-deaf" because of the "broken speech of his characters."[31] And though Ralph Ellison, Wright's friend, colleague, and fellow migrant, titled his review of Wright's autobiography *Black Boy* "Richard Wright's Blues," his articulation of Wright's work as blues stresses metaphoric connections rather than aesthetic ones, such as his ability to use art to keep "fingering [the] jagged grain" of black life.[32] Forty years later, Houston Baker provided a critical reexamination of Wright's aesthetic skill after decades of critical neglect. Baker treats Wright's blues influence tropologically, addressing Wright's repeated representation of what Baker dubs "black (w)holes," sites where Wright expresses "black blues life's pressing desire."[33] Despite Baker's call for a rehearing of Wright in the context of a blues-centered vernacular theory of form, few subsequent scholars engaged with the sonic elements of Wright's fiction—blues or otherwise—aside from recent work by Tom McEnaney, Stephen Tracy, and Erich Nunn, who examine Wright's aurality in terms of radio and real estate, "King Joe," and representations of the phonograph, respectively.[34] In what follows, I contribute to this conversation by amplifying the off-the-record undertones of Ledbetter's personal and musical influence on Wright—as an urban migrant, a theorist, an activist, a fiction writer, and, importantly, a listener—an influence keenly heard in Wright's interventions toward an expanded understanding of lynching and segregation as sonic terrorism and sound as a medium enabling lynching's terrible mutation and expansion into the North's segregated cities. The reverberations begin with Wright's challenges to John Lomax's packaging of Lead Belly as a "to-be-lynched" body, a calculated visual stunt turning the sonic color line into a tripwire, with Lead Belly's voice signalling the robustness of the black masculine threat for the white Northern listening ear and viscerally conditioning how black male voices would be incorporated into the nation during the Great Depression's racial upheaval.

"These Hands Once Killed a Man": Lead Belly, Lomax, and the Sound of the "To-Be-Lynched" Body

Wright spoke candidly about Lomax and Ledbetter's exploitative relationship as "one of the most amazing cultural swindles in American history." He called out Lomax's economic mistreatment as well as his profit-fueled and "vicious tirade of publicity to the nation's leading newspapers about the Negro folk singer."[35] Beginning in 1935, Lomax demanded Ledbetter perform and take promotional photographs dressed in prison stripes and/or bandannaed and barefoot in sharecropper's overalls. Even Angola's prisoners no longer wore stripes; in 1930, then-governor of Louisiana R. G. Pleasant censured the practice because it "degrade[d] and humiliate[d] them unnecessarily."[36] Ledbetter—a fastidious dresser, particularly while performing—found Lomax's representational demands demeaning and offensive to his sense of dignity, masculinity, and professional musicianship. A symptomatic example from *LIFE*'s 1937 feature depicts Lead Belly sitting amidst bulging sacks and stacks of barrels—raw materials of the rural South, the picture implies, much like himself—open-mouthed in midsong, barefoot,

Promotional photograph from *LIFE*. The accompanying caption incorporated visual dialect: "Huddie Ledbetter, better known as Lead Belly, calls himself 'de king of de twelve-string guitar players of de worl.'"

and clad in denim overalls with a red bandanna around his neck. The spread's bluntly racist title, "Bad Nigger Makes Good Minstrel," frames Lead Belly's images within lynching discourse and plays revealingly on words; "makes" suggests both Lead Belly's transformation and a crude recipe to "make" good music using black hypermasculinity and pain as necessary ingredients.

While early press featured Lead Belly in sharecropper attire, the reviews rarely, if ever, commented on his sartorial theatrics, an omission suggesting audiences naturalized Lomax's carefully calibrated representation of Lead Belly as, in Wright's words, "a half-sex mad, knife-toting, big Black buck from Texas."[37] Wright went on to critique Lead Belly's press—and U.S. media representation of black men more generally—through allusions in both "Big Boy Leaves Home" and *Native Son*, where white-authored ALL CAPS headlines stalk his protagonists.

Lomax's costuming staged Lead Belly in the visual protocol of lynching, which, in turn, altered white Northern listeners' experience toward the threatening sonics they imagined emanating from a "to-be-lynched" body. Music scholars usually read Lomax's costuming of Lead Belly as simply an obvious sign of Ledbetter's exploitation. However, Lomax's visual commodification also relied upon and helped construct the sonic color line; Lomax hoped that the sight of Lead Belly would affirm the sound of his racialized performance, and the sound of his racialized performance would confirm his visual display of race, gender, and regional identities, activating the feedback loop between racialized sight and sound. In other words, Lomax wanted audiences to *hear* Lead Belly's overalls and bare feet, even—especially—when they couldn't see them. Lomax's visual objectification and sonic commodification also revealed how the American sonic color line sought to fix and limit black voices, defining their value only in relation to white desire, a practice connected to the practice of lynching as the most extreme form of white silence and black silencing.

Lomax's exploitation of the sonic color line's feedback loop also normalized his vision of "authenticity" and hid his active shaping of Ledbetter's sound as well as the way Ledbetter challenged Lomax's hegemony. Lomax deliberately thwarted Ledbetter's attempts to become a pop singer, for example, by slowing down his tempos, shunning set lists with dance numbers and Gene Autry covers, discouraging songwriting about recent inventions and events, and refusing to allow performances in venues that did not fit Lomax's idea of traditional blues/folk. However, Ledbetter skillfully used "code switching and subterranean parody," as McGinley's analysis reveals, to upstage Lomax and link his songster tradition to vaudeville—playing with tempo and continuing to dance onstage—strategies demonstrating practiced skill and knowing artistry belying prison stripes, bare feet, and stereotypes of "natural" musicality.[38]

Lomax's relentless marketing of Ledbetter as a "to-be-lynched" body pressured the sonic color line's dynamics toward characterizing black male voices as dangerous and hypersexual to "match" the visual framing of their bodies as inherently criminal, sexual, and strong. A white Southerner born only two years after the Civil War and raised in Bosque County, Texas, Lomax grew up within what William Carrigan calls Central Texas's "lynching culture," intensified through the recent war with Mexico, white Texans' valorization of the Texas Rangers' attacks on Native Americans, and its role as a key Western outpost of slavery. Biographers report that Lomax claimed to have witnessed a lynching as a boy. While a Harvard student, he wrote about the incident—in which white men hauled a black man accused of raping a white woman out of a courtroom and hanged him—several times, and he recalled the story "almost obsessively" in his later years (Lomax died the same year as Ledbetter, 1948). For Lomax, the Bosque County lynching was "a violent story that he could not stop seeking out and transmitting."[39] The control Lomax exerted over Lead Belly's body, sound, and image tapped into the long U.S. history of white brutalization—and brutification—of the black male body and extended the process into the sonic domain. That Ledbetter himself narrowly escaped a white lynch mob in 1930 undoubtedly made his audiovisual costuming all the more harrowing. According to the *Shreveport Times*, "Only the prompt response of the sheriff's office for help saved the negro [Ledbetter] from mob violence at the hands of a band of men who stormed the Mooringsport Jail."[40] Performing onstage offered Ledbetter a chance, however, to audibly speak back to white crowds and the opportunity to hear himself sounding what McGinley calls "a series of flights and escapes."[41]

Since the development of portable photography in the late-nineteenth century, whites circulated images of twisted, eviscerated, and silenced black bodies as a technology of social control offering whites voyeuristic pleasure in their perceived dominance. Whites used photographs of spectacle lynchings as terrorism, instructive scenes reaching far beyond the local mob to regional and national imagined communities.[42] These largely staged images weren't mere documentation but rather a part "of the entire production that is a lynching."[43] White men often carried out lynchings under the guise of "protecting" white women; many of the men they murdered stood falsely accused of raping white women and white mobs carried them from their homes or out of jail before a trial could occur, sending the message that no one was safe. More often than not, whites targeted black men who had managed to gain some type of social, economic, or political power or who refused to diminish themselves as Jim Crow law demanded. Between 1877 and 1950—roughly Lead Belly's life span—whites lynched fifty-four black men in his hometown of Caddo Parish, Louisiana, the second highest number of lynch victims in the country.[44] While lynching declined significantly after 1890, whites revived the practice in the 1930s—whites lynched ten black people in 1920 but twenty-eight in 1933—a resurgence fueled by the Great Depression's scarcity and scapegoating and enabled by a mass media–saturated environment spreading news of alleged black criminality via radio, wire services, and print. The Southern Commission on the Study of Lynching estimated that over 75,000 whites participated in lynch mobs in 1930 alone. Ashraf A. Rushdy argues that although public "lynch carnivals" began to fade during this period due to anti-lynching activism—which I discuss in a moment—the practice shifted to a more covert, impromptu practice deliberately difficult to formally call a "lynching."[45] The new form of "underground" lynching, as the National Association for the Advancement of Colored People (NAACP) described it in 1940, sent shockwaves of terror throughout America's black communities, and the ritual continued to affectively bind white people as a racial power bloc across boundaries of social class, gender, and region. Especially as antiracist activism increased during the Depression and notions of a "color-blind" public began to take hold, whites diffused the practice of lynching into other acts of white supremacy: police brutality, restrictive covenants, and segregated tenement housing. The sonic color line enabled lynching's dispersal, allowing the sounds of white supremacy intoned at lynchings to morph and circulate. Lynching's shift, as Wright's work shows, created new auditory experiences and demanded new forms of listening.

We can better hear, for example, the dangerous stakes of Lomax's "aesthetics of the folk" once we properly contextualize Lead Belly's stage(d) costuming within America's visual discourse of lynching. If we place *LIFE*'s 1937 promotional image of Lead Belly beside the 1935 photo *LIFE* ran of the dead body of lynch victim Rubin Stacy surrounded by white lynchers, uncanny resemblances surface. I reprint the Stacy image here with great care, not as "evidence" but to enable me to contextualize his life with other black men's in the 1930s to show him as a historical agent who, among many other concerns, daily negotiated white supremacy's legal and extralegal acts of diminishment, disappearance, and death. Whites murdered Stacy, a homeless sharecropper facing the precarious, itinerant life wrought by racist labor laws, in Fort Lauderdale, Florida, after a white woman named Marion Jones accused him of rape; subsequent investigations revealed he had come to her door asking for water. A group of masked white men wrested Stacy from six marshals and shot and hanged him in view of Jones's farm. His body remained on display for three hours while thousands of white people took photos and souvenirs.

LIFE's image centers and foregrounds Stacy's corpse, perhaps to reverse the heroic scale of the many lynching photos emphasizing the

Whites lynch Rubin Stacy, Fort Lauderdale, Florida, July 19, 1935.

largeness of the white mob in contrast to a solitary black body. However, the photographer's perspective also heightens the sense of Stacy's body as a trophy on display for white spectators, both within and without the photo. In placing the triumphantly smiling white girl in triangular composition with Stacy, the photographer captures white supremacy in formation. Her grin evokes horror at such acculturation, yet the angle symbolically evokes the alleged delicacy of white womanhood; the girl's smallness and crisp white "Sunday Best" contrast with the close-up of Stacy in work shirt and tattered sharecroppers' overalls, the noose taut around his broken neck where a neckerchief might have been.[46] By the hot July day in 1935 when whites killed Rubin Stacy, an overalls and workshirt–clad Ledbetter had been performing for white audiences with John Lomax for six months and a *March of Time* newsreel dramatizing Ledbetter and Lomax's meeting had been playing in movie houses nationwide for five months. In the crucial scene where a newly freed Ledbetter surprises a nervous Lomax in his hotel room, Ledbetter wears overalls, a workshirt, and a neckerchief. This is how Lomax and *Time* introduced Lead Belly's persona to the nation.

Before leaving Stacy to rest and moving on to consider the impact of Lead Belly's costuming upon the white elite listening ear of the 1930s, I mention one last similarity between the *LIFE* photos pertinent to the sonic color line's contouring of the sonics of "blackness": an emphasis on hands as a metonym for black masculinity. Reducing the complex humanity of black men and women to a collection of fleshly parts has a long genealogy back to slavery and the racial discourse enabling and undergirding it. Whites exerted power over black bodies by discursively fragmenting them and objectifying various parts as useful but ultimately fungible.[47] Hands, in particular, came to stand in for anonymous black bodies at perpetual work, adding the Americanism "fieldhand" to the English language, which the *Oxford English Dictionary* contextualizes as "*spec.* a slave working on a plantation."[48] Leigh Raiford argues that lynching continued white fragmentation of the black body postemancipation, offering a "leisure time activity" palliating white anxiety about the rise of America's new "raceless" consumer culture—theoretically, anyone could now buy anything anywhere—that threatened the white South's fantasy of blanket segregation. Lynching's photographic traces reinforced a segregated consumer economy, quite literally separating whites as consumers and black people as the consumed.[49] A crucial symbolic element in lynching photographs, black hands metonymically stood in for the larger white project of subduing black agency, manhood, and power. Stacy's hands, for example—paradoxically potent and impotent, powerful and powerless, cuffed even though arrested by death—remain pointedly in the forefront of most images from this event. Stacy's hands hang over and stand in for his phallus, a visual gesture displacing white violence onto the black body, offering up "rape" as the justification for the mob's murder (and castration as the punishment); focusing the gaze on Stacy's hands also evokes whites' fixation on fantasies of unbridled black masculinity and the perceived threat of white emasculation.

Both Ledbetter and Wright engage with lynching's representation of black hands. An additional image from Lead Belly's *LIFE* photo spread focuses specifically on Ledbetter's hands as they grip his guitar neck. In the first image, Lead Belly's hands strum so fast they register as a blur, but here his hands remain fixed and literally silenced. The accompanying caption, "These Hands Once Killed a Man," links the two images indelibly to each other, to Ruben Stacy, and to lynching's resurgence, as well as to whites' fear of black agency in America's growing recording industry, which threatened segregation's seeming totality by privatizing listening, circulating black voices in places where whites refused their material bodies safe passage, and offering black people a potentially profitable alternative to farm and factory work (along with the wherewithal accompanying American fame). Contextualizing Lead Belly's promotional images within lynching's well-established visual politics

Promotional photograph from *LIFE*: "These Hands Once Killed a Man."

recenters the music industry's power on whites as consummate listeners and consumers of blackness, a racialized economy of sound scripted by the sonic color line's invisible hand. Wright's use of the imagery of black hands challenges and reverses this process, particularly in his 1934 poem "I Have Seen Black Hands," which sweeps historically from slavery through lynching to the rising black activism of his contemporary moment. "Black hands fought and scratched and held back but a thousand white hands / took them and tied them," he writes in a middle stanza. "And some day—and it is only this which sustains me"—he prophesies at poem's end—"some day there shall be millions and millions of them [black hands] / On some red day in a burst of fists on a new horizon!"[50]

In a historical moment when, as Rushdy argues, lynchings became more "subterranean and secret," the sudden white interest in a black ex-convict's music indicates a sonic rerouting of lynching's erotic potency.[51] Combining the provocation of violence with the titillation of phallic suggestion, the *LIFE* image fetishizes Lead Belly's hands as powerful, sexual, and potentially deadly: the hands of a walking, talking, singing, "to-be-lynched" black man, but one hemmed in by the sonic color line. Lomax's framing of Ledbetter's body in relation to lynching imagery impacted how white audiences heard, interpreted, and represented his voice. Lead Belly's arrival in the late-1930s represented a shift in the sonic color line toward fetishizing a husky, emotive black male voice, beginning with blues and folk and culminating midcentury with rock and roll. What the dominant listening ear once dismissed as hopelessly flawed and in need of "cultivation," it now marked as irresistibly authentic and perpetually, delightfully inassimilable. Lynching, then, offered whites a particular way of "seeing blackness,"[52] and it produced new forms of discipline for the white listening ear seeking "a voice to match all that."

"The Miracle Voice Which Has Melted Prison Walls": Lead Belly's Press Reception

White audiences' unfamiliarity with Lead Belly did not mean they approached his sound without expectation. Ledbetter's white Northern press reception from his Lomax tours reveals how the sonic color line offered up shared understandings of Lead Belly's voice as "sweet," "charming," "husky," "enchanting," "rich," and "inarticulate"—adjectives sonifying white male sexuality, violence, and desire, disavowing and displacing it onto the bodies and voices of black male performers. Bob Steck, the white emcee for Lead Belly's 1936 performance at the leftist summer retreat Camp Unity, recalled that white listeners made immediate connections between Lead Belly's visible blackness and their audiovisual perceptions: "All of us easily recalled the sturdy, well-built, muscular man with the massive arms and a voice to match all that."[53] In what follows, I flip the script a bit on Alexandra Vazquez's concept of "the detail" to offer that specific moments of musical perception are not solely due to the performer's aesthetic choices, but that foci and fixations also result from the choices of differently positioned listeners. As Vazquez's work helps us understand, the sonic color line's emphasis on particular racialized details—timbre, volume, and affect, in the case of Lead Belly—offered white listeners a shorthand solution to the "too muchness" of black humanity, agency, and citizenship, as well as black people's increasing representation and popularity in American musical culture. I find her observation that details "also carry what can feel like unbearable reminders of past violences" particularly useful as the details of Lead Belly's voice that white listeners amplified resonated with affective visceral echoes of white lynching practice and carried traces of the sonic color line's representational violence.[54]

White press reviewers used loaded terms such as "sweet" to describe Lead Belly's voice, a term carrying dominant anxieties about black masculinity and sexual power. One of the first pieces published upon Ledbetter's arrival in New York City set the tone for much early press: the infamous *New York Herald Tribune* article "Sweet Singer of the Swamplands Here to Do a Few Tunes between Homicides." "Sweet" feminizes Lead Belly, in that it echoes traditional descriptions of female operatic voices and connects his voice to his body, but here "sweet" had less to do with vocal tone and much more with assumptions about sexual prowess and his voice as an instrument of pleasure. Short for "sweetback," "sweet" described pimps, good lovers, and/or men financially supported by women in exchange for sexual satisfaction: a "sweet man" or "sweet papa." The blues culture of the 1930s often valorized the sweetback, especially because musicians with "sweet" voices could ply their trade without toiling long hours at dangerous, dead-end "straight" jobs, which for black men largely meant demeaning service work or grueling factory and farm labor. Being a "sweetback" turned the representational tables on the high unemployment rate for black men during the Depression, which hovered around 50 percent in 1935 (compared with 32 percent for white men). Cultivating a reputation as a "sweetback" implied a choice to live outside white masculine expectations rather than submit to economic discrimination and/or accept white gender norms. However, the *Herald Tribune* article uses "sweet" to play on white stereotypes of black hypersexuality, constructing a racialized masculinity unavailable to white men and therefore representing a continued source of fear and fascination. The article represents Lead Belly's "sweet" voice as the sonic equivalent of his phallus:

> Lead Belly's voice causes brown-skinned women to swoon and produced a violently inverse effect upon their husbands and lovers. A large scar bears witness to his dreadful charm and a knife that was fortuitously dull. Big Boss [how the article refers to John Lomax, allegedly because Lead Belly did so himself] fears that in Harlem something catastrophic may happen when Lead Belly starts to sing.[55]

For the benefit and discipline of their readership, the paper evokes Lead Belly's sweetness as a "catastrophic" potency and "dreadful charm" threatening the social order. It also represents black audiences as particularly susceptible to sweetness, an image of the sonic color line framing whites as controlled observers of black licentiousness, a move I will discuss further in the next chapter in regard to radio.

In particular, the white press uses "husky" to heighten the racialized sexuality in Lead Belly's voice, a term linked to charm, enchantment, and emotional release. The same *Tribune* review describes his voice as a "husky tenor" that "ineluctably charm[s] the ears of those who listen."[56] In addition to masculine heft, "husky" implies emotiveness and a related vocal aberrance. The *OED* defines "husky" as a specific reference to "persons and their voice," particularly the sound of being "dry in the throat, so that the timbre of the voice is lost, and its sound approaches more or less a hoarse whisper (an effect of continued speaking, laryngeal inflammation, or violent emotion)."[57] "Husky" encompasses the mystical, "raw," and "weird" sounds whites heard in black voices in the nineteenth century, while layering on hypersexuality, violence, and emotional spectacle. While the sounds of "plaintive[ness]" and "pathos" link Lead Belly's performances to dominant Reconstruction-era conceptions of the black voice, "huskiness" genders and sexualizes Lead Belly's sound much more directly. While not explicitly masculine, "husky" implies girth and mass. After Lead Belly's Harvard performance, the *Boston Globe* noted his "plaintive, husky, voice . . . the miracle voice which has melted prison walls and wrung pardons from Governors."[58] And if even the seemingly sturdy government institutions limiting black mobility fell prey to his titillating sound, what other walls might "melt" (with all sexual connotations implied)?

Widely varying opinions on the depth of Lead Belly's voice reveal the distortions of the listening ear, connecting vocal depth to the perceived violent criminality and mesmerizing hypersexuality of the "to-be-lynched" body. The *Herald Tribune* claimed it was a "husky tenor" and the *New Yorker* an "enchanting baritone."[59] Other reviews depict his voice as a spellbinding, palpable sonic force of black masculinity that white audiences must be wary of while indulging in its allegedly transformational power. Such descriptions give a sexual charge to the notion of enchantment, simultaneously hypermasculinizing Lead Belly and feminizing him as a seductress, an erotics Niambi Carter calls "intimacy without consent" in her study of lynching as sexual violence.[60] Listening to Lead Belly was not just a way for whites to hear black manhood but to touch and be touched by it too.

One of the most common details white critics mentioned while describing the mesmerizing depth of Lead Belly's voice is "rich," an adjective rife with sonic, technological, and racialized resonance. According to the *OED*, "rich" had already marked a sound "full and mellow in tone" for hundreds of years. However, the sonic color line enabled the notion to proliferate in American entertainment culture that black voices were "richer" than white voices, a stereotype that accelerated with the development of recording technology and the rise of the recorded music industry. Alice Maurice, Tim Brooks, and Stadler all cite white recording engineers and equipment salespeople's beliefs that black voices made superior recordings because they possessed a "richness" uniquely suited to early acoustic recording, a process dogged by limited sensitivity, nonexistent dynamics, and poor frequency ranges.[61] Early recording and broadcasting equipment amplified, propagated, and commodified the emergent ideal of the listening ear: a baritone voice coded as masculine and authoritative, resulting in the "husky" "richness" of Lead Belly's voice sounding a dangerous, enchanting excess.

Because music and broadcast industries opened up new forms of agency to black performers—threatening whites with consumption by the very voices they so desired—the sonic color line worked to thwart the deep, rich, husky black voice's disruptive potential by reducing its sonic and lyrical detail to inarticulate sound, thereby enabling the white listening ear full rein/reign to experience pleasure without fear of enthrallment. White reviewers claimed Lead Belly's vocals could not be understood, let alone as meaningful words; white audience accounts emphasize how Lead Belly "sang with an intensity and a passion that swayed an audience many times unable to understand a word of his songs."[62] The sonic color line marking the racialized border between articulate and inarticulate resonates strongly with the power dynamics Charles Chesnutt represented via Uncle Julius's storytelling persona and his interactions with his white Northern listeners. In his critique of Chesnutt, John Edgar Wideman argues segregation worked to create "two distinct types of speech," and its "consequent rituals" attempted to amplify "the *seams* of mutual intelligibility" between them.[63] However, while Julius's white listeners asserted their power by disparaging his speech—which they perceived as idiosyncratic and incorrect—Lead Belly's listeners attempted to secure their control by revelling in their refusal to work to understand him and finding pleasure (and profit) in stripping his sound of meaningful detail. As Pete Seeger remembered, "Sometimes audiences couldn't understand [Lead Belly's] Louisiana accent"; however, he noted that the element whites claimed made him unintelligible was what aspiring (white) folk singers sought to reproduce.[64] Part of Lead Belly's "authenticity" depended on his inaudibility—and iterability—to the listening ear of white cultural elites, amplifying their linguistic privilege and granting them access to his body. Here the listening ear marks the Other as always already culturally deficient; he must transform himself to be heard as articulate yet, once this shift occurs, can no longer be culturally "authentic."

The inarticulate authenticity many white listeners craved also represents a refusal to hear Lead Belly's music as present-oriented. The listening ear thus buried potential notes of protest, hearing Lead Belly's songs as enchantingly unintelligible and inarticulate. White audiences often lamented the passing of the "authentic" black musical culture they heard in Lead Belly's voice and, through sound recording, sought to preserve and revive; Lomax frequently objectified Lead Belly as a "walking archive." Black press coverage, on the other hand, stressed the potentially resistant sonics and contemporary elements of Ledbetter's repertoire, which the *Pittsburgh Courier* found powerful because his songs "often sound a note of protest, of sarcasm, of bitterness, or revolt, which is precisely the point of view that the Negro's sensitive exploiters do not wish to hear expressed."[65] White listeners tuned out elements of protest in blues along with its "exuberant expression of survival and endurance," while the listening ear attuned itself to folklorists and record producers' marketing of blues as a "product of black misery."[66]

Lead Belly's different reception in the black press reveals "enchantment" as a classed, raced, gendered, and historically contingent response to black male voices, one showing how the sonic color line's selective listening habits tune out and/or mishear sounds of black agency. The *New York Amsterdam News* downplayed the purported enchantment of Ledbetter's voice, debunking the "spectacular and romantic story concerning the pardon which Governor Pat Neff of Texas had granted to a man who had been convicted of murder." While white press accounts granted Lead Belly's mystical voice the power to hold the governor spellbound, black press coverage depicted the governor as merely an arbiter of talent rather than a thrall: "So impressed by a song Lead Belly had written in his honor, the governor immediately signed his pardon."[67] This account made clear that although Lead Belly's voice expressed agency, it remained distinct from the very different sort of power wielded by the pardoning governor and the prison system.

By and large, Ledbetter the man received more attention in Northern black papers than Lead Belly the persona, a decision that emphasized black audience responses and recentered black listening practices at the heart of black performance. Emphasis on the matchless qualities of Lead Belly's talents challenged the sonic color line's stereotype of the essential (and excessive) musicality of black people. The black press highlighted Lead Belly's voice as a deliberately disciplined instrument, not an essentially raced and gendered sound. McGinley also argues that such emphasis was partly due to the black middle class's "questioning whether or not Ledbetter was a fit representative of black uplift," but it also tactically challenged Lomax's insistence on "the myth of blues' *terroir*—its inexorable tie to agricultural labor." Black newspapers emphasized Ledbetter as a professional who played mainly for black audiences and his Harlem performances as both a logical outcropping of his musical career and a steep challenge, as black audiences in New York favored the "urban, microphoned modernist" sound of jazz performers such as Lena Horne, whom I discuss in the next chapter.[68] Critic Joe Bostic suggested the urbane scat stylings of jazz vocalist and bandleader Cab Calloway—slated to perform the week after Lead Belly—as a sonic antidote "to make me (and you too) forget his sour show."[69] And while historical consensus has deemed the Apollo performance a "failure," McGinley compellingly argues that Lead Belly's lackluster reception should be considered as a "performance out of time" instead, one that amplified the sonic impact of Ledbetter's years of imprisonment and confronted Northern migrants with the sounds of times, places, and people left behind.[70] Furthermore, Ledbetter's sound echoed a warning that migration alone did not guarantee safe passage; the sonic color line reached beyond any regional boundary, wedding the white gaze to the listening ear in the construction of black people as "to-be-lynched" bodies.

Re-presenting Lynching and Racial Violence in the 1930s

Ledbetter's musical example offered Wright, a politically active migrant escaping Southern "lynching culture"—in addition to the close calls he details in "The Ethics of Living Jim Crow," whites in Elaine, Arkansas, murdered Wright's uncle Silas Hopkins, a prosperous saloon owner, in 1918—a method of sonified black agency refocusing lynching's gaze onto white supremacy itself. After he met Ledbetter, Wright's personal listening practices shifted; he became much more interested in Southern black music, studying it and recalibrating his embodied ear to hear more than misery in the genre. In his *Daily Worker* article, Wright subtly positioned himself as Ledbetter's ideal listener, opening the piece with Lead Belly on a porch "strumming his 12-string guitar" and the writer at his feet. Wright goes on to emphasize the virtuostic diversity and expansiveness of Ledbetter's sound and musical knowledge, not as an old-timey repository but as a living force: "It seems that the entire folk culture has found its embodiment in him," Wright wrote. "It seems he knows every song his race has ever sung."[71] Wright pursued knowledge of black folk music back through the nineteenth century, studying the same Jubilee Singers archive at Fisk University that I did for the previous chapter. Drawing from Fisk's materials, he wrote a screenplay about the Jubilee Singers shortly after publishing *Native Son*, called *Melody Limited*. Although the screenplay is fascinating on many levels, I'll limit my discussion to one: the insight it offers into how Wright came to listen differently to the black folk tradition. He tells the Jubilee Singers' story through a fictional band manager, the "young Negro Bob Simms," a Northerner frustrated by the sound of Southern black culture. "Hears Shortning Bread song," Wright directs, "hears a spiritual sung in church as he passes, looks at stars. Why do they make so much noise? he asks himself. If it wasn't for that hollering this would be ideal, a paradise."[72] However, inspired by the singers, Simms eventually sheds most of the fear, pain, and discomfort the spirituals sparked in him and, by the end of the screenplay, begins to merge this musical tradition with his Northern urban identity.

In prose fiction written prior to *Melody Limited*, Wright used the trope of the listener to examine how white supremacy colonized listening, how and why black men came to hear themselves as noise—"to-be-lynched" bodies out of place and time—and hear black folk culture as an embarrassing remnant rather than a powerful legacy capable of fuelling contemporary resistance. By underscoring how white supremacy interpolated a diverse array of whites as listeners—Northern and Southern, liberal and conservative, male and female, young and old—Wright revealed lynching to have an even wider range of terror, a stronger role in white racial formation, and a deeper impact on U.S. social and political structures than previously thought. Wright's early fiction emphasized the profoundly aural aspects of lynching and other forms of white racial violence, signifying on the trope of the listener to expand "lynching" (and black perception of the practice) to include sham trials, hyperaggressive policing, the prison system, sharecropping, segregation, predatory landlording, and political corruption.

To better understand the stakes of Wright's aural representations of lynching, I contextualize them within contemporary conversations about representational politics in antilynching responses, in particular the art exhibitions in New York City in the mid-1930s organized by the NAACP and the Communist Party—of which Wright was an active member throughout the 1930s. Antilynching activists debated whether or not to utilize lynching photos as a counterrepresentational strategy ever since Ida B. Wells published one in *A Red Record* (1895).[73] Was it desirable—or even possible—to reframe white supremacist photographs as proof of lynching's systemic terrorism? During their respective tenures as leadership of the NAACP, W. E. B. Du Bois (editor of *The Crisis* from 1910 to 1934), James Weldon Johnson (secretary from 1920 to 1930), and Walter White (secretary from 1931 to 1955) labored over decisions to republish intercepted photographs in antilynching material, fearing republication might unleash precisely the type of violence, anger, and fear they protested.[74] By the 1930s, black political groups remained wary of recirculating lynching images but developed strategies such as pointed and ironic captioning to unsettle the image's initial intent: "Do not look at the Negro," read the caption on the protest flyer circulated by the NAACP after Rubin Stacy's lynching, ". . . instead, look at the SEVEN white children who gaze at this gruesome spectacle." Other outlets used image cropping to evoke a sense of complicity in their readers, zooming in to the white mob or focusing on the victims' bodies.[75]

The NAACP and the Communist Party explored other avenues of visual protest against lynching. The same year Wright published the antilynching poem "Between the World and Me" and began to write "Big Boy Leaves Home," the NAACP flew a black flag emblazoned with "A MAN WAS LYNCHED YESTERDAY" twenty times from the window of their New York office; then NAACP director Walter White also organized the controversial *An Art Commentary on Lynching* at the Arthur U. Newton Galleries in uptown Manhattan. White commissioned at least one of the pieces to comment on the Scottsboro case.[76] The exhibit, and others like it, exploded lynching photographs' documentary claims, mediated lynching through color, perspective, light, composition, and other representational strategies, and refocused the juridical gaze onto the white mob rather than the lynched black figure. However, the process of mediation fixed these counterrepresentations in a tense referential relationship to the "original" photographs; to contest the images, they featured graphic depictions of the black male body victimized and in pain, leaving many critics to wonder if the artwork accentuated racial subordination despite its intentions to the contrary.[77] Overall, visually re-presenting lynching proved to be fraught, operating within the politics of looking that constituted lynching itself.

The Soundtrack

New developments in sound cinema intrigued Wright and intensified his literary engagement with America's politics of looking.[78] Despite— and perhaps because of—childhood memories of segregated movie houses without bathrooms for black patrons and an interminable parade of stereotypical black characters, Wright told writer and friend Margaret Walker "he felt like movies were like life itself, and he openly admitted to [her] that he modeled his dramatic and melodramatic fiction after the movies."[79] Farah Jasmine Griffin also understands Wright's fiction cinematically, positioning it against the "nostalgia of Hollywood in films like *Gone With the Wind* (1939) and *Stormy Weather* (1943)."[80] With *Melody Limited*, Wright attempted to work more directly with film, but as biographer Hazel Rowley delicately explains, "it was not an idea that easily found funding" in the Jim Crow entertainment industry of the 1940s.[81] Wright found Hollywood's resistance to his screenplay for *Native Son* equally insurmountable, despite the novel's popularity. Eventually, Argentina Sono Film shot the movie in Buenos Aires with Wright in the role of Bigger Thomas; the film was successful in South America, but American censors defanged it both politically and aesthetically before its arrival in the States. Feeling like commodified grist for Hollywood's racial propaganda mill instilled a sense of the medium's power in Wright, along with a desire to hijack the camera from the white gaze and enlist it in antiracist struggle. Wright first began his cinematic experiments via prose fiction, using sensory imagery to create powerful audiovisual literary experiences. Several critics have noted Wright's desire to create a cinematic experience for *Native Son's* readers; however, rarely do they look beyond its visuality.[82] I make a distinction here between visuality—which refers only to sight—and the cinematic, which references the interplay between visual and audio techniques.

Given sound's multidirectional qualities, cinema's auditory dimension comes closest to enacting Wright's desire to create a story that could "'enclose' the reader's mind in a new world," particularly in the earliest days of "Talkies."[83]

In 1933, the year Wright turned 25, new editing technology signalled the death of the "talkie" and the beginning of "sound cinema": dialogue could now be mixed with music and background sounds without losing sound quality. Rick Altman argues that, "throughout the thirties, nearly every important technological innovation can be traced back to the desire to produce a persuasive illusion of real people speaking real words." He describes this relationship as "sound cinema's fundamental lie," a falsehood insinuating "that the sound is produced by the image when in fact it remains independent from it."[84] Merging these two sensory modalities and limiting aurality's role in cinematic narrative reified vision as the dominant sense in film and beyond. When Wright began *Uncle Tom's Children*, the notion of the "sound track"—called thus because sound information was etched directly onto celluloid film alongside the visual images—had only recently come into being. Therefore, we must locate Wright's aesthetics within specific realist developments in cinematic technique during the 1930s, specifically the dramatic increase in synchronous sound's clarity, the "inaudibility" of sound editing, and contemporary iterations of the sonic color line.

Operating within the same supremacist regime that produced lynching, the cinematic practice of wedding "real" people to "real" words abetted the construction of the racial "reality" of both visual and sonic color lines. As Maurice argues, filmmakers found the notion of the "black voice" essential to the illusion of synchronous sound, especially when new sound technologies remained clunky, unsettling, and distracting to mainstream white audiences accustomed to silent films. Many a silent film star's career ended because their singular "real" voice couldn't "match" the infinite array audiences had imagined. However, because of the sonic color line, white audiences felt they knew precisely what a "black voice" sounded like, an American cultural yardstick the film industry exploited to mainstream its newest technology. Filmmakers relied upon the sonic color line to "match" black voices with black bodies to sell audiovisual cinema as realistic to white American audiences. Using black personalities and lavish performance numbers featuring black casts, Maurice argues, became a "common strategy of the early sound era: selling the sound cinema via black performers and selling black performers (primarily to white audiences) via the sound cinema."[85] As synchronous technology improved, and better microphone placement enhanced the illusion of spatial depth, the realism of cinematic sound took on two powerful new valences: that of appearing not to deviate from what Mary Ann Doane describes as the "ideology of the visible"—what you hear is what you see and vice versa—while at the same time carrying meaning in its own right.[86]

By juxtaposing aural and visual "tracks" in his work, Wright's early fiction resists the tyranny of the "ideology of the visible" and the sonic color line, using vivid metaphoric representations of sound to expose its ability to contest the gaze's ideological and psychological freight, even as it so often bears its weight. Motivated by Ledbetter's life and sound and the challenge of sonifying black literary representation, Wright's early fiction tweaked realist forms to reckon with the sound track of the Great Migration for black men, using the trope of the listener to explore black male subject formation, racial terror, and avenues of resistance at Jim Crow's height. I use "sound track" both as a literal referent to cinema's aurality and as a metaphor positing sound as potentially autonomous from sight even as it remains inextricably intertwined. Particularly when contracted into its contemporary spelling and usage, the term "soundtrack" encapsulates the cinematic and phonographic—Lead Belly's timbres and Wright's words—while contesting the sonic color line's naturalized match between sound and body.

Witnessing the Sonic Color Line: "Big Boy Leaves Home"

Wright's "Big Boy Leaves Home" soundtracks the spectacular violence of Southern lynching as well as the everyday terror apprehended by black boys as they grow into "to-be-lynched" American bodies. Within the short story, slavery's aural imagery—singing voices, screams, barking bloodhounds, pastoral insect drones, and bird songs[87]—familiar from Douglass, Jacobs, and Chesnutt, reveals how black subjectivity continued to be wrought by terror in a Jim Crow regime built on (and nostalgic for) antebellum power dynamics. However, in signifying on the trope of the listener, Wright atomizes, reconstructs, and reassembles many key audiovisual moments from Douglass's *Narrative*, remixing it as a cinematic soundtrack of segregation: the pastoral for-whites-only landscape, the murder of a man at water's edge, a woman's scream, the scene of enforced listening to violence, and the sound of song rising out of covering woods. Wright's soundtrack links segregation to slavery while showing how the terror of lynching diffuses itself moment by moment into one's everyday life through listening.

Wright's literary soundtrack amplifies how black boys came to understand the codes of the sonic color line as lifesaving yet paradoxically self-destructive. Terror frames and permeates "Big Boy Leaves Home," even as the five-part story opens in an Edenic setting, depicting Big Boy and friends Larry, Bobo, and Buck playing hooky from school. In section one, Wright constructs a sense of black male preadolescent community through sound, a vulnerable site of "easy laughter" and private joy that the boys imagine beyond white surveillance. Wright connects the boys' stolen afternoon with the long tradition of African American expressive culture he writes of in his Lead Belly review: "stolen sounds" that have carved out community, history, and shared space in the face of white regimes of power. As the boys walk to the forbidden swimming hole on a white man's property, Big Boy, Bobo, Larry, and Buck revel in the pleasant sound of one another's voices, a quartet "blending in harmony." Wright doesn't distinguish between the speaking boys for several pages; he depicts their voices as unified, each an "echo" of the other.[88] Composed almost entirely of sound—dialogue, song, laughter, and a train whistle—the scene envelops the boys in intimacy. Through the sound of "shrill, cracking, adolescent" male voices, Wright presents a fantasy of male identity construction that excludes and resists the maternal, which Cheryl Higashida describes as "another instrument of Jim Crow socialization."[89] Their intertwined voices sing, "Yo mama don wear no drawers / Ah senna when she pulled em off / N she washed em in alcohol, / N she hung em out in the hall / N then she put 'em back on her QUALL!" performing symbolic violence by reducing the "mama" to her sexualized, reproductive body.[90] These sexually charged lyrics—coupled with the boys' pubescent cracks—show how black boys mobilized sound to claim and gender space, sonifying the politics of exclusion pressuring and pressured by black masculinity.

In sounding out a black masculine space against the spatial codes and cues of the sonic color line, Wright's opening tableau amplifies the boys' vulnerability and the fragility of their claims on the Southern landscape, especially in relationship to the established literary tradition of the (white) American Southern pastoral.[91] As I discussed in the previous chapter, white Southern writers used the pastoral to idealize, preserve, and mythologize plantation slavery as a "more healthful, life-sustaining time" for all.[92] These stories combined an idyllic rural landscape with stock representations of honorable paternal whites and cheerful and subservient black people. In the antebellum era, slaveholders imagined a quiet, "idealized and romanticized" plantation life in opposition to a noisy industrial North, a process only intensifying after the war.[93] Operating at the intersection of the Southern pastoral and the sonic color line, harmony and quietude continued to be aural metaphors for a segregationist social order.

The stakes of the black boys' vocal resistance to white quietude only increase as Wright's soundtrack amplifies the racial violence already audible in the boys' fugitive pastoral afternoon. In Wright's reworked pastoral, the history of slavery, racism, and lynching (and resistance against them) is as endemic to the landscape as the trees, rivers, birds, and cricket songs.[94] Big Boy suggests they "go to the creek fer a swim," but the boys initially refuse: "N get lynched? Hell naw!" Once they arrive at Old Man Harvey's fence—a Jim Crow version of Colonel Lloyd's forbidden garden in Douglass's *Narrative*—they share an unspoken realization: no more singing and playing without concern for volume. The fence makes the sonic color line manifest; crossing it places the boys within white earshot, and the meaning of their voices rapidly shifts from pleasurable harmony to potentially dangerous noise. As they begin to police one another's sound, their temporary Eden dissipates. "Don holler so loud!" one boy reprimands. Another seconds: "They kin hear yo ol big mouth a mile erway!"[95] An aural form of Du Boisian double-consciousness, the boys no longer hear themselves *as* themselves, but rather they imagine themselves through a colonized listening practice, internal projections of how the white listening ear hears and understands them as "to-be-lynched" bodies.

However, as Wright's plot unfolds, the boys learn that even self-policing cannot save them when confronted with the sound hierarchized above any other in the Southern quietude: a white woman's scream. Within moments of stripping down and diving in, a young white woman named Bertha spots the boys and screams for her boyfriend, Old Man Harvey's son, who arrives with rifle in hand. To the dominant white listening ear, the sound of the white female scream—whether heard, rumored, or imagined—enabled the practice of lynching. Key to the "mythology of the [black] rapist," the aural screen of the white female scream effectively masked lynching's political and institutional agenda, enabling white men to use lynching in combination with segregation and disenfranchisement to maintain their ascendancy in the face of African American citizenship privilege and rising social, economic, and legal power.[96] The aural image of the scream also objectified white female sexuality as white male property,[97] circumscribing white female identity as fragile even as the public power ascribed to this sound muffled the shouts of lynching's victims and the cries of black women, whom white men frequently subjected to physical and sexual violence (including lynching) with little to no recourse.[98] In "Big Boy Leaves Home"—and, I argue, in *Native Son*—Wright exposes how the sonic color line valorizes the white female scream and embeds it within lynching's visual representation as the sound that truly enchants the listening ear.[99]

The naked black boys know the code of the sonic color line, immediately connecting the white woman's scream to their probable castration—a central component of the ritual of lynching—and/or death. Upon seeing Bertha on the embankment, Big Boy's voice drops to a fearful whisper: "It's a woman ... A *white* woman!" Big Boy's "*white*" causes the boys to anticipate the ensuing racial performance; they "instinctively cove[r] their groins." The boys try to explain that they merely want to get their clothes, but Bertha refuses to listen; she stands mute "with her hand covering her mouth" as if waiting for her cue. As soon as Big Boy moves toward his clothes—in Bertha's narrative a move toward *her*—she screams. Wright repeats "the woman screamed" three times in a matter of sentences, constructing it as the soundtrack shaping the violence that follows. Wright also uses the italics signalling a vocal inflection on "*white*" as a leitmotif. When Big Boy's father rushes home to help his son, all Big Boy's mother has to say is "Saul, it's a *white* woman!" Her tone shift as she says "*white*" *is* the sonic color line; the sound embeds the white woman's scream in the word, spatializing segregation's reach into their home. Big Boy reacts to the sound as if struck.[100]

Also qua Douglass, Wright represents how the sonic color line enables divergent listening experiences for white and black men in the face of a white woman's scream—as well as how differently it impacts the Southern soundscape. To the white male listening ear, Bertha's scream demands, enables, and excuses immediate violence. Old Man Harvey's son, Jim, announces his presence not with his voice but with the "CRACK!" of his rifle, a sound fixing what Jim "sees"—a gang rape scene—as the official narrative. The first "CRACK!" of the white man's rifle/voice is met with the "grunt" of Lester's dying exhalation; with the second "CRACK!" comes the creek's "bubbling" as it swallows Buck's lifeless body.[101] Hearing the contrast between the loud noise of white power and the return of quietude, Big Boy immediately apprehends that he will be next and that whites will secret away the boys' murders. Suddenly, he wrests the gun from Jim's hands. The final "CRACK!" in this scene brings Jim's death, saving Big Boy's life but giving him only fleeting power. Bertha's screams redouble, metaphorically and literally signalling the lynch mob soon to be after him.

From section three of the story on, Wright limits the readers' experience of the soundscape to Big Boy's point-of-audition, a move linking the landscape's pastoral quietude with the racial horror undergirding its placidity, while dramatizing how the sonic color line colonizes and terrorizes black people, disciplining them to apprehend the quieter signs of white violence lurking in the sonic details of what Patricia Yaeger calls the South's "unseen everyday."[102] Wright's soundtrack performs this tension; Big Boy hears the brutality intrinsic in the quietude. Once the boys arrive home, any sound breaking the silence potentially signals the lynch mob's approach. Wright's aural montage of minute household sounds emphasizes the vulnerability of black domestic space to white power. No omniscient narrator alerts readers to the actions of the white community, replicating how the family dreads the terror-laden sound of footsteps and door knocks. Even the typical domestic sounds add to the tension mounting within the small house, which Wright literalizes with aural imagery: "They were quiet, thinking. The water kettle on the stove sang." The singing kettle eases no pressure; rather, it directs attention to the increasing intensity.[103]

As the sky darkens and Big Boy eventually hides away in an outdoor kiln hoping to survive the night, Wright increasingly restricts his protagonist's sensory perception to listening, attuning black readers to the trope of the listener and refusing white readers the familiar panoramic gaze of the lynching photograph and its voyeuristic privilege. When Big Boy overhears the lynch mob arrive and capture his friend Bobo, Wright uses aural imagery to place readers into his moment-by-moment experience. Wright's layered soundtrack mixes Bobo's "shrill screams" with the mob's joyful singing and the "cricket cries" of the countryside, amplifying the suppressed sonics of Lead Belly's music while exposing lynching and the white Southern pastoral as interdependent systems of power. By representing Big Boy's terror-filled listening experience as the soundtrack to whites' lynching of Bobo, Wright recasts the practice as white criminality rather than extralegal justice.

In addition to challenging white voyeurism, Wright's aural imagery unravels the sonic color line's naturalized matches between sounds and racialized bodies. Wright links white bodies to sounds grotesque in their mundane glee: "They had started the song again. '*We'll hang every nigger t a sour apple tree . . .*' There were women singing now. Their voices made the song round and full. Song waves rolled over the top of the pine trees . . ." Wright also represents Bobo's screams of pain, but Big Boy's point-of-audition disembodies their sound: "*A* scream quivered," "*the* scream came again," or simply "screams, one on top of the other, each shriller and shorter than the last."[104] Whereas Douglass's representation of Hester's scream tied the sound even more firmly to her body—seeking a semblance of Hester's agency and attempting to sensitize his audience to slave suffering—Wright refuses to locate the screams within Bobo's throat, emphasizing lynching as a technology for producing these sounds as an object of desire—and of sexual climax—for the gathered mob. As Carter argues, "The act of lynching, particularly castration, is a demonstration of male-on-male sexual abuse," although rarely discussed as such.[105] BoBo's screams, emanating from everywhere, bear the representational weight of hundreds of lynchings—both as a communal expression of black outrage and as an aural symbol of whites' standardization of the process.

For the young black male protagonists of "Big Boy Leaves Home," listening functions simultaneously as a disciplining force, a conduit of terror, a tool of survival, and a purveyor of resistant knowledge about white supremacy, particularly how the sonic color line enabled the regional fluidity of American racial regimes of power. For black readers of the Great Migration generation, Big Boy's night in the kiln—simultaneously grave and womb—embodied the "bloodstained gate" so many passed through on their way out of the South, a reminder of the death they left behind and its continued visceral impact on their daily lives and listening practices. Wright's evocation of the trope of the listener sounded a provocative alarm about the difficult necessity of decolonizing one's listening, particularly in a Northern urban soundscape that seemed deafeningly different yet hauntingly similar. While Wright leaves readers wondering as to Big Boy's ultimate destiny once he arrives up north smuggled inside a laundry truck—literally the South's "dirty laundry"—he leaves no question as to the fate of *Native Son*'s protagonist Bigger Thomas, whose own mother describes him as bound for the gallows.

When Wright himself moved from Jackson, Mississippi, to the city of Memphis, Tennessee, in 1925, he noticed immediately how "here my Jim Crow education assumed a quite different form. It was no longer brutally cruel, but subtly cruel." The feeling only intensified upon moving to Chicago in 1927. In order to make palpable the ways in which Northern "forces of oppression are less visible," Wright combined aural imagery and the trope of the listener with a realist aesthetic in *Native Son*, showing how the sonic color line spatialized race in American cities and revealing lynching's long reach across the Mason-Dixon Line.[106] Like Big Boy, Bigger is a Southern migrant driven north by racial violence; a white lynch mob killed his father five years before the novel begins. Chicago proves not to be the promised land Big Boy and his friends envisioned when they sang of "a train bound for Glory."[107]

Wright refines his point-of-audition technique in *Native Son*, representing Bigger as a listener to amplify the criminalized topography of his life in South Side Chicago. While Chicago's soundscape differs qualitatively and quantitatively from the tense quietude of "Big Boy"'s rural setting, Wright uses the same descriptive palette to embed a similar sense of danger in the urban landscape: droning bees become droning furnaces; whirring rattlesnakes transform into whirring fire hoses; howling dogs resound in Chicago's howling winds; the "fitful song" of the cricket is amplified in the police siren's "terror-song." As in *Uncle Tom's Children*,

Native Son's soundtrack represents not an omniscient catalogue of all audible sounds, but rather its imagery vivifies how Bigger apprehends the environment that envelops and entraps him.[108] And while Bigger's ability to apprehend the sonic color line enables his day-to-day survival, his migrant's ears disciplined to hear the lynch mob's roar in everyday urban cacophony ultimately exact a terrible toll.

"Magic Whiteness without Sound": *Native Son*

In contrast to "Big Boy Leaves Home," *Native Son* immediately barrages the reader with mechanical sounds signifying the sonic color line's spatialization of black urban space. Perhaps one of the most iconic aural images within African American literature, the onomatopoeic "Brrrrrriiiiiiinnnnnng"—ripping across the page with a grating seven r's and seven shrill i's—opens the novel in medias res, thrusting readers into a segregated world where time has already run out; the alarm's urgent howl proved a harbinger of the many urban uprisings in the Depression's wake. Griffin examines the alarm's resonance as a marker of the Southern migrant's interpellation into the industrial Northern economy driven by time clocks rather than sun cycles.[109] In addition to its symbolic work, the clanging clock alerts readers to the importance of listening as a critical modality for reproducing, apprehending, and resisting racist violence. As Bigger and his family reluctantly arise, the alarm's piercing howl fuses with the high-pitched squeal of a predatory rat scampering across the floor and contrasts with the screams of his mother and sister as they scramble for safety; the Thomases are inundated with screaks, screams, squeals, and raspy skitters. The clanging alarm, the shrill scream, and the shriek of the doomed black rat resonate with the unequal power relations shaping Bigger's life, prefiguring the ending of Wright's novel. Born into noise and defined as dissonance by the powers that be, Wright's protagonist will be hunted, trapped, and doomed to a living death behind the cell door's clang.

Evoking the trope of the listener, Wright likens Bigger's vulnerability to a "giant ear that can never close," then proceeds to unfold the narrative in moment-to-moment temporality over three parts representing three consecutive days: "Fear," "Flight," and "Fate."[110] In section one, Bigger's mother gets him a job as chauffeur to the wealthy Dalton family, where

Bigger stands out as a noisy intrusion into their quiet, white world. His first night on the job finds him alone with Mary Dalton, the liberal daughter who gets so drunk Bigger has to carry her upstairs. When Mrs. Dalton checks in on her, Bigger panics at the thought of being caught in a white woman's bedroom and suffocates Mary to muffle her potential scream (and the violence it would almost certainly bring him). He then smuggles her body downstairs, dismembers it, and places it in the furnace. After her body is eventually discovered in section two, Bigger flees with his girlfriend, Bessie, through the snowy Chicago streets, hiding in abandoned buildings as the police cordon tightens. That night he rapes, then kills Bessie and thrusts her body down an air shaft. The police eventually surround him on the roof of a building as an angry white mob roars below. In section three, "Fate," the novel details Bigger's trial and eventual death sentence, focusing on the sound of his legal proceedings.

Wright's characterization of Bigger pushes the trope of listening even farther than "Big Boy Leaves Home," using repetition to dramatize how black men internalize the sonic color line in order to detect and survive subtle landmines of white racist violence, a running mental script that profoundly limits Bigger's self-worth, emotional well-being, and sensory experience of the world as a whole. Feelings of entrapment and isolation follow Bigger on either side of the spatial boundaries of segregation. Wright pairs Bigger's visual experience with an extremely limited palette of sound—again denaturalizing the "match" between audio and visual—showing segregation to be about so much more than lines on a map or stark visual contrasts between "separate but equal" neighborhoods. Sonically, Wright constructs Chicago through two simultaneous, overlapping soundtracks. Wright describes the first as "noisy crowded [and] filled with the sense of power and fulfillment" of those not bound by the color line.[111] The second is Bigger's limited city. His narrow sonic experience of Chicago contests representation of the urban North as a space of visible freedom and equal rights. For example, Wright describes almost all the sounds Bigger apprehends in *Native Son* with a repetitive combination of six adjectives: "clanging," "droning," "rattling," "rumbling," "roaring," and "creaking." As Wright detailed in "How Bigger Was Born"—now a standard addition to reprints of *Native Son*—he chose the "clanging" of the alarm to "convey the motif of the entire scheme of the book," using it to "sound, in varied form, the note that was to be resounded throughout [the book's] length." He turns a signal of danger into *Native Son*'s keynote, emphasizing the constant trauma and stress "bearing hourly" upon Bigger while simultaneously putting the reader on constant alert.[112] Bigger struggles to hear beyond the "clanging" of the alarm reverberating throughout the text, in the "far away clang" of passing street cars, the "clanging of the shovel against iron" as the reporters unearth Mary's charred bones, and the bell he hears while fitfully dreaming in the Dalton home, which "clanged so loud that he could hear the iron tongue clapping against the metal sides." In horrific symmetry, the clanging alarm echoes the cell door "clanging" at novel's end. Bigger hears "droning"—another of Wright's repeated sonic adjectives with all its implications of meaningless, repetitive labor—in the furnace that houses Mary's bones, in the fire hose the police use to capture him, and in the voices of the mob, preacher, and lawyers. He also hears repeated metallic "rattling" across disparate moments: in the rattling of the coal down the furnace chute, in the sound of passing street cars, in gusts of wind that rock the city the night Bigger is captured, and in the horrifying noise of Bessie's murder.[113] Wright's repetition envelops Bigger and constructs his subjectivity as both a product of his urban environment and an interactive process of listening to it.

Wright often uses aural imagery to show how the sonic color line provides segregated space with a distinct affect while exposing the listening ear as a racialized spatial protocol, extending white privilege to control over common soundscapes. Bigger hears, understands, and acts on the contrasting sounds in spaces deemed "white" and "black" by Chicago's racist real estate covenants (legalized in 1919 and, by 1940, in effect on over 50 percent of the housing stock—the most in the nation).[114] In contrast to the cacophonous representation of the Thomases' apartment, the spaces of white privilege emit measured sound. When Bigger walks toward the Dalton home on "quiet and spacious" Drexel Avenue, he crosses a physical threshold of the sonic color line and a hush falls around him: "The streets were empty, save for an occasional car that zoomed past on swift rubber tires. This was a cold and distant world; a world of secrets carefully guarded." Unlike public streetcars clanging their way down fixed tracks, quiet private automobiles head wherever they please at any speed. "The opposition between the steel of the streetcars and the 'swift rubber tires' of automobiles," Alessandro Portelli argues, "divides two universes of sounds and two types of space (the crowded streetcars and the privacy of the automobile)."[115] Drexel's stillness represents whites' power over the sonic protocols of certain key public spaces; the street's secretive (and privatized) silence within the heart of the city requires the repression of racial and socioeconomic Others. The Daltons' silent mansion literally depends upon the Thomases' noisy rat-infested kitchenette for its existence; Mr. Dalton owns the company that holds their lease. In the midcentury political economy of Chicago's South Side, the Daltons' silence is not merely the absence of sound but an act of power determining who belongs where—and when, how, and by whom they should be heard.

Like an auditorium using absorbent material to suppress echoes, the entire Dalton home is muffled, padded, and deadened against the noise of the black outer world, a physical manifestation of the listening ear that represents how whites construct it against the perceived threat of blackness. When Bigger arrives, the silence of the Daltons' mansion frightens him, seeming loud in its difference from his own grating world. "He was startled to hear a soft gong sound within," when he rings the bell, then later, as his listening intensifies, "the slow ticking of a clock" and "a faint sound of piano music." *Native Son* melds audio with visual here; these tones are both heard and seen throughout the house's "smooth walls," its "softly lighted hallway," "dim lights," "rug so soft and deep," and its terrifying "big white cat, pacing without sound."[116] The auditory negative of the squealing black rat, the Daltons' mute cat's silent gaze increasingly haunts Bigger throughout the novel. Wright's symbolic soundscapes show that the Daltons' power extends beyond the mansion's door. As the story unfolds, Chicago's streets fill with snow, which Bigger describes as "magic whiteness without sound." This blizzard, a "sort of great natural force," climactically symbolizes far-reaching white control over the city: "All around him were silence and night and snow falling, falling as though it had fallen from the beginning of time and it would always fall till the end of the world."[117] Wright's *Native Son* uses sound to underscore whiteness as a normative and proprietary material presence, as well as an oppressive structure of privilege with tremendous economic, political, and psychic rewards—quiet and powerful.

Akin and, as Wright's novel shows, related to the quietude of the Southern pastoral, the muted sonics of privileged white domesticity enact for Bigger the racial terror that reminds him that, even among liberal whites in the North, he remains a "to-be-lynched" body. This knowledge begins to physically transform his body and the way he feels within it. Bigger moves through this cold, alien world "conscious of every inch of his black body."[118] Similar to Jacobs's experience in *Incidents in the Life of a Slave Girl*, sound and space offer epistemological access to the self, but here listening offers self-annihilation rather than self-making. Bigger physically embodies noise, which historian Peter Bailey spatializes as "sound out of place."[119] Feeling noticeably out of sorts the moment he enters the white neighborhood—unconsciously clamping his jaw tight— Bigger becomes hyperaware of his sound. Like Big Boy and his friends at the swimming hole, Bigger slips into an automatic mode of listening and responding; he suddenly feels "involuntarily" compelled to whisper rather than speak. On edge during the interview with the frequently "word-less" Mr. Dalton, Bigger notices the house itself trying to muffle, mute, and consume him. Under the listening ear's classed and raced surveillance, Bigger becomes hyperaware of his bodily difference and psychic alienation.[120]

Although the sonic color line enables their mansion to resound with white privilege, Mr. and Mrs. Dalton tune out their knowledge of precisely how white supremacy metes out benefits and punishments. Wright satirizes the wealthy Northern white elites who characterized racism in the South as crude, ignorant, and barbaric yet enacted laws that not only created vast urban ghettoes, a prison system overflowing with black men, and industries dependent on the labor of underpaid, undereducated people working in substandard conditions, but also profited by such violence and inequity. "Daltonism" was actually the term for color blindness in Great Britain. Wright symbolizes this meta-phoric blindness through Mrs. Dalton's visual impairment. Mrs. Dalton's physical blindness coupled with a "white" view of the world attests to the shift in U.S. racial formation in Wright's contemporary moment, one no longer dependent on visual articulations of difference. Almost always in a state of "intense listening," Mrs. Dalton understands racial identity predominately through the sonic color line and its attendant lis-tening ear. Bigger feels a heightened sense of himself as noise whenever in the presence of Mrs. Dalton's hyperdeveloped listening ear. Mrs. Dalton's listening practice offers Bigger two options: to become inaudible by mimicking her expectations—walking where she wants him to, putting his glass down precisely when he finishes, going to night school—or to be exposed as a "to-be-lynched" body, a dangerous sound out of place. Bigger's sudden perception of himself as noise viscerally links Chicago to Mississippi.

Mrs. Dalton's racialized listening expectations dictate in no small way—to paraphrase Elizabeth Alexander—the parameters in which Bigger's body moves.[121] He associates her presence with the power of "unseen" racial terror and its hold over him. Bigger chooses to smother Mary Dalton rather than be caught with her by Mrs. Dalton's listening ear. Wright constructs a gothic mélange of a soundscape to record and transmit Bigger's terror and titillation that night in Mary's room: creaky floorboards, soft rustles, pounding hearts, mumbled prayers, last gasps, and expectant silences.[122] After killing Mary, Bigger imagines Mrs. Dalton can hear every sound his body makes. He is only able to evade her exacting ears by mirroring her: "With each of her movements toward the bed his body made a movement to match hers, away from her, his feet not lifting themselves from the floor, but sliding softly and silently over the smooth deep rug."[123]

Wright's Native Son depicts the ability to define and repress noise as only one facet of how the sonic color line constructs racialized space via sound and listening. The flip side of the icy silence of whiteness is the power to make noise with impunity. When whites cross spatial color lines to capture Bigger, he hears the silence accede to the apocalyptic "terror song of the siren," the overwhelming noise announcing the arrival of eight thousand white policemen in the South Side. In an all-too-familiar sonic performance of police brutality, the inordinately massive squad uses its overwhelming audio resources to intimidate Chicago's black residents. Bigger's capture allows whites to perform their power over the soundscape by penetrating Bigger with a horrific sound—here, an echo of Big Boy in the hole, listening—a sound that literally pins Bigger in his place:

He listened; there were throbs of motors; shouts rose from the streets; there were screams of women and curses of men. . . . The siren died and began again, on a high, shrill note this time. It made him want to clutch at his throat; as long as it sounded it seemed he could not breathe. . . . a medley of crashing sounds came, louder than he had thought that sound could be: horns, sirens, screams. There was hunger in those sounds as they crashed over the roof-tops and chimneys.[124]

Policing noise functions here as a sonic lynch mob; Bigger begins to suffocate and clutch at his throat as the siren encapsulates him.

The sonic color line's extremes of controlled silence and controlling noise connect the extralegal practice of lynching in the South with state-sanctioned segregation, police brutality, and biased courts in Northern states. The noise of the police capture accedes to the "roaring mob" of spectators gathered outside the courthouse, an aural image that threatens to dominate the third part of *Native Son*. Their "mighty roar" echoes throughout Bigger's trial; the "roar of [their] voices" penetrates the walls of Bigger's jail cell; and the "roar gr[ows] louder" when he is led through to the courtroom. The description here is reminiscent of the dialogue Big Boy overhears as Bobo is lynched: "As soon as [Bigger] was visible the roar reached a deafening pitch and continued to rise each second. . . . 'You black ape! Shoot that bastard!'" Even more troubling, the vociferous noise of this would-be lynch mob penetrates the courtroom during Bigger's trial. When Buckley, the state's attorney, first takes the floor, "the room was quiet as a tomb. Buckley strode to the window and with one motion of his hand hoisted it up. The rumbling mutter of the vast mob swept in. The court room stirred." With this action, Buckley (re) constructs the courtroom as a giant echo chamber filled by the mob's rumbling hate. The judge ultimately ignores Bigger's lawyer's impassioned closing statement, and Max's voice, as he feared, goes unheard above mob's "thirsty screams and hungry shouts."[125] In "Big Boy Leaves Home," Wright constructs a soundtrack to contest lynching's violent visual representations; in *Native Son*, Wright's soundtrack enables readers to hear Bigger's capture and sham trial *as* lynching.[126]

Wright's literary representation of lynching's soundtrack enabled him to create individual characters whose experiences extended beyond the narrative of singularity rapidly obscuring documented acts of lynching in the late 1930s. He used the trope of the listener to widen lynching's definition beyond death by mob hanging, expand its terrorist geography beyond the backwoods of the American South, and reveal its terrible ability to manufacture "to-be-lynched" bodies while making culpable the whites whose imaginations produced them. Wright's use of sound, in particular, exposes lynching's horrific diffusion into everyday life—into frequent (and frequently violent) encounters with police, hostile courtrooms, overcrowded prisons, and devastated families—and its stubborn defiance of temporality. Rushdy argues that lynching continued precisely because, right around the time that *Native Son* was published, the nation declared "lynching was a dying, if not dead, practice."[127] But the drones and clangs, and screams Wright recorded and re-sounded through his listeners Bobo and Bigger, allow us to listen beyond this rhetorical boundary, to hear simultaneously the intertwined past and presentness of lynching, so that we can protect ourselves while fighting—and hopefully eradicating—any future iterations. When we embed Wright's work in the genealogy of the sonic color line, we can hear how the bubbling of the water as Buck's body sinks underneath its surface ripples outward from Douglass's master's murder of Demby in the lake, and we can hear Demby's refusal to treat listening as obedience as it radiates forward through Lead Belly's defiance to Eric Garner telling the police, "It stops today." Wright's early work reminds us that black lives matter and that we honor the dead—and decolonize our listening—by listening, really listening to them, freeing ourselves from the listening ear's distorted discipline.

As I read and reread Wright's chilling representation of Bigger's fictional law-and-order lynching, I cannot help but hear the novel's far-reaching resonance in our contemporary moment, echoing in the last words of the unarmed black men and women killed by American police over the seventy-five years since *Native Son*'s publication. "I can't breathe!" sputtered Eric Garner (September 15, 1970–July 17, 2014) as NYPD officer Daniel Pantaleo held him in an illegal chokehold restraint. The screams and cries of Freddie Gray (August 16, 1989–April 19, 2015) echoed off the brick buildings of Baltimore's Gilmor Homes as officers dragged his slackened body over to the police van where Officer Cesar Goodson would deliver the "rough ride" that severed Freddie's spine. "All of this for a traffic ticket," Sandra Bland (February 7, 1987–July 13, 2015) repeated, with rising intensity, as Texas Trooper Brian T. Encinia yanked her from her car and threw her to the ground. With hands up, Michael Brown (May 20, 1996–August 9, 2014) said "OK, OK, OK, OK" as Ferguson, Missouri officer Darren Wilson shot him six times. "Call the ambulance," Shantel Davis (May 26, 1989–June 14, 2012) cried out to bystanders after Brooklyn Detective Phil Atkins shot her through the chest: "Please don't let me die." And the voices of these men and women—these last sonic acts of agency—keep shouting in the silence their living voices should have filled.[128]

Wright's artistry in *Native Son* allows us to connect how he wielded his fictional art in the 1930s with the acts of the brave men and women who record police brutality with their cell phone cameras today, such as Kevin Moore, who took footage of Baltimore police dragging Freddie Gray into their van, or Ramsey Orta, who recorded Eric Garner's last words. Working at a newspaper himself, Wright well knew how both the sonic color line and dominant media narratives limited documentary representation; literature offered Wright a way to record lynchings whose soundtracks could not be stripped. I want to be clear that my consideration of how Wright's novel may have resonated with black readers as a historical recording and as part of a tradition of literary witnessing does not reduce the novel to sociology or journalism, particularly considering that both Moore and Orta narrated their videos, weaving into the record their own stories of police brutality and analysis of racialized violence as their cells capture Gray's and Garner's murders. "Shorty, that was *after* they Tasered the shit out of him," Moore says, correcting the timeline of events, perhaps even to one of the officers on the scene. "Once again the police beating up on people," Orta narrates as an officer presses Garner's face into the pavement, "look right here."[129] Tellingly, media outlets often mute such commentary; they edit the men's voices out, or they frame the videos with discrediting disclaimers describing Moore and Orta as "amateur" and encouraging viewers to look rather than listen. Most egregiously, they simply turn the soundtrack down and layer their own commentary over Moore's and Orta's voices.

Bigger Thomas's own final words in *Native Son*, "Good bye!" shouted down the prison hallway to his retreating lawyer, return us to Wright's relationship with Ledbetter and the intimacy that may have passed between them, particularly as the novel ends with the image of Bigger "hear[ing] the ring of steel against steel as a far door clanged shut."[130] Readers often assume the "ring of steel against steel" and the prison door "clang[ing] shut" are one and the same, but given Wright's love and knowledge of film—not to mention how his literary soundtracking reimagines the relationship between the auditory and the visual—it is quite possible Bigger hears two sounds here: the door shutting *and* a blues soundtrack, the ring of Lead Belly's steel pick plucking his guitar's steel strings. As the cell closes on death row, Bigger *finally* hears the blues—one of many elements of black folk culture he either tuned out or could not access—the sound of the guitar rising not as commodity or amusement but as accompaniment, a fellow traveller of his aural imagination. While Wright's closing imagery represents blues as masculine and sites it uncomfortably close to that clanging prison door, careful listeners remember that *Native Son*'s end is in the beginning, in the clang of the alarm that sonically connects kitchenette to jail cell. Contra Lomax, who thought segregated prisons fostered "authentic" blues for collection, Wright depicts segregation *as* prison and blues as a method, both for expressing this truth and for decolonizing listening to hear it.

In the process of making meaning from what Carla Kaplan calls the "failed exchange" between Bigger and his lawyer, Max, at novel's end,[131] scholars have muffled the powerful moment of imagined sonic and haptic connection among incarcerated people that Bigger brings to life while in his cell, one that imagines an escape from the walled-in "screams and curses and yells of suffering" that "nobody heard" via the connection of electrical wires. Through a realization of shared isolation—that steel on steel again—Bigger imagines a "union, identity," that begins by extending his hands, beyond the "to-be-lynched" body, beyond labor, beyond fetishization, toward others doing the same. "If he reached out with his hands, and if his hands were electric wires, and if his heart were a battery giving life and fire to those hands, and if he reached out with his hands and touched other people, reached out through those stone walls and felt other hands connected with other hearts—if he did that, would there be a reply, a shock?"[132] And here again is the touch of Lead Belly, whose resolute hands sounded his isolation against the cells of Angola, the walls of segregation in the North and West, and, eventually, the isolation booths of WNYC as the host of Folksongs of America, bringing "to-be-lynched" bodies to new lives and identities over those electrical wires. The passage also suggests that while Wright continued to pursue cinematic aesthetics, he also began to articulate sound's unique powers.

The crackling of electricity Bigger imagines as the spark enabling new possibilities of connection resembles the newly electrified mass medium of radio—the subject of the next chapter—especially the potential for its elaborate networks to "reach out through those stone walls" and create new communities of listeners with hearts connected through hands on the dial.

Finally, in this image of mass media connection I also hear future echoes of the Civil Rights Movement, whose musical methods and movements Shana Redmond brilliantly amplifies in *Anthem*,[133] as well as the #blacklivesmatter movement in our contemporary moment, where protestors use "lock boxes" to chain their hands together so that the police cannot remove them, chanting "I Can't Breathe" and "Hands up, Don't Shoot" amidst the noise of riot police and the profound silence of the state regarding racialized and increasingly militarized policing.

5.

Broadcasting Race

Lena Horne, W. E. B. Du Bois, and Ann Petry

"Almost every day, I hear someone on the radio hailing America as the home of democracy. Yet almost every network is guilty of discrimination against the Negro performer. There are a few isolated cases of Negroes in broadcasting, but the lily-white policy is seldom violated."
—Lena Horne, *The Chicago Defender*, September 20, 1947

In 1937, Huddie Ledbetter recorded his new song "Turn Yo' Radio On" for the Library of Congress, an ode he composed upon arriving in New York City. The tune enthusiastically depicts radio as a powerful medium creating new forms of sociality via speedy information delivery. "Turn yo' radio on," Lead Belly repeatedly appeals, just before he propels his yodel into the space where a breath usually occurs: "Whooooooo." Cut short by the next line, his burst of sound replicates the wonder, heat, and sheer velocity engendered by radio transmissions: "Turn yo radio on / so you hear what's goin' on."[1]

Ledbetter's song powerfully (and joyfully) reconciles black folk traditions with new technologies and the rapid pace of postmigration urban life. Merging technological optimism with lyrics detailing the exploits of various trickster animals—including the "little red rooster," a symbol of masculine prowess Lead Belly also evokes with his "Whoooo"— the song heralds radio's significance in black life and the centrality of black people and black culture to American modernity. "Oh the little red rooster said to the hen," Lead Belly sings, "Buy yourself a radio so we all can listen in / Turn yo' radio on." Preceding the radio, and still necessary in a post-radio world, the rooster's word-of-mouth network operates with and against the broadcast medium, offering enthusiasm at some moments and subtle critique at others: "Times, baby, ain't like they useta," retorts the hen, taking stock of the Great Migration's disjunctures and radio's potential for disruption. As Ralph Ellison explained in 1948's "Harlem is Nowhere," black migrants transitioned "from slavery to the condition of man in a space of time so telescoped (a bare 85 years), that it is literally possible for them to step from feudalism into the vortex of industrialism simply by moving across the Mason Dixon line."[2] Lead Belly's "whoooo" soundtracks the exhilaration of this movement—and genders it, much like Ellison—while the hen's character expresses hesitance to embrace what may just be the latest way for marginalized peoples to "listen in" to (white) American life.

Ledbetter's "Turn Yo' Radio On" remains important to his songbook as an example of music made once free of John Lomax's contract, but I argue it is also key to media history as well. The song sonically archives a black-authored representation of black radio listening during the medium's so-called American golden age, a term and time period intertwined with the legacies of whiteness and nostalgia in the national collective memory. Ledbetter's song reminds listeners that American radio audiences were far more diverse in the 1930s and 1940s than its programming, imagery, archives, or much of its scholarship depicts— how could they not be with 90 percent of American households owning at least one radio and listening to an average of three to four hours of broadcasting daily?—yet the industry actively ignored black listeners until morale became an issue for recruitment as Americans geared up to World War II.[3] Frustratingly, African Americans did find themselves listening in as white American broadcasters, networks, advertisers, radio stations, writers, casting agents, musicians' and actors' unions, newspaper critics, and media theorists excised them from contemporary conversations about radio and its role in shaping "modern" citizens.

This chapter shows the culmination of the sonic color line's rise to significance as a central force of racialization in American life and the increasing entanglement of the listening ear with sound reproduction technologies. I articulate how the sonic color line connected U.S. radio's so-called golden age to legal segregation, arguing that this relationship enabled the construction of liberal color blindness as a citizenship ideal following World War II. Post-1945, the white listening ear increasingly demanded conformity to white middle-class sonic norms as the price of full citizenship.[4] Because assimilation threatened white supremacy and control, however, the dominant culture became even more invested in the sonic color line, which then became more fine-grained and subtle. The rise of standardized radio speech and state-sponsored color blindness subjected racialized groups to new forms of aural body discipline because as technology and pedagogy increasingly considered vocal tones and speech patterns to be changeable traits—unlike skin color, for example, which can only be "overlooked"—those that would not (or could not) conform to white sonic norms risked not only increased discrimination but the blame for it too. Bolstered by scientific discoveries confirming race to be biological fiction, proponents of color blindness began to shut down conversation about the nation's (still very apparent) visual color line and the historical impact of race on U.S. institutions. While color blindness held out an elusive promise of fairness and equity, the sonic color line enabled the ongoing racial shell game, one where racial signifiers shuffle interminably between sight and sound. The notion that race can be overlooked equated racism almost solely with visible skin color, a limitation that simply intensified the use of sonic cues to stereotype, exclude, segregate, discriminate against, and justify violence against people of color—all while declaring race invisible and racism eradicated.

Through archival analysis of the racial politics of U.S. radio and close readings/listenings of black radio performance and radio criticism by singer Lena Horne, scholar W. E. B. Du Bois, and writer Ann Petry, this chapter shows how, from its earliest manifestations, color blindness never seriously threatened the link between "whiteness" and "Americanness," because it did not challenge—or even acknowledge—the sonic color line disciplining American listening over the past one hundred and fifty years to "match" certain sounds, voices, and environments to visual markers of race. Because the sonic color line historically contoured, identified, and marked mismatches between "sounding white" and "looking black," it continued to make the abstraction of race *palpable*—both blackness *and* whiteness—even when it could no longer officially be "seen." In fact, the sonic color line actually enabled the rise of what Eduardo Bonilla-Silva identified as "color-blind racism" because it allowed conservative, liberal, *and* progressive whites a method of continuing to perceive race and enact discrimination without *seeming* to do so (or, for some, without perceiving or consciously recognizing it), while making it more difficult for people of color and antiracist advocates to prove the continued existence of racial violence and institutional inequity.[5] After all, in Western culture, looking implies active, meaningful intent, while listening connotes passivity and a lack of control; it just naturally *happens*. I have argued throughout this book, however, that listening is a dynamic historical and cultural practice, an embodied critical sense shaping how and what we think, *and* an ethical act shaped by our thoughts, beliefs, experiences, and ideologies, one both subject to discipline and offering agency.

This last chapter focuses specifically on black radio listeners' entanglements with racial subjection and assertions of agency during and after World War II, showing the impact of the sonic color line's genealogy on U.S. radio programming and identifying an explicit tension between the color-blind assimilation of the listening ear and race-conscious efforts to decolonize listening. Much remains at stake in arguments about who has been tuned out of "old time" radio's legacy, especially as its visual images and sonic traces have retroactively become some of the most potent aesthetic renderings of racial segregation, gender inequality, and heteronormativity as the "golden age" of America itself: a time when whiteness aligned perfectly with "American citizen," domestic gender roles remained clear and unassailable, "family values" went unquestioned, and national unity and patriotism for the "good war" never flagged. I argue it is no coincidence that U.S. radio's golden age overlaps so neatly with both Jim Crow and the rise of state-sponsored color blindness; therefore, we must consider both the sonic color line and the material realities of segregation—its social, spatial, emotional, and psychological impacts—as a frame for understanding representations of radio from this period. Scholars recognize but largely take for granted the lack of black performers and behind-the-scenes workers in 1930s–1940s network radio; few consider how white-authored fantasies of the "black radio listener" enabled the norming of white listening practices, and fewer still consider how black listeners heard and challenged the palpable whiteness of radio's form.

"Lofty Aerials, Symbols of Freedom": Radio and the Rise of Color-Blind Nationalism

Understanding and challenging the pull of the "golden age" narrative on American memory has emerged as a key critical conversation in radio studies' recent fluorescence. In Neil Verma's superb account of 1930s and 1940s radio aesthetics, he discusses how "the dizzying outpouring of radio plays that filled the airspace of the twentieth century left a residue on modern understanding. For one thing, it made the golden age fully imaginable and worthy of a degree of nostalgia bordering on mawkishness."[6] Fan and retail websites such as OTRCAT.com, www.mysteryshows.com, and www.radiolovers.com have revived and accelerated radio nostalgia by digitizing and selling copies of selected shows and cementing a certain brand of "old time radio" visual iconography: black-and-white images of predominately white radio stars performing live on air—clutching scripts and standing in a semicircle around outsized RCA microphones—and Norman Rockwell-esque reprints of white extended families—parents, children, and grandparents—huddled near gleaming cathedral radio sets. Fan distribution of digitized radio shows has greatly enabled contemporary radio scholarship, and new research has rightfully complicated several problematic golden age fantasies: its ever-absorbed listener, its seemingly anything-can-happen liveness, its domination by national networks, and its ability to bring about national unity and consensus. Kate Lacey details how radio quickly "became defined as a secondary medium with fragmentary, ephemeral content listened to while doing other things," a form of listening quickly denigrated as both "distracted" and feminine because of its association with domestic labor.[7] Historian Alexander Russo's study of radio infrastructure reveals the inaccuracy of nostalgic notions characterizing golden age radio as an entirely "live, national and networked" medium bringing about "unification and centralization" in American life. By the 1940s, in particular, Russo argues "this definition of radio [was] functional as ideology only."[8] But as this book lays bare in regard to listening and race, ideologies have powerful material consequences, both in their own moment and beyond.

This section articulates America's changing racial milieu in the 1940s with its growing culture of technological optimism, particularly the nation's symbolic investment in radio as a medium of truth, freedom, and color blindness. Eric Porter dubs this period America's "first post-racial moment" because of the rapid dissemination of conclusive evidence that race had no biological basis by the sciences, government, and the liberal Left, a watershed that "made possible both racial transcendence and racial inequalities cloaked within this transcendence."[9] New understandings stopped short, however, in accounting for the persistence of racial inequities, both globally and in the United States. While propagating the largely metaphorical gesture that racial difference should no longer be "seen"—the stance we now call color blindness—"race as fiction" disavows the long historical legacy of white supremacy's impact on sensory perception that I have traced in this book, ensuring its continuance by making it difficult for whites to perceive and for people of color to publicly challenge.[10]

Long discussed as a "blind" medium because it lacked an overt visual dimension and depended heavily on ambient sounds and vocal tones, radio became a primary technology of so-called color blindness, uniquely suited to make the optics of race disappear through omission. White network executives often pointed to radio's aurality as an example of color blindness already achieved, particularly when challenged about the industry's almost complete lack of black workers. For example, former actor and longtime network programmer Tom McAvity, then network production supervisor for CBS, told University of California Los Angeles researcher Estelle Edmerson in 1954: "Since radio is oral, Negroes' chances should be greater. Radio is less limited in theory. I don't feel that the lack of Negroes in radio is due to discrimination . . . the lack of Negroes in radio is due to the lack of competent Negro actors."[11] With their simplistic calculus, McAvity's dismissive remarks show how the period popularly considered that American radio's "golden age" readily overlapped with racial segregation. Network radio, in particular, enabled the emergence of color blindness, helping to make race invisible via exclusion, omission, and silencing while simultaneously expanding the sonic color line's repertoire of aural codes representing and hierarchizing racial difference. Liberal white Americans could safely claim color blindness as a reality without losing their privileged status because the sonic color line continued to inform their perception and perform its racial labor.

Network radio's location as a site of color-blind nationalism must be heard, as the work of Horne, Du Bois, and Petry tells us, through the materialities of American segregation and implicated in the racially transcendent racism emerging on air. While African Americans organized against domestic racism via the *Pittsburgh Courier*'s Double V Campaign and later the Civil Rights Movement, many liberal whites perceived these struggles as opportunities to affirm black people's eventual cultural conformity to the brand of (white) Americanness broadcast on the radio. The process of "wartime racial realignment," Michele Hilmes argues, meant that "for blacks, a rhetoric of inclusion [was] deployed strategically that *denies* racial distinctions in favor of a democratic national identity; for whites a discourse of fear that *depends* upon racial distinctions was used to excite white participation."[12] The double meaning of the term color-blind—overlooking race, looking obsessively at race—served this Janus-faced agenda well, and radio, in which race could not be seen but was everywhere heard, enabled its mass broadcast. In the American run-up to World War II, radio functioned as a technology of the sonic color line, propagating racialized aural representations, mediating racial discourse, and practicing racial exclusion while depicting itself as incapable of racialization.

Ruth Benedict and Gene Weltfish's influential public affairs pamphlet *The Races of Mankind* (1943) exemplified America's shift toward considering physical signs of racial difference "nonessential" while constructing audible differences at the same time. Commissioned by the Office of War Information and the United Service Organizations to aid American soldiers headed overseas, the pamphlet contributed to the transformation in American racial ideology relegating racism to a primitive past and locating U.S. statecraft in a "scientifically grounded, modernizing, and universalizing antiracist discourse," even as its domestic audience remained racially segregated.[13] Both Benedict and Weltfish studied with prominent anthropologist (and longtime friend of Du Bois) Franz Boaz, who advocated for the abolition of any scientific validity lent to "race." After characterizing all visual markers of race as "nonessentials," Benedict and Weltfish asserted that qualities such as language are not a matter of race either. However, two of the pamphlet's cartoonish illustrations, "An American Brought Up in China Will Speak Chinese" and "Anyone Can Learn Any Language," reveal the sonic color line at work.

AN AMERICAN BROUGHT UP IN CHINA WILL SPEAK CHINESE.

"An American Brought Up in China Will Speak Chinese," *The Races of Mankind* (1943).

Ostensibly representing the malleability of culture, "An American Brought Up in China Will Speak Chinese" entertains the idea that disconnects can occur between how someone looks and how he or she talks; however, it also normalizes the expectation of "racial surprise" at the perceived mismatch via the slack-jawed speaker in the second panel, signifying the two men's Americanness via an identical 1940s white middle-class masculinity. The second cartoon involving sound, "Anyone Can Learn Any Language," depicts an array of brown-skinned "foreigners" simultaneously saying "yes" in Babel-like confusion.

Like the first cartoon, the drawing seeks to create color blindness by unsettling immediate connections between language and visual racial appearance, but the sheer shock and confusion on all of the men's faces ironically begs the question: If language is malleable, wouldn't better communication be ensured by monolingualism? While the first cartoon suggests white Americanness transcends cultural and linguistic divergences, the second implies that citizenship reveals the circular logic

ANYONE CAN LEARN ANY LANGUAGE.

"Anyone Can Learn Any Language," *The Races of Mankind* (1943).

of the sonic color line: it demands that people of color discipline their sound to be considered full citizens, yet white Americans are encouraged to exhibit "racial surprise" when they do, ensuring the continuation of racial difference.[14]

The color-blind unity/aural difference dynamic of new social science thinking about race permeated the American airwaves and informed writing and thinking about radio as intrinsically free of race. Network broadcasting made direct interventions into domestic race issues at the beginning of World War II, developing sustaining programs such as CBS's *Americans All, Immigrants All* (1939), sponsored by the Federal Radio Education Committee and the U.S. Office of Education—which I discuss later in the context of Du Bois's involvement—*I'm an American* (1941), also sponsored by the federal government, and NBC's *Freedom's*

People (1941), focused specifically on African American history and culture. Taken together, these programs asserted a new perspective on race that strategically included the "claims of African Americans to full rights and citizenship along with those of Americans of European descent" while evoking audible difference: racialized music, sounds, and exaggerated dialect.[15]

As with the networks' high-profile sustaining programs, radio critic Orrin Dunlap's writing from this period imbued American radio with a color-blind progressivism that marked the United States as a nation whose freedom, equality, and unity contrasted with conditions in rising totalitarian regimes in Europe and Asia. "America's radio is out in the open," Dunlap wrote in a 1939 *Times* article: "Lofty aerials, symbols of freedom, dot the hills from coast to coast. They are not long-range nozzles through which to spray propaganda."[16] Dunlap proclaimed, without irony, that the American microphone "breathed sound freely" because listeners could choose between President Roosevelt's "fireside chats" and the minstrel antics of *Amos 'n' Andy*—a popular program whose black titular characters were played by two white men, a juxtaposition representing radio's racialized power dynamics in sharp relief.[17] Shortly after evoking such stark aural difference, Dunlap argued that listeners' freedom cannot threaten national unity because broadcasts are necessarily "modulated with what the American ear wants and chooses to hear." Dunlap's singular "American ear" presents the flip side of Benedict and Weltfish's representation of color blindness, tuning out racialized aural difference and norming listening.

Dunlap's "American ear" closely aligns with what I have theorized as the listening ear, creating an aural imaginary aligning whiteness with Americanness through language of inclusion, openness, and choice, and radio's "color-blind" aurality. Radio then disseminates color blindness while aspiring to unified listening, exemplified in the 1942 ad, developed by Chicago's Sheldon-Claire Company, depicting a white family huddled around their radio. The ad exemplifies both Dunlap's technological patriotism and Hilmes's notion of "wartime racial realignment" through its inclusive second-person rhetorical address—"This is *your* America"—combined with its fear-mongering tone and limited visual imagining of the American citizenry. Images such as the Sheldon-Claire ad have become metonymic stand-ins for the "golden age of radio"—as

This is America...

...where you can listen to your radio in your living room – – not in a hideout. Where you are free to hear both sides of a question and form your own opinion ★ This is your America

... Keep it Free!

Ad developed by the Sheldon-Claire Company, 1942.

a Google image search for this phrase instantly affirms—effecting the erasure of black people as "Americans," let alone radio listeners, during this period. Perhaps the biggest irony of Dunlop's commentary and the Sheldon-Claire ad is that, by 1942, the newly formed Office of War Information had already instituted a systemic propaganda program, one so well integrated that most Americans remained unaware of its existence even while "openly" listening to favorite radio personalities discuss gas rationing.

Building from the belief in American radio as an unmediated purveyor of freedom, radio documentarian and dramatist Norman Corwin argued for black inclusion in the industry via a technological color blindness that also relied upon the sonic color line's distinctions. In a 1945 *Chicago Defender* interview, Corwin argued that the physical mechanics of radio itself worked as a direct technological representation of color blindness. His statements—reprinted by *Negro Digest* as "A Microphone Is Color Blind"—assured black readers that his "feeling about Negroes in radio is that they belong as surely as the microphone."[18] Corwin's odd simile likens black participation in radio not to whites' proprietary ownership but rather to the microphone's mute utility, which, while fundamental to broadcasting, can only amplify others' voices. Corwin then affirms some of the historic assumptions wrought by the sonic color line regarding "black" voices and sound reproduction: "I have found the same thing that makes Negroes supremely great artists in song makes them great in speech. The color and warmth conveyed in the performance of a Negro artist is directly communicable by air. The microphone is a faithful reporter and says exactly what it hears."[19] While celebrating black voices, Corwin's use of "communicable" rather than "communicated" also tinges "black sound" with infectiousness. The passage assures white listeners that black speakers' voices are simultaneously naturally different and easily identifiable over the "color-blind" airwaves. Forwarding the belief in the microphone's objectivity also problematically labelled the voices of the few black radio actors as faithful representations rather than performances. But whereas radio listeners heard a wide range of white voices on air in a spectrum of roles, the sonic color line circumscribed the sound *and* content of black speech. As John Hutchens wrote for the *New York Times* in 1944: "To nine radio listeners out of ten the Negro is one of several stock characters—the comical servant, the vaudeville hoofer, the flashy loafer, or old Uncle Tom bowing and scraping under the magnolia trees—and his home is usually the Harlems of the musical comedies."[20] Corwin goes on to argue that elocution courses would improve black radio presence. With no comment on educational segregation, Corwin proclaimed: "Negro schools should have in their curriculum courses in public speaking, radio, theater. There is no reason why there should not be Negro announcers. It is important to study diction so that distinction in speech cannot be noted."[21] On one hand, Corwin argues black voices should retain the racial markings that the sonic color line makes legible (and pleasurable) to white listeners. On the other, he suggests that black announcers must sound enough like their white colleagues to go on air. This is not to say that white announcers did not take elocution courses or that white ethnic accents were not also silenced, only that the standard for "indistinct" American remained an aspirational middle-to-upper-class white masculine sound.

There remained, then, a profound disconnect in the 1940s between the full exercise of American citizenship, the idealized discourse of color-blind radio, and the actual presence of African American radio producers, performers, and listeners. As state-sponsored color blindness rose to prominence, the United States' network programming became almost exclusively white, behind the scenes and over the airwaves. Little opportunity existed for black engineers and audio technicians, especially as segregation made training opportunities scarce. No black writers were regularly employed by any national station during the 1940s; the Los Angeles Radio Writers Guild had *not a single* black member. Black sports announcer Joe Bostic—the same critic who once blasted Lead Belly's performance at the Apollo—said he could find "not a single Negro entertainer placing in the first ten of any branch of radio entertainment" in the trade publications.[22] Regular on-site broadcasts that featured black performers all but vanished after 1940, meaning most black musical performances were mediated by white announcers and sponsors. *The Camel Caravan* regularly featured Benny Goodman, and orchestra leader Sammy Kaye hosted *Sunday Serenade*, while big-name black artists such as Horne, Cab Calloway, Duke Ellington, Hazel Scott, and Nat King Cole relied on sporadic guest appearances.[23] Finally, while a smattering of local programs with black DJs and announcers existed, only ten African American performers were steadily employed by the national radio industry at its height, 1943–1953, a steady and marked decline from radio's first decades. These performers were concentrated almost exclusively in the traditionally racialized genres of comedy or musical variety. As actor, musician, and assistant casting director Fluornoy Miller detailed, "The Negro characters are practically all comedians. . . . [the] white man's conception of what he thinks, or likes to think, the Negro is like." In addition to comedy roles, black actors occasionally found work on sustaining programs specifically targeted toward racial issues; however, as Barbara Savage details, these programs' messages remained constrained and unable to push racial boundaries too far.[24]

While confirming white racial imaginings, national network radio constructed aural representations of "blackness" in terms of music as well as voice. Booking agents shunted black performers to blues and jazz gigs, believing them incapable of playing other genres. The Los Angeles branch of the American Federation of Musicians remained segregated until 1953, and the branch's white president channeled LA radio contracts almost exclusively to white union musicians because "stringed instruments were prominently used in radio." With few jobs available for black classical musicians after years of extensive (and expensive) study, only a determined few trained to make what black violinist William Hadnot called radio's "intensified sympathetic music," which radio producers felt appealed to the listening ear. The rest remained confined to clearly racialized jazz and blues breaks.[25] However, because of the ascendance of color blindness—and the fact that musical proclivity does not directly reference visual racial qualities—gatekeepers could claim that "calls are very rare for dance musicians who are not all-around musicians. This may be the cause of the Negro musicians' lack of employment. I don't think they are excluded because of race."[26] The sonic color line's feedback loop circulated preconceived notions regarding black musicality, and, in turn, the listening ear affirmed and honed racialized musical divisions.

In addition, white booking agents, casting directors, and executives often required black radio performers to speak in scripted dialect, what actors Maidie Norman and Wonderful Smith referred to as "Negroid Sounds" and scholar Alain Locke called the "cornfield voice." White producers and scriptwriters exaggerated black voices with "poor grammar, poor diction, and certain voice qualities"—a practice characterized by Savage as "aural blackface"—no matter the character's regional location or education.[27] Norman reported being "told repeatedly that I don't sound like a Negro"—and she was therefore ineligible for black roles—but when she sought jobs "not requiring this special voice quality," casting directors stonewalled her.[28] Despite white executives' insistence that black people had a recognizable "voice quality," many black radio actors needed instruction to speak in this racialized manner. Lillian Randolph, known for playing Birdie on *The Great Gildersleeves* and Madame Queen on *Amos 'n' Andy*, said white *Lone Ranger* producer George Treadle "taught [her] Negro dialect."[29] Johnny Lee, who played the "comic lawyer" Algonquin C. Calhoun on *Amos 'n' Andy*, "had to learn how to talk as white people believed Negroes talked. Most of the directors take it for granted that if you're a Negro actor, you'll do the part of a Negro automatically."[30] Lee's experience confirms that whites used the sonic color line to match the visibility of blackness with a corresponding aural counterpart signifying its unambiguous presence on "color-blind" radio.

White-scripted sonic stereotypes also limited the content and frequency of black speech. Randolph, for example, summed up her lines on the first three years of *The Great Gildersleeves* as "mostly 'yes sir,' and 'no, sir.'" Horne—a controversial figure because many listeners could not immediately race her voice—almost lost her job when she fought for the right to address the white star of *Duffy's Tavern* by his first name. "The script had to be revised so that I wouldn't address the star as 'Archie,'" Horne remembered. "They wanted me to call him 'Mr. Gardner.' It wasn't considered proper for a Negro girl to speak a white man's first name. But I refused to consent to the change. So the earth-shaking problem was finally solved by deleting the name from the script."[31] On the one hand, Randolph's and Horne's experiences show how whites attempted to reaffirm the sonic color line by scripting black actors' lines to aurally communicate their disempowered social position vis-à-vis white actors, naturalizing both the sounds and the relations. On the other hand, Horne's resistance to the sonic color line's "earth-shaking" minutiae amplifies how black performers used their voices—off air and on—to rescript sonic stereotypes, challenge the limitations of their roles, and decolonize listening.

"You Were Wonderful": Lena Horne Fights the Sonic Color Line

Black performers intervened in the sonic color line's imposition of the "colored voice" in complex and multifaceted ways, combining conformity, negotiation, outright refusal, and the nurturing of a race-conscious, self-defined "black voice." Some black actors, such as *Beulah*'s Hattie McDaniel, the first African American radio lead, publicly conformed to the sonic color line, arguing that only by remaining on air could black actors exercise agency. Others, such as Randolph, negotiated with the sonic color line, learning the so-called Negro dialect but audibly revealing its artifice whenever she could. Butterfly McQueen publicly refused to play maids; she quit her job on the *Jack Benny Show* when writers changed her role from Rochester's girlfriend to Mary Livingstone's maid. "I didn't mind playing a maid the first time because I thought that was how you got into the business," McQueen said. "But after I did the same thing over and over I resented it. I didn't mind being funny, but I didn't like being stupid." McQueen's refusal ended her radio career.[32]

Other black radio performers challenged the sonic color line *and* the hegemony of color blindness by insisting that some black performers did sound distinct from their white colleagues, a cultural rather than biological difference signifying creative innovation and communal connection. Fluornoy Miller cited a different rubric for cultural authenticity than the white listening ear's minstrel exaggerations, expressing pride in black cultural difference and urging his colleagues to avoid pressures to assimilate to normative white speech patterns or exaggerate to white-authored Negro dialect. "The Negro's effort to break down social prejudice," Miller bemoaned, "has cost him his heritage—his music, dances, etc."[33] *The Red Skelton Show*'s Johnny Lee concurred:

> We have phrases, idioms—that is, speech habits, etc. that are ours. I can't explain, but there is something distinctive about most Negroes' speech technique. A lot of us are trying to throw away a quality that the white man is picking up and using . . . all races have certain similarities of voice and speech qualities. We are normal individuals and should not be made ashamed of our distinguishing assets.[34]

By possessively asserting the distinction and attractiveness of black voices, Lee redraws the sonic color line, flipping its hierarchical script to decolonize listening from the white listening ear's conditioning, a practice Sidonie Smith and Julia Watson call "countervalorization."[35] Almost twenty years before "Black Is Beautiful" became a worldwide diasporic slogan, black radio performers and thinkers challenged the sonic erasures of color blindness and the long history of the sonic color line's normalized assessments, asserting the beauty, power, and diversity of the sounds of their voices.

By the mid-1940s, Lena Horne wielded one of the most distinct voices in American culture, let alone radio. The smooth sound she crafted shifted strategically across the sonic color line and back again, vexing white definitions of "black" sound while signalling her social and political commitments to black people through vocal phrasing and sonic detail. Black radio performers, in particular, heard and respected her crossover abilities yet remained conflicted about the meaning of Horne's success. In Edmerson's assessment of black radio in 1954, several radio personalities described Horne as an exception to radio's racialized soundscape. Edmerson interrogates the assertions of white radio executives that black actors' voices possess an undeniably recognizable tone and that, for black actors, voices must "match" bodies: "This theory, of course, was disproved long ago when such Negro actors and actresses as: Maurice Ellis, Frank Wilson, Juano Hernandez, Frank Silvera, Lena Horne, Maidie Norman, and others were presented in various non-Negro radio presentations." Ernest Whitman—host of *Jubilee*, an armed services radio show for black servicemen that regularly welcomed Horne as a guest— asserted that Horne's voice and bearing crossed a heavily guarded and culturally dangerous border for some white listeners. "If Negroes were presented on the same level as whites," Whitman worried, referencing Horne's demeanor, "the South would not accept him. They would probably boycott the sponsor's products. There has been evidence of this, especially in motion pictures; example: Lena Horne and Rochester [Eddie Anderson]."[36] Notorious Memphis censor Lloyd Binford cut Horne's and Anderson's scenes so often that it became standard practice for Metro-Goldwyn-Mayer to isolate Horne's performances from white cast members' so editors could excise her songs without disrupting the plot, splicing a literal sonic color line into the film and protecting the white listening ear with a tiny piece of clear adhesive tape.[37] Horne's work in white-oriented programs such as *Mail Call* and *G.I. Journal* also possessed a hermetically sealed quality; Horne rarely banters with the cast or does anything but sing.

Whitman's comment addresses the stakes Horne faced for performing with a voice that white listeners assumed as their possession, even as they demanded that Others sonically assimilate for full citizenship rights. Other entertainers concurred, mentioning Horne in the same breath as Marian Anderson as one of the few artists whom white audiences accepted in categories other than "Negro," but they also thought that, overall, white audiences had little interest in boundary-breaking sonic performances. In fact, argued Miller—who helped Horne get her gig with Noble Sissle's orchestra—might not Horne's fame be due to the politics of respectability that demanded her "appeasement" of black middle-class activists uncomfortable with vernacular art forms? "Great performers have been pushed into the background," Miller asserted, "while performers who featured a certain brand of performance which has been associated with the Negro were brought forward."[38] In honing a sound that defied white *and* black audiences' expectations, might Horne's voice further silence black vernacular practices?

Echoing the racially transgressive performances of Elizabeth Taylor Greenfield in the 1850s, Horne's smooth vocal stylings again confirm, one hundred years later, that neither vocal timbre nor listening is biologically grounded; rather, they are performative practices at the intersection of culture, ideology, body discipline, and agency. Horne herself attributed the crispness of her diction and her lack of perceptible regional accent to her Grandmother Cora's strict discipline. An active "race woman" and a pillar of the black middle class in Bedford-Stuyvesant, Cora put her faith in respectability politics, and she sought to disentangle black voices from the sonic color line's associations by imposing standard English pronunciation and banning most black music from her home. According to Horne's biographer, "Even the lusty sounds of gospel and blues made Cora cringe; in her home, anything that signified a loss of control was shunned. Instead she listened to Bach and Georgian chants, cutting off the musical part of Lena's black heritage."[39] Not quite as strict, Horne's grandfather, former editor of the *Freeman* and the *Bee*, allowed Horne some Bert Williams and Florence Mills, but not blues. Horne internalized her grandparents' concerns about how race, class, and respectability structured her voice. However, Horne also spent some formative years with her mother, an itinerant actress, in the South, exposing her to a wider vocal and musical array and pushing her to express herself more openly. Although Horne felt she "couldn't sing" and "was a *bad* dancer," she began performing at age sixteen at the Cotton Club, honing her craft alongside Aida Ward, Leitha Hill, and Adelaide Hall, first as a chorine and eventually as a soloist.[40] Although I focus on her early radio years, the long and illustrious history of her voice and the many changes Horne put it through tells a larger story about her struggles to decolonize her listening from betwixt and between her grandmother's sense of control and propriety and the request of her mother (and many a stage director) to put more "feeling" into her work.[41] Scholar Shane Vogel traces the alleged "coldness" of Horne's early performances to her onstage "impersona," her guarded, controlled, and calculated refusal of intimacy and exposure, particularly in settings where audiences expected "feeling."[42] Horne's radio work locates another important source of Horne's performances of isolation in the genealogy of the sonic color line—after all, "cold" in the nineteenth century applied to the "white" sound of Jenny Lind—as well as a new cultural anxiety over the role of the voice in black assimilation in "colorblind" America. While radio's so-called blindness theoretically offered Horne more opportunity for experimentation and expression than either film or cabaret—which placed her visually raced identity front and center—her radio roles provoked different racial dilemmas, regarding her defiantly liminal voice.

Although America's black and white presses heard Horne's voice as racially indeterminate to some degree—or at least radically adaptable—both ultimately raced Horne's voice as "black," although with different strategies and divergent motivations. Black critics argued over the strength and quality of Horne's singing voice but nonetheless "matched" her voice to her body, realigning the sonic color line rather than reaffirming it and decolonizing their readers' listening by challenging dominant aesthetics and widening the sound of a "black" voice. Even though Horne herself claimed she "couldn't sing the blues," the black press occasionally described her as a "beautiful blues singer" or a "blues beauty," a race-conscious claim expanding the blues genre even if only awkwardly describing Horne's repertoire.[43] The black press connected Horne's unique singing voice with her (beautiful) black body to celebrate her racial identity in the face of the white press's tendency to bifurcate her voice, whitening its sound yet fetishizing her "coolness" as tonal mask for raging racialized sexuality.

Unlike many white reviewers, who pondered her voice's ability to cross the sonic color line, many black critics grounded Horne's voice firmly in her raced and gendered body, a move simultaneously empowering and limiting. The Chicago Defender glibly called her "one of the best chirpers in the business and the most attractive to 'sell' songs in Broadway or Harlem history." By referencing segregated New York's white downtown and black uptown, the *Defender* intimates the sonic color line–crossing abilities of her voice but then suggests Horne can only mobilize this vocal agency because her female beauty can "sell" such race crossing, an uncomfortable knot of capitalism, racism, colorism, and the long history of racializing black women's sexuality in America. To the *Atlanta Daily World* she was simply a "beautiful, sweet-voiced leading lady" with a "clear and bell-like" voice, imagery again reminiscent of qualities the listening ear hears as "white" and "feminine" vocal styles.[44] However, the *Daily World* links Horne's beautiful voice with her "beautiful" body, describing her skin in rich detail: she is a "café-au-lait songstress," a "bronze goddess," a "light-bronze beauty," and "MGM's honey brown queen."[45] Exchanging the terms "black" and "negro" for a range of chromatic adjectives claims Horne through colloquial descriptive terms of praise, even as such words call attention to Horne's lighter skin tone and proximity to white beauty standards. As ambivalent as it was celebratory, Horne's early black press matched her sound to her skin and struggled with how Horne's particular embodiment of beauty enhanced her agency as a singer, particularly in what Priscilla Peña Ovalle calls the "new era of (white) female sexuality during and after World War II," enabling her voice to travel over the airwaves and across the sonic color line.[46]

However, the listening ear also evolved in concert with Horne's vocal defiance, much as it did when faced with the boundary-crossing Jubilee Singers. Horne's white reviewers worked hard to rhetorically isolate her voice in its own unique racial category rather than relying on clear rhetorical emphases and repeated descriptors, such as "weird," "raw," etc., used for other singers this book discussed. Many white critics actually defined Horne's sound by the qualities they did *not* hear; Horne's voice may not have sounded entirely "white," yet it did not sound black (or, to some, black *enough*). For example, *Coronet*—a general interest offshoot of *Esquire*—linked Horne's fame to her seeming lack of vocal adornment: "She just sang the old songs simply, with no tricks, no shouting, nothing fancy," a description associating black singing styles with excessive embellishment.[47] Shortened from "coon shouting," "shouting" was by 1940 a flat racial terminology describing a wide range of African American singing practices whites considered emotive, ornamental, and untutored: falsetto, melisma, vocal dynamics, and what Ethel Waters described as the ability to "riff and jam and growl."[48] While shouting did not always refer to phenotypically black singers—many prominent "coon shouters" in the early twentieth century were Jewish women such as Fanny Brice—the term maintained its racial referent. *PM*, New York's short-lived liberal daily, also used the sonic racial code word "shouting": "Lena Horne can shout with the best of them when she's singing that kind of song . . ." the ellipses implying Horne can change her entire musical approach—and racial emphasis—with a simple change of the repertoire.[49]

While the black press contextualized Horne's voice in terms of race consciousness, white press reviews of Horne revealed how the listening ear had shifted with color blindness to listen for the "right kind of black." "Chocolate Cream Chanteuse," the title of *TIME*'s 1943 feature, offers a synesthetic image positioning Horne for consumption—visually, sonically, culturally, and sexually—what bell hooks calls "eating the Other." "Chanteuse" lends a European cast to Horne's nightclub performances, which the writer diametrically opposed to the blues: "Unlike most Negro chanteuses," *TIME* describes, "Lena Horne eschews the barrelhouse manner, claws no walls, conducts herself with the seductive reserve of a Hildegarde."[50] Like "shouting," "barrelhouse" is also a racialized sonic term from the nineteenth century, referring to illicit bars hosting entertainment (often blues) and prostitution. The idea that Horne "claws no walls" evokes the sonic color line to economically construct an image of a "typical" black woman singer—animalistic, hypersexual, and excessively emotional—while lauding Horne for controlling her sexuality according to white standards of bodily comportment (which, as discussed in chapter 2, are also a nineteenth-century legacy). *TIME* evokes Hildegarde, a German-American cabaret singer from Milwaukee, Wisconsin, as an interracial comparison and foil; clad in ball gowns and elbow-length gloves, Hildegarde performed a second-generation, "melting pot," white, middle-class femininity, "sing[ing] the way Garbo looks."[51] But unlike Garbo's and Hildegarde's fit, Horne's voice and body are not something *TIME* can unify, nor can it make peace with the listening ear's perceived mismatch; her voice cannot ultimately be contained by her bodily reserve. In another move echoing Greenfield's reception, *TIME* queers the sound of Horne's sexuality, declaring her voice redolent with "high lavender virtuosity," a too-intense femininity—excessive to the point of camp or drag—that belies restraint. Symptomatic of Horne's widely vacillating white press, the *TIME* review shows the listening ear in flux, shifting to contain crossings of the sonic color line through increasingly more fine-grained attention to the sound of race in the voice, particularly as aligned with sexuality, and emphasis on black assimilation to white speech habits.

Horne's early white press reviews also used "torch singer" to gesture toward whiteness while retaining a sonic referent to black female sexuality. This racially ambiguous term placed Horne in a canon of white ethnic female singers including Hildegarde and "the hottest torch singer of them all," Dinah Shore, who claimed she learned to sing by imitating her black nursemaid's "noodling" ("Dinah" became Frances Rose Shore's stage name early on, giving her voice a more "Southern" cast).[52] On turn-of-the-century vaudeville stages, the torch song was "considered to be exotic," along with the Jewish women performing it.[53] When Horne and Shore debuted, "torch singing pioneered the use of these black vocal techniques in singing aimed at a white middle-class audience by singers who, claiming whiteness, performed without any pretense of being black."[54] The mainstream white press often compared Horne and Shore as mirrored images of each other across (and crossing) the sonic color line: the black singer who sounded "white" and the white singer who sounded "black." Horne's voice—which the white press heard as tending toward whiteness—was often called "cold," while both the white and black presses represented Shore's personality and voice—heard to echo "blackness"—as "sultry voiced," "mellow," and "warm."[55] In a review of Horne's 1942 album *Moanin' Low*, the *Washington Post*'s swing critic asserted, "In this collection of torch songs, Lena—who had done stints with name bands like Artie Shaw's—is very much in the Dinah Shore groove. Miss Horne hasn't got that low, smooth delivery down as pat as has titillating Dinah; but in her own quiet way, Lena manages to dig into the wax with a bit more heat than you can get from the Shore gal."[56] The *Post* review performed the sonic color line's feedback loop: no matter how "smooth" and white Lena sounded, her public identity as a black woman left the listening ear yearning to discover, even invent, a little more "lowness" and "a bit more heat" within her timbre. The sonic impact of color blindness enabled whites' mobility across the sonic color line and back again—Shore never lost her "America's Sweetheart" label—while creating a neither/nor "no person's land" for black people whose bodies do not "match" the sounds the listening ear has been disciplined to expect.

However, through a close reading of Horne's 1944 guest appearance on the CBS network thriller *Suspense*, I detail her resistance to color-blind categorizations of her voice, using intonation, phrasing, and vocal versioning to enhance her agency, challenge the sonic color line's connection of white speech patterns with American nationalism, and align her voice with other black performers who defied sonic stereotyping, such as Marian Anderson.[57] A pulp- and gothic-inspired program, *Suspense* cultivated a prestigious reputation through quality sound, original scripts, and first-rate guest performances, from the likes of Shore, Orson Welles, Frank Sinatra, Lucille Ball, and Peter Lorre. *Suspense* specialized in creating dangerous, unpredictable, and transgressive situations, titillating audiences by encouraging actors to play against type and "to take center stage as complex subjective protagonists in their own twisted narratives."[58] Horne crafts her *Suspense* character against several intertwined facets of her established persona—particularly her alleged "coldness" and cultivated black middle-class respectability—to challenge, if not decolonize, her listeners' habits, especially regarding the whiteness of American sonic citizenship.

As written by Robert L. Richards, Horne's role in "You Were Wonderful," nightclub singer "Lorna Dean," invites a pseudobiographical performance, yet she uses her voice to co-script the role and the racial limitations she faced on air and off. As Daphne Brooks argues, black female vocalists of this era did not simply follow scripts; rather, they used the materiality of their voices to transcend limited roles, cocreate their characters through performance, *and* craft "a poetics of modern black womanhood."[59] Heretofore, Horne appeared predominately in singing-only roles on variety-style programs, unless part of an all-black cast as in *Stormy Weather* (1943) or *Cabin in the Sky* (1942). Lorna Dean, her first and only starring role in a radio drama—let alone on a national network playing a potential romantic lead opposite a white man, all but unheard of in the 1940s—offered Horne access to a wide audience without the immediate corporeal tensions white audiences created at her cabaret performances. *Suspense* raced Horne's character, not so much through her diction—evoking the rapid-fire style of a noir detective—nor her (non-existent) dialect, but through plot points, other characters' descriptions, and the content of her monologues. Horne's own subtle phrasing and vocal emphases, however, sounded her agency within and without the role to disrupt monolithic conceptions of black womanhood. Reviews suggest many black listeners heard Horne loud and clear; the National Newspaper Publishers Association, a black wire service, said "listeners throughout the country were amazed at the dramatic role and the punch lines assigned to Lena Horne. . . . It was a new departure in commercial programs, featuring Miss Horne in the principal dramatic role." Furthermore, "her lines gave her an opportunity to take several swipes at the 'master race theory,' which she did superbly."[60]

As the first black actor and professional singer cast on *Suspense*, Horne called attention to the whiteness of the previous 116 episodes, broadcast between 1942 and 1944. *Suspense*'s audible whiteness meant any episode featuring a black performer would appear to introduce race into the show's "color-blind" universe. Unlike the white characters guesting on the show, free to connect their voices to "unfamiliar bodies, deviant bodies, bodies marked by trauma and perversion,"[61] Horne came to *Suspense* always already bearing blackness's deviance and trauma; even the allegedly "invisible" and "disembodied" medium of radio could not—or would not—uncouple her voice from her body. Instead, plot and aural context cues heightened and naturalized the relationship between the two, even as the program also unsettled stereotypes about blackness and womanhood.

The assertive, fast-talking tone Horne uses for Lorna Dean both inhabits and sends up Horne's aloof reputation while playing on white audiences' expectations of sonic sultriness from black women. The title "You Were Wonderful" operates as a triple entendre, blurring the boundaries between Dean's performance onstage and her (potential) performance as a lover, setting the listener up for a tale of romance and lust instead of World War II espionage. The episode opens with Dean, a famous black American singer, arriving in Buenos Aires, Argentina. Her hard-edged voice gives her an air of icy opportunism from the moment she shouts "Mr. Reynaldo!" across the still-warm corpse of the nightclub's previous singer: "I want the job. Now!" When Johnny—the white American antihero expatriate played by Wally Maher—censures her for bad timing, Horne-as-Dean retorts, "Did I ask you anything?" and then, after a long pause, "now, Mr. Reynaldo, I am sorry for the girl, but I'm a singer, not a sob sister." While her biographer claims her stiltedness at the episode's outset pointed to her "weakness at delivering lines," the sonic color line provides an enhanced filter, revealing Horne's performance as something other than failed vampishness.[62] Rather, Horne's delivery crafts an audible, double-voiced "impersona" expressing her agency and anger over America's segregated airwaves.

Horne's guarded delivery created the episode's true suspense: Does Dean's tough talk sound her disloyalty to the U.S. war effort? Put another way, given how whites treat black people in the United States, does Dean have any motivation *not* to become a spy? Buenos Aires hosts an assortment of unsavory Axis powers, signalled by overly genteel European accents: the Austrian Mr. Harlins and the German Stengel. Harlins approaches Dean with a large sum to sing "One Dozen Roses," at a specified time. Johnny tries to talk Dean out of it, but she blows him off. On the night of her performance, Johnny barges into her dressing room, telling Dean that Harlins intends to use her song to tip off a U-boat of an American ship's departure. After a heated exchange, Dean goes onstage, ostensibly to sing as planned. However, when the moment arrives, she performs a defiant "My Country 'Tis of Thee," which, depending on the audiences' assumptions about Dean's character, operates as a twist ending that thwarts the listening ear's expectation of betrayal.

The conclusion of "You Were Wonderful" reveals Dean's—and perhaps Lena's—coldness as a performance of heroism and heroic self-protection. Operating alone until the very end, Dean never trusts Johnny or relies on him to save her; she believes *him* to be the spy until he shoots Harlins and Stengel. Dean's steely tone enabled her "to displac[e] herself from discursive and representational systems, even while appearing within them," as Vogel argues regarding Horne's aloofness.[63] It also sounds the character's fatalism; from the moment Dean steps into the cabaret, her hard-edged voice signifies her readiness to die fighting. "When I found out what you boys were doing," Dean proudly reveals to an enraged Harlins, "I arranged for a little tip-off of my own and that song you heard was it." Johnny, who has been working for the government all along, breaks in and saves her life, asking her why she risked "playing a lone hand like that." She responds, with audible satisfaction, to "get in *my* licks at the master race."

Horne-as-Dean's triumphant switcheroo performance, "My Country 'Tis of Thee," sends out an important broadcast signal within the story while subverting the sonic color line outside of it. Just five years before, Marian Anderson sang this song as her own broadcast signal live to millions by NBC's Blue network on the steps of the Lincoln Memorial, protesting the Daughters of the American Revolution's exclusion of her from their venue. Gayle Wald notes the importance of the technological mediation of Anderson's voice: "Also listening, we can surmise, were many who would have hesitated to welcome into their homes black women who were not also domestics, or black voices that did not speak in the tones of radio characters such as 'Amos and Andy.'"[64] Offstage or on, Horne embodied neither of these identities; the president of the NAACP, Walter White, who had a hand in organizing Anderson's concert, organized behind Horne's refusals to play menial roles onstage or speak "the cornfield voice." According to Wald, Anderson had planned to begin with "The Star-Spangled Banner," but White suggested "My Country" because more people knew the words and because of its "ironic implications," which Horne plays to the hilt in "You Were Wonderful."[65]

Horne's version bears striking similarities to Anderson's, and I argue it amplifies the politics of what Wald describes as "shared vibrations."[66] Though Horne does not trill her r's or replicate Anderson's famous alteration of the lyrics to "of thee *we* sing," her performance sonically nods to Anderson's; unlike Dean's other orchestral numbers in the episode, she performs "My Country 'Tis of Thee" with only piano accompaniment as Anderson did, and sings with a similar stridency. If, as Wald convincingly argues, Anderson's performance sounds a vibrational call to listen, Horne's performance audibly calls back to Anderson, signalling that she has indeed heard. Dean prefaces her performance with: "I want to sing something by special request. It's a song that is very popular in my own country and I am sure it is with many of you down here," highlighting Dean's claim to America and framing the stakes of her double cross. As the Germans whisper frantically over the song's triumphant tones, listeners realize Dean honors her own country's "special request." The song's echoes of Anderson, however, prevent Dean's defiance from being interpellated into a neat-and-tidy nationalism. In amplifying Anderson's resonant vibration as a radical act of inclusion and an opportunity to "get in [one's] licks at the master race," Dean achieves a double victory against the sonic color line and the listening ear.

Or at least she would have, had Johnny not decided to cut the radio lines before Dean approached the microphone. Only the nightclub audience (and *Suspense*'s listeners) hears Dean's sonic defiance, not the American sailors nor the world's shortwave radios within the context of the plot. An act of mistrust cloaked as patriotism, Johnny's silencing nullifies Dean's self-sacrifice and allows him, in the narrative's waning seconds, to regain the hero's role that American culture and convention construct as his due.

"You Were Wonderful" offers a potent reminder of the sonic color line's shifting politics amidst the new cultural landscape of color blindness. Whereas radio drama permitted Horne to defy aural stereotypes, call attention to her persona as performance, strategically mobilize aural markers of race, draw unexpected sonic lineages, and meaningfully embed her raced voice in a site usually "lily white," *Suspense*'s twist ending paradoxically reminded listeners of the barriers black people faced to be heard. The dead wires dangling at the end of "You Were Wonderful" sound out the connections between the golden age of U.S. radio and segregation, encouraging listeners to notice—and really listen to—the silences invisibly but palpably constructing their world.

African American artists created powerful images of silence (and silencing) across media and genres during the 1940s. Visceral and often terrifying, these representations of silence connected segregation's everyday indignities with the institutionalized and increasingly "color-blind" forms of power constructing and benefitting from racism: America's media, army, court system, and, most fundamentally, capitalism itself. Du Bois and Petry evoke silence as the synesthetic experience of life on the other side of the sonic color line, the visual, aural, and tactile feelings of exclusion, of being tuned out, dismissed, and misheard by the listening ear. Silence can look like a white boss or a government agent, sound like a cacophony of screams or a western playing on the radio, and it can feel like fingers clutching your throat. Du Bois, for example, translates experiences like Johnny cutting the wires at the end of "You Were Wonderful" into new social theorizations of race influenced by his experiences as a radio guest and producer. The color line he had understood to be porous and malleable forty years before hardened into the implacable plate-glass walls of a vacuum tube, a barrier sound cannot cross. It silences black people within it, while enabling the white people outside to either ignore them or find amusement in their silent gestures of fury and frustration. While undoubtedly offering grim perspectives on black life in the United States, the dystopic prose of black writers of this era resisted the seductive discourse of "color-blind" wartime inclusion and helped readers connect the personal and the political as well as the sensory and the systemic that would prove foundational to the Civil Rights Movement and remain resonant in our contemporary moment.

"Screaming in a Vacuum Unheard": Du Bois behind the Scenes

Since radio's inception, Du Bois had been fascinated with its possibilities for mass influence, especially because it created an immediacy that challenged the listening ear's distanced perspective. He gave his first long-range broadcast from Boston, Massachusetts, on January 10, 1926, a speech called "The Civilization of White People"; the response, he wrote, "astonished and gratified him."[67] Several letters from black audience members complimented how "the whole lecture came in to us so clearly and distinctively that one could almost imagine themselves as being one of the gathering."[68] "Imagine you in Philadelphia hearing me speak in Boston," responded Du Bois. "It is almost witchcraft, isn't it?"[69] Shortly after the Boston broadcast, he wrote structural engineer Charles S. Duke: "I am very much interested in radio broadcasting. I had my first experience with it about a month ago in Boston and I have received letters from as far as West Virginia. The National Association for the Advancement of Colored People must go into this but I am afraid it is going to cost too much."[70] Duke responded with disappointing news: not only would a competitively powerful station cost around 125,000 dollars, but also the U.S. government had suspended new licensing.[71]

While Du Bois's vision of a black-owned station would not be realized until Atlanta's WERD in 1949, he continued seeking opportunities to propagate the sound and influence of black discourse on the radio throughout the 1920s and 1930s. In 1927, the *Forum* magazine paid him to argue the "positive side" in "a corker" of a radio debate in New York City with notorious white supremacist eugenicist (and fellow Harvard alum) Lothrop Stoddard. Because of Du Bois's increasing audibility—and his role as editor of the *Crisis* and later *Phylon*—he was sought after by local radio stations such as New York's WEVD to increase black participation on the radio and to "get over to the public, a truer picture of events in the fields of unemployment, disarmament, labor struggles, civil liberties violations, and so forth, than the public may glean from the headlines and editorials of the vested press."[72] Until the Depression, when radio networks consolidated and almost totally whitened America's airwaves, Du Bois considered the radio a potential avenue of self-representation and social change.

While the sonic color line influenced U.S. radio from its beginnings, after the Depression fundamental shifts occurred that tightened an already-limited black access. In a trajectory opposite what Frantz Fanon would observe in 1950s Algeria, where radio began as the "instrument of colonial society and its values" and then transformed into the "Voice of the Revolution" when long-range broadcasts challenged Radio-Alger's authority, American radio became more heavily censored, segregated, and propaganda-laden. In Du Bois's purview, its potential role shifted from an acousmatic truth-teller to an echo chamber for power.[73] He told the National Advisory Council on Radio in Education as much when they contacted him for the "You and Your Government" program:

> I made no reply to your proposal concerning the Committee on Civic Education by Radio. I am in deepest sympathy with the general idea but my experience, so far, has been that anything connected with the radio in the United States is a part of widespread propaganda by the rich. In that, I'm naturally not interested.[74]

The veil-like "blindness" of radio now seemed better suited to producing the illusions and distortions necessary to maintain white hegemony.[75] These feelings only intensified when Du Bois toured Germany in 1936, where Third Reich broadcasts profoundly impressed him with the "enormous power of radio for good and evil."[76] Upon returning to the United States, Du Bois continued to intervene in the racial propaganda perpetrated on air, but in a much more limited way.

Given the networks' intensified segregation, Du Bois's radio work took a behind-the-scenes turn and, I argue, influenced his shift toward a sonic color line in *Dusk of Dawn*, described by Porter as a "jumping off point for a new stage of thinking in which long established ideas, roles, and rhetoric are reworked and imbued with new meanings in a changing social context."[77] In this text, Du Bois shifts his primary racial metaphor from an obscuring yet porous veil between the darker and lighter races—capable of being lifted—to an impenetrable, hermetically sealed plate-glass wall—not unlike a soundproof radio booth. As he drafted *Dusk of Dawn* in 1939, Du Bois served as an unpaid advisor for "The Negro" episode of the nationally broadcast program *Americans All, Immigrants All*, along with Howard professor Alain Locke. At the urging of the show's creator, Rachel Davis DuBois (no relation), U.S. Commissioner of Education J. W. Studebaker begrudgingly invited the two scholars to give feedback on the script about black life, which Davis DuBois admitted "f[e]ll far short." The controversial twenty-six-part series, cosponsored by CBS, the Federal Security Agency, and the U.S. Office of Education, represented various groups' individual histories while incorporating them into a larger national narrative of assimilation that would ideologically unite the nation in preparation for impending war. While cordial, Studebaker's letter to Du Bois firmly limits his participation to the "subjects upon which you might be able to cooperate with us."[78] Given how much of Gilbert Seldes's script concentrates on slavery's benefits to the nation's growth, Du Bois's notes show agonizing restraint, concentrating on correcting gross historical inaccuracies involving Reconstruction. Du Bois also urged producers that "something ought to be inserted here to show the reaction of the slave himself toward slavery."[79] Locke suggested *Americans All* remove dialect that aurally raced black actors. The writers accepted few of their revisions but agreed to reconceive the ending around contemporary black achievement.

Du Bois and Locke's struggle was akin to what black radio producers faced when they challenged the sonic color line by cultivating and propagating counterimages to aural blackness. In the small slots of opportunity provided by the occasional network program such as "The Negro" episode—only one black-themed recurrent series, NBC's *Freedom's People*, aired between 1939 and 1945—black producers and casting directors fought to select narrators, announcers, and actors whose voice signalled blackness to black audiences rather than the white listening ear. Savage depicts *Freedom's People* as a key site of aural resistance that sought to "avoid present[ing] the 'class' of African Americans that had been created by radio itself."[80] Refusing to speak white-imagined "Negro dialect," popular narrators such as Paul Robeson and Canada Lee represented aural blackness with deep tones, crisp diction, and an assertive seriousness. However, black construction of an aural analogue to the modernist "New Negro" created new challenges, particularly because it emphasized masculinity and a middle-class urban respectability that muted other forms of black expression deemed less respectable.

Du Bois and Locke faced similar challenges as they clashed with *Americans All* writers, facing the sonic color line off air that muted their critiques and shaped the show for the white audiences' comfort. Even with their efforts, "the final script for 'The Negro,'" Du Bois biographer David Levering Lewis declares, "omitted, bowdlerized, and backtracked."[81] None of Du Bois's changes made it live on air. At the last minute, CBS added a musical number, "Black Boy" sung by *Showboat* star Jules Bledsoe, that lasted a third of the program. It was later panned by Locke as a "mammy interpolation," a gendered insult revealing anxiety over sonic representation of black voices on the radio as well as implicitly connecting masculinity to the sound of vocal power.[82] However, mechanical difficulties involving CBS's transcription machine—and persistent protests by Locke, Du Bois, and Davis DuBois—meant the scripted version would be rerecorded for the educational aftermarket. Exasperated but resolute, Du Bois reminded Davis DuBois that it could have been worse; after all, he wrote, "it's not so much what you actually get in as what you keep out."[83]

Du Bois's struggle to keep aural stereotypes and misinformation from America's airwaves could only have contributed to his feeling that, by 1940, making reasoned arguments against racism was akin to "screaming in a vacuum unheard."[84] Shut out from the means of mass dissemination of information, Du Bois transduced his palpable feelings of isolation and inaudibility into a new structuring metaphor for race. Particularly when he contextualized it within the devastating new realities of racially motivated global warfare, Du Bois could no longer conceive of race as a mere idea to overturn, as the ideology of liberal color blindness would have it, but rather he "insisted on remaining attuned to the persistence and complexity of race," especially "white supremacy's survival in the first postracial moment."[85] While the U.S. government circulated the language of racial inclusion via programming such as *Americans*

All, the physical, cultural, social, and economic isolation of black people into segregated ghettos only intensified.

Du Bois's shift to a sonically oriented color line challenged how American broadcasting represented and embodied color blindness. In Du Bois's new account, listening—as both epistemology and technology— also produces race, and ideologies of race have a profound (and widely divergent) impact on how people listen, how they imagine others to listen, and, most importantly, whose screams they deem worth heeding. Because this passage is not as well known as his discussion of the veil, I quote Du Bois at length:

> It is as though one, looking out from a dark cave in a side of an impend-
> ing mountain, sees the world passing and speaks to it; speaks courteously
> and persuasively, showing them how these entombed souls are hindered
> in their natural movement, expression, and development; and how their
> loosening from prison would be a matter not simply of courtesy, sym-
> pathy, and help to them, but aid to all the world. One talks on evenly
> and logically in this way, but notices that the passing throng does not
> even turn its head, or if it does, glances curiously and walks on. It gradu-
> ally penetrates the minds of some of the prisoners that the people pass-
> ing do not hear; that some thick sheet of invisible but horribly tangible
> plate glass is between them and the world. They get excited; they talk
> louder; they gesticulate. Some of the passing world stops in curiosity;
> these gesticulations seem so pointless; they laugh and pass on. They still
> either do not hear at all, or hear dimly, and even what they hear, they
> do not understand. Then the people within may become hysterical. They
> may scream and hurl themselves against the barriers, hardly realizing in
> their bewilderment that they are screaming in a vacuum unheard and
> that their antics may seem funny to those outside looking in. They may
> even, here and there, break through in blood and disfigurement, and find
> themselves faced by a horrible, implacable, and quite overwhelming mob
> of people frightened for their very existence.[86]

Inverting Plato's allegory of the cave, Du Bois's metaphor challenges visually centered epistemologies. Under this model, black people are soundproofed yet hypervisible, constantly on display for the curiosity of the white gaze; the plate glass offers a clarity of sight without any aural information, which gives whites a false certainty in their perceptions. However, his story also pulls back from the idea that sound, by its very nature, operates as a medium to challenge vision's hold on truth. Unlike Plato's version, in which the underground prisoners are conditioned to a distorted sense of reality—viewing shadows cast on the wall as truth and truth as "nothing but the shadows of images"—in Du Bois's new allegory of race, it is the "passing throng" outside the cave who operate on their false assumptions of the prisoners within.[87]

Now blind *and* deaf to the realities of black life—but ever more convinced of their understanding—whites outside the cave exhibit a willful, conditioned configuration of the senses that allows them to maintain power and privilege without acknowledging their culpability or its human costs. While white supremacist ideology constructed the plateglass chamber—the topic of *Dusk of Dawn*—its visual clarity enabled segregation to seem natural (and pre-existing) to the whites outside, yet those outside fail to realize that they "either do not hear at all, or hear dimly, and even what they hear, they do not understand." As no sound escapes the chamber, whites see the wails of the imprisoned as spectacle: entertaining but otherwise "pointless" gesticulations.

By calling attention to the multiple, simultaneous sensory modalities of race, Du Bois imparted important new knowledge: white supremacy's opaque veils and plate-glass enclosures were not due to "unconscious habit and irrational urge," as he had once thought but rather were products of conscious, deliberate, and strategic perceptual misinformation, one that, inspired by Du Bois, I have traced in this book.[88] In a pointed reference to his earlier writing—and to his experience with "The Negro" episode—Du Bois describes how, at first, it appears that the imprisoned only have to put forth reasoned appeals to leave the cave. However, as these repeated attempts fail and the whites "laugh and pass on," hysteria mounts within. Wails of humanity become futile screams of imprisonment, causing "bewilderment" and frenzied attempts to escape, even at a severe cost to themselves. If they are able to break the glass, the fugitives become unrecognizable to themselves—devastated by "blood and disfigurement"—and/or they find themselves facing an "overwhelming" white mob—an image combining European fascism with the white American practice of lynching. For the glass to be removed, fundamental shifts in listening must occur on either side—a dismantling of the listening ear outside the glass and a decolonizing of listening on the inside.

Published six years after *Dusk of Dawn*, Ann Petry's *The Street* signifies on the suffocating isolation of Du Bois's theories of race, as protagonist Lutie Johnson struggles to escape her racial and economic entrapment within a Harlem tenement whose walls echo with its residents' screams of frustration and cries of pain, enhanced by the ever-present sound of the radio. Petry's novel dramatizes the relationship between the sound of black suffering and radio's ubiquity, invoking the trope of the listener to meditate on an ethics of listening for a mass-mediated age and to consider the agency of black radio listeners under segregation, laying bare the impact of America's "golden age" of radio upon its "forgotten 15,000,000" listeners.[89]

Black Radio Listeners: From the Airwaves to *The Street*

Petry's bestseller offers a rare representation of black radio listeners from the "golden age," one that emerged from a regular, lively discourse about radio in black newspapers and journals that actively resisted limited mainstream white understandings of black listenership. Petry often discussed radio programming in her weekly *Lighter Side* column for *The People's Voice*; she recommended the National Urban League's *Heroines in Bronze* to her readers, for example, commending the national broadcast's focus on African American women.[90] Elsewhere in *The People's Voice*, columns such as When to Listen, The Listening Post, and Bostic's Dial Time highlighted programming black listeners enjoyed, curated schedules of the few shows regularly featuring black performers, and urged activism against the industry's misrepresentation.

In Dial Time, Bostic listed corporate-sponsored shows featuring black performers so that readers could "buycott" their products and write in with suggestions, critiques, and praise when merited. "Don't fail to write or wire to the sponsors at Columbia Broadcast System," Bostic wrote after a Fred Allen Texaco broadcast, "to let them [Texaco] know how much you appreciate their presenting a Negro performer, minus the burlesque and the bandanna."[91] After a particularly egregious episode of *March of Time* featuring a segment lampooning black folk music, Bostic announced he "received nearly a hundred calls from incensed

listeners Saturday morning, which shows that we are on the alert."
Media critiques by Bostic and others had a far-reaching impact; a 1942
report from the Office of Facts and Figures estimated that "the overwhelming majority of blacks—more than eight out of ten—read some
black newspaper, usually either the *Amsterdam News* or *The People's
Voice*."[92] Bostic's curatorial reportage created a public venue for black
media critique and engaged readers in a collective project to actively
decolonize listening—identifying and challenging the default whiteness
of radio while simultaneously cultivating a sense of alertness to how the
American radio industry normalized the sonic color line.

Petry—women's editor of *The People's Voice* and Bostic's colleague—
also examined American enthusiasm for radio in her fiction. While only
one aspect of *The Street*'s multilayered realist portrait of a black woman's
struggle to physically, financially, and psychologically escape a dismal
Harlem tenement, the radio's persistent, ubiquitous presence suggests it
has a much larger role in the novel (and in Lutie Johnson's tragic down-
fall) than previous scholarship has afforded it.[93] Setting *The Street* in
her contemporary moment, Petry details the intersecting struggles of
Lutie and her neighbors in the 116th Street tenement—the omnipres-
ent madam Mrs. Hedges; the lascivious attempted rapist, building super
Jones; Jones's self-effacing girlfriend, Min; and Lutie's bright young son,
Bub—along with radio's role in sounding out their segregated lives.

Petry's representation of the physical spaces of segregation as the
material contexts of reception for black radio audiences provides a
rare archival interpretation of black radio listening in the 1940s, along
with another key moment of signifyin(g) on the African American literary trope of the listener/listening as epistemology that I have traced
throughout this book. Through her stream-of-consciousness representation of Lutie's listening, Petry echoes the trope and extends it to consider the relationship between the sonic color line and black women's
experiences of isolation, oppression, and depression in midcentury
urban modernity. Petry dialogues most directly with Richard Wright's
inattention to black female listeners in crafting *Native Son*'s horrific
urban soundscape as well as Du Bois's graphic sonification of America's racial echo chamber. Muted strains remain, however, of Douglass's
notion of radical openness and Brent's evocation of community listening as decolonizing epistemology, if only because Petry's characters'

listening habits seem all but blocked to both possibilities by the ruth-less atomization of racial capitalism and the sonic color line's relentless body discipline. Recently separated from her husband and raising her son alone, a desperate but determined Lutie moves into a dark, dingy apartment in an overcrowded building whose brick structure seals off its residents so tightly that not even sound vibrations escape, while its "flimsy" interior walls "echo and reecho" with sobs, screams, fights, and blaring radio broadcasts, overexposing the residents' intimate sufferings and "fits of violent elation."[94]

While Lutie often feels trapped in and suffocated by racialized do-mestic space, her radio provides a portal to other times, places, experi-ences, affects, and moods. Yet, Lutie's experiences show the imagined travel of radio as a double-edged sword for black women, whom Hilmes describes as "the most completely marginalized group in radio's prac-tices."[95] Radio also functions as a sonic brick through Lutie's apartment window, allowing the intertwined ideologies of white supremacy and patriarchy to flood her intimate space. In the 1940s many critics and industry professionals regarded "intimacy" as both goal and product of American radio, whether referring to the "warm, personal feeling" of announcers' voices or the "relationship to radio entertainers and pro-grams characterized by intimacy and loyalty" that blurred boundaries between private and public spaces.[96] Radio's perceived ability to pierce and recode domestic space both mimics *and* enables the encroachment of segregation into black lives and homes. As GerShun Avilez theorizes in his work on segregation narratives, "The attempt to confine a subject to a particular place . . . can paradoxically engender a feeling of hav-ing no place for that subject inside and outside of the segregated area. The sense of having no place travels, as it were, and has the motility of a policing force."[97] Like (and through) radio broadcasts, white valu-ation of black space enters, shapes, and surveilles black homes, while the feelings of isolation and entrapment segregation engenders follow black people outside their homes. The sonic color line's long genealogy enabled such intimate and invisible sensory traffic across what Avilez calls segregation's "value-laden boundaries," increasing segregation's portability through affect and bringing the effect of racial hierarchy into newly "integrated" public spaces.[98] In turn, American radio trans-duced the once-bold boundaries of the sonic color line into the subtle static, muffled suppressions, and silent omissions of state-sponsored color blindness.

Petry connects radio listening to race, nationalism, and identity formation via the "color-blind" listening experiences of Lutie's son, Bub, who spends much of his time alone in their apartment. The novel's sole character to enjoy radio listening, Bub counts their set among the familiar possessions stabilizing his lonely world in the necessary absence of his working mother, along with "the big chair, the card table . . . [and] the congoleum rug."[99] As Lutie remembers, "Bub usually listened to one of those interminable spy hunts or cowboy stories, and at night the living room was filled with the tumult of a chase, loud music, and sudden shouts. And Bub would yell, 'Look out! He's in back of you.'"[100] Many parents complained of the poor quality of children's radio programming, especially in a one-set household like Lutie's.[101] However, Petry's novel details Bub's specific context of reception to make a deeper critique than one pointing out the vapidity or violence of kids' radio. Lutie flashes back to Bub's listening habits on the night of his arrest for stealing mail from the neighboring buildings as she sits alone in their silent apartment, inviting readers to connect American radio's alleged "color-blind" interpellation with Bub's incarceration. What damage occurs when radio waves cross the physical boundaries of segregation while broadcasting the sonic color line's protocols as normalcy? Bub listens to the radio very differently from the way the adults around him do, and not just because of his eager imagination. Although he understands the desperation of his class situation—in fact, his desire to help out financially at home makes him susceptible to the super's manipulation—Bub has yet to fully comprehend its connection to his racial identity, in part because of Lutie's misplaced confidence in the American Dream (and her desire to protect Bub from racial injury). On the one hand, Bub's immersive listening experiences exemplify the social, legal, and sonic boundaries that radio's aurality could cross; when Bub listens to the radio, he freely imagines himself at the center of its normative plots. On the other hand, the passage reveals the fragility of Bub's radio reveries, positioned on the heels of his arrest.

While *The Street* does not directly blame radio for Bub's incarceration, the novel reveals his vulnerability in the fantasy of a color-blind America. Believing that American radio programming speaks to and for him certainly increases his gullibility to the super's revenge plot against Lutie; Jones easily convinces Bub that his stealing mail is part of "some detective work catching crooks" for the police.[102] Bub has not yet realized that the agency he playacts through the radio's "interminable spy hunts or cowboy stories" will be unavailable to him once the black boy becomes a black man. And with exclusion comes erasure; American culture *relies* on these interconnected imperial narratives of patriarchal white supremacy to justify various forms of violence perpetrated against black men. Until the moment of his arrest, Bub fails to recognize the New York Police Department has little use for black boys, except as suspects, inmates, and, in his case, wards of the state.

Unlike Bub, Lutie hears her exile from radio's address and apprehends the sonic color line barring her from color-blind citizenship, yet she relies on the radio to ease segregation's acute loneliness. Radio provides her with feelings of connection, experienced through sound but activated by the temporality of simultaneous listening. Lutie seeks out the radio whenever she feels the most alone in her struggles at the intersection of racism, sexism, and classism, snapping her set on after nearly every setback the novel details: after she catches Bub shining shoes; after she finds out she will not be able to make money singing because of her white boss (and landlord) Junto's proprietary sexual interest in her; after she returns from visiting Bub at the juvenile detention center; and after a predatory lawyer tells Lutie she has to pay him 200 dollars to help Bub. In her lowest moments, Lutie listens out through her sorrow, frustration, and desperation, seeking the materiality of her radio set and its vibrations perhaps even more than its sounds; she usually turns it on "full blast" and sits "down close to it, so that the dance music would shut out the silence."[103] Paradoxically, Lutie seeks to decrease her "aware[ness] of the silence under the sound of the radio" and the "stillness that crept through all the rooms," yet all the while "listening, straining to hear something *more* under the sound of the radio."[104] Lutie's attempts to tune into "something *more*" beyond radio's omissions cultivates a critical awareness of the sonic color line's suppressions and misrepresentations; yet, by continuing to tune in at her loneliest moments, Lutie redoubles segregation's silences rather than banish them. Radio, marketed as a technology capable of closing massive global communication gaps in space and time and "banishing isolation,"[105] held out a ready and inexpensive source of electronically reproduced sounds affecting simultaneity and approximating companionship to those most in need. Yet, as Lutie's experience demonstrates, radio mediated rather than automatically eased social, cultural, political, and economic isolation; inviting the sounds of a party she was not invited to—and a sonic citizenship she was not a party to—into her living room often heightens her isolation, giving it weight, heft, and a ferocious staying power, especially because she tunes out other possible sources of solace, such as her neighbors. Through Lutie's pained and strained listening, Petry reveals black people's everyday struggle to enact a decolonizing listening practice in the face of radio's sonic simultaneity, offering the feeling of listening together as a balm for overwhelming isolation.

Not only does Petry show the qualitative gap between simultaneous and community listening, but she also uses aural imagery that shows how, for black listeners hemmed in by segregation *and* the sonic color line, radio can act as a sonic silencer, drowning out the connections that would foster and sustain a resistant community listening practice. When Lutie finds out Bub has been arrested, for example, she sinks, sobbing to the floor, and

> all through the house radios went on full blast in order to drown out this familiar, frightening, unbearable sound. But even under the radios, they could hear it, for they had started crying with her when the sound first assailed her ears. . . . The thin walls shivered and trembled with the music. Upstairs, downstairs, all through the house, there was music, any kind of music, turned up full and loud—jazz, blues, swing, symphony surged through the house.[106]

While the residents' snapping their radios to drown Lutie out offers a form of agency—and amplifies sound's ability to carve out private spaces within the hyperaudibility and surveillance of segregation's overcrowding—tuning out has consequences. The scene echoes Douglass listening to the "unbearable" screams of his Aunt Hester, but with a very different ethical stance. Rather than remaining radically open—an act Douglass describes as maintaining a resistant humanity in the face of slavery's abjection—Lutie's neighbors respectively sequester themselves through sound, closing themselves off from her grief, disavowing the parts of themselves that continue "crying with her" as a survival method. But what of the self survives such autosuppression, let alone of a community? Petry's twist on the trope of the listener shows that the mere material presence of radio and/or music does not automatically create a cohesive community. The context of reception and the agency of the listeners matter greatly, as Lutie's neighbors use the illusory, intangible intimacy of radio's mélange of "jazz, blues, swing, symphony" to thwart physical and emotional connection, momentarily waylaying their own blues by banishing hers.

Although Petry's depiction of radio listening underscores that tuning in does not automatically translate into listening out, her characters do practice a variety of listening strategies to resist radio's ideological whiteness and its sensory assault on blackness. Petry editorially flattens the sound of the radio in *The Street*, for example, representing how, for many black listeners, what critics, historians, and fans deemed American radio's golden age registered largely as a sonic wallpaper of (white) sameness. Characters rarely describe specific radio content, referring mainly to "the radio" or "the sound of the radio" and occasionally to its volume, sometimes "blaring," "full blast," and "turned up full and loud" and at other times merely making a "faint tinny sound."[107] Residents of 116th Street frequently listen askance to the radio—over it, or under it, but rarely directly to it—valuing the medium for its material manifestations of music and voice and the space such sounds clear for interiority, access to one's "inner reservoir of thoughts, feelings, desires, fears, ambitions that shape a human self."[108] Listening askance—a cultivated distance akin to Lena Horne's performance of impersona—enables Lutie to find pleasure in a medium perpetrating racial exclusion and to insulate herself from psychic injury while maintaining the affective link to simultaneity radio provided.

Other characters decolonize their listening by recoding radio's material with alternate meanings and sonic emphases. For instance, when Lutie performs an impromptu rendition of a radio standard in Junto's bar—Frances Reckling's "Darlin'," written by a friend of Petry's and made a hit by Lucky Millinder's orchestra in 1944—she makes sure "it was of something entirely different that she was thinking and putting into the music: she was leaving the street with its dark hallways, its mean, shabby rooms . . . she and Bub were getting out and they would never be back."[109] Listeners familiar with this transformational praxis would be able to hear, in this moment, Lutie performing her listening *through* the song. Like Horne and Billie Holiday, both famous for rephrasing the lyrics of postwar love songs, transforming so-called sentimental ditties into resistant expressions of black women's sentiment, Lutie shapes her voice as a tool of resistant black female self-making within segregation's confines. Lutie's decolonial listening practice sidesteps and transfigures radio's exclusion into what Jayna Brown calls "a utopian impulse of black expressive forms that is as momentary, ephemeral, and elusive as it is physically, historically, and politically placed."[110] Lutie's performance recalls the sonic defiance of Dean in "You Were Wonderful," especially her use of vocal detail as communication medium.

Significantly, Petry's novel begins (rather than climaxing) with Lutie's breakthrough singing performance, dramatizing both the stakes and the necessity of decolonizing listening. Petry pits Lutie's voice against the white supremacist institutional forces arrayed to silence it, including "color-blind" broadcasting. Petry collects various modes of radio programming together in one horrifying extended aural image near the end of the novel—advertising, music, and a religious service—mingling these sounds with Lutie's sobs and screams to show, in a very granular way, how listening to the whiteness of U.S. radio confuses and isolates Lutie. Coming home after the bandleader, Boots, informs her that she has to have sex with Junto in order to get paid for singing, Lutie begins a sad, frightful ascent up her tenement's staircase—a material analogue for Du Bois's echo chamber—and as she stops to sob in the hallways, she hears snatches of her neighbors' radios. At this point, Lutie has almost lost everything: her husband, her dreams of becoming a singer, her plans to leave 116th Street, and, ultimately, the hope in meritocracy, what she now calls "that obscuring cloud of dreams," that had been her guiding narrative toward economic success. Thematically, this scene uses sound to interweave the novel's main motifs: Lutie's occluded fight for full citizenship privileges and monetary success, the interplay between the seeming clarity of the color-blind American Dream and its deeper ideological distortions (delivered here via the radio), as well as the way radio heightened segregation's entrapment. Guided by sound, Lutie felt that, finally, "she could see this hall in reality."[111]

Becoming aware of the tenement as both prison and echo chamber shifts Lutie's listening practice dramatically. She now pays careful attention to the contradictory and conflicting content of radio's broadcasts rather than just tuning in to its affect of inclusion:

> Radios were playing on the third and fourth floors. She tried to walk faster to get away from the medley of sound, but her legs refused to respond to her urging. "Buy Shirley Soap and Keep Beautiful" was blared out by an announcer's voice. The sounds were confusing. Someone had tuned in the station that played swing records all night, and she heard, "Now we have the master of the trumpet in 'Rock, Raleigh, Rock.'"

Lutie consciously tries to escape the "medley of sound," a cacophony of "confusing" sounds masking pain and "blar[ing] out" a trio of dubious quick-fix solutions to America's institutional problems. Lutie's legs resist her mind's willful attempt to tune out by slowing her down, forcing her to listen through her embodied ear. This first sound, an advertisement for the skin-lightening company Shirley Soap reminds Lutie that, whatever American radio's other uses, its primary purpose is to sell. Although ostensibly color-blind, the context of the ad's reception—a black woman listening through her tenement's walls, shortly after fending off a white man's claim on her body—and the announcer's demand that Lutie "Keep Beautiful" exacerbate the interlocking pressures Lutie faces regarding gender, sexuality, and race. The Shirley Soap pitch genders the radio's sound—slyly revealing the origin of the term "soap operas" for female-oriented serials—and portrays how marketers for those programs needled insecurities about physical beauty, one of women's primary markers of value in a patriarchal society. As a black woman, Lutie faces the additional burden of colorism—pressure to lighten her skin toward whiteness to be "truly" beautiful—and the stereotype of black hypersexuality that makes her even more vulnerable to rape, sexual abuse, and unwanted attention from black and white men. The Shirley ad airs a "confusing" message of race and gender as indelible-yet-removable flaws and equivocally holds out the limiting beauty norms that condition (white) American womanhood as universal and accessible.

Next, Lutie hears some swing layered over the advertisement, an image that shocks her into recognition of how the sonic color line and the listening ear have circumscribed her musical ambitions. By 1944, swing had moved far beyond its initial flowering in black urban culture and into the phase Joel Dinerstein describes as corporate "white-facing."[112] The recording industry dubbed Benny Goodman the "King of Swing" in the late 1930s; the "Lindy Hop" appeared on Broadway by 1943; and U.S. government–sponsored "swing bands" entertained military troops. Unlike "Darlin'," the song Lutie performs, "Rock, Raleigh, Rock" provides neither comfort nor an opportunity for Lutie to express herself through listening; the song's title refers to one of the nation's most completely segregated cities, a reminder of the links between Southern and Northern racisms.[113] The sound itself conveys how white American capitalism appropriates, reworks, and profits from sounds authored by black cultural producers for the sensibility of the dominant white listening ear, arranging not only the aural markers of self-authored blackness out of the mix but also the musicians themselves. Particularly because Lutie listens on the night Boots and Junto effectively end her musical ambition—and her dream of escaping the street—she hears the lack of opportunity in the cultural industry for black female musicians.

The culminating broadcast battling for Lutie's attention is a revival church service, a sound that positions the black church as potential salve for Lutie's wounds. The preacher's call interpellates her as a fellow "lost soul" in need of "the way" to salvation:

> [The song] mingled with the sounds of a revival church which was broadcasting a service designed to redeem lost souls: "This is the way, sisters and brothers. This is the answer. Come all of you now before it's too late. This is the way." As she walked along, she heard the congregation roar, "Preach it, brother, preach it." Suddenly a woman cried loud above the other sounds, "Lord Jesus is a-coming now."
>
> The congregation clapped their hands in rhythm. It came in clear over the radio. And the sound mingled with the high sweetness of the trumpet playing "Rock, Raleigh, Rock" and the soap program joined in with the plunking of a steel guitar, "If you wanta be beautiful, use Shirley Soap."
>
> A fight started on the third floor. Its angry violence echoed up the stairs, mingled with the voices on the radio.[114]

Lutie's indifference to the church broadcast—and the violence in the volatile "mingle" between capitalism, culture industry, and religion—at first suggests a critique of religious salvation via radio broadcast.

However, the service's sonic details—the rhythmic clapping, the roaring congregation, the intensity of the woman's cry for Jesus, the steel guitar's suggestive Southernness—render the image more ambiguous. Media historian Suzanne Smith has recovered archived broadcasts of revival preacher Elder Lightfoot Solomon Michaux—the "Happy Am I" preacher—who performed weekly national services from 1932 through the early 1950s to millions of listeners; she highlights his activist mission to reach people where and how they were: "I wanted to give people religion over the air so they might have it at home. Then they couldn't have an excuse for not going to church. . . . They could get God and his teachings right in their own parlor." Smith argues that dismissing his listeners as easily misled or cultish—as some critics did—misses how racially transgressive Michaux's sermons could be, "in ways that complicate our understanding of how modern religious movements navigated Jim Crow segregation."[115] The popularity and intensity of Michaux's broadcasts correlate with the importance of black churches as hotbeds of resistance, a key force in the growing Civil Rights Movement. Black church membership also provided agency and community for many black women, which Lutie desperately seeks.[116] Like Bigger Thomas, Lutie cannot find solace in historically black folkways. If the sermon sounds a moment of connection—black hands reaching through segregation's walls, electrifying each other—Lutie keeps on walking. Petry's imagery of the stairwell filled with competing broadcasts resonates strongly with Du Bois's description of racial segregation as an echo chamber, and as Lutie attempts to climb her way upward through it— literally and symbolically—no clear path of uplift emerges. Without a decolonized listening practice, Lutie fixates on the perpetual echoes that sound out her imprisonment.

In *The Street*, however, the echo chamber's loud mélange eventually cedes to a palpable silence, the gendered flip side of blackness as "noise." In *The Street*, silence registers as a creeping, gothic-styled sensation, a void threatening Lutie with dissolution. The more trapped Lutie feels—because of her indebtedness, the legal system, her divorce, the misogyny of various men, white and black—the more she perceives silence as intrusive, even predatory. Upon visiting Bub, for example, she notices a "dangerous silence" following her, becoming so strong it takes on a smell. The silence trails her back home, showing itself as an audible "pool" filling her apartment. Like the wind that circumscribed her path at the novel's beginning, the silence chases her down 116th Street, causing increasingly erratic and restricted movements. She ducks into the movies, only to find silence "crouched along the aisles . . . waiting, waiting." At the beauty parlor, Lutie hears silence "under the words" of her beautician; she fears it "would walk down the street with her and into the apartment." The radio can no longer keep oppression's silence at bay—in fact, the radio only redoubles silence, here a pervasive material experience of whiteness and white supremacy in the absence of white people. At one point, Lutie imagines the silence taking on Junto's form. Petry's dynamic and synesthetic representation of silence shows how the listening ear and the sonic color line form a highly portable affect of segregation, one difficult to dismantle.[117]

Within Petry's Harlem soundscape, silence does not delineate sound's absence; rather, it amplifies the sound of absence in Lutie's life and calls attention to her continued exile from America's "color-blind" national narratives. At the end of the novel, she eventually breaks the silence with an act of rage, killing the bandleader in self-defense after he attempts to rape her by smashing his face with a candlestick. Lutie has lost everything—her "goodness," her husband, her singing gig, her civil service job, her home, her dreams of a meritocratic America, even her son, still in juvenile detention—and she decides to flee. Petry signifies heavily on *Native Son* in the closing pages by reversing the imagery of Bigger killing Bessie, sending Lutie to Bigger's Chicago—which Wright has already told us offers no solution to Lutie's problems—and by closing with the image of Harlem's streets filling with snow. Lutie, however, hears not a howling storm but a quiet dusting:

> The snow fell softly on the street. It muffled sound. It sent people scurrying homeward, so that the street was soon deserted, empty, quiet. And it could have been any street in the city, for the snow laid a delicate film over the sidewalk, over the brick of the tired, old buildings; gently obscuring the grime and the garbage and the ugliness.[118]

The noisy snowfall in *Native Son* exposed white control over Chicago and announced white supremacy's penetration of spatial segregation's borders. *The Street's* soft snowfall—all the more nefarious in its silence and beauty—*masks* white supremacy in America's new color-blind regime. The snow knows no "white" and "black" boundaries; it falls everywhere equally, making even poverty-stricken streets appear as if they "could have been any street in the city." The snow's "delicate film" functions analogously to the sonic color line; it "muffled sound" and "gently obscure[ed] the grime and the garbage and the ugliness" of racial inequity, all the while sending people "scurrying" toward disparate privileges and punishments. Petry encourages readers to listen out beyond the color-blind listening ear's discipline and distortion, to sound out racism's "tired, old buildings" hiding just below America's smooth white surface.

Through deafening silence, Petry reveals the crucial difference between identifying racism and decolonizing perception. Although Lutie understands racism, sexism, and classism and lives the material consequences of their intersection, awareness alone does not liberate her—in fact, it joins with her isolation to cause depression and self-destruction. Staring at the snow, Lutie comes to the devastating conclusion that her life does not matter, even to herself. "What possible good," she wonders, "has it done to teach people like me to write?" And with that question, Lutie cuts her own wires and falls silent, disappearing into another segregated street in another segregated city. Ironically, of course, Lutie's musings call attention to Petry's authorial agency, an act that weaponizes words against white silencing of black lives. Petry's metacommentary offers up her novel as a memorial to the "many Lutie Johnsons" she knew, "women whose experiences and tragedies followed a similar pattern,"[119] and an echolocative dispatch to black women, telling them their lives do matter, and urging them to find themselves and one another and to listen, together, to and through the "similar patterns" that restrict but do not define them.

Listening as Petry's novel encourages—sounding out whiteness while amplifying the sounds it has masked—reveals a different understanding of 1930s and 1940s American radio, one decidedly less nostalgic but central to American modernity. Although the discipline of radio studies has always considered the medium more than "just" entertainment, it has yet to fully reckon with how "golden age" U.S. network radio represented—and shaped—segregation. Given the growing enthusiasm for a "new radio studies" to identify new archives to expand the field's research horizons, a unique opportunity exists for a radical shift in historiography, one that no longer privileges white listeners yet labors to understand the impact of radio's aural whiteness over time.[120] Accounting for the industry's physical exclusion of black performers, writers, and listeners is only the beginning; we must continue to articulate the sonic color line's impact on radio's sound as well as radio's impact on the sonic color line and its ties to "color-blind" American citizenship.

Chicana/o studies and radio scholar Dolores Inés Casillas's ¡Sounds of Belonging! reminds us of the racial and linguistic biases of U.S. media historiography while exploring Spanish-language radio's ability to construct cultural citizenship and belonging in tension with and often outside of the exclusionary discourse and practices I explored in this chapter. She, too, researches toward a different perspective from which to listen to U.S. radio history, arguing that radio scholars should "reconsider calling the earlier half of the last century the 'Golden Era' since the contemporaneous era proves that radio is thriving, especially Spanish language radio." And while my analysis of the sonic color line pauses chronologically where Casillas's book begins, I hear our work in dialogue regarding American network radio's marginalization of listeners of color. While I deliberately operate within the "monolingual and black/white cultural approaches to radio studies" Casillas rightly critiques,[121] I do so to show how the sonic color line's long history (and entanglement with sound reproduction technologies) facilitated the standardization of particular sounds as simultaneously "white" and "American," enabling American radio to broadcast race even in what Horne called the most "lily white" of programming, solidifying the very black/white binaries that further marginalize Latina/o audiences. In other words, 1930s and 1940s radio did not just passively reflect the racial temperature of the times—as so many of its passionate defenders claim[122]—but also worked from a familiar sonic recipe to set a new iteration of race to boil. Taken together, the work of Horne, Du Bois, and Petry helps us hear the breadth, depth, and profundity of America's many forms of radio silence regarding race, enabling a more complex understanding of the unique—but related—struggles of various racialized groups to decolonize their listening practices from the sonic color line's hegemony, over the airwaves and in everyday life.

Afterword

"I had a student email me and he said, 'There's invisible flashing white-only signs everywhere!'"
—Nia Nunn Makepeace, Ithaca College, New York, Black Lives Matter Teach-In, October 24, 2015. Over 1,000 students marched in a protest calling for a no-confidence vote for IC President Tom Rochon on November 11, 2015.

"We do not speak 'Yo' or 'Bro' here" and "We do not play rap, hip hop or R&B here."
—Signs that hung for years at Dillinger's Bar and Grill, Binghamton, New York, removed in November 2013 following protest marches by community members and Broome Community College and Binghamton University students and faculty

"That's how I speak, you cannot hear me that well."
—Earwitness to Trayvon Martin's murder Rachel Jeantel to Don West, defense attorney representing George Zimmerman, July 2013

I wrote this book to name and explain how racism works through sound and how American listening habits are shaped by our experiences as raced subjects and by dominant ideologies of "correct," "proper," and "sensitive" listening. I wanted to provide a thorough historical context and genealogy for the sonic color line's stereotypes—the "deep" black voice, the "noisy" neighborhood, the "loud" music—to show that incidents of racist listening cannot be dismissed, laughed off, or chalked up to white ignorance and/or innocence. I sought to provide useful language to think and talk about listening and the agency inherent within it, amplifying the work performed toward decolonizing listening by Frederick

Douglass, Harriet Jacobs, Elizabeth Taylor Greenfield, the Jubilee Singers, Charles Chesnutt, Richard Wright, Huddie Ledbetter, Lena Horne, W. E. B. Du Bois, Ann Petry, and so many others, so that we may liberate ourselves and our society from the continuing racial hierarchies and material inequities structured by the sonic color line and the listening ear. Americans come of age within a racialized soundscape that enables segregation and racism through sonic cues that vibrate under the radar of visually based discrimination laws and affects. In the allegedly color-blind post–Civil Rights Movement United States, there are "invisible, flashing white-only signs everywhere,"[1] and we hear them loud and clear—paradoxically when we seem the most not to.

Sounds have histories, and how we hear and understand them can, without exaggeration, mean life or death. Scholar Regina Bradley describes the painful burden of self-policing and the way it travels with her: "As a loud, squeaky black woman I am especially attuned to how my sonic footprint plays into how I live and if I should die. As a black woman, the bulk of my threat is associated with my loudness. My blackness sonically and culturally codes me as threatening due to the volume of my voice."[2] When asked to connect my historical work with our contemporary struggles, I often define the sonic color line like this: when you know that in order for you to stay alive, "to listen" must become "to obey," no matter what; when you know your irritated tone of voice at a traffic ticket stop might mean your death, as happened to Sandra Bland in Texas; when the police hear "OK OK OK" as aggression, and it costs you your life like it did Mike Brown in Ferguson, Missouri. It is when you are a 19-year-old girl (Rachel Jeantel, Sanford, Florida) testifying about the loss of your good friend—Trayvon Martin, shot to death by neighborhood vigilante George Zimmerman—a death you *heard* through Martin's cell phone, but you cannot get through a sentence of testimony without being tone-policed, told to repeat yourself, reprimanded to speak louder, and essentially asked to serve as your own translator for a predominately white jury. When witnesses do not—or cannot—aurally conform to the sonic color line—Bradley describes Jeantel's resistant performance as "sonic rachetness"[3]—the stakes are high; they risk being silenced by lawyers, reprimanded by judges, misinterpreted by court reporters, and tuned out by predominately white middle-class jurors. The sonic color-line almost certainly contributes to a penal system where black men are six times as likely to be incarcerated as white men.[4]

The listening ear also creates situations compelling people of color to police themselves in order to gain entry to white spaces and, all too often, to make it out healthy, whole, and alive. Until November 2013, for example, Dillinger's Celtic Pub and Eatery in Binghamton, New York, posted signs that the bar "officially" did "not speak 'Yo' or 'Bro.'"[5] Most immediately, this communicated to speakers of African American Vernacular English that white ways of listening, being, and speaking—culturally coded as "proper"—controlled this space. By evoking the racialized hierarchy of speech sounds, the sign created a hostile space for black patrons, one where the doorman might arbitrarily deny you entry, slam you to the ground, and call you "nigger," as happened to Kyle Lovett-Pitts on August 25, 2013.[6]

Perhaps most insidiously, Bradley's and Lovett-Pitts's experiences tell us, the sonic color line fractures Americans' *simultaneous* experiences of the same spaces. It enables segregation via sonic protocol as we live, work, study, and raise children side by side in fractured, unequal spaces that seem ostensibly—and legally—"free," "open," and "equitable" for everyone. And the sonic color-line impacts our campuses just as it does our streets. On February 25, 2015, the Binghamton University group Students for Change went to a town hall meeting about racial injustice on campus. There, they were met with armed police.[7] Though the university later claimed the officers were at the meeting only to listen, that the police chose—and were permitted—to listen bearing visible firearms during a time of nationwide #blacklivesmatter protests over police brutality spoke silent volumes about whose safety—whose lives—mattered in that moment. That row of uniformed white men with guns and Kevlar vests charged the allegedly neutral space of a public university with racialized affect before a word was said, bifurcating the room into "the threatening" and "the threatened" and silently blaming the students for the very hostility and lack of safety they were there to protest.

However, it is my fondest wish that the historical examples of black agency and decolonizing practices in the face of racism through soundscape control remind us that the listening ear's limited range creates the conditions for its own undoing. As I write, university students all over the country—Binghamton, University of Mississippi, Ithaca College,

Yale, Tufts, Princeton, Brown, Claremont McKenna—are challenging the institutional racism of American higher education and their respective institutions' wholesale refusal to do anything about it (while lauding "diversity"). And while we do not yet know where the nascent #blacklivesmatter movement will be in five or ten years—or even next year—it is important to note that these students, in unity with protestors in Ferguson, Missouri, Staten Island, New York, Baltimore, Maryland, and many other U.S. cities, are sounding the most recent crisis erupting from a long-standing form of sonic white supremacy. Some protests have mobilized silent die-ins, while others have wielded a wide spectrum of sound—bullhorn call-and-response chants, shouts, screams, YouTube videos, well-timed questions—to demand new relations of speaking and listening, particularly the right to listen freely to themselves and *as* themselves.

As Rachel Jeantel told Zimmerman defense attorney Don West, "That's how I speak, *you* cannot hear me that well."[8]

As the span of this book shows, the sonic color line and the listening ear accreted over time and have continued to evolve, with sometimes-frightening efficacy, in tandem with technology and racial ideologies. The difficult, necessary work of decolonizing listening and dismantling race's sonic architecture will take much time, awareness, discomfort, and steady, conscious, meticulous effort. In the long tradition of the trope of the listener, may we challenge, multiply, and amplify our listening, in order that we, paraphrasing Ice Cube, check ourselves before we wreck ourselves. May we also offer one another something more and something better: an ethics of listening where we are all, at long last, as Frederick Douglass imagined, "witnesses and participants," hearing beyond the narrowed lives racialized listening has wrought, and amplifying the community listening that sustained Harriet Jacobs, listening out to and for one another.

NOTES

INTRODUCTION

1 Breanna Edwards, "Texas Department of Public Safety Director: Escalation of Sandra Bland's Traffic Stop Was Trooper's Fault," *The Root*, 20 January 2016, http://www.theroot.com/articles/news/2016/01/texas_department_of_public_safety_director_says_escalation_of_sandra_bland.html. Black Americans also experience nonlethal force and threats of violence at the hands of police twice as often as whites do. Jon Swaine, "Black Americans Twice as Likely as Whites to Face Use of Non-fatal Police Force, US Study Says," *Guardian*, 14 November 2015, http://www.theguardian.com/us-news/2015/nov/14/black-americans-twice-as-likely-as-whites-to-face-use-or-threat-non-fatal-police-force-us-study.

2 Amy Davidson, "What Niya Kenny Saw," *New Yorker*, 30 October 2015, http://www.newyorker.com/news/amy-davidson/what-niya-kenny-saw.

3 Richard Dyer, *White* (London: Routledge, 1997), 45.

4 Mark M. Smith, *How Race Is Made: Slavery, Segregation, and the Senses* (Chapel Hill: University of North Carolina Press, 2006).

5 Les Bull and Michael Back, "Introduction," in *The Auditory Culture Reader* (Oxford: Berg, 2003), 14; and Fred Moten, *In the Break* (Minneapolis: University of Minnesota Press, 2003), 191.

6 Kara Keeling, *The Witch's Flight: The Cinematic, the Black Femme, and the Image of Common Sense* (Durham, NC: Duke University Press, 2007), 10; Michel Foucault, *Discipline and Punish: The Birth of the Prison*, trans. Alan Sheridan (1977; New York: Vintage Books, 1995), 27. My thinking is also influenced by Trevor Pinch and Frank Truocco's *Analog Days* (Cambridge, MA: Harvard University Press, 2004) and Trevor Pinch and Karin Bijisterveld's "Introduction" to *The Oxford Handbook of Sound Studies* (Oxford: Oxford University Press, 2011), particularly for their user-centered and historically contextualized theories of technological development.

7 Jonathan Sterne, *The Audible Past: Cultural Origins of Sound Reproduction* (Durham, NC: Duke University Press, 2003), 8; Myles W. Jackson, "From Scientific Instruments to Musical Instruments: The Tuning Fork, the Metronome, and the Siren," in *The Oxford Handbook of Sound Studies* (Oxford: Oxford University Press, 2011), 201–223.

8 Nicole Hodges Persley calls this "post-minstrel performance" in "Sampling Blackness: Performing African Americanness in Hip-Hop Theater and Performance" (PhD dissertation, University of Southern California, 2009), 59.

9   W. E. B. Du Bois, *The Souls of Black Folk* (1903; New York: Penguin, 1989); and Du Bois, *Dusk of Dawn* (1940; New York: Transaction Publishers, 1984).

10 Alexander Weheliye, *Phonographies: Grooves in Sonic Afro-Modernity* (Durham, NC: Duke University Press, 2005), 102. For others on Du Bois and music, see Paul Gilroy, *The Black Atlantic: Modernity and Double-Consciousness* (Cambridge, MA: Harvard University Press, 1993); Kevin Thomas Miles, "Haunting Music in *The Souls of Black Folk*," *Boundary 2: An International Journal of Literature and Culture*, Fall 2000, 199–214; Steve Andrews, "Toward a Synaesthetics of Soul: W. E. B. Du Bois and the Teleology of Race," in *Re-Cognizing W. E. B. Du Bois in the Twenty-First Century: Essays on W. E. B. Du Bois*, ed. Mary Keller and Chester J. Fontenot (Macon, GA; Mercer University Press, 2007), 142–185; Virginia Whatley Smith, "They Sing the Song of Slavery: Frederick Douglass's *Narrative* and W.E.B. Du Bois's *The Souls of Black Folk* as Intertexts of Richard Wright's *12 Million Black Voices*," in The Souls of Black Folk: *One Hundred Years Later*, ed. Dolan Hubbard (Columbia: University of Missouri Press, 2003), 85–125; Christopher A. Brooks, "The 'Musical' Souls of Black Folk: Can Double Consciousness Be Heard?" in The Souls of Black Folk: *One Hundred Years Later*, 269–283; and Carter Mathes, *Imagine the Sound: Experimental African American Literature after Civil Rights* (Minneapolis: University of Minnesota Press, 2015).

11 Judith Jackson Fossett and Jeffrey A. Tucker, "Preface: In Medias Race," in *Race Consciousness: African American Studies for the New Century*, ed. Judith Jackson Fossett and Jeffrey Tucker (New York: New York University Press, 1997), xiii–xviii.

12 For an extended analysis of the veil as "acousmatic," see Jennifer Stoever, "Fine-Tuning the Sonic Color-line: Radio and the Acousmatic Du Bois," *Modernist Cultures* 10, no. 1 (March 2015): 99–118.

13 Charles Hirschkind, *The Ethical Soundscape: Cassette Sermons and Islamic Counterpublics* (New York: Columbia University Press, 2009), 13.

14 Du Bois, *Souls*, vii.

15 Du Bois, *Dusk of Dawn*, 6 and 131.

16 Nina Sun Eidsheim, "Marian Anderson and 'Sonic Blackness' in American Opera," *American Quarterly* 63, no. 3 (September 2011): 641–671; and Lisa Gitelman, *Scripts, Grooves, and Writing Machines: Representing Technology in the Edison Era* (Stanford, CA: Stanford University Press, 1999), 135. Barbara Dianne Savage dubbed the vocal tone of minstrelsy as "aural blackface" in *Broadcasting Freedom: Radio, War, and the Politics of Race, 1938–1948* (Chapel Hill: University of North Carolina Press, 1999), 74. For more of Eidsheim's understanding of the impact of race on the voice as a performative "technology of selfhood," see "Synthesizing Race: Towards an Analysis of the Performativity of Vocal Timbre," *Trans: Transcultural Music Review* 13 (2009). I engage further with Eidsheim in chapter 2.

17 Savage, *Broadcasting Freedom*, 74.

18 Dyer, *White*.

19 See Derrick Valliant's discussion of the "sounds of whiteness" as the baseline for U.S. radio broadcasting in "Sounds of Whiteness: Local Radio, Racial Formation,

and Public Culture in Chicago, 1921–1935," *American Quarterly* 54, no. 1 (March 2002): 25–66. See also Geoff Mann, "Why Does Country Music Sound White? Race and the Voice of Nostalgia," *Ethnic and Racial Studies* 31 (2008): 73–100.

20 John Baugh, "Linguistic Profiling," in *Black Linguistics: Language, Society, and Politics in Africa and the Americas,* ed. Sinfree Makoni, Geneva Smitherman, Arnetha F. Ball, and Arthur K. Spears (London: Routledge, 2003), 155–168.

21 For additional theoretical discussions of "noise," see R. Murray Schafer, *The Soundscape: Our Sonic Environment and the Tuning of the World* (Rochester, VT: Destiny Books, 1994); Barry Truax, *Acoustic Communication* (Norwood, NJ: Ablex, 1984); Jacques Attali, *Noise: The Political Economy of Music* (Minneapolis: University of Minnesota Press, 1985); Tricia Rose, *Black Noise: Rap Music and Black Culture in Contemporary America* (Middletown, CT: Wesleyan University Press, 1994); Douglas Kahn, *Noise, Water, Meat* (Cambridge, MA: MIT Press, 1999); Emily Thompson, *The Soundscape of Modernity: Architectural Acoustics and the Culture of Listening in America, 1900–1933* (Cambridge, MA: MIT Press, 2002); Steve Goodman, *Sonic Warfare: Sound, Affect, and the Ecology of Fear* (Cambridge, MA: MIT Press, 2010); Hillel Schwartz, *Making Noise: From Babel and the Big Bang & Beyond* (New York: Zone Books, 2011); Garret Keizer, *The Unwanted Sound of Everything We Want* (New York: Perseus Book Group, 2010); and Moten, *In the Break.*

22 Tony Schwartz, quoted in Alan L. Otten, "Noise?," *Wall Street Journal,* 31 May 1973.

23 Cornel West, *Prophesy Deliverance! An Afro-American Revolutionary Christianity* (Philadelphia: Westminster Press, 1982), 28.

24 Noise Free America, "Rochester Overrun by Boom Cars," 1 September 2002, http://www.noisefree.org/newsroom/pressrelease-display.php?id=50. In 2006, I attended a meeting of the Rochester Soundscape Society where citizens spoke directly to the police chief about the "boom car" threat.

25 Judith Butler, *Bodies That Matter: On the Discursive Limits of "Sex"* (London: Routledge, 1993), xi.

26 Foucault, *Discipline and Punish,* 24.

27 Bull and Back, "Introduction," 5.

28 Leon Botstein, "Toward a History of Listening," *Musical Quarterly* 82 (1998): 427–431; David Suisman, "Thinking Historically about Sound and Sense," introduction to *Sound in the Age of Mechanical Reproduction,* ed. David Suisman and Susan Strasser (Philadelphia: University of Pennsylvania Press, 2010): 1–12; and Gustavus Stadler, "Introduction: Breaking Sound Barriers," *Social Text* 102 (Spring 2010): 1–12. Other studies of listening as historically, socially, and materially grounded include: Frances Aparicio, *Listening to Salsa: Gender, Latin Popular Music, and Puerto Rican Cultures* (Hanover, NH: University Press of New England, 1998); James H. Johnson, *Listening in Paris* (Berkeley: University of California Press, 1995); Bruce R. Smith, *The Acoustic World of Early Modern England: Attending to the "O" Factor* (Chicago: University of Chicago Press, 1999); John Picker, *Victorian*

Soundscapes (Oxford: Oxford University Press, 2003); Richard Cullen Rath, *How Early America Sounded* (Ithaca, NY: Cornell University Press, 2003); Josh Kun, *Audiotopia: Music, Race, and America* (Berkeley: University of California Press, 2005); Mark M. Smith, *Listening to Nineteenth-Century America* (Chapel Hill: University of North Carolina Press, 2000); Nichole T. Rustin and Sherrie Tucker, eds., *Big Ears: Listening for Gender in Jazz Studies* (Durham, NC: Duke University Press, 2008); and Joanna Demers, *Listening through the Noise: The Aesthetics of Experimental Electronic Music* (Oxford: Oxford University Press, 2010).

29 Jean-Luc Nancy, *Listening* (New York: Fordham University Press, 2007), 6.

30 The term "embodied ear" emerged from discussions in my fall 2012 How We Listen course at Binghamton University.

31 Steph Ceraso, "Sounding Composition, Composing Sound: Multimodal Listening, Bodily Pedagogies, and Everyday Experience" (PhD dissertation, University of Pittsburgh, 2013); Cara Lynne Cardinale, " 'Through the Eyes': Reading Deafened Gestures of Look-Listening in Twentieth Century Narratives" (PhD dissertation, University of California, Riverside, 2010). For more at the juncture of sound studies, deafness/Deaf studies, and dis/ability studies, see Mara Mills, "Deaf Jam: From Inscription to Reproduction to Information," in *"The Politics of Recorded Sound,"* special issue, *Social Text* 102 (Spring 2010): 35–58. On deafness, see Mara Mills, "Deafness," in *Keywords in Sound*, eds. *David* Novak and Matt Sakakeeny, (Durham, NC: Duke University Press, 2015), 45–54; and Trevor Boffone, "Deaf Latin@ Performance: Listening with the Third Ear," *Sounding Out! The Sound Studies Blog*, 3 August 2015, http://soundstudiesblog.com/2015/08/03/deaf-latin-performance-listening-with-the-third-ear/.

32 Mathes, *Imagine the Sound*, 6.

33 Houston A. Baker Jr., *Blues, Ideology, and Afro-American Literature: A Vernacular Theory* (Chicago: University of Chicago Press, 1984); Henry Louis Gates Jr., *The Signifying Monkey: A Theory of African-American Literary Criticism* (Oxford: Oxford University Press, 1988); Paul Gilroy, *The Black Atlantic: Modernity and Double Consciousness* (Cambridge, MA: Harvard University Press, 1993); Hazel V. Carby, "It Jus Be's Dat Way Sometime: The Sexual Politics of Women's Blues," in *The Jazz Cadence of American Culture*, ed. Robert O'Meally (New York: Columbia University Press, 1998), 470–483; Stuart Hall, "What Is Black in Black Popular Culture?," *Stuart Hall: Critical Dialogues in Cultural Studies*, ed. David Morley and Kuan-Hsing Chen (London and New York: Routledge, 1996), 470.

34 Emily Lordi, *Black Resonance: Iconic Women Singers and African American Literature* (New Brunswick, NJ: Rutgers University Press, 2013), 18.

35 Ibid., 6; Alexandra Vazquez, *Listening in Detail: Performances of Cuban Music* (Durham, NC: Duke University Press, 2013).

36 Shana Redmond, *Anthem: Social Movements and the Sound of Solidarity in the African Diaspora* (New York: New York University Press, 2013), 1.

37 Mathes, *Imagine the Sound*, 11.

38 Ann Petry, "The Novel as Social Criticism," *The Writer's Book*, ed. Helen Hull (New York: Harper and Brothers, 1950), 35 (emphasis mine).

39 Gates, *Signifying Monkey*, xxii.

40 Some exceptions: Damien Keane, *Ireland and the Problem of Information: Irish Writing, Radio, Late Modernist Communication* (University Park: University of Pennsylvania Press, 2014); Kun, *Audiotopia*; Moten, *In the Break*; Picker, *Victorian Soundscapes*; Tom McEnaney, "Acoustic Properties: Radio, Narrative, and the New Neighborhood of the Americas" (PhD dissertation, University of California, Berkeley, 2011); Weheliye, *Phonographies*; Elizabeth Wood, "Sapphonics," in *Queering the Pitch: The New Lesbian and Gay Musicology*, ed. Philip Brett, Elizabeth Wood, and Gary C. Thomas (New York: Routledge, 1994); and Philipp Schweighauser, *The Noises of American Literature, 1890–1985: Toward a History of Literary Acoustics* (Gainesville: University of Florida Press, 2006).

41 David Novak and Matta Sakakeeny, "Introduction," *Keywords in Sound*, 6.

42 Ibid.

43 Gustavus Stadler, "On Whiteness and Sound Studies," *Sounding Out!*, 6 July 2015, http://soundstudiesblog.com/2015/07/06/on-whiteness-and-sound-studies/.

44 Gustavus Stadler, ed., "*The Politics of Recorded Sound*," special issue, *Social Text* 102 (Spring 2010); Josh Kun and Kara Keeling, eds., "*Sound Clash: Listening to American Studies*," special issue, *American Studies* 63 (Fall 2011); Daniel Bender, Duane Corpis, and Daniel J. Walkowitz, eds., "Sound Politics: Critically Listening to the Past," special issue, *Radical History Review* 121 (March 2015).

45 Hall, "What Is Black," 470.

46 Marta Savigliano, *Tango and the Political Economy of Passion* (New York: Westview Press, 1995), 13.

47 Baugh, "Linguistic Profiling."

48 Jennifer Stoever-Ackerman, "Splicing the Sonic Color-Line: Tony Schwartz Remixes Postwar *Nueva York*," *Social Text* 102 (Spring 2010): 59–85; Jennifer Stoever-Ackerman, "Reproducing U.S. Citizenship in *Blackboard Jungle*: Race, Cold War Liberalism, and the Tape Recorder," *American Quarterly* 63, no. 3 (September 2011): 781–806; and Jennifer Stoever-Ackerman, "The Noise of SB 1070 or Do I Sound Illegal to You?," *Sounding Out!*, 10 August 2010, http://soundstudiesblog.com/2010/08/19/the-noise-of-sb-1070/.

49 Sharon Patricia Holland, *The Erotic Life of Racism* (Durham, NC: Duke University Press, 2012), 7.

50 Ibid.; Eduardo Bonilla-Silva, *Racism without Racists: Color-Blind Racism and the Persistence of Racial Inequality in America* (Oxford: Rowman and Littlefield, 2009); Douglass Massey and Nancy Denton, *American Apartheid: Segregation and the Making of the Underclass* (Cambridge, MA: Harvard University Press, 1993); and Michelle Alexander, *The New Jim Crow* (New York: The New Press, 2012).

51 Cheryl Harris, "Whiteness as Property," *Harvard Law Review* 106, no. 8 (June 1993): 1707–1791; and George Lipsitz, *The Possessive Investment in Whiteness: How*

White People Profit from Identity Politics (Philadelphia: Temple University Press, 2006).

52 Christine Ehrick, "Vocal Gender and the Gendered Soundscape: At the Intersection of Gender Studies and Sound Studies," *Sounding Out!*, 2 February 2015, http://soundstudiesblog.com/2015/02/02/vocal-gender-and-the-gendered-soundscape-at-the-intersection-of-gender-studies-and-sound-studies/.

53 Kimberly Foster, "Daniel Holtzclaw, Police Sexual Assault, and the Terror of Being Uncared for," *For Harriet*, 9 November 2015, http://www.forharriet.com/2015/11/daniel-holtzclaw-police-sexual-assault.html#axzz3r08oStbz.

54 Ibid.

55 Liana Silva, "As Loud As I Want to Be: Gender, Loudness, and Respectability Politics," *Sounding Out!*, 9 February 2015, http://soundstudiesblog.com/2015/02/09/as-loud-as-i-want-to-be-gender-loudness-and-respectability-politics/.

56 Bruce R. Smith, "Listening to the Wild Blue Yonder: The Challenges of Acoustic Ecology," in *Hearing Cultures: Essays on Sound, Listening, and Modernity*, ed. Veit Erlmann (Oxford: Berg, 2004), 24.

57 Moten, *In the Break*; and Smith, *Acoustic World*.

58 I use "aural imagery" to describe literary representations of sound—dialogue, music, screams, cries, laughter, and extraverbal sounds, as well as a full range of ambient sounds—that activate a reader's "inner hearing." Aural imagery implies both the literary representation of sound and the transmission of it.

59 Roland Barthes, "The Grain of the Voice," in *Image, Music, Text* (London: Fontana, 1977), 179.

60 "Sonic Protocols" is adapted from Rath, *How Early America Sounded*, 152. Marjorie Garber, *A Manifesto for Literary Studies* (Seattle, WA: Walter Chapin Simpson Center for the Humanities, 2003), 12.

61 Schweighauser, *Noises of American Literature*.

62 Weheliye, *Phonographies*, 74.

63 Weheliye, *Phonographies*, 73 and 74. Raymond Williams's "structure of feeling" describes the "pre-emergence" of "active and pressing but not yet fully articulated" cultural formations in *Marxism and Literature* (New York: Oxford University Press, 1978), 126.

64 Mary Ann Doane, "Ideology and the Practice of Sound Editing," in *Film Sound: Theory and Practice*, ed. Elisabeth Weis and John Belton (New York: Columbia University Press, 1985), 59.

65 Michele Hilmes, *Radio Voices: American Broadcasting 1922–1952* (Minneapolis: University of Minnesota Press, 1997), 256.

66 Michael Omi and Howard Winant, *Racial Formation in the United States: From the 1960s to the 1990s* (1986; New York: Routledge, 1994); Avery Gordon and Christopher Newfield, *Mapping Multiculturalism* (Minneapolis: University of Minnesota Press, 1996); Lipsitz, *Possessive Investment in Whiteness*; Vijay Prashad, *Everybody Was Kung Fu Fighting* (New York: Beacon Press, 2001); Bonilla-Silva, *Racism without Racists*.

CHAPTER 1. THE WORD, THE SOUND, AND THE LISTENING EAR

1 "Fifty Dollars to Stop the Runaways!" *The Greensborough Patriot*, 15 June 1836, retrieved 7 June 2016 from UNCG Digital Collections, libcdm1.uncg.edu/compound object/collection/GSOPatriot/id/5406/rec/4. Hortense Spillers, "Mama's Baby, Papa's Maybe: An American Grammar Book," *Diacritics* 17, no. 2 (Summer 1987): 206.

2 Charles Pickering and John Charles Hall, *The Races of Man* (London: H. G. Bonn, 1854), xxxi.

3 Michael Chaney, *Fugitive Vision: Slave Image and Black Identity in Antebellum Narrative* (Bloomington: Indiana University Press, 2008), 10 and 9.

4 Jonathan Crary, *Techniques of the Observer: On Vision and Modernity in the Nineteenth Century* (Boston: MIT Press, 1990).

5 Richard Cullen Rath, *How Early America Sounded* (Ithaca, NY: Cornell University Press, 2003).

6 Daniel Cavicchi, *Listening and Longing: Music Lovers in the Age of Barnum* (Middletown, CT: Wesleyan University Press, 2011).

7 Saidiya Hartman, *Scenes of Subjection: Terror, Slavery and Self-Making in Nineteenth-Century America* (New York: Oxford University Press, 1998), 148.

8 Robert B. Stepto, *From Behind the Veil: A Study of Afro-American Narrative* (Urbana: University of Illinois Press, 1979); Henry Louis Gates Jr., *The Signifying Monkey: A Theory of African-American Literary Criticism* (Oxford: Oxford University Press, 1988); Houston A. Baker Jr., *Blues, Ideology, and Afro-American Literature: A Vernacular Theory* (Chicago: University of Chicago Press, 1984); Mae Gwendolyn Henderson, "Speaking in Tongues: Dialogics, Dialectics, and the Black Woman Writer's Literary Tradition," in *Reading Black, Reading Feminist: A Critical Anthology*, ed. Henry Louis Gates Jr. (New York: Meridian, 1990), 116–142; Barbara Johnson, "Metaphor, Metonymy, and Voice in *Their Eyes Were Watching God*," in *A World of Difference* (Baltimore: Johns Hopkins University Press, 1987), 160–167; and Michael Awkward, *Inspiriting Influences: Tradition, Revision, and Afro-American Women's Novels* (New York: Columbia University Press, 1989).

9 Jon Cruz, *Culture on the Margins: The Black Spiritual and the Rise of American Cultural Interpretation* (Princeton, NJ: Princeton University Press, 1999).

10 Rachel Banner, "Surface and Stasis: Re-reading Slave Narrative via *The History of Mary Prince*," *Callaloo* 36, no. 2 (Spring 2013): 301.

11 Mark M. Smith, *Listening to Nineteenth-Century America* (Chapel Hill: University of North Carolina Press, 2001), 175 and 174.

12 Ralph Ellison, *Invisible Man* (1952; New York: Vintage, 1995), 16.

13 R. Murray Schafer, *The Soundscape: Our Sonic Environment and the Tuning of the World* (Rochester, VT: Destiny Books, 1994), 12.

14 David Pantalony, *Altered Sensations: Rudolph Koenig's Acoustical Workshop in Nineteenth-Century Paris* (New York: Springer, 2009), 20.

15 Veit Erlmann, *Reason and Resonance: A History of Modern Aurality* (Brooklyn, NY: Zone Books, 2010), 219 and 220.

16 Smith, *Listening to Nineteenth-Century America*, 29.

17 Spillers, "Mama's Baby," 225.

18 Smith, *Listening to Nineteenth-Century America*, 148, 149.

19 "The Fugitive Slave Act, September 18, 1850," *Internet Modern History Sourcebook*, Fordham University, http://www.fordham.edu/halsall/mod/1850fugitive.asp.

20 Mark M. Smith, *How Race is Made* (Chapel Hill: University of North Carolina Press, 2006), 34.

21 Caleb Bingham, *The Columbian Orator* (1797; Boston, MA: Philip H. Nicklin, 1811), 13–14, retrieved 20 June 2011 from Google Books, http://books.google.com/books?id=n64CAAAAYAAJ&printsec=frontcover&dq=the+columbian+orator&hl=en&ei=yY8oToCRNMSBtgf9xZmMDQ&sa=X&oi=book_result&ct=result&resnum=1&ved=0CCkQ6AEwAA#v=onepage&q&f=false.

22 Jacques Attali, *Noise* (Minneapolis: University of Minnesota Press, 1977), 61.

23 Oxford English Dictionary Online, s.v. "ecstasy," accessed 17 October 2012, http://www.oed.com/view/Entry/59423.

24 See Karl Otfried Müller's description in *Introduction to a Scientific System of Mythology* (Edinburgh: William Tait, 1844), 222: "Note . . . the ecstatic dance, the wild *charivari* of unharmonious music, the frantic gesticulations, with which the negro nations worship their gods."

25 Bingham, *The Columbian Orator*, 14.

26 Rath, *How Early America Sounded*, 143 and 124.

27 Alex Black, "Abolitionism's Resonant Bodies: The Realization of African American Performance," *American Quarterly* 63, no. 3 (September 2011): 619.

28 Smith, *Listening to Nineteenth-Century America*, 175.

29 Granville Ganter, " 'He Made Us Laugh Some': Frederick Douglass's Humor," *African American Review*, 37, no. 4 (Winter 2003): 544.

30 Frederick Douglass, *Narrative of the Life of Frederick Douglass, An American Slave* (1845, New York: Modern Library, 2004), 52.

31 Douglass, *Narrative*, 83, 117, and 118.

32 When Douglass quotes his masters, he portrays their vocabulary as limited and crude: "Now you d——d b—h, I'll learn you how to disobey my orders!" screams Captain Anthony at Hester. Douglass, *Narrative*, 22.

33 Ibid., 20, 25, and 26. As Diana Fuss has shown, last words were an important sound in antebellum culture, valued for "spiritual, social, and familial functions," making Douglass's depiction of Severe especially damning. Fuss, "Last Words," *ELH* 76, no. 4 (2009): 878.

34 Douglass, *Narrative*, 26.

35 Ibid., 34. In refuting the association of nonverbal sound with blackness, Douglass is careful not to simply reattach it as an intrinsic characteristic of whiteness. Rather, Douglass uses nonverbal imagery to denaturalize the slave masters' power, disclosing the habitual processes by which whites assumed and performed it.

36 Douglass, *Narrative*, 25, 31, and 36.

37 Elizabeth Alexander, " 'Can You Be BLACK and Look at This?': Reading the Rodney King Video(s)," in *Black Male: Representations of Masculinity in Contemporary Art*,

ed. Thelma Golden (New York: Whitney Museum of Art, 1994), 91–110. Anthony's beating of Aunt Hester has been identified as a "primal scene" by L. S. Person, "In the Closet with Frederick Douglass: Reconstructing Masculinity in *The Bostonians*." *Henry James Review* 16, no. 3 (1995): 292–298; Gwen Bergner, "Myths of Masculinity: The Oedipus Complex and Douglass's 1845 *Narrative*," in *The Psychoanalysis of Race*, ed. Christopher Lane (New York: Columbia University Press, 1998), 241–260; Hartman, *Scenes of Subjection*; M. O. Wallace, *Constructing the Black Masculine: Identity and Ideality in African American Men's Literature and Culture 1775–1995* (Durham, NC: Duke University Press, 2002); Fred Moten, *In the Break: The Aesthetics of the Black Radical Tradition* (Minneapolis: University of Minnesota Press, 2003); Harryette Mullen, "Runaway Tongue: Resistant Orality in *Uncle Tom's Cabin, Our Nig, Incidents in the Life of a Slave Girl,* and *Beloved*," in *The Culture of Sentiment: Race, Gender, and Sentimentality in Nineteenth-Century America*, ed. Shirley Samuels (New York: Oxford University Press, 1992), 244–264; A. Abdur-Rahman, "The Strangest Freaks of Despotism: Queer Sexuality in Antebellum African American Slave Narratives," *African American Review* 40, no. 2 (2002): 223–237; Alexander Weheliye, "After Man," *American Literary History* 20, nos. 1–2 (Spring/Summer 2008): 321–336; and Dwight McBride, *Impossible Witnesses: Truth, Abolitionism, and Slave Testimony* (New York: New York University Press, 2001). Moten, Hartman, and McBride all deem this a "primal scene" because it respectively intertwines knowledge with traumatic sex/violence, enacts a spectacular representation of African American bodies, and functions as a moment of conversion. However, these critics do not overtly implicate listening in this process.

38 Alexander, "Can You Be BLACK," 96. Moten, *In the Break*, 21, 22, 6, and 191.

39 Smith, *Listening to Nineteenth-Century America*, 78.

40 Douglass, *Narrative*, 22.

41 David Messmer, "'If Not in the Word, in the Sound': Frederick Douglass's Mediation of Literacy through Song," *American Transcendental Quarterly* 21, no. 1 (March 2007): 15.

42 Douglass, *Narrative*, 20 and 22.

43 Alexander, "Can You Be BLACK," 97.

44 Douglass, *Narrative*, 20 and 22.

45 Ibid., 21.

46 Ibid.

47 Mullen, "Runaway Tongue."

48 My reading of Douglass's narrative strategy is bolstered by Dwight McBride's discussion of the "self-consciousness with which [Douglass] understands, profiles, and addresses the reader" in *Impossible Witnesses*, 158. It also takes into account Douglass's revision in *My Bondage and My Freedom* (1855; New York: Modern Library, 2003), where he explains Hester's situation in more detail and her beating in much less. Douglass quotes Hester: "Each blow, vigorously laid on, brought screams as well as blood. '*Have mercy; Oh! have mercy*' she cried; '*I won't do so no more.*'" *My Bondage and My Freedom*, 38 (emphasis in original).

49 Cruz, *Culture on the Margins*, 49.

50 Douglass, *Narrative*, 21.

51 Messmer, "If Not in the Word," 6.

52 "Aural literacy" comes from the discipline of education, where it refers to the diverse learning styles that students bring to the classroom besides text-based skills. I borrow it here to use in the context of African American literature.

53 Joseph Roach, *Cities of the Dead: Circum-Atlantic Performance* (New York: Columbia University Press, 1996), 11.

54 Douglass, *Narrative*, 28.

55 Ibid., 28.

56 Whereas Hartman views these passages as discrete entities—one as ultimate debasement and the other as potentially insurgent—Moten sees them as connected: "passionate utterance and response." Hartman, *Scenes of Subjection*; and Moten, *In the Break*, 21.

57 Douglass, *Narrative*, 28 and 27.

58 Ibid., 27.

59 Ibid., 27 and 28.

60 Ibid., 28.

61 Ibid., 27.

62 Cruz, *Culture on the Margins*, 7.

63 Carla Kaplan, "The Erotics of Talk: 'That Oldest Human Longing' in *Their Eyes Were Watching God*," *American Literature* 67, no. 1 (1995): 118.

64 Douglass, *Narrative*, 28.

65 Like Jean Fagin Yellin, I believe it is important to distinguish between Linda Brent, the "black fugitive slave narrator," and Harriet Jacobs, the "black fugitive slave author." Yellin, "Introduction," in *Incidents in the Life of a Slave Girl* (1861; Cambridge, MA: Harvard University Press, 2009), xliii.

66 Yvon Bonenfant, "Queer Listening to Queer Vocal Timbres," *Performance Research* 15, no. 3 (2010): 77.

67 Harriet Jacobs, *Incidents in the Life of a Slave Girl*, 218.

68 Ibid., 190.

69 Marilyn Lake, "Sounds of Power: Oratory and the Fantasy of Male Power," in *Talking and Listening in the Age of Modernity: Essays on the History of Sound*, ed. Joy Damousi and Deasley Deacon (Canberra, Australia: Australian National University E Press, 2007); Holly Blackford, "Figures of Orality: The Master, the Mistress, the Slave Mother in Harriet Jacobs's *Incidents in the Life of a Slave Girl: Written By Herself*," *PLL* 37, no. 3 (Summer 2001): 332.

70 Mark M. Smith's *Listening to Nineteenth-Century America* and Shane White and Graham White's *The Sounds of Slavery* (New York: Beacon Press, 2005) are helpful as comprehensive renderings of slavery's soundscapes. I present a more targeted examination of antebellum soundscapes specifically focused on the dynamics of listening. For a discussion of how African American music came to be labelled as "black" sound by whites, see "First Truth, Second Hearing" in Ronald Radano's *Lying Up a Nation* (Chicago: University of Chicago Press, 2003).

71 Don Idhe, *Listening and Voice: Phenomenologies of Sound*, 2nd ed. (Albany, NY: SUNY Press, 2007), 131, 132, and 134 (emphasis in original).

72 Neil Campbell, *The Cultures of the American New West* (Chicago: Fitzroy Dearborn, 2000), 29. "Re-storying" has three main tenets: (a) the sense of creating new stories that "counter and displace the mythic ones" framing dominant understanding; (b) the power of stories to heal, inspire, and regenerate communities; and (c) the sense of remapping spaces depicted as monoracial or monocultural as sites where cultures "collide, fuse, intermingle and interrelate." Campbell adapts the term from Gary Paul Nabhan and Paul Klett's *Desert Legends: Re-Storying the Sonoran Borderlands* (New York: Henry Holt, 1994).

73 Jacobs, *Incidents*, 233.

74 Blackford, "Figures of Orality," 329.

75 Hartman, *Scenes of Subjection*, 7.

76 Jacobs, *Incidents*, 137 and 234.

77 Cavicchi, *Listening and Longing*, 60.

78 Jacobs, *Incidents*, 234.

79 Ibid., 195.

80 Ibid., 295.

81 John Howard Payne, *"Home Sweet Home"* (Boston: Lee and Shepard, 1882).

82 Jacobs, *Incidents*, 254.

83 Moten, *In the Break*, 194.

84 Pauline Oliveros, *Deep Listening: A Composer's Sound Practice* (New York: iUniverse, 2005), xxii.

85 Jacobs, *Incidents*, 137.

86 Ibid., 136–137.

87 Stephanie Li, "Motherhood as Resistance in Harriet Jacobs's *Incidents in the Life of a Slave Girl*," *Legacy* 23, no. 1 (2006): 15.

88 Jacobs, *Incidents*, 141.

89 Andrew Levy, "Dialect and Convention: Harriet A. Jacobs's *Incidents in the Life of a Slave Girl*," *Nineteenth-Century Literature* 45, no. 2 (September 1990): 211.

90 Jacobs's detailed descriptions of Johnkannaus, a regional antebellum Christmas celebration, present a more complex rendering than Douglass's depictions of debilitating debauchery. Jacobs, *Incidents*, 268. See Karen E. Beardslee, "Through the Slave Culture's Lens Comes the Abundant Source: Harriet A. Jacobs's *Incidents in the Life of a Slave Girl*," *MELUS* 24, no. 1 (Spring 1999): 37–58.

91 Jacobs, *Incidents*, 211–212.

92 Ibid., 141.

93 Ibid.

94 Ibid, 167; Lydia Marie Child, "Introduction," in *Incidents in the Life of a Slave Girl* (1861; New York: Modern Library, 2004): 128; Jacobs, *Incidents*, 126.

95 Jacobs, *Incidents*, 147.

96 Li, "Motherhood as Resistance," 21.

97 Jacobs, *Incidents*, 187.

98 Ibid., 188.

99 Child, "Introduction," 128.

100 Ibid., 363; Hartman, *Scenes of Subjection*, 50.

101 Jacobs, *Incidents*, 149.

102 Kevin Quashie, *The Sovereignty of Quiet: Beyond Resistance in Black Culture* (New Brunswick, NJ: Rutgers University Press, 2012), 22.

103 Jacobs, *Incidents*, 200.

104 Ibid., 229.

105 Ibid., 287.

106 In the contemporary moment, isolation chambers have become standard procedure in many American "supermax" prisons. Deborah Sontag, "Video Is a Window Into a Terror Suspect's Isolation," *New York Times*, 6 December 2006.

107 Jacobs, *Incidents*, 263.

108 Ibid., 304, 268, 271, and 259.

109 Ibid., 304 and 287.

110 Bonenfant, "Queer Listening," 77.

111 Jacobs, *Incidents*, 303.

112 Ibid., 320.

113 Ibid., 326 and 342.

114 Ibid., 351.

115 Roland Barthes, "Listening," in *The Responsibility of Forms* (Berkeley: University of California Press, 1985), 260.

116 Jacobs, *Incidents*, 326.

117 Ibid., 346.

118 Hartman, *Scenes of Subjection*, 19.

119 Jacobs, *Incidents*, 189.

120 Cruz, *Culture on the Margins*, 7; José Esteban Muñoz, *Disidentifications: Queers of Color and the Performance of Politics* (Minneapolis: University of Minnesota Press, 1999).

121 Cruz, *Culture on the Margins*, 7. Cruz does not mention Jacobs's observations.

CHAPTER 2. PERFORMING THE SONIC COLOR LINE
IN THE ANTEBELLUM NORTH

1 Nina Sun Eidsheim, "Marian Anderson and 'Sonic Blackness' in American Opera," *American Quarterly* 63, no. 3 (September 2011): 651. See also Carla L. Peterson, *"Doers of the Word": African-American Women Speakers and Writers in the North (1830–1880)* (New Brunswick, NJ: Rutgers University Press, 1995); Daphne A. Brooks, *Bodies in Dissent* (Durham, NC: Duke University Press, 2006); Julia Chybowski, "The 'Black Swan' in England: Abolition and the Reception of Elizabeth Taylor Greenfield," *American Music Research Center Journal* 14 (2004): 7–25; Julia Chybowski, "Becoming the 'Black Swan' in Mid-Nineteenth-Century America: Elizabeth Taylor Greenfield's Early Life and Debut Concert Tour," *Journal of the American Musicological Society* 67, no. 1 (Spring 2014): 125–165; and Alex Black,

"Abolitionism's Resonant Bodies: The Realization of African American Performance," *American Quarterly* 63, no. 3 (September 2011): 619–639.

2 Chybowski, "Becoming the 'Black Swan,'" 140.

3 Chybowski details Greenfield's Northern upbringing and training in "Becoming the 'Black Swan'" and discusses how and why the white American press ignored it. "Kingdom of culture" is a reference from W. E. B. Du Bois, *The Souls of Black Folk* (1903; New York: Penguin, 1996), 5.

4 Daphne A. Brooks, "'Puzzling the Intervals': Blind Tom and the Poetics of the Sonic Slave Narrative," *The Oxford Handbook of the African American Slave Narrative*, ed. John Ernest (Oxford: Oxford University Press, 2014), 393.

5 Kyla Wazana Tompkins, *Racial Indigestion: Eating Bodies in the Nineteenth Century* (New York: New York University Press, 2012), 55.

6 Chybowski, "Becoming the 'Black Swan,'" 125.

7 *Brief Memoir of the "Black Swan," Miss E. T. Greenfield, the American Vocalist* (London, 1853), 4, Rush Rhees Library Special Collections, Rochester, New York.

8 Christina Sharpe, *Monstrous Intimacies: Making Post-Slavery Subjects* (Durham, NC: Duke University Press, 2012), 24.

9 Brooks, "'Puzzling the Intervals,'" 411; Eric Gardner, "Slave Narratives and Archival Research," in *Oxford Handbook*, 17.

10 Hortense Spillers, "'Mama's Baby, Papa's Maybe': An American Grammar Book," in *Black, White, and in Color: Essays on American Literature and Culture* (Chicago: University of Chicago Press, 2003), 203. The Compromise of 1850, enacted by Congress in the wake of conflict over the land seized in America's war with Mexico, allowed California to enter the Union as a free state and enact the Fugitive Slave Law requiring citizens to turn suspected runaways over to the authorities, in essence, a nationwide endorsement of slavery.

11 Quoted in Arthur La Brew, *The Black Swan: Elizabeth T. Greenfield, Songstress* (Detroit, MI, 1969), 23. The clipping is from 10 September 1850. This may be the performer whom Greenfield's brief 1853 *Memoir* mentions as another "person of colour [who] had visited London and other European cities, and sung at HER MAJESTY's Theatre. . . . [Greenfield] naturally desires to avoid the probability of any misunderstanding as to her identity, or confusion that might arise from *that* fact." *Brief Memoir of the "Black Swan,"* 1.

12 Bluford Adams, *E Pluribus Barnum: The Great Showman and the Making of U.S. Popular Culture* (Minneapolis: University of Minnesota Press, 1997), 43. The *Oxford English Dictionary* traces the use of "Barnum" as a noun back to 1856, especially as a synonym for "humbug, nonsense; showmanship." Oxford English Dictionary Online, s.v. "Barnum," accessed 29 August 2011, http://www.oed.com/view/Entry/15642.

13 Eric Lott, *Love and Theft: Blackface Minstrelsy and the American Working Class* (Oxford: Oxford University Press, 1995), 41; Michael Rogin, *Blackface, White Noise* (Berkeley: University of California Press, 1998); William J. Mahar, *Behind the Burnt Cork Mask: Early Blackface Minstrelsy and Antebellum American Popular Culture* (Chicago: University of Illinois Press, 1998); and Jayna Brown, *Babylon*

Girls: Black Women Performers and the Shaping of the Modern (Durham, NC: Duke University Press, 2008).

14 Mahar, *Behind the Burnt Cork Mask*, 350. Mahar describes Lind as a frequent target for minstrels, particularly as operatic burlesques became more popular in the 1850s. However, Greenfield's presence on American stages—which he does not mention—greatly complicates his claim that "the many parodies of opera had nothing to do with black culture, but with upper-class whites' appropriation of European cultural traditions." Mahar, "Black English in Early Blackface Minstrelsy: A New Interpretation of the Sources of Minstrel Show Dialect," *American Quarterly* 37, no. 2 (Summer 1985): 284.

15 Article 2 [Untitled], *The Albion: A Journal of News, Politics, and Literature*, 11 June 1853.

16 Quoted in the *Cleveland Plain Dealer*, quoted in La Brew, *Black Swan*, 53.

17 Quoted from the *New York Morning Express* in *Brief Memoir of the "Black Swan,"* 15.

18 Rebeccah Bechtold, "'She Sings a Stamp of Originality': Sentimental Mimicry in Jenny Lind's American Tour," *ESQ: A Journal of the American Renaissance* 58, no. 4 (2012): 502 and 505.

19 Susan McClary, *Feminine Endings: Music, Gender, and Sexuality* (Minneapolis: University of Minnesota Press, 1991), 54.

20 Ibid., 68.

21 Ibid., 99.

22 Bechtold, "Stamp of Originality," 502.

23 Quoted in *Brief Memoir of the "Black Swan,"* 11; quoted in La Brew, *Black Swan*, 70; quoted in *The Black Swan at Home and Abroad: A Biographical Sketch* (Philadelphia: W.S. Young, 1855), 24.

24 Spillers, "Mama's Baby," 214.

25 "Music—Concert," *New York Daily Tribune*, 2 April 1853. Nell Irvin Painter points out that black women's rights speaker Sojourner Truth's voice was "so low that listeners sometimes termed it masculine." Painter, *Sojourner Truth: A Life, a Symbol* (New York: W. W. Norton, 1996), 3.

26 McClary, *Feminine Endings*, 65. Rachel Adams, *Sideshow U.S.A.: Freaks and the American Cultural Imagination* (Chicago: University of Chicago Press, 2001); Linda Frost, *Never One Nation: Freaks, Savages, and Whiteness in U.S. Popular Culture, 1850–1870* (Minneapolis: University of Minnesota Press, 2005).

27 Lott, *Love and Theft*, 235. To add another layer of sonic meaning, the song "Lucy Neale" was part of an opera burlesque of Bellini's *La sonnambula*, which both Lind and Greenfield regularly performed. Greenfield was not the inspiration for "Lucy Neale," as Eidsheim suggests in "Marian Anderson," 653.

28 Chybowski, "Becoming the 'Black Swan,'" 155.

29 Washington Irving to Miss Mary Hamilton, 12 November 1850, in *The Life and Letters of Washington Irving, vol. 3*, ed. Pierre Munroe Irving (London: Richard Bentley, 1865), 60.

30 "Report from the Women's Temperance Meeting," *Frederick Douglass's Paper*, 29 October 1852.

31 "Speech of Rev. Antoinette Brown, at the Women's Temperance Meeting," *Frederick Douglass's Paper*, 25 February 1853.

32 Quoted in *Brief Memoir of the "Black Swan,"* 10.

33 Carla Peterson argues black female singers and speakers were aware of this and tried to de-emphasize the body. Peterson, *"Doers of the Word,"* 122–124.

34 "Jenny Lind's Voice," *Water-Cure Journal*, September 1850.

35 Bechtold, "Stamp of Originality," 506.

36 George Lipsitz, "The Possessive Investment in Whiteness: Racialized Social Democracy and the 'White' Problem in American Studies," *American Quarterly* 47, no. 3 (September 1995): 369–387.

37 Lott, *Love and Theft*, 74; Nell Irvin Painter, *The History of White People* (New York: W. W. Norton, 2010), 164; Mark Harris, quoted in Daniel Cavicchi, *Listening and Longing: Music Lovers in the Age of Barnum* (Middletown, CT: Wesleyan University Press, 2011), 38.

38 Gustavus Stadler, *Troubling Minds: The Cultural Politics of Genius in the United States* (Minneapolis: University of Minnesota Press, 2006), 46.

39 Chybowski, "Becoming the 'Black Swan,'" 144.

40 Lott, *Love and Theft*, 91. Bearing visible traces of Irish-inflected English, "B'hoys" and "G'hals" referred to members of the Bowery subculture that rose to notoriety in the 1840s through representations in minstrel shows.

41 Steve Waksman, "Selling the Nightingale: P.T. Barnum, Jenny Lind, and the Management of the American Crowd," *Arts Marketing: An International Journal* 1, no. 2 (2011): 2. Lind did have a black audience, which I discuss later.

42 "Jenny Lind's First Concert," *New York Daily Tribune*, 12 September 1850.

43 "Jenny Lind's First Concert in New York," *New York Herald*, 12 September 1850.

44 Cavicchi, *Listening and Longing*, 35. "Audiencing" is Cavicchi's term.

45 "The Lind Fever," *Saturday Evening Post*, 14 September 1850.

46 Waksman, "Selling the Nightingale," 10.

47 "Jenny Lind's First Concert," *New York Daily Tribune*, 12 September 1850.

48 "Music: Jenny Lind and Her First Concert," *The Albion*, 14 September 1850.

49 Cavicchi, *Listening and Longing*, 135.

50 "A Complaint from the Country," *Dwight's Journal of Music: A Paper of Art and Literature*, 21 March 1857, 195.

51 "Music: Mademoiselle Jenny Lind at Castle Garden," *The Albion*, 21 September 1850 (emphasis mine).

52 "Some Remarks on Jenny Lind's Singing," *The Albion*, 2 November 1850 (emphasis mine).

53 Bechtold, "Stamp of Originality," 503.

54 Ibid., 506. German opera was on the rise during this period, championed by the influential *Dwight's Journal of Music*, which printed a letter from Lind in which she calls Germany *"the land of real music"* and distinguishes between "Italian *song*

and German *music,*" a distinction that Dwight proclaims "is the whole story in a nutshell." "Voice Teaching in Italy—Italian Song and German Music—Jenny Lind," *Dwight's Journal of Music,* 6 October 1855.

55 For a detailed discussion of the racial classification of Italians in the nineteenth century, see Paul Spickard, *Almost All Aliens: Immigration, Race, and Colonialism in American History* (London: Routledge, 2007), 248–249.

56 Richard Dyer, *White* (London: Routledge, 1997), 24.

57 Kyla Schuller, "Taxonomies of Feeling: The Epistemology of Sentimentalism in Late-Nineteenth-Century Racial and Sexual Science," *American Quarterly* 64, no. 2 (June 2012): 282.

58 Eliza Farnham, quoted in Barbara Welter, "The Cult of True Womanhood: 1820–1860," *American Quarterly* 18, no. 2 (Summer 1966): 156.

59 "Some Remarks on Jenny Lind's Singing," *The Albion,* 2 November 1850.

60 Sherry Lee Linkon, "Reading Lind Mania: Print Culture and the Construction of Nineteenth-Century Audiences," *Book History* 1, no. 1 (1998): 97.

61 Welter, "The Cult of True Womanhood," 151–174.

62 W.H.F., "Jenny Lind in Europe and America," *New York Daily Tribune,* 11 October 1850.

63 Quoted in Welter, "Cult of True Womanhood," 166; Illustration 1 [Untitled], *Godey's Lady's Book,* June 1850.

64 Wazana Tompkins, *Racial Indigestion,* 103.

65 Gillen D'Arcy Wood, *Romanticism and Music Culture in Britain, 1770–1840: Virtue and Virtuosity* (Cambridge: Cambridge University Press, 2010), 9.

66 Bechtold, "Stamp of Originality," 511.

67 Schuller, "Taxonomies of Feeling," 282; Jenny Lind to Professor Bystrom, "Learning How to Sing," 2 June 1868, reprinted in *The Etude,* February 1948, 64. Courtesy of special collections at the Sibley Music Library, Rochester, New York.

68 Lind, "Learning How to Sing," 124–125.

69 "Jenny Lind's Voice"; Alice B. Neal, "A Reminiscence of Jenny Lind," *Godey's Lady's Book,* December 1850; and "Jenny Lind," *United States Magazine and Democratic Review,* October 1850.

70 Quoted in Dyer, *White,* 75 (emphasis Dyer's).

71 Ziad Fahmy, *Everyday Egyptians: Creating the Modern Nation through Popular Culture* (Palo Alto, CA: Stanford University Press, 2011), 15. Fahmy replaces "imagined community" with "media capitalism."

72 Elizabeth McHenry, *Forgotten Readers: Recovering the Lost History of African American Literary Societies* (Durham: Duke University Press, 2002), 91.

73 *North Star,* 16 March 1849. The quotations Jerrold uses are from Isaiah 55:8–9, suggesting a fusion of Christianity and whiteness, particularly the notion of being chosen by God.

74 Quoted in "Ludicrous and Pitiable!," *The Liberator,* 24 January 1851.

75 "Letter from New York," *National Era,* 31 October 1851; "Letter from Cincinnati," *National Era,* 1 May 1851.

76 "The Respectable Man of Boston: Row at Faneuil Hall," *New York Daily Tribune*, 18 November 1850. Daniel Webster, the new secretary of state to President Millard Fillmore, helped negotiate the Compromise of 1850. Lewis Cass was a military officer and a politician who promoted the Doctrine of Popular Sovereignty, which would have allowed newly acquired states to vote on their slave status. Robert Charles Winthrop, who had just taken over Webster's vacated senatorial seat, espoused anti-abolitionist views. Bunker Hill was a Revolutionary War battle fought in Boston, and "the ladies in the gallery" referred to the women segregated by sex at the event. While more women spoke at political events—Abigail Folsom tried unsuccessfully to speak before Douglass at Faneuil Hall—their presence was by no means standard.

77 Harriet Jacobs, *Incidents in the Life of a Slave Girl* (New York: Modern Library, 2004), 358.

78 For a full listing of Greenfield's 1851–1853 tour and a sample of her repertoire, see Chybowski, "Becoming the 'Black Swan,'" 157–158.

79 Lott, *Love and Theft*, 40–41.

80 *New York Herald*, quoted in *Brief Memoir of the "Black Swan."*

81 For discussions of the Astor Place riots, see Lawrence Levine, *Highbrow/Lowbrow* (Cambridge, MA: Harvard University Press, 1988), 66–70; and Lott, *Love and Theft*, 66–67.

82 *The Rochester Paper*, quoted in *Brief Memoir of the "Black Swan,"* 8.

83 "Mann and Phillips," *The Liberator*, 8 April 1853.

84 Lott, *Love and Theft*, 131–135.

85 *Brief Memoir of the "Black Swan,"* 8.

86 Chybowski, "Becoming the 'Black Swan,'" 133.

87 Levine, *Highbrow/Lowbrow*; Timothy D. Taylor, *Beyond Exoticism: Western Music and the World* (Durham, NC: Duke University Press, 2007), 34.

88 This quote is from an unidentified Rochester, New York newspaper as quoted in *Brief Memoir of the "Black Swan,"* 8. It was a common descriptor of her voice in white newspapers, although by no means universal.

89 Greenfield's repertoire issued similar challenges to Anna Bishop (Greenfield performed her signature song "On the Banks of the Guadaliver"), Mademoiselle Parodi (also known for "Do Not Mingle"), the "Irish Swan," and Catherine Hayes.

90 *Oxford English Dictionary Online*, s.v. "black swan," accessed 7 November 2015, http://www.oed.com/view/Entry/282957?redirectedFrom=black+swan.

91 Black, "Abolitionism's Resonant Bodies," 623.

92 Eidsheim, "Marian Anderson," 207.

93 Black, "Abolitionism's Resonant Bodies," 620; Eidsheim, "Marian Anderson," 201.

94 *Boston Evening Transcript*, quoted. in James Trotter, *Music and Some Highly Musical People* (New York: Lee and Shepherd Publishers, 1878), 77. Rife with Christian and political symbolism and identified with Ancient Rome, nineteenth-century racial science considered the Adriatic Sea and its environs an ancestral site of one of Western Europe's white racial types, identified by the aquiline or "Roman nose."

95 Quoted in *Brief Memoir of the "Black Swan,"* 7; *Boston Evening Gazette,* 31 January 1852.

96 R. Murray Schafer, *The Soundscape: Our Sonic Environment and the Tuning of the World* (Rochester, VT: Destiny Books, 1993), 88.

97 Steven Connor, *Dumbstruck: A Cultural History of Ventriloquism* (Oxford: Oxford University Press, 2000), 23.

98 Peterson, "Doers of the Word," 124.

99 Quoted in *Brief Memoir of the "Black Swan,"* 15, 9.

100 Quoted in *Brief Memoir of the "Black Swan,"* 12 and 13. For more on Joice Heth, see Uri MacMillan's *Embodied Avatars* (New York: New York University Press, 2015). Zola Maseko's *The Life and Times of Sara Baartman* (Icarus Films, 1999) is an excellent resource on Baartman.

101 Quoted in *Brief Memoir of the "Black Swan,"* 12.

102 Chybowski, "Becoming the 'Black Swan,'" 146, 151.

103 Quoted in *Brief Memoir of the "Black Swan,"* 15.

104 Alexander Melville Bell, *A New Elucidation of the Principles of Speech and Elocution* (Edinburgh: Thorton and Collie, 1849), iii, retrieved on 15 January 2012 from Google Books, http://books.google.com/books?id=ODIEAAAAQAAJ&pg=PR2#v=snippet&q=listening&f=false. See also Mara Mills, "Deaf Jam: From Inscription to Reproduction to Information," in *"The Politics of Recorded Sound,"* special issue, *Social Text* 102 (Spring 2010): 35–58.

105 Chybowski, "Becoming the 'Black Swan,'" 144.

106 Quoted in La Brew, *Black Swan,* 45 and 69.

107 Spillers, "Mama's Baby," 229.

108 *New York Herald,* quoted in *Brief Memoir of the "Black Swan,"* 9 (emphasis mine).

109 Harriet Beecher Stowe, quoted in Trotter, *Music and Some Highly Musical People,* 82.

110 Annie McKay, "Speaking Up: Voice Amplification and Women's Struggle for Public Expression," *Technology and Women's Voices: Keeping in Touch,* ed. Cheris Kramarae (New York: Routledge and Kegan Paul, 1988), 188.

111 *The Black Swan at Home and Abroad,* 8.

112 Quoted in *Brief Memoir of the "Black Swan,"* 11; Quoted in La Brew, *Black Swan,* 70.

113 Cavicchi, *Listening and Longing,* 106.

114 Letter to Elizabeth Taylor Greenfield from G., 8 March 1853, quoted in *The Black Swan at Home and Abroad,* 39.

115 Elizabeth Wood, "Sapphonics," *Queering the Pitch: The New Gay and Lesbian Musicology,* ed. Philip Brett, Elizabeth Wood, and Gary C. Thomas (New York: Routledge, 1994), 32, quoted in the *Cleveland Plain Dealer,* in LaBrew, *Black Swan,* 53.

116 Brooks, *Bodies in Dissent,* 298.

117 Sharpe, *Monstrous Intimacies,* 3. Brooks discusses Greenfield briefly as an ancestor figure whose "resoundingly transgressive" style "gave birth to a genealogy of black women's cultural play," in Brooks, *Bodies in Dissent* (312–313).

118 Chybowski, "Becoming the 'Black Swan,'" 132.

119 "The Black Swan," *Provincial Freeman*, 18 November 1854.

120 Robert S. Levine, *Martin Delany, Frederick Douglass, and the Politics of Representative Identity* (Chapel Hill: University of North Carolina Press, 1997), 10.

121 Martin Delany, *The Condition, Elevation, Emigration, and Destiny of the Colored People of the United States* (1852; New York: Humanity Books, 2004), 137.

122 Letter from M. R. Delany, *Frederick Douglass's Paper*, 22 April 1853.

123 "MISS ELIZABETH T. GREENFIELD—'The Black Swan,'" *Frederick Douglass's Paper* (26 February 1852).

124 J.G., "The BLACK SWAN," *Frederick Douglass's Paper* (6 May 1852).

125 *The Voice of the Fugitive*, quoted in La Brew, *Black Swan*, 63.

CHAPTER 3. PRESERVING "QUARE SOUNDS," CONSERVING THE "DARK PAST"

1 W. E. B. Du Bois, *The Autobiography of W. E. B. Du Bois* (New York: International Publishers, 1968), 122.

2 Gustavus D. Pike, *The Jubilee Singers and Their Campaign for Twenty Thousand Dollars* (Boston: Lee and Shephard, 1873), 108.

3 Quoted in "Fisk Choir's Precursors," *New York Times*, 22 January 1933.

4 Eric Foner, *Forever Free* (New York: Vintage Books, 2005), xix.

5 Alexander Weheliye, *Phonographies: Grooves in Afro-Sonic Modernities* (Durham, NC: Duke University Press, 2005), 25. According to the *Oxford English Dictionary*, the term "spiritual"—shortened from "Negro Spiritual"—did not come into vogue until after the Civil War. *Oxford English Dictionary Online*, s.v. "spiritual" accessed 31 July 2013, http://www.oed.com.proxy.binghamton.edu/view/Entry/186900?redirectedFrom=spiritual#eid.

6 I use "technique of the self" from Gavin Kendall and Gary Wickham's reading of Michel Foucault in *Understanding Culture: Cultural Studies, Order, Ordering* (London: Sage, 2001).

7 Stephen Best, *The Fugitive's Properties: Law and the Poetics of Possession* (Chicago: University of Chicago Press, 2004), 54. Blind Tom Wiggins was a popular nineteenth-century performer, an enslaved man with amazing musical acuity whom many now consider a savant. See also Stephanie Jensen-Moulton, "'Specimens' and 'Peculiar Idiosyncrasies': Songs of 'Blind Tom' Wiggins," *American Music Review* 40, no. 2 (Spring 2011), accessed 23 April 2016, http://www.brooklyn.cuny.edu/web/academics/centers/hitchcock/publications/amr/v40-2/moulton.php. The Compromise of 1877—also called "The Great Betrayal"—was an unwritten agreement between the Democrat and Republican parties following the controversial 1876 presidential election. The Democrats awarded Rutherford B. Hayes the presidency on the condition that he would remove the federal troops from the South, returning state and local control to white Southern elites.

8 Charles Chesnutt, *The Conjure Woman*, in *The Conjure Stories*, Norton Critical Editions, ed. Robert B. Stepto and Jennifer Rae Greeson (1899; New York:

W. W. Norton, 2011). The Norton edition includes the original text of *The Conjure Woman* along with newly-recovered unpublished tales from the cycle.

9 For more theoretical discussion of double-voicedness, see Henry Louis Gates Jr., *The Signifying Monkey: A Theory of African-American Literary Criticism* (Oxford: Oxford University Press, 1989).

10 Thomas DeFrantz and Anita Gonzales, "Introduction," *Black Performance Theory*, ed. Thomas DeFrantz and Anita Gonzales (Durham, NC: Duke University Press, 2014), 14 and 8.

11 Gayle Wald, "Soul Vibrations: Black Music and Black Freedom in Sound and Space," *American Quarterly* 63, no. 3 (September 2011): 675 and 692.

12 Ibid., 676.

13 Daniel Cavicchi, *Listening and Longing: Music Lovers in the Age of Barnum* (Middletown, CT: Wesleyan University Press, 2011), 127.

14 Ella Sheppard, journal entry, 30 March 1874, Jubilee Singers Collection, box: Clippings, Histories, Writings, Etc., John Hope and Aurelia E. Franklin Library Special Collections, Fisk University.

15 Ella Sheppard Moore, "Historical Sketch of the Jubilee Singers," in "Fisk Jubilee Singers after 40 Years 1871–1911," special issue, *Fisk University News* 49, 50, in Jubilee Singers Collection, box: Clippings, Histories, Writings, Etc., John Hope and Aurelia E. Franklin Library Special Collections, Fisk University; Fred Moten, *In the Break: The Aesthetics of the Black Radical Tradition* (Minneapolis: University of Minnesota Press, 2003); Daphne Brooks, *Bodies in Dissent: Spectacular Performances of Race and Freedom 1850–1910* (Durham, NC: Duke University Press, 2006).

16 Charles Chesnutt, copy of a letter sent to the *Christian Union*, in *The Journals of Charles Chesnutt*, ed. Richard Brodhead (Durham, NC: Duke University Press, 1993), 107.

17 Charles Chesnutt to George Washington Cable, Charles Chesnutt Papers, box 1, folder 16, John Hope and Aurelia E. Franklin Library Special Collections, Fisk University.

18 John Edgar Wideman, "Charles Chesnutt and the WPA Narratives: The Oral and the Literate Roots of Afro-American Literature," in *The Slave's Narrative*, ed. Charles T. Davis and Henry Louis Gates Jr. (Oxford: Oxford University Press, 1985), 59.

19 *Journals of Charles Chesnutt*, 121 and 71.

20 Ibid., 121 and 122.

21 Glenda Carpio, "Black Humor in the Conjure Stories," in *The Conjure Stories*, Charles W. Chesnutt, ed. Robert B. Stepto and Jennifer Rae Greeson, Norton Critical Editions (New York: W. W. Norton, 2011), 333.

22 John Wesley Work, "The Jubilee Songs Today; Their Collection and Rendition," *Fisk University News*, Fisk Jubilee Singers after 40 Years 1871–1911, 21. Jubilee Singers Collection, box: Clippings, Histories, Writings, Etc., John Hope and Aurelia E. Franklin Library Special Collections, Fisk University.

23 Molly McGarry, *Ghosts of Futures Past: Spiritualism and the Cultural Politics of Nineteenth-Century America* (Berkeley: University of California Press, 2008), 20.

24 Ibid., 39.

25 Thomas A. Edison, "The Phonograph and Its Future," *The North American Review* 126, no. 262 (May–June 1878): 527; Jonathan Sterne, *The Audible Past: Cultural Origins of Sound Reproduction* (Durham, NC: Duke University Press, 2003), 290 (emphasis in original).

26 Unnamed doctor, quoted in Gustavus Pike, *The Jubilee Singers and Their Campaign*, 43.

27 George White, quoted in Andrew Ward, *Dark Midnight When I Rise* (New York: Farrar, Strauss, and Giroux, 2000), 117.

28 Maggie Porter Cole, quoted in Ibid., 129.

29 Georgia Gordon, "Reminisces of the Jubilee Singers," in "Fisk Jubilee Singers after 40 Years 1871–1911," *Fisk University News*, 30, in Jubilee Singers Collection, box: Clippings, Histories, Writings, Etc., John Hope and Aurelia E. Franklin Library Special Collections, Fisk University. That White's pitch pipe is one of scant material items besides clippings in the archive underscores his perfectionist listening practices.

30 Maggie Porter Cole, "Remembrance of Maggie Porter Cole, Written to Mr. Allison on the occasion of Jubilee Day in 1934, written from Detroit Michigan," in "Fisk Jubilee Singers after 40 Years 1871–1911," *Fisk University News*, 3. Jubilee Singers Collection, box: Clippings, Histories, Writings, Etc., John Hope and Aurelia E. Franklin Library Special Collections, Fisk University.

31 Moore, "Historical Sketch of the Jubilee Singers," 43.

32 Maggie Porter Cole, quoted in Lynn Abbott and Doug Seroff, *Out of Sight: The Rise of African American Popular Music, 1889–1895* (Jackson: University Press of Mississippi, 2009), 22.

33 Adam Spence, quoted in Ward, *Dark Midnight*, 110.

34 Fred Moten and Stefano Harney, *The Undercommons: Fugitive Planning and Black Study* (New York: Autonomedia, 2013), 65.

35 Saidiya Hartman, *Scenes of Subjection: Terror, Slavery, and Self-Making in Nineteenth-Century America* (Oxford: Oxford University Press, 1998), 25.

36 Brooks, *Bodies in Dissent*, 297.

37 Frederick Douglass, *Narrative of the Life of Frederick Douglass, An American Slave* (1845; New York: Modern Library, 2004), 27; Moten and Harney, *The Undercommons*, 26.

38 Moore, "Historical Sketch of the Jubilee Singers," 43.

39 Daphne Brooks, "Afro-Sonic Feminist Praxis: Nina Simone and Adrienne Kennedy in High Fidelity," in DeFrantz and Gonzalez, *Black Performance Theory*, 301.

40 Moten and Harney, *Undercommons*, 63.

41 Sheppard, journal entry, February 20, 1874, Jubilee Singers Collection, box: Clippings, Histories, Writings, Etc., John Hope and Aurelia E. Franklin Library Special Collections, Fisk University.

42 Moten and Harney, *Undercommons*, 64.

43 Ralph Ellison, "Change the Joke and Slip the Yoke," in *The Collected Essays of Ralph Ellison*, ed. John F. Callahan (New York: Modern Library, 2003), 100–112.

44 *Journals of Charles Chesnutt*, 121.

45 Charles Chesnutt, "Some Uses and Abuses of Shorthand," in *Charles W. Chesnutt: Essays and Speeches* (Stanford, CA: Stanford University Press, 1999), 74.

46 Charles Chesnutt, "Self-Made Men," in *Charles W. Chesnutt: Essays and Speeches*, 37.

47 Charles Chesnutt, "Some Uses and Abuses of Shorthand," in *Charles W. Chesnutt: Essays and Speeches*, 74.

48 Ibid., 87.

49 Ibid., 75.

50 Veit Erlmann, *Reason and Resonance: A History of Modern Aurality* (Brooklyn, NY: Zone Books, 2010), 220, 221, and 220.

51 Frederick Nast, "Music and Musicians in New York," *Harper's*, May 1881, 818. Apollo gave Midas an ass's ears after the king judged Pan a better musician than Apollo, "merely giving to ears so dull and dense the proper shape." Edith Hamilton, *Mythology: Timeless Tales of Gods and Heroes* (1942; New York: Grand Central Publishing, 2011), 412.

52 "The Jubilee Singers," *London Times*, 7 May 1873.

53 *Independent*, 14 March 1872.

54 *London Times*, 7 May 1873; *Hartford Courant*, 16 February 1872; and the rest *London Times*.

55 *Independent*, 14 March 1872.

56 "The *Christian Recorder*," *Accessible Archives*, accessed 7 May 2015, www.accessible-archives.com/collections/african-american-newspapers/the-christian-recorder/.

57 Julius H. Bailey, *Race Patriotism: Protest and Print Culture in the AME Church* (Knoxville: University of Tennessee Press, 2012), xvii.

58 T.S.M., "Missionary Singers," *Christian Recorder*, 8 May 1873; and Rev. Newman Hall, "The Jubilee Singers in England," *Christian Recorder*, 12 June 1873.

59 "The Jubilee Singers," *Christian Recorder*, 15 April 1875.

60 "Missionary Singers," *Christian Recorder*, 8 May 1873.

61 "Washington Correspondent," *Christian Recorder*, 10 July 1873.

62 Carrie, "Professor Gilliard's Lecture," letter to the editor, *Christian Recorder*, 20 February 1873.

63 "Personal Notes," *Christian Recorder*, 11 February 1875.

64 "The Jubilee Singers," *Christian Recorder*, 15 April 1875.

65 "The Jubilee Singers Will Be Coming Home Soon," *Christian Recorder*, 4 June 1874.

66 "The Jubilee Singers," *Christian Recorder*, 15 April 1875.

67 "From the January Number," *Christian Recorder*, 15 January 1874; "The Jubilee Singers," *Christian Recorder*, 19 April 1877; and "The Jubilee Singers," *Christian Recorder*, 29 January 1874.

68 Katie Graber, "'A Strange, Weird Effect': The Fisk Jubilee Singers in the United States and England," *American Music Research Center* 14 (2004): 27–52.

69 "Select Reading Central Yorkshire," *Christian Recorder*, 22 February 1877; "The Jubilee Singers Have Recently Gone to Germany," *Christian Recorder*, 6 December 1877; and "General Mention," *Christian Recorder*, 23 August 1877.

70 Loudin quoted in Ward, *Dark Midnight*, 311.

71 "The Dumb Witness," which remained unpublished as a stand-alone story in Chesnutt's lifetime, is a notable exception. It appears in Stepto and Greeson's Norton edition of *The Conjure Stories*.

72 Chesnutt, "The Goophered Grapevine," in *The Conjure Stories*, 7.

73 Ibid., 5.

74 The *Cleveland Gazette* (Cleveland's largest black newspaper) covered Julius McAdoo's tour. Chesnutt's daughter befriended Orpheus's wife, singer Mattie Hall, who toured with the troupe. For press clippings and archival material concerning Orpheus McAdoo, see Josephine Wright, "Orpheus Myron McAdoo: Singer, Impresario," *The Black Perspective in Music*, August 1976, 320–327. For an analysis of McAdoo's shift to minstrelsy revival (and his influence on South African music), see Veit Erlmann, "'A Feeling of Prejudice': Orpheus M. McAdoo and the Virginia Jubilee Singers in South Africa 1890–1898," *Journal of Southern African Studies* 14, no. 3 (April 1988): 331–350.

75 Barbara McCaskill and Caroline Gebhard, "Introduction," *Post-Bellum, Pre-Harlem: African American Literature and Culture 1877–1919* (New York: New York University Press, 2006).

76 W. E. B. Du Bois, *The Souls of Black Folk* (1903; New York: Barnes and Noble, 2003), 181.

77 A frame narrative, often called a "story within a story," opens with a story that exists in part to occasion another story and provide a comment on it. The frame narrative was popularized within the English tradition in the fourteenth century via Chaucer's *Canterbury Tales*.

78 Charles Chesnutt, typed manuscript copy of "The Future American," published in three installments in *The Boston Transcript*, 18 August 1900, 25 August 1900, and 1 September 1900, n.p., box 5, folder 6, Charles Chesnutt Papers, John Hope and Aurelia E. Franklin Library Special Collections, Fisk University.

79 Booker T. Washington to Charles Chesnutt, 28 October 1901, box 1, folder 16, Charles Chesnutt Papers, Fisk University Special Collections; Charles Chesnutt to Booker T. Washington, 5 November 1901, box 1, folder 16, Charles Chesnutt Papers, Fisk University Special Collections.

80 Wideman, "Charles Chesnutt," 60.

81 Houston Baker, *Modernism and the Harlem Renaissance* (Chicago, The University of Chicago Press, 1987), 41.

82 Charles Chesnutt, Letter to Walter Hines Page, 20 May 1898, in *To Be an Author: Letters of Charles W. Chesnutt, 1889–1905*, ed. Joseph McElrath and Robert C. Leitz (Princeton, NJ: Princeton University Press, 1997), 105.

83 Gavin Jones, *Strange Talk: The Politics of Dialect Literature in Gilded Age America* (Berkeley, CA: University of California Press, 1999), 1.

84 "The Dumb Witness" is the only conjure tale written entirely in standard English.

85 Epigraphs from Zora Neale Hurston and Geneva Smitherman, quoted in Carla Kaplan, *Miss Anne Goes to Harlem* (New York: Harper and Row, 2013), n.p.

86 Wideman, "Charles Chesnutt," 66.

87 Chesnutt, "The Goophered Grapevine," *The Conjure Stories*, 6.

88 Ibid., 16 and 17.

89 Ibid., 15.

90 Ibid.

91 Jean Harvey Baker, *Mary Todd Lincoln: A Biography* (New York: W. W. Norton, 2008), 328–339.

92 Chesnutt, "Po' Sandy," *The Conjure Stories*, 15.

93 Ibid.

94 Ibid.

95 Ibid.

96 Hartman, *Scenes of Subjection*, 139.

97 Chesnutt, "Po' Sandy," *The Conjure Stories*, 19.

98 Ibid., 20.

99 Fred Moten, *In the Break* (Minneapolis: University of Minnesota Press, 2003).

100 Chesnutt, "Po' Sandy," *The Conjure Stories*, 20.

101 Ibid., 21.

102 Ibid.

103 Oliver Laughland, Jessica Glenza, Steven Thrasher, and Paul Lewis, "'We Can't Breathe': Eric Garner's Last Words Become Protesters' Rallying Cry," *Guardian*, 4 December 2014, http://www.theguardian.com/us-news/2014/dec/04/we-cant -breathe-eric-garner-protesters-chant-last-words.

104 Chesnutt, "Po' Sandy," *The Conjure Stories*, 21.

105 Vorris Nunley, *Keepin' It Hushed: The Barbershop and African American Hush Harbor Rhetoric* (Detroit, MI: Wayne State University Press, 2011), 2.

106 Dean McWilliams, *Charles W. Chesnutt and the Fictions of Race* (Athens: University of Georgia Press, 2002); and Wiley Cash, "'Those Folks Downstairs Believe in Ghosts': The Eradication of Folklore in the Novels of Charles W. Chesnutt," in *Charles Chesnutt Reappraised: Essays on the First Major African American Writer*, ed. David Garrett Izzo and Maria Orban (Jefferson, NC: McFarland, 2009), 69–80.

107 Chesnutt, "Po' Sandy," *The Conjure Stories*, 21.

108 Ibid., 21 and 22.

109 Chesnutt, "The Conjurer's Revenge," *The Conjure Stories*, 30–31.

110 Ibid., 31.

111 Du Bois, *The Souls of Black Folk*, 1.

CHAPTER 4. "A VOICE TO MATCH ALL THAT"

1 "Bad Nigger Makes Good Minstrel," *LIFE*, 19 April 1937, 39.

2 Kip Lornell and Charles Wolfe cite MLA organizers referring to Lead Belly as a "talented aborigine" in correspondence with Lomax in *The Life and Legend of Lead Belly* (New York: Da Capo Press, 1999), 130.

3 Hazel Rowley, *Richard Wright, The Life and Times* (Chicago: University of Chicago Press, 2008), 128–129. Rowley estimates Wright's numbers in the "dozens." In *The Unfinished Quest of Richard Wright* Michel Fabre cites the total at 200 plus. Fabre, *Unfinished Quest* (Urbana: University of Illinois Press, 1993), 148.

4 Richard Wright, *Uncle Tom's Children*, (1938; New York: Harper and Row, 1965); Richard Wright, *Native Son* (1940; New York: Harper Perennial, 2005); Richard Wright, *12 Million Black Voices* (1941; New York: Thunder's Mouth Press, 2002).

5 Richard Wright, "Huddie Ledbetter, Famous Negro Folk Artist, Sings the Songs of Scottsboro and His People," *Daily Worker*, 12 August 1937, 7.

6 Hazel V. Carby, *Race Men, The W. E. B. Du Bois Lectures* (Cambridge, MA: Harvard University Press, 2000), 109. Carby uses the one-word spelling "Leadbelly," which is common, although Ledbetter himself insisted on two words, also the spelling used by the Lead Belly Foundation and Richard Wright. I move between uses of Ledbetter (the man) and Lead Belly (his performance identity) as context dictates.

7 Huddie Ledbetter, "Scottsboro Boys," *The Library Of Congress Recordings: Lead Belly—Let It Shine On Me* (Nashville: Rounder Records, 1991).

8 Richard Wright, "Blueprint for Negro Writing," reprinted in *Race and Class* 21, no. 403 (1980): 403–412.

9 Ibid., 407.

10 Ibid., 404 and 407.

11 Eric Lott, "Howlin' Wolf and the Sound of Jim Crow," *American Quarterly* 63, no. 3 (September 2011): 701 and 709.

12 Brandon LaBelle, *Acoustic Territories* (New York: Continuum, 2010), 109.

13 Hilton Als, "GWTW," in *Without Sanctuary: Lynching Photography in America*, James Allen (Santa Fe, NM: Twin Palms, 2000), 39.

14 Gustavus Stadler, "Never Heard Such a Thing: Lynching and Phonographic Modernity," *Social Text* 102 (Spring 2010): 102.

15 Ibid., 98.

16 Paige A. McGinley, *Staging the Blues: From Tent Shows to Tourism* (Durham, NC: Duke University Press, 2014), quote from 19, paraphrase from 6.

17 Jodi Roberts, "Panel 22," in *Jacob Lawrence: The Migration Series*, ed. Leah Dickerman and Elsa Smithgall (New York: The Museum of Modern Art and The Phillips Collection, 2015), 90.

18 Richard Wright, "The Ethics of Living Jim Crow," *Uncle Tom's Children*, 5.

19 Isabelle Wilkerson, *The Warmth of Other Suns: The Epic Story of America's Great Migration* (New York: Vintage Books, 2011), 10 and 9.

20 Farah Jasmine Griffin, *"Who Set You Flowin'?": The African-American Migration Narrative* (Oxford: Oxford University Press, 1996), 5 and 98.

21 Anonymous answers to Chicago Commission on Race Relations Survey from 1922, quoted in Wilkerson, *Warmth of Other Suns*, 350.

22 Quoted in Ibid., 291.

23 Jennifer Stoever-Ackerman, "Splicing the Sonic Color-Line: Tony Schwartz Remixes Postwar *Nueva York*," *Social Text* 102 (Spring 2010): 59–85; and Jennifer Stoever, "'Just Be Quiet Pu-leeze': The *New York Amsterdam News* Fights the Postwar 'Campaign against Noise,'" *Radical History Review* 121 (Spring 2015): 145–168.

24 Wilkerson, *Warmth of Other Suns*, 333; Roberts, "Panel 22," 126.

25 Wright lived in Harlem in late 1939 and early 1940, with first wife, Dhimah Meadman's family, but returned to Brooklyn after marrying white activist Ellen Poplar. They bought a house in Greenwich Village in 1945 hoping to find less discrimination against mixed-race families; Wright was the first African American to own property in the Village, although he had to hide his identity through a dummy corporation to purchase it. They lived there two years, suffering daily discrimination until they left permanently for Paris in 1947. Jerry W. Ward and Robert J. Butler, *The Richard Wright Encyclopedia* (Westport, CT: Greenwood, 2008), 56–57 and 161–162.

26 Lornell and Wolfe, *The Life and Legend of Lead Belly*, 200. I discussed findings in an email exchange with Lornell in January 2012.

27 Howard Taubman, "'Firing Line' Songs Thrill Audience," *New York Times*, 27 June 1942, 9.

28 Fabre, *Unfinished Quest*, 150. Wright also wrote blues songs, collaborating with Langston Hughes, Josh White, Count Basie, and Paul Robeson, but not officially with Ledbetter.

29 The Lead Belly Foundation possesses the originals. I am working with Ledbetter's grandnephew Alvin Singh to assign authorship. In a letter to Wright biographer Michel Fabre dated 22 June 1992, archivist Sean Killeen believed that even without "specific reference about date and authorship," "it doesn't sound like Lead Belly's style of composing, nor does it resemble other pieces he 'composed' (e.g., Hitler, Titanic, Jean Harlow, Howard Hughes)." Sean Killeen Papers, box 20, Richard Wright folder, Kroch Special Collections, Cornell University.

30 Richard Wright, "How Bigger Was Born," in *Native Son* (1940; New York: Harper Perennial, 2005), 434. Demonized by the white press, Robert Nixon was arrested in Chicago for allegedly murdering white women; white mobs repeatedly called for his lynching outside the courtroom. During Nixon's trial, writer Margaret Walker sent Wright clippings in New York. Robert Nixon was executed in 1939. Wright, "How Bigger Was Born," 455–456.

31 Zora Neale Hurston, "Stories of Conflict," *Saturday Review of Literature*, 2 April 1938, 32.

32 Ralph Ellison, "Richard Wright's Blues," *Shadow and Act* (New York: Signet, 1966), 78.

33 Houston Baker, *Blues, Ideology, and Afro-American Literature: A Vernacular Theory* (Chicago: University of Chicago Press, 1984), 151.

34 Tom McEnaney, *Struggling Words: Public Housing, Sound Technologies, and the Position of Speech* (Minneapolis: University of Minnesota, forthcoming); Erich Nunn, *Sounding the Color Line: Music and Race in the Southern Imagination* (Athens: University of Georgia Press, 2015); Stephen Tracy, "A Wright to Sing the Blues: King Joe's Punch," in *Richard Wright in a Post-Racial Imaginary*, ed. William Dow, Alice Craven, and Yoko Nakamura (London: Bloomsbury, 2014), 197–215.

35 Wright, "Huddie Ledbetter," 7.

36 Letter from Pleasant quoted in John Pleasant Jr.'s "Ruffin G. Pleasant and Huey P. Long on the Prisoner-Stripe Controversy," *Louisiana History: The Journal of the Louisiana Historical Association* 15, no. 4 (Autumn, 1974): 364–365.

37 Wright, "Huddie Ledbetter," 7.

38 McGinley, *Staging the Blues*, 85 and 91.

39 Nolan Porterfield, *Last Cavalier: The Life and Times of John A. Lomax, 1867–1948* (Chicago: University of Illinois Press, 2001), 12; Tim Armstrong, *The Logic of Slavery: Debt, Technology, and Pain in American Literature* (Cambridge: Cambridge University Press, 2012), 164.

40 Quoted in Mark Allen Jackson, *Prophet Singer: The Voice and Vision of Woody Guthrie* (Jackson: University of Mississippi Press, 2007), 156.

41 McGinley, *Staging the Blues*, 81.

42 Grace Elizabeth Hale, *Making Whiteness: The Culture of Segregation in the South* (New York: Pantheon Books, 1998); Dora Apel, *Imagery of Lynching: Black Men, White Women, and the Mob* (New Brunswick: Rutgers University Press, 2004); Jonathan Markovitz, *Legacies of Lynching: Racial Violence and Memory* (Minneapolis: University of Minnesota Press, 2004); Leigh Reighford, "Lynching, Visuality, and the Un/making of Blackness," *Nka: Journal of Contemporary African Art* no.20 (Fall 2006): 22–31; and Carby, *Race Men*, 2000.

43 Ashraf H. A. Rushdy, *The End of American Lynching* (New Brunswick, NJ: Rutgers University Press, 2012), 92.

44 "Map of 73 Years of Lynchings," Equal Justice Initiative, reprinted in the *New York Times*, 9 February 2015, http://www.nytimes.com/interactive/2015/02/10/us/map-of-73-years-of-lynching.html?_r=0. Ledbetter lived from 1888 to 1948.

45 Rushdy, *The End of American Lynching*, 98.

46 Allen, *Lynching Photography*, 185.

47 Leigh Raiford, *Imprisoned in a Luminous Glare: Photography and the African American Freedom Struggle* (Chapel Hill: University of North Carolina Press, 2010), 36.

48 Oxford English Dictionary Online, s.v. "field," accessed 19 October 2015, http://www.oed.com/view/Entry/69922?redirectedFrom=fieldhand.

49 Raiford, *Imprisoned*, 36.

50 Richard Wright, "I Have Seen Black Hands," *New Masses*, 26 June 1934, 16.

51 Rushdy, *The End of American Lynching*, 94.

52 Raiford, *Imprisoned*, 63.

53 Letter from Bob Steck to Sean Killeen (undated), #6789. Box 9, Folder 9-18, Sean Killeen Lead Belly Collection, Kroch Special Collections, Cornell University.

54 Alexandra Vazquez, *Listening in Detail: Performances of Cuban Music* (Durham: Duke University Press, 2013), 19 and 29.

55 "Sweet Singer of the Swamplands," *New York Herald Tribune*, 3 January 1935.

56 Ibid.

57 *Oxford English Dictionary Online*, s.v. "husky," http://www.oed.com/view/Entry /89719, accessed 22 April 2016.

58 *Boston Globe*, 15 March 1935, Box 4, Folder 19, Sean Killeen Lead Belly Collection, Kroch Special Collections, Cornell University.

59 "I'm in New York City," *New Yorker* (1935), collected in *Lead Belly: A Life in Pictures*, ed. Tiny Robinson and John Reynolds (Göttingen: Steidl, 2008), 44.

60 Niambi M. Carter, "Intimacy without Consent: Lynching as Sexual Violence," *Politics & Gender* 8, no. 3 (September 2012): 414.

61 Tim Brooks, "'Might Take One Disc of This Trash as a Novelty': Early Recordings by the Fisk Jubilee Singers and the Popularization of 'Negro Folk Music,'" *American Music* 18, no. 3 (Autumn 2000): 278–316; Alice Maurice, "'Cinema at Its Source': Synchronizing Race and Sound in the Early Talkies," *Camera Obscura* 17, no. 1 (2002): 31–71; and Stadler, "Never Heard Such a Thing," 2010.

62 Bill Schauer's firsthand account of Lead Belly's performance in Berkeley is quoted in *Lead Belly: A Life in Pictures*, 55.

63 John Edgar Wideman, "Charles Chesnutt and the WPA Narratives: The Oral and the Literate Roots of Afro-American Literature," *The Slave's Narrative*, ed. Charles T. Davis and Henry Louis Gates Jr. (Oxford: Oxford University Press, 1985), 65–66.

64 Pete Seeger, quoted in *Lead Belly: A Life in Pictures*, 11–12.

65 "The Songs of the Negro," *Pittsburgh Courier*, 26 September 1936.

66 McGinley, *Staging the Blues*, 115.

67 "Ex-convict is Apollo's Star," *New York Amsterdam News*, 4 April 1936.

68 McGinley, *Staging the Blues*, 107, 109, and 115.

69 Joe Bostic, "Seeing the Show," *New York Age*, 11 April 1926, Box 1, Apollo Theater folder, Sean Killeen Lead Belly Collection, Kroch Special Collections, Cornell University. The white papers, too, picked up the narrative of a Lead Belly–Calloway rivalry, although championing Lead Belly as more authentic.

70 McGinley, *Staging the Blues*, 117.

71 Wright, "Huddie Ledbetter," 7.

72 Richard Wright, "*Melody Limited*," unfilmed screenplay, p. 10, Richard Wright Papers, Box 67, Folder 793, Beinecke Rare Book and Manuscript Library, Yale University. With thanks to Tom McEnaney.

73 Ida B. Wells, *Southern Horrors and Other Writings: The Anti-Lynching Campaign of Ida B. Wells, 1892–1900*, ed. Jacqueline Jones Royster (Boston: Bedford Books,

1997). Also see Leigh Reighford's "Lynching, Visuality, and the Un/making of Blackness."

74 Jacqueline Goldsby, *A Spectacular Secret: Lynching in American Life and Culture* (Chicago: University of Chicago Press, 2006), 250–251.

75 National Association for the Advancement of Colored People and J. W. Johnson, *N.A.A.C.P. Rubin Stacy Anti-lynching Flier*, box 280, fol. Lynching (1935–1946), Yale Collection of American Literature, Beinecke Rare Book and Manuscript Library; Rushdy, *The End of American Lynching*, 72.

76 Apel, *Imagery of Lynching*, 118. Also Margaret Rose Vendryes, "Hanging on Their Walls: An Art Commentary on Lynching, the Forgotten 1935 Art Exhibition," in *Race Consciousness: African-American Studies for the New Century*, ed. Judith Jackson Fossett and Jeffrey A. Tucker (New York: New York University Press, 1997), 153–176; and Helen Langa, "Two Anti-Lynching Art Exhibitions: Politicized Viewpoints, Racial Perspectives, Gendered Constraints," *Nka: Journal of Contemporary African Art* 20 (Fall 2006): 96–117.

77 Langa, "Two Anti-Lynching Art Exhibitions."

78 Margaret Walker, *Daemonic Genius: A Portrait of the Man and a Critical Look at His Work* (New York: Warner Books, 1988); Vincent Pérez, "Movies, Marxism, and Jim Crow: Richard Wright's Cultural Criticism," *Texas Journal of Literary Studies* 43, no. 2 (Summer 2001): 142–168.

79 Walker, *Daemonic Genius*, 222.

80 Griffin, *"Who Set You Flowin'?,"* 28.

81 Hazel Rowley, *Richard Wright, The Life and Times*, 279.

82 McEnaney's work is a notable exception. Ross Pudaloff, "Celebrity as Identity: *Native Son* and Mass Culture," in *Richard Wright: Critical Perspectives Past and Present*, ed. Henry Louis Gates Jr. and K. A. Appiah (New York: Amistad, 1993), 156–170; Damon Marcel DeCoste, "To Blot It All Out: The Politics of Realism in Richard Wright's *Native Son*," *Style* 32, no. 1 (Spring 1998): 127–147; and Pérez, "Movies, Marxism, and Jim Crow."

83 Wright, "How Bigger was Born," 537.

84 Rick Altman, "The Evolution of Sound Technology," in *Film Sound: Theory and Practice, ed.* Elisabeth Weis and John Belton (New York: Columbia University Press, 1985), 47 and 46.

85 Maurice, "Cinema at Its Source," 31.

86 Mary Ann Doane, "Ideology and the Practice of Sound Editing," in Weis and Belton, *Film Sound: Theory and Practice*, 59.

87 See Mark M. Smith's *Listening to Nineteenth-Century America* (2001); and Shane White and Graham White's *The Sound of Slavery* (New York: Beacon Press, 2005).

88 Wright, "Big Boy Leaves Home," *Uncle Tom's Children* (New York: Harper Perennial, 1965), 17.

89 Cheryl Higashida, "Aunt Sue's Children: Re-viewing the Gender(ed) Politics of Richard Wright's Radicalism," *American Literature* 75, no. 2 (June 2003): 401.

90 Wright, "Big Boy Leaves Home," 18.

91 The pastoral literary tradition dates to Virgil's *Eclogues,* and the genre functions to resolve tensions between an idealized past and a changing present. Lucinda MacKethan, "Genres of Southern Literature," *Southern Spaces: An Internet Journal and Scholarly Forum,* 16 February 2004, http://southernspaces.org/2004/genres-southern-literature.

92 Ibid. Reconstruction-era Southern pastoral writers include Joel Chandler Harris, Thomas Nelson Page, George W. Cable, Grace King, and Thomas Dixon, whose novel *The Clansman* was the basis for D. W. Griffith's 1915 silent film *Birth of a Nation.*

93 Smith, *Listening to Nineteenth-Century America,* 19 and 30.

94 Anissa J. Wardi, "Inscriptions in the Dust: A Gathering of Old Men and Beloved as Ancestral Requiems," *African American Review* 36, no. 1 (Spring 2002): 36.

95 Wright, "Big Boy Leaves Home," 27, 20, 26.

96 Robyn Weigman, *American Anatomies: Theorizing Race and Gender* (Durham, NC: Duke University Press, 1995): 96. See also Shawn Michelle Smith, "Afterimages: White Womanhood, Lynching, and the War in Iraq," *Nka: Journal of Contemporary African Art* 20 (Fall 2006): 72–85; Hazel Carby, *Reconstructing Womanhood* (New York: Oxford University Press, 1987); and Sandra Gunning, *Race, Rape, and Lynching: A Red Record of American Literature 1900–1912* (New York: Oxford University Press, 1996). For a discussion of the role of white women in the Klu Klux Klan of the 1920s, see Kathleen M. Blee's *Women of the Klan: Racism and Gender in the 1920s* (Berkeley: University of California Press, 1992); Nancy MacLean, *Behind the Mask of Chivalry: The Making of the Second Klu Klux Klan* (New York: Oxford University Press, 1994); and Tara McPherson, *Reconstructing Dixie: Race, Gender, and Nostalgia in the Imagined South* (Durham, NC: Duke University Press, 2003).

97 MacLean, *Behind the Mask of Chivalry,* 114.

98 Hortense Spillers describes this as "ungendering" in "'Mama's Baby, Papa's Maybe': An American Grammar Book," in *Black, White, and in Color: Essays on American Literature and Culture* (Chicago: University of Chicago Press, 2003).

99 Philip Brophy argues the female scream is "one of the most iconic sound effects in cinema" next to the sound of gunfire. "I Scream in Silence: Cinema, Sex and the Sound of Women Dying," in *Cinesonic: The World of Sound in Film* (Sydney: Southwood Press, 1999), 52.

100 Wright, "Big Boy Leaves Home," 28 and 27. Wright uses italics to aurally inflect *white* in "The Ethics of Living Jim Crow" and *12 Million Black Voices.*

101 Wright, "Big Boy Leaves Home," 28.

102 Patricia Yaeger, *Dirt and Desire: Reconstructing Southern Women's Writing, 1930–1990* (Chicago: University of Chicago Press, 2000), xii.

103 Wright, "Big Boy Leaves Home," 31, 36, 37, and 39.

104 Wright, "Big Boy Leaves Home," 48 (emphasis mine).

105 Carter, "Intimacy without Consent," 418. See also Weigman, *American Anatomies;* and Carby, *Race Men.*

106 Wright, "The Ethics of Living Jim Crow," 13; Griffin, *"Who Set You Flowin'?,"* 98.

107 Wright, "Big Boy Leaves Home," 19.

108 Several critics argue Wright's conception of Bigger's point of view is *Native Son's* supreme achievement. See Louis Tremaine, "The Disassociated Sensibility of Bigger Thomas," in *Richard Wright's* Native Son, ed. Harold Bloom (New York: Chelsea Home Publishers, 1988), 89–104; and John M. Reilly, "Giving Bigger a Voice: The Politics of Narrative in *Native Son*," in *New Essays on* Native Son, ed. Kenneth Kinnamon (Cambridge: Cambridge University Press, 1990), 35–62. I am the first to discuss Bigger's "point of audition."

109 Griffin, *"Who Set You Flowin'?,"* 95.

110 Wright, "How Bigger Was Born," 529.

111 Ibid., 516.

112 Ibid, 534.

113 Wright, *Native Son*: "Clang": "far away clang" (91, 351, and 353), "clanging of the shovel against iron" (250), "clanged so loud" (189), and "clanging" cell door (391, 487, and 502); "Drone": Mary's bones (140, 180, 177, and 213), fire hose (311), the voices of the mob (384), the preacher (328), and the courtroom lawyers (385); and "Rattling": coal chute (134), passing street cars (20), gusts of wind (268), and Bessie's murder (276). The "roaring" of the Dalton's furnace is another significant recurring sound. This blisteringly hot machine is one of the most active elements of Wright's audible terrain, moaning (146), humming (171), whispering (236, 241), and singing (175, 178) with the torrid, "droning" rage that Bigger cannot express. Most often, the furnace simply roars with a consuming fear and a ferocity that often blots out sound entirely (105, 107, 133, 137, 185, 248, 251). Until the reporters discover Mary's bones, this sound haunts Bigger.

114 Beryl Salter, *Family Properties: Race, Real Estate and the Exploitation of Black Urban America* (New York: Metropolitan Books, 2009), 40–41. A typical covenant read: "At no time shall said premises . . . be sold, occupied, let or leased . . . to anyone of any race other than the Caucasian, except that this covenant shall not prevent occupancy by domestic servants of a different race domiciled with an owner or tenant." Quoted by Salter, *Family Properties*, 40.

115 Wright, *Native Son*, 44; Alessandro Portelli, "On the Lower Frequencies: Sound and Meaning in *Native Son*," *Critical Essays on Richard Wright's* Native Son, ed. Kenneth Kinnamon (New York: Twayne Publishers, 1997), 234.

116 Wright, *Native Son*, 51, 50, 51, and 57.

117 Ibid., 135 and 211.

118 Ibid., 51 and 52.

119 Peter Bailey, "Breaking the Sound Barrier," *Popular Culture and Performance in the Victorian City* (Cambridge: Cambridge University Press, 1998), 185.

120 Readings of Bigger's arrival in the Dalton home have largely focused on: 1) its visual aspects, e.g., in James Nagel, "Images of 'Vision' in *Native Son*," in Kinnamon, *Critical Essays on Richard Wright's* Native Son, 86–93; and Robert J. Butler, "Seeing *Native Son*," in *Approaches to Teaching Wright's* Native Son, ed. James A. Miller

(New York: MLA of America, 1997), 22–27; 2) the "racializing gaze" of Mr. Dalton, in Mikko Juhani Tuhkanen, "'A [B]igger's Place': Lynching and Specularity in Richard Wright's 'Fire and Cloud' and *Native Son*," *African American Review* 33, no. 1 (Spring 1999): 125–133; and 3) the literal blindness and metaphoric color blindness of Mrs. Dalton, in Jonathan Elmer, "Spectacle and Event in *Native Son*," *American Literature* 70, no. 4 (December 1998): 767–798.

121 Elizabeth Alexander, "Can you be BLACK and Look at This? Reading the Rodney King Video(s)," in *Black Male: Representations of Masculinity in Contemporary American Art*, ed. Thelma Golden (New York: Harry Abrams, 1994), 100.

122 Wright, *Native Son*, 95. Although he does not discuss sound, Robert Butler characterizes *Native Son* as gothic in "Farrell's Ethnic Neighborhood and Wright's Urban Ghetto: Two Visions of Chicago's South Side," *MELUS* 18 (Spring 1993): 103–111, and in "Urban Frontiers, Neighborhoods, and Traps: The City in Dreiser's *Sister Carrie*, Farrell's *Studs Lonigan*, and Wright's *Native Son*," in *Theodore Dreiser and American Culture: New Readings*, ed. Yoshinobu Hakutani (Newark: University of Delaware Press, 2000), 274–290. James Smethurst asserts *Native Son* is actually an antigothic novel using gothic conventions ironically. Smethurst, "Invented by Horror: The Gothic and African American Literary Ideology in *Native Son*," *African American Review* 35, no. 1 (Spring 2001): 29–40.

123 Wright, *Native Son*, 98.

124 Ibid., 260 and 257–258.

125 Ibid., 312, 337, 373, and 267.

126 The fact that Wright based *Native Son* on the newspaper coverage of the 1938 Robert Nixon case supports this reading.

127 Rushdy, *The End of American Lynching*, 2.

128 Mychal Denzel Smith, "Eric Garner's Death and the Exasperation With Police Violence," *The Nation*, 21 July 2014, http://www.thenation.com/article/eric-garners -death-and-exasperation-police-violence/; Manny Fernandez, "Freddie Gray's Injury and the Police 'Rough Ride,'" *New York Times*, 30 April 2015, http://www .nytimes.com/2015/05/01/us/freddie-grays-injury-and-the-police-rough-ride.html; "Sandra Bland Dashcam Video," Police Center—News and Pursuits, Youtube, 21 July 2015, https://www.youtube.com/watch?v=Dkqw_7mrJnU, accessed 23 April 2016. Bland, whom I discuss in more detail in the book's conclusion, was found dead in her prison cell; Monica Davey, Michael Wines, Erik Eckholm, and Richard A. Oppel Jr., "Raised Hands and the Doubts of the Grand Jury," *New York Times*, 29 November 2014, http://www.nytimes.com/2014/11/30/us/raised-hands -and-the-doubts-of-a-grand-jury-.html; and Jamie Schram, "Cop Shoots Woman, Charged with Attempted Murder, Dead in Brooklyn," *New York Post*, 15 June 2012, http://nypost.com/2012/06/15/cop-shoots-woman-charged-with-attempted-mur der-dead-during-struggle-in-brooklyn/#ixzz1xs3t78BP.

129 Kevin Moore video footage embedded in Katherine Rentz, "Videographer: Freddie Gray Was Folded Like 'Origami,'" *Baltimore Sun*, 23 April 2015, http:// www.baltimoresun.com/news/maryland/freddie-gray/bs-md-gray-video

-moore-20150423-story.html, accessed 23 April 2016; and "Eric Garner Video—
Unedited Version," *New York Daily News*, 12 July 2015, https://www.youtube.com
/watch?v=JpGxagKOkv8, accessed 23 April 2016.

130 Wright, *Native Son*, 430.

131 Carla Kaplan, *The Erotics of Talk: Women's Writing and Feminist Paradigms*
(Oxford: Oxford University Press, 1991), 136.

132 Wright, *Native Son*, 362.

133 Shana Redmond, *Anthem: Social Movements and the Sound of Solidarity in the
African Diaspora* (New York: New York University Press, 2014); and Dave Id and
Julia Carrie Wong, "Audacious Black Lives Matter Shutdown of Oakland Police
Headquarters," *East Bay*, 29 December 2014, https://www.indybay.org/news
items/2014/12/29/18766146.php.

CHAPTER 5. BROADCASTING RACE

1 Lead Belly, "Turn Yo' Radio On," in *Gwine Dig a Hole to Put the Devil In: Library
of Congress Recordings* (1938; Rounder Records, 2011). Lyrical transcription by the
author.

2 Ralph Ellison, "Harlem Is Nowhere," *The Collected Essays of Ralph Ellison* (New
York: Modern Library, 2003), 55.

3 Gerd Horten, *Radio Goes to War: The Cultural Politics of Propaganda during
World War II* (Berkeley: University of California Press, 2003), 2.

4 Jennifer Stoever-Ackerman, "Reproducing U.S. Citizenship in a *Blackboard Jungle*:
Race, Cold War Liberalism, and the Tape Recorder," *American Quarterly* 63, no. 3
(September 2011): 781–806; and Jennifer Stoever-Ackerman, "Splicing the Sonic
Color-Line: Tony Schwartz Remixes Postwar *Nueva York*," *Social Text* 102 (Spring
2010): 59–85.

5 Eduardo Bonilla-Silva, *Racism without Racists: Color-Blind Racism and the Persistence of Racial Inequality in America* (Lanham, MD: Rowman & Littlefield,
2013).

6 Neil Verma, *Theater of the Mind* (Chicago: University of Chicago Press, 2012), 223.

7 Kate Lacey, *Listening Publics: The Politics and Experience of Listening in the Media
Age* (Cambridge: Polity Press, 2013), 128.

8 Alexander Russo, *Points on the Dial* (Durham, NC: Duke University Press, 2010),
14.

9 Eric Porter, *The Problem of the Future World: W. E. B. Du Bois and the Race Concept at Midcentury* (Durham, NC: Duke University Press, 2010), 3.

10 Avery Gordon and Christopher Newfield describe color blindness as a fundamental
"white indifference to the racialized dimension" of the seemingly "neutral" category
of citizen in "Multiculturalism's Unfinished Business," in *Mapping Multiculturalism*, ed. Avery Gordon and Christopher Newfield (Minneapolis: University of
Minnesota Press, 1996), 89.

11 Quoted in Estelle Edmerson, "A Descriptive Study of the American Negro in
the United States Professional Radio, 1922–1953" (Master's thesis, University of

California, Los Angeles, August 1954), 101. I am grateful for Edmerson's groundbreaking oral history work.

12 Michele Hilmes, *Radio Voices: American Broadcasting 1922–1952* (Minneapolis: University of Minnesota Press, 1997), 256.

13 Porter, *Problem of the Future World,* 49.

14 Ruth Benedict and Gene Weltfish, *The Races of Mankind* (Washington, DC: Public Affairs Committee, 1943), 5, 16, 15, and 17.

15 Hilmes, *Radio Voices,* 250. For a production history of *Freedom's People* and *Americans All,* see Barbara Dianne Savage's *Broadcasting Freedom: Radio, War, and the Politics of Race* (Chapel Hill: University of North Carolina Press, 1999).

16 Orrin Dunlap, "The Pilgrim's Pride," *New York Times,* 19 November 1939.

17 For a discussion of black protests against *Amos 'n' Andy,* see Savage, *Broadcasting Freedom,* 7–9.

18 Ramona Lowe, "More Negroes in Radio Urged By Norman Corwin," *The Chicago Defender,* 17 February 1945; and Norman Corwin, "A Microphone Is Color Blind," *Negro Digest,* May 1945, 17–18.

19 Corwin, "A Microphone Is Color Blind," 18.

20 John E. Hutchens, "This is Service," *New York Times,* 19 March 1944.

21 Corwin, "A Microphone Is Color Blind," 18.

22 Joe Bostic, "Radiograph," *The People's Voice,* 14 February 1942.

23 According to conductor Marl Young, "by 1945 and 1946, almost all of the Negro musicians' regular radio performances had been discontinued" in Edmerson, "Descriptive Study," 217.

24 Quoted in Edmerson, "Descriptive Study," 79; Savage, *Broadcasting Freedom.*

25 John Te Groen, president of white Local 47, quoted in Edmerson, "Descriptive Study," 263; William Hadnot, black violinist, quoted in Ibid., 282.

26 Maury Paul, recording secretary of LA white musicians' Local 47, quoted in Edmerson, "Descriptive Study," 264.

27 Quoted in Edmerson, "Descriptive Study," 39 and 46; quoted in Savage, *Broadcasting Freedom,* 74; Savage, *Broadcasting Freedom,* 7.

28 Quoted in Edmerson, "Descriptive Study," 69.

29 Charles Whitbeck, " 'Madame Queen' Joins Cosby," *Evening Independent,* 1 September 1969. Randolph also discussed this with Edmerson, although she cites James Jewell, another of *The Lone Ranger*'s producers. Edmerson, "Descriptive Study."

30 Quoted in Edmerson, "Descriptive Study," 29–30.

31 Lillian Randolph, quoted in Edmerson, "Descriptive Study," 95; Lena Horne, quoted in Alvin Moses, "Lena Horne Swats Jim Crow," *The Chicago Defender,* 20 September 1947.

32 Stephen Bourne, *Butterfly McQueen Remembered* (Lanham, MD: Scarecrow Press, 2008), 64; quoted in "Actress Butterfly McQueen Is Killed in Fiery Accident," *Los Angeles Times,* 23 December 1995.

33 Quoted in Edmerson, "Descriptive Study," 66.

34 Quoted in Ibid., 80–81.

35 Sidonie Smith and Julia Watson, "Introduction," *De/Colonizing the Subject: The Politics of Gender in Women's Autobiography*, ed. Sidonie Smith and Julia Watson (Minneapolis: University of Minnesota Press: 1992), xx.

36 Edmerson, "Descriptive Study," 104; Ernest Whitman, quoted in Ibid., 84.

37 Lena Horne and Richard Schickel, *Lena* (Garden City, NY: Doubleday, 1965), 139–140.

38 Miller, quoted in Edmerson, "Descriptive Study," 88 and 66.

39 James Gavin, *Stormy Weather: The Life of Lena Horne* (New York: Atria paperback, 2009), 14.

40 Quoted in Ibid., 3.

41 Lena Horne to Jonathan Schwartz, quoted in Ibid., 86.

42 Shane Vogel, "Lena Horne's Impersona," *Camera Obscura* 23, no. 1 (2008): 11–45.

43 Horne and Schickel, *Lena*, 95; *The Chicago Defender*, 30 August 1941; and *The Chicago Defender*, 30 August 1941.

44 *The Chicago Defender*, 30 August 1941; and *Atlanta Daily World*, 28 February 1938.

45 *Atlanta Daily World*, 17 November 1942; *Atlanta Daily World*, 6 May 1942; *Atlanta Daily World*, 24 August 1942; and *Atlanta Daily World*, 27 August 1944.

46 Priscilla Peña Ovalle, *Dance and the Hollywood Latina: Race, Sex, and Stardom* (New Brunswick, NJ: Rutgers University Press, 2010), 3.

47 "Tall, Tan, and Terrific," *Coronet*, January 1944, 31.

48 Jon Stratton, *Jews, Race, and Popular Music* (Farnham, Surrey, United Kingdom: Ashgate, 2008), 28; and Ethel Waters, quoted in Ibid., 29.

49 Robert Rice, "The Real Story of Lena Horne," *PM's Sunday Picture News*, 10 January 1943, 22.

50 "Chocolate Cream Chanteuse," *TIME*, 4 January 1943; and bell hooks, *Black Looks: Race and Representation* (Boston: South End, 1992). A chanteuse is "a female singer of popular songs, esp French." OED Online, s.v. "chanteuse," accessed 12 January 2013, http://www.oed.com/view/Entry/30523?redirectedFrom=chanteuse.

51 "Music, Deep or Not," TIME, 27 November 1950.

52 Louella O. Parsons, "Real Singer to Play the Role of One," *Washington Post*, 25 March 1943; Bruce Cassiday, *Dinah!* (New York: Berkeley Books, 1979), 17.

53 Stratton, *Jews, Race, and Popular Music*, 13–14.

54 Ibid., 15.

55 "Just Send It to Dinah," *New York Times*, 12 July 1942; "Song Queen," *Los Angeles Times*, 23 November 1941; and "Warm, Witty Dinah Shore Stars in Mahalia's Program," *Chicago Daily Defender*, 25 January 1968.

56 Bill Gottlieb, "Swing Sessions," *Washington Post*, 26 April 1942.

57 "You Were Wonderful," *Suspense*, episode aired 9 November 1944 on CBS, recording obtained from Otrcat.com in February 2010.

58 Alison McCracken, "Scary Women and Scarred Men: *Suspense*, Gender Trouble, and Postwar Change, 1942–1950," in *Radio Reader: Essays in the Cultural History of Radio*, ed. Michele Hilmes and Jason Loviglio (New York: Routledge, 2002), 184.

59 Daphne A. Brooks, "'One of These Mornings, You're Gonna Rise Up Singing': The Secret Black Feminist History of the Gershwins' *Porgy and Bess*" (paper, Experience Music Project Conference, New York City, 25 March 2012).

60 "Lena Horne Heard in New Kind of Role on Network," *Atlanta Daily World*, 19 November 1944.

61 McCracken, "Scary Women," 184.

62 Gavin, *Stormy Weather*, 173.

63 Vogel, "Lena Horne's Impersona," 36.

64 Gayle Wald, "Soul Vibrations: Black Music and Black Freedom in Sound and Space," *American Quarterly* 63, no. 3 (September 2011): 673–696.

65 Ibid., 684. On this point, Wald paraphrases Raymond Arsenault, author of *The Sound of Freedom: Marian Anderson, the Lincoln Memorial, and the Concert that Awakened America* (New York: Bloomsbury Press, 2009).

66 Ibid.

67 The date and title are taken from E. Pearl Bailey to W. E. B. Du Bois, 11 January 1926, W.E.B. Du Bois Papers (MS312), Special Collections and University Archives, University of Massachusetts Amherst Libraries. The remark is taken from W. E. B. Du Bois to George Coleman, 10 March 1926, W. E. B. Du Bois Papers (MS213).

68 Irene Remillard to W. E. B. Du Bois, ca. January 1926, W. E. B. Du Bois Papers (MS312); and Maybelle L. Gunn to W. E. B. Du Bois, 13 January 1926, W. E. B. Du Bois Papers (MS213). E. Pearl Bailey describes a more uneven listening experience: "At times your voice more than filled the room, then again it would fade into almost nothingness." E. Pearl Bailey to W. E. B. Du Bois, 11 January 1926, W. E. B. Du Bois Papers (MS213).

69 W. E. B. Du Bois to E. Pearl Bailey, 13 January 1936, W. E. B. Du Bois Papers (MS312).

70 W. E. B. Du Bois to Charles S. Duke, 5 February 1926, W. E. B. Du Bois Papers (MS213).

71 Charles S. Duke to W. E. B. Du Bois, 26 February 1926, and W. E. B. Du Bois to Charles S. Duke, 12 March 1926, W. E. B. Du Bois Papers (MS 312).

72 The Forum to W. E. B. Du Bois, 27 September 1927, W. E. B. Du Bois Papers (MS213); and financial statement to W. E. B. Du Bois, 27 September 1927. Transcripts of the Du Bois–Stoddard debates are available in the Du Bois Collection at the Fisk University Library Special Collections, Nashville, Tennessee, box 19, fol. 24. Correspondence from Norman Thomas, president of New York's WEVD, "The Debs Memorial Station," 7 July 1931, Du Bois Collection, Fisk University, box 1, fol. 19. For a discussion of post-1940 appearances of Du Bois on radio, see Gerald Horne's *Black and Red: W. E. B. Du Bois and the Afro-American Response to the Cold War, 1944–1963* (Albany, NY: SUNY Press, 1986).

73 Frantz Fanon, "This is the Voice of Algeria," *A Dying Colonialism* (New York: Grove Press, 1965), 69–98. For a discussion of government involvement with radio during World War II, see Horten, *Radio Goes to War*, although Horten does not include an extensive conversation about race.

74 W. E. B. Du Bois to the Committee on Civic Education by Radio, 11 August 1932, W. E. B. Du Bois Papers (MS 312).

75 I reluctantly use the term "blind" for its historicity and resonance with Du Bois's language of the veil rather than its accuracy as a descriptor of the medium. See Rudolph Arnheim, "In Praise of Blindness," partially reprinted in *Radiotext(e)*, ed. Neil Strauss (New York: Semiotexte, 1993), 20–25. Martin Shingler and Cindi Weiringa speak eloquently about radio's visuality in *On Air: Methods and Meanings of Radio* (London: Arnold Press, 1998).

76 David Levering Lewis, *W. E. B. Du Bois: The Fight for Equality and the American Century, 1919–1963* (New York: Henry Holt, 2000), 460.

77 Porter, *Problem of the Future World*, 34.

78 He also misspells his name as "DuBois" throughout their correspondence, save one letter. J. W. Studebaker to W. E. B. Du Bois, 7 November 1938, in *The Correspondence of W. E. B. Du Bois, vol. 2*, ed. Herbert Aptheker, (Amherst: University of Massachusetts Press, 1976), 175–176; and Rachel Davis DuBois to W. E. B. Du Bois, October 1938, W. E. B. Du Bois Papers (MS 312).

79 Columbia Broadcasting Systems, script for "The Negro," December 1938, 24 pages; W. E. B. Du Bois, "Criticism of *Americans All, Immigrants All*," 30 November 1938, W. E. B. Du Bois Papers (MS 312).

80 Savage, *Broadcasting Freedom*, 74.

81 Levering Lewis, *W. E. B. Du Bois*, 461.

82 Locke, quoted in Savage, *Broadcasting Freedom*, 41. That Bledsoe was asked to perform by NAACP President Walter White makes the story even more complex, especially given Du Bois's strained relationship with the NAACP.

83 Rachel Davis DuBois wrote a letter to Alain Locke three days after the broadcast explaining she had no control over Bledsoe's participation and urging him and Du Bois to write a letter asking that the song not go out on the recorded version. Du Bois annotated a copy of this letter with names and addresses. Rachel Davis DuBois to Alain Locke, 21 December 1938, W. E. B. Du Bois Papers (MS 312); and Du Bois, quoted in Levering Lewis, *W. E. B. Du Bois*, 461.

84 Du Bois, *Dusk of Dawn*, (1940; New York: Transaction Publishers, 1984), 131.

85 Porter, *Problem of the Future World*, 22 and 23.

86 Du Bois, *Dusk of Dawn*, 131.

87 Plato, *The Republic*, trans. Benjamin Jowett (Digireads, 2011), 224. Plato also refers to the distortion of the sound in this parable: "And suppose further that the prison had an echo which came from the other side, would they not be sure to fancy when one of the passers-by spoke that the voice they had heard came from the passing shadow?" Ibid.

88 Du Bois, *Dusk of Dawn*, 296.

89 This phrase comes from "The Forgotten 15,000,000: Ten Billion a Year Negro Market Is Largely Ignored by National Advertisers," *Sponsor*, October 1949, 24.

90 Ann Petry, "The Lighter Side," *People's Voice*, 27 March 1943, 22. For a full history and analysis of *Heroines in Bronze*, see Savage's *Broadcasting Freedom*.

91 Joe Bostic, "Dial Time," *The People's Voice*, 2 May 1942.

92 Ibid.; Farah Jasmine Griffin, *Harlem Nocturne: Women Artists and Progressive Politics During World War II* (New York: Basic Civitas, 2013), 91–92.

93 Thus far, Petry's critics scarcely mention radio, if at all. The main strands of criticism of *The Street* deal with:

   1) the interconnections of segregation and the body, e.g. Larry R. Andrews, "The Sensory Assault of the City in Ann Petry's *The Street*," in *The City in African-American Literature*, ed. Yoshinobu Hakutani (Madison, NJ: Fairleigh Dickinson University Press, 1995), 196–211; Meg Wesling, "The Opacity of Everyday Life: Segregation and the Iconicity of Uplift in *The Street*," *American Literature* 78, no. 1 (March 2006): 117–140; and Evie Shockley, "Buried Alive: Gothic Homelessness, Black Women's Sexuality, and (Living) Death in Ann Petry's *The Street*," *African American Review* 40, no. 3 (Fall 2006): 439–460;

   2) the novel's critique of the American dream and black labor, e.g. Richard Yarborough, "The Quest for the American Dream in Three Afro-American Novels: *If He Hollers Let Him Go, The Street*, and *Invisible Man*," *MELUS* 8, no. 4 (Winter 1981): 33–59; Gayle Wurst, "Ben Franklin in Harlem: The Drama of Deferral in Ann Petry's *The Street*," in *Deferring a Dream: Literary Sub-Versions of the American Columbiad*, ed. Gert Buelens and Ernst Rudin (Basel: Birkhauser, 1994), 1–23; Michele Crescenzo, "Poor Lutie's Almanac: Reading and Social Critique in Ann Petry's *The Street*," in *Reading Women: Literary Figures and Cultural Icons from the Victorian Age to the Present*, eds., Jennifer Phegley and Janet Badia, (Toronto: University of Toronto Press, 2005), 215–235; and Bill V. Mullen, "Object Lessons: Fetishization and Class Consciousness in Ann Petry's *The Street*," in *Revising the Blueprint: Ann Petry and the Literary Left*, ed. Alex Lubin (Jackson: University Press of Mississippi, 2007), 35–48;

   3) its representations of Harlem and mid-century urban space, e.g., Carol E. Henderson, "The "Walking Wounded": Rethinking Black Women's Identity in Ann Petry's *The Street*." *Modern Fiction Studies* 46, no., 4 (Winter 2000): 849–867; and Tyrone Simpson, *Ghetto Images in Twentieth-Century American Fiction: Writing Apartheid* (New York: Palgrave MacMillan, 2012;

   4) Petry's relationship to Richard Wright and/or social realism, e.g., Kecia Driver McBride, "Fear, Consumption, and Desire: Naturalism and Ann Petry's *The Street*," in *Twisted from the Ordinary: Essays on American Literary Natural-ism*, ed. Mary Papke (Knoxville: University of Tennessee Press, 2003), 304–322; Stacy Morgan, *Rethinking Social Realism: African American Art and Literature 1930–1953* (Athens: University of Georgia Press, 2004); Heather Hicks, "Rethinking Realism in Ann Petry's *The Street*," *MELUS* 27, no. 4 (Winter 2002): 89–105; and Don Dingledine, "It Could Have Been Any Street: Ann Petry, Stephen Crane, and the Fate of Naturalism," *Studies in American Fiction* 34, no. 1 (Spring 2006): 87–106;

   5) the interrelationship of domesticity, motherhood, and the black female body, e.g. Nellie Y. McKay, "Ann Petry's *The Street* and *The Narrows*: A Study of

the Influence of Class, Race, and Gender on Afro-American Women's Lives," in *Women and War: The Changing Status of American Women from the 1930s to the 1950s*, ed. Maria Diedrich and Dorothea Fischer-Hornung (New York: Berg, 1990): 127–140; You-Me Park and Gayle Wald Park, "Native Daughters in the Promised Land: Gender, Race, and the Question of Separate Spheres," *American Literature* 70, no. 3 (1998): 607–633; and A.J. Davis, "Shatterings: Violent Disruptions of Homeplace in *Jubilee* and *The Street*," *MELUS* 30, no. 4 (Winter 2005): 25–51;

6) gendered forms of resistance including music and reading, e.g., McKay, "Ann Petry's *The Street*"; Kimberly Drake, "Women on the Go: Blues, Conjure, and Other Alternatives to Domesticity in Ann Petry's *The Street* and *The Narrows*," *Arizona Quarterly* 54, no. 1 (1998): 65–95; Joanna X. K. Garvey, "That Old Black Magic?: Gender and Music in Petry's Fiction," *Black Orpheus: Music in African American Fiction from the Harlem Renaissance to Toni Morrison*, ed. Saadi Simawe (New York: Garland, 2000), 119–152; Jürgen E. Grandt, *Kinds of Blue: The Jazz Aesthetic in African American Narrative* (Columbus: Ohio State University Press, 2004); Cresenczo, "Poor Lutie's Almanac"; and William Scott, "Material Resistance and the Agency of the Body in Ann Petry's *The Street*," *American Literature* 78, no. 1, (2006): 89–116;

7) the novel's representation of black attitudes about and experiences of World War II, e.g., Maureen Honey, *Bitter Fruit: African American Women in World War II* (Columbia, MO: University of Missouri Press, 1999). Griffin's treatment of the novel in *Who Set You Flowin'?* and *Harlem Nocturne* is unique in that it bridges many of these categories, bringing in other key strands such as the Great Migration, practices of ancestor remembrance, and Ann Petry's consumer activism.

94 Ann Petry, *The Street* (1946; Boston: Beacon Press, 1985), 3–4.

95 Hilmes, *Radio Voices*, 258. This remains true critically as well. Outside of Hilmes's work and Barbara Savage's *Broadcasting Freedom*, I have found only passing references to black women in the context of radio (usually referring to performances).

96 Erik Barnouw, *Hand Book of Radio Writing* (New York: Little, Brown, 1947), 62; Hilmes, *Radio Voices*, 186.

97 GerShun Avilez, "Housing the Black Body: Value, Domestic Space, and Segregation Narratives," *African American Review* 42, no. 1 (2008): 145 and 135.

98 Ibid.

99 Petry, *The Street*, 218.

100 Ibid., 401.

101 For an extended discussion of daytime radio programming during this period, comprised of children's shows and programs marketed to women, see Hilmes, *Radio Voices*, 151–182.

102 Petry, *The Street*, 298.

103 Ibid., 80.

104 Ibid., 80 and 418 (emphasis mine).

105 Christine Frederick, "Radio for the Housekeeper," *Good Housekeeping*, 1922, quoted in Hilmes, *Radio Voices*, 147.

106 Petry, *The Street*, 390.

107 Ibid., 144, 390, and 411.

108 Kevin Quashie, *The Sovereignty of Quiet: Beyond Resistance in Black Culture* (New Brunswick, NJ: Rutgers University Press, 2012), 23.

109 Petry, *The Street*, 222. For a more detailed music-focused reading of this scene, see Grandt, *Kinds of Blue*, 35–37. Griffin details the friendship between Petry and Reckling, in *Harlem Nocturne*, 88, as does Elisabeth Petry in *At Home Inside: A Daughter's Tribute to Ann Petry* (Jackson: University Press of Mississippi, 2003), 165–166.

110 Jayna Brown, "Buzz and Rumble: Global Pop Music and Utopian Impulse," *Social Text* 102 (Spring 2010): 125.

111 Petry, *The Street*, 313.

112 Ibid.; Joel Dinerstein, *Swinging the Machine: Modernity, Technology, and African American Culture between the Wars* (Amherst: University of Massachusetts Press, 2003), 173.

113 Like Yemisi Jemoh and Jürgen Grandt, I have been unable to find any extradiegetic references to "Rock, Raleigh, Rock." A. Yemisi Jimoh, *Spiritual, Blues, and Jazz People in African American Fiction: Living in Paradox* (Knoxville: University of Tennessee Press, 2002); and Grandt, *Kinds of Blue*.

114 Petry, *The Street*, 312–313.

115 Quoted in Suzanne Smith, "Tuning Into the 'Happy Am I' Preacher: Researching the Radio Career of Elder Lightfoot Solomon Michaux," *Sounding Out!*, 5 March 2015, http://soundstudiesblog.com/2015/03/05/tuning-into-the-happy-am-i-preacher-researching-the-radio-career-of-elder-lightfoot-solomon-michaux/.

116 See Anthea Butler, *Women in the Church of God in Christ: Making a Sanctified World* (Durham: University of North Carolina Press, 2008).

117 Petry, *The Street*, 409, 411, 413, and 418.

118 Ibid., 436.

119 Petry, *The Street*, 436; "Ann Petry: First Novel, Ann Petry Defies Tradition and Hits Jackpot in 'The Street,'" *EBONY*, April 1946, 35–36. Ann Petry Collection #1391, Box 8, printed material, no folders, Howard Gotlieb Archival Research Center, Boston University.

120 Neil Verma, "From Mercury to Mars: Introducing Antenna's New Radio Studies Series," *Antenna*, 9 August 2013, accessed 3 November 2015, http://blog.commarts.wisc.edu/2013/08/09/from-mercury-to-mars-introducing-antennas-new-radio-studies-series/. See also, Jason Loviglio and Michele Hilmes, eds., *Radio's New Wave: Global Sound in the Digital Era* (London: Routledge, 2013).

121 Dolores Inés Casillas, *Sounds of Belonging: U.S. Spanish-Language Radio and Public Advocacy* (New York: New York University Press, 2014), 13.

122 For examples of apologies and virulent defenses for the "golden age" of radio, see the comments section for Jennifer Stoever, "On the Lower Frequencies: Norman

Corwin, Colorblindness, and the 'Golden Age' of U.S. Radio," *Sounding Out!*, 10 December 2012, http://soundstudiesblog.com/2012/09/10/on-the-lower-frequen cies_corwin_colorblindness_radio/.

AFTERWORD

1 Nia Nunn Makepeace, quoted in Josh Brokaw, "If You're Black in Ithaca, Your Blood Is Boiling," *Ithaca Times*, 28 October 2015, http://www.ithaca.com/news /if-you-re-black-in-ithaca-your-blood-is-boiling/article_d69dea44–7cf8–11e5-bd51 -b32852b04195.html.

2 Regina Bradley, "SANDRA BLAND: #SayHerName Loud or Not at All," *Sounding Out!*, 16 November 2015, http://soundstudiesblog.com/2015/11/16/sandra-bland -sayhername-loud/.

3 Regina Bradley, "To Sir, With Ratchety Love: Listening to the (Dis)Respectability Politics of Rachel Jeantel," *Sounding Out!*, 1 July 2015, https://soundstudiesblog .com/2013/07/01/disrespectability-politics-of-rachel-jeantel/.

4 Bruce Drake, "Incarceration Gap Widens between Whites and Blacks," *Pew Research Center*, 6 September 2016, http://www.pewresearch.org/fact -tank/2013/09/06/incarceration-gap-between-whites-and-blacks-widens/.

5 CRCC Binghamton, "To Students and Faculty," *Nzinga*, 12 October 2013, http:// www.nzinga.org/2013/10/12/to-students-and-faculty/.

6 Stacey Lovett-Pitts, "Mother of a Young Black Male," *Nzinga*, 23 October 2013, http://www.nzinga.org/2013/10/23/mother-of-a-young-black-man/.

7 "Faculty in Support of 'Students for Change,'" letter to the editor, *The Pipe Dream*, 6 March 2015, http://www.bupipedream.com/opinion/50211/letter-to-the-editor -faculty-in-support-of-students-for-change/.

8 "George Zimmerman Trial Day 14: Live Updates," *News 13*, 27 June 2013, http:// www.mynews13.com/content/news/cfnews13/news/article.html/content/news /articles/cfn/2013/6/27/zimmerman_opening_statements.html. Italics mine.

INDEX

ABOUT THE AUTHOR

Jennifer Lynn Stoever is Associate Professor of English at the State University of New York at Binghamton. She is co-founder and editor-in-chief of *Sounding Out!: The Sound Studies Blog.*

CPSIA information can be obtained
at www.ICGtesting.com
Printed in the USA
LVHW09s1944140818
586955LV00006B/961/P